# The Rule of Moderation

Why was it that, whenever the Tudor-Stuart regime most loudly trumpeted its moderation, that regime was at its most vicious?

This ground-breaking book argues that the ideal of moderation, so central to English history and identity, functioned as a tool of social, religious and political power. Thus *The Rule of Moderation* rewrites the history of early modern England, showing that many of its key developments – the *via media* of Anglicanism, political liberty, the development of empire and even religious toleration – were defined and defended as instances of coercive moderation, producing the 'middle way' through the forcible restraint of apparently dangerous excesses in Church, state and society. By showing that the quintessentially English quality of moderation was at heart an ideology of control, Ethan Shagan illuminates the subtle violence of English history and explains how, paradoxically, England came to represent reason, civility and moderation to a world it slowly conquered.

ETHAN H. SHAGAN is Professor of History and Director of the Center for British Studies at the University of California, Berkeley. He is the author of *Popular Politics and the English Reformation* (Cambridge, 2002), which won numerous prizes including the Royal Historical Society's Whitfield Prize and the American Historical Association's Morris Forkosch Prize, and is editor of *Catholics and the 'Protestant Nation': Religious Politics and Identity in Early Modern England* (2005).

# The Rule of Moderation

*Violence, Religion and the Politics of Restraint in Early Modern England*

Ethan H. Shagan

CAMBRIDGE UNIVERSITY PRESS
Cambridge, New York, Melbourne, Madrid, Cape Town,
Singapore, São Paulo, Delhi, Tokyo, Mexico City

Cambridge University Press
The Edinburgh Building, Cambridge CB2 8RU, UK

Published in the United States of America by Cambridge University Press,
New York

www.cambridge.org
Information on this title: www.cambridge.org/9780521135566

First published 2011

Printed in the United Kingdom at the University Press, Cambridge

*A catalogue record for this publication is available from the British Library*

*Library of Congress Cataloguing in Publication data*
Shagan, Ethan H., 1971–
The rule of moderation : violence, religion, and the politics of restraint
in early modern England / Ethan H. Shagan.
     p.   cm.
Includes bibliographical references and index.
ISBN 978-0-521-11972-6 (hardback)
1. Moderation.   2. Great Britain – History.   I. Title.
BJ1533.M7S53   2011
942.05 – dc23      2011023029

ISBN 978-0-521-11972-6 Hardback
ISBN 978-0-521-13556-6 Paperback

For Hannah and Noah

For Hannah and Micah

# Contents

# Figures

# Acknowledgements

Near the beginning of Woody Allen's 1980 film *Stardust Memories*, a fan tells the newly middle-aged film director played by Allen that she really loves his films, especially the 'early, funny ones'. This comment is much on my mind as this book goes to press, since readers who enjoyed my first book, *Popular Politics and the English Reformation*, may be puzzled to find such a different work in their hands now. One reader who emphatically did not enjoy that earlier book described me in a review as the '*enfant terrible*' of early modern British history, so perhaps in an autobiographical sense this new book, like Allen's film, is about the very *un*golden mean of incipient middle age and the desire to do something different and larger than the work of one's youth. What lies between *enfant terrible* and *éminence grise*? In my case, apparently, an obsessive rejection of mediocrity.

My first book was so narrowly focused on the 'voices of the people' that I emerged from its publication as a gainfully employed historian of early modern Britain who had never read Hobbes's *Leviathan* or Hooker's *Lawes*, not to mention Aristotle's *Politics*. At a personal level, then, the goal of this second project was to write a learned book, to read deeply in the cultural and intellectual production of early modern England in order to make sense of the largest problem that I had discovered in my encounter with the subject: the apparent contradiction between England's obsession with moderation and its violent national history. The result, for good or ill, is a Big Book in a way that *Popular Politics* was not: it spans more years and more subjects over more pages using more methodologies, and it makes large arguments about the cultural dynamics and fault lines of early modern England. That is not to say that this book represents the final word. I am painfully aware of how much more remains to be said on so capacious a subject; my only excuse is that I hope this book opens more doors than it closes.

Given the many different issues at stake in this book, I have necessarily sought advice and criticism from a wide range of scholars who have been kind enough to offer their comments. Robert Harkins, Peter Marshall,

Anthony Milton, John Morrill, Alec Ryrie and Jonathan Sheehan all read complete drafts of this book. Individual chapters were read by Tim Breen, Rachel Foxley, Polly Ha, Carla Hesse, Chris Hodson, Kinch Hoekstra, Peter Lake, Tom Laqueur, Ed Muir, Mark Peterson, Sharon Stimson and James Vernon. Their ideas offered new insights which, besides saving me from countless errors, forced me to abandon the notion of 'paradox' that had structured earlier versions, convinced me to move and rewrite my discussions of social theory and spurred the substantial rewriting of the chapter on 'social moderation'. In addition, draft chapters were read by large groups of scholars at professional seminars at Berkeley, Yale and the Newberry Library, and I owe thanks to all the participants, particularly Jim Epstein, Vicky Kahn, Jeff Knapp and Steve Pincus, for their insightful comments.

I have also given oral presentations on this material at many scholarly meetings and seminars: the Sixteenth Century Studies Conference in Montreal in 2010 and in Salt Lake City in 2006; the Reformation Studies Colloquium in St Andrews in 2010; the University of Reading Early Modern Studies Conference in 2010; the annual Lecture in Early Modern History at the Newberry Library in 2010; the Early Modern Britain Seminar in Cambridge University in 2009; the Oxford University Seminar on Early Modern British History in 2007; the North American Conference on British Studies in 2006; the Medieval and Renaissance Seminar in the Department of English and Comparative Literature at Columbia University in 2006; a conference entitled 'Redefining the National Interest' at the Newberry Library in 2005; the Seminar in Early Modern History at the Huntington Library in 2005; and the Seminar on the Ecclesiastical History of Britain at the Institute of Historical Research in London in 2004. I owe thanks to all the participants who endured and helped to refine earlier versions of my ideas.

Generous financial support for research leave was provided by Northwestern University and the University of California, Berkeley. The Mellon Foundation also provided generous funding for a year of research at the Newberry Library in Chicago, and I cannot imagine a more genial place to work. I am indebted to the intellectual stimulation of my colleagues at the Newberry, especially Matt Cohen, Jim Epstein, Jim Grossman and Carla Zecher. I also want to note the extraordinary support of colleagues at both Northwestern and Berkeley; their willingness to talk to me about my obsessions over lunch, coffee or beer has been truly heroic. At Northwestern, Tim Breen, Bill Heyck, Eric Klinenberg, Sarah Maza, Ed Muir and Regina Schwartz helped me to get this project off the ground. At Berkeley, Carla Hesse, Kinch Hoekstra, Tom Laqueur, Mark Peterson, Jonathan Sheehan and James Vernon are largely responsible for me being able to finish it. In particular, the Gang of Five has given me a level of intellectual stimulation about which most scholars only dream.

There are four colleagues and friends in particular who have made this book possible. Peter Lake is the intellectual inspiration for the whole project and he has stood by me throughout; as I wrote in the preface to my first book, his generosity in encouraging me to find my own voice is a model for mentors everywhere. John Morrill has since 1999 offered me not only exemplary mentoring but also extraordinary friendship. Ed Muir has been like an older brother to me, and having someone to argue with about early modern history while sitting at Wrigley Field made my years in Illinois uniquely stimulating. Finally, if it were not for my daily coffees with Jonathan Sheehan, digging as deeply as we could into whatever he or I happened to be working on that day, I would never have figured out what this book was really about.

I also owe enormous thanks to Michael Watson, Liz Friend-Smith and Chloe Howell at Cambridge University Press for all their hard work to make this the best book it could be. The images are reproduced by permission of the Cambridge University Library, with the exception of Figure 3, which is reproduced by permission of the British Library, and Figure 9, which is reproduced by permission of the Library of Congress.

At a personal level, it is hard to imagine putting into words the thanks I owe to all the people who have helped me over the last eight years. Academic books take so many years that while you are writing them, life happens to you; in my case, since I started work on this project my daughter was born, my father died, I moved across the country, my father-in-law died, and my son was born. It seems hopeless to try to list all the people who have helped me survive these years while remaining a productive scholar. So let me just thank my family (including, but not limited to, Rena, Jillian, Henry, Robynn, Gary, Diana and Yeta), Sarah's family, whom I am happy to call my family, too (including, but not limited to, Vivian, David, Rachel, James and Joan) and all the friends who have stood by us over the last eight years. Most importantly, I wish that I could express the thanks I owe to four special people: my wife Sarah Paul for her love and patience; the late Mike Shagan for a lifetime of love and support; and my children Hannah Shagan and Noah Shagan for reminding me of the joys of excess. Hannah and Noah, this book is for you.

# Abbreviations

| | |
|---|---|
| *AHR* | *The American Historical Review.* |
| BL | British Library. |
| CUL | Cambridge University Library. |
| *EHR* | *The English Historical Review.* |
| *HJ* | *The Historical Journal.* |
| *JBS* | *Journal of British Studies.* |
| *LP* | J. S. Brewer *et al.* (eds.), *Letters and Papers, Foreign and Domestic, of the Reign of Henry VIII* (London, 21 vols. in 33, 1862–1932). |
| LPL | Lambeth Palace Library. |
| *NAW* | David Quinn (ed.), *New American World: A Documentary History of North America to 1612* (New York, 5 vols., 1979). |
| *ODNB* | *Oxford Dictionary of National Biography.* |
| *P&P* | *Past & Present.* |
| PRO | The National Archives, Public Record Office. |
| *SCJ* | *The Sixteenth Century Journal.* |
| *SR* | *The Statutes of the Realm (1225–1713) Printed by Command of His Majesty George the Third* (London, 12 vols., 1810–28). |
| *WJW* | John Whitgift, *The Works of John Whitgift*, ed. John Ayre (Cambridge, 3 vols., 1851–3). |
| *WMQ* | *The William and Mary Quarterly.* |
| *WRH* | Richard Hooker, *The Folger Library Edition of the Works of Richard Hooker*, ed. W. Speed Hill (Cambridge, Mass., 7 vols. in 8, 1977–98). |

# Prologue

> First she tasted the porridge of the great, huge bear, and that was too
> hot for her; and she said a bad word about that. And then she tasted
> the porridge of the middle bear, and that was too cold for her; and she
> said a bad word about that too. And then she went to the porridge of
> the little, small, wee bear, and tasted that; and that was neither too hot
> nor too cold, but just right; and she liked it so well she ate it all up: but
> the naughty old woman said a bad word about the little porridge pot,
> because it did not hold enough for her.
>
> Robert Southey, 'The Three Bears'[1]

There was no Goldilocks in the earliest written versions of the tale, only
an 'impudent, bad old woman'. In the 1837 version by Robert Southey,
the old woman's invasion of the three bears' domestic tranquility was nar-
rated as a cautionary tale of moderation versus excess. The 'good natured
and hospitable' bears were the very image of civilised moderation. Each
bear had only what he (significantly, they were all male) needed: 'Each a
chair to sit in; a little chair for the little, small, wee bear, and a middle-
sized chair for the middle bear, and a great chair for the great, huge
bear.' In proper control of their bodily appetites, they 'walked out into
the wood while the porridge was cooling, that they might not burn their
mouths by beginning to eat it too soon'. In keeping with their modest
condition, they ate their porridge with wooden spoons. The old woman,
by contrast, was an avatar of excess, a greedy and foulmouthed beggar
rather than the innocent child of later interpretations. When she located
the porridge that was 'neither too hot nor too cold, but just right', instead
of appreciating its moderation she gobbled it up and cursed it because
the pot 'did not hold enough for her'. When she located the chair that
was 'neither too hard nor too soft, but just right', she sat down until
'the bottom of the chair came out, and down came hers, plump upon
the ground. And the naughty old woman said a wicked word about that
too.' And it was lucky the bears used wooden spoons, for 'if they had

---

[1] Robert Southey, *The Doctor, &c.* (London, 7 vols., 1834–47), IV, pp. 318–26.

been silver ones, the naughty old woman would have put them in her pocket'. At the end of the tale, then, the old woman reaped the fruits of her immoderation, a process described as the purgation of 'ugly, dirty' matter by 'good, tidy bears': having lazily fallen asleep, she was forced by the return of the bears to hurl herself out of a second-floor window, 'and whether she broke her neck in the fall, or ran into the wood and was lost there, or found her way out of the wood and was taken up by the constable and sent to the house of correction for a vagrant as she was, I can not tell'.

We know little about the origins of 'The Three Bears', but we do know that it had been circulating in England long before it was written down in the 1830s. It seems likely, though it is not certain, that, like many other folktales collected in the nineteenth century, it had roots deep in the early modern era.[2] Certainly its emphasis on moderation fed upon an older preoccupation with virtuous mediocrity that has long been noticed by scholars, and helped inaugurate modern stereotypes of Englishness, but has received little serious historical scrutiny. If we might thus tentatively take 'The Three Bears' as a projection of early modern England's cultural imagination, it is worth noticing several things about the ideal of moderation it embodies. First, moderation here is a relative rather than an absolute conception of virtue: 'just right' is defined in contrast to encroaching extremity, represented not just by hot and cold porridge but by the excesses of the bad old woman. Second, its defence of moderation is an aggressive and even violent exercise: the story plainly attacks certain forms of social behaviour even as it defends others, and the bad old woman ends the tale at best rotting in prison and at worst lying dead on the forest floor. Third, while the violence of the denouement might seem to belie the bears' ethical superiority, their expulsion of the old woman is in fact described as an example of moderation rather than an exception to it. Fourth, the identity of the antagonist is no coincidence: the poor, vagrant crone embodies centuries of stereotypes of immoderation in need of restraint, while moderation is normatively associated with male, middle-sort householders – the three bears themselves. The story thus depends upon a profound tension within

---

[2] Evidence for the story's antiquity is threefold: first, two wholly independent versions in distant parts of England were produced in the 1830s; second, both versions at least claim that the story was an oral folktale, although this claim is more robust in Eleanor Mure's version than in Robert Southey's; third, the story bears considerable family resemblance to the folktale 'Scrapefoot', which much more clearly has early modern origins. See Iona Opie and Peter Opie, *The Classic Fairy Tales* (Oxford, 1974); Alan Elms, '"The Three Bears": Four Interpretations', *The Journal of American Folklore* 90, no. 357 (July–September 1977), pp. 257–73. The 1831 ms version has been printed in facsimile as Eleanor Mure, *The Story of the Three Bears* (Toronto, 1967).

the ideal of moderation it depicts: moderation was simultaneously a state of equipoise and an act of control, both self-restraint and the restraint of others to produce a golden mean.

"The Three Bears' therefore suggests in broad strokes the thesis of this book: in early modern England, the ubiquitous moral principle of moderation was a profoundly coercive tool of social, religious and political power. Beginning in the reign of Henry VIII, a cluster of Aristotelian ethical ideals centred on 'moderation', the 'golden mean' and the 'middle way' became a standard moral language by which power in state, Church and society was justified.[3] Of course, the preceding period also had its share of speculation on moderation. The middle ages were nothing if not Aristotelian, and besides numerous attempts to reconcile Peripatetic ethics with Christianity, concepts of 'balance' or 'equilibrium' brought moderation to the core of medieval science and economics.[4] Yet rarely in the middle ages did these ideas shape public discourse the way they did in Tudor-Stuart England. There were several important reasons for this new emphasis – besides the exponential growth of public discourse itself – on ideals of moderation available since antiquity. First was the Reformation principle that restraint in the world, rather than monkish abnegation of the world, was the epitome of virtue; in English culture, moderation was often coded Protestant. Second was the Renaissance principle of the *vita activa*, stressing that classical wisdom was not merely a private pursuit but an instrument of public policy; in Tudor England, moderation became the business of government. Third was the peculiar institutional configuration of the English Reformation, which subsumed crucial questions of ecclesiastical moderation within the politics of the English state. In light of these developments, from the second quarter of the sixteenth century onwards the ideal of moderation became central to the authorisation of public action in England. It retained this pre-eminent position until the later seventeenth century, but even long afterwards moderation continued to hold a privileged place in the nation's discourse.

This book argues that the early modern preoccupation with moderation shaped the development of English history in profound but deeply

---

[3] The most sophisticated discussion of this phenomenon is Joshua Scodel, *Excess and the Mean in Early Modern English Literature* (Princeton, 2002).

[4] Joel Kaye, 'The (Re)Balance of Nature, *c.*1250–1350', in Barbara Hanawalt and Lisa Kiser (eds.), *Engaging with Nature: Essays on the Natural World in Medieval and Early Modern Europe* (Notre Dame, 2008); see also Joel Kaye, *Economy and Nature in the Fourteenth Century: Money, Market Exchange, and the Emergence of Scientific Thought* (Cambridge, 1998). There were also more popular works on moderation like *The ABC of Aristotle*, a startlingly popular didactic poem for children that survives in no fewer than fourteen manuscripts: Martha Rust, 'The ABC of Aristotle', in Daniel Kline (ed.), *Medieval Literature for Children* (New York, 2003).

counterintuitive ways. For the idea of the 'middle way' defined ethical spectrums, delineating not only moral centres but also immoral peripheries: arguments for moderation routinely incorporated attacks upon immoderate, excessive, immoral others. Moreover, according to prevailing views of the human condition, moderation was extremely difficult to achieve, beyond the capacity of most if not all subjects; its maintenance thus required aggressive new interventions by authority in the social world. Most importantly, moderation meant government, with no firm boundary between the ethical governance of the self and the political governance of others; it referred simultaneously to the internal restraint of wayward passions by reason and the external restraint of wayward subjects by authority. Thus, assertions of moderation in early modern England – from the *via media* of Anglicanism, to the rise of the middle sort, to the idea of liberty – were in significant measure arguments for government, authorising the forcible restraint of dangerous excesses in Church, state and society. This book thus analyses how moderation was claimed in early modern England, arguing that such claims were the instruments by which politics was conducted, power was sought and domination was justified.

*Part I*

# Moderate foundations

# Introduction

This book began as an attempt to answer a deceptively simple question: why was it that whenever the Tudor-Stuart regime most loudly trumpeted its moderation, that regime was at its most vicious? The question had first occurred to me in the context of Henry VIII's remarkable, simultaneous execution of three Catholics and three Protestants in July 1540 as a (literally) flamboyant statement of the Church of England's moderation. But over years of teaching English history, I found that the question seemed to recur in a wide variety of contexts: the claim to punish religious dissidents for their conduct but not to make windows into men's souls; the use of writs of the peace to enforce order and punish offenders without resorting to the courts; claims for the moderation of the English empire compared to the excesses of New Spain; laws promoting religious toleration that established new penalties for blasphemy. The common thread running through these examples was that they were all cases where power was authorised and even amplified by its limitation. My deceptively simple question, I realised, led deep into the ideological heart of early modern England.

My first answer to this question was that moderation was an intrinsically relational and comparative ethical framework, so that every claim to the moderate centre involved the construction and vilification of extremists on the margins. I still stand by this initial answer, and while I am hardly the first scholar to notice it, the intrinsically aggressive character of moderation is far too rarely emphasised. As a historian, however, I soon became unsatisfied with such an ahistorical, structural thesis. If moderation were 'always already' aggressive, then there seemed little point in isolating one specific example of it or studying its ideological resonances in a particular time and place. I was uninterested in practising philosophy without a licence; I wanted to understand what made moderation so peculiarly important to early modern England.

My second answer, then, was much more historically specific. In a Protestant religious context, where original sin cast such a long shadow upon human morality, ethical moderation was seen as virtually impossible to achieve, so moderation was constantly externalised: human beings naturally tended to sinful excesses, hence the *via media* required the coercive power of ministers and magistrates. Moreover, the Renaissance ideal of the *vita activa*, in which Tudor lawmakers adopted an activist impulse to improve the commonwealth, provided a context in which the ancient ethical ideal of moderation was made central to public policy and modes of governance for the first time. In this sense, I came to see the peculiarly aggressive moderation of the Tudor-Stuart regime as the bastard child of Renaissance and Reformation, a glaring example of Margo Todd's dictum that 'internal contradictions are to be expected from an intellectual milieu which in England combined humanist optimism with the Calvinist doctrine of human depravity'.[1] Again, I still stand by this answer: the presumed moral incapacity of its subjects allowed the English government to justify acts of breathtaking repression as instances of moderation. But I soon realised that this could not be the whole answer because, while it explained how moderation became an exercise of power, it failed to explain how power was authorised by its moderation.

My third and final insight, then, was that the state's prerogative to moderate its subjects reflected deeper habits of thought, first noticed by historians of gender and empire as well as historians of political philosophy, in which the ethical government of the self was understood as a microcosm or synecdoche of the political government of subjects.[2] Within a Renaissance mentality that presumed interconnections and dependencies between human beings and their environments, *moderation meant government* with no clear boundary between inward and outward. Hence, if moderation were the active force by which excesses were controlled and reduced to a mean, then the 'moderation of gentlemen' could mean simultaneously control of their passions and control of their servants, while the 'moderation of the Church of England' could mean simultaneously a middle way between Catholicism and Anabaptism and the requirement of obedience and conformity it enforced upon its subjects. If internal and external moderation were so profoundly linked, in other words, then power could be authorised and amplified by its limitation: the moderation of the government legitimated its use of coercive force, but that use of coercive force was itself an example of the government's moderation. In this model, moderation subsumed two concepts that today

---

[1]  Margo Todd, *Christian Humanism and the Puritan Social Order* (Cambridge, 1987), p. 18.
[2]  See e.g. Susan James, *Passion and Action: The Emotions in Seventeenth-Century Philosophy* (Oxford, 1997); Carolyn Merchant, *The Death of Nature: Women, Ecology, and the Scientific Revolution* (San Francisco, 1980); Richard Tuck, *Philosophy and Government, 1572–1651* (Cambridge, 1993); James Tully, *An Approach to Political Philosophy: Locke in Contexts* (Cambridge, 1993), ch. 6.

are incompatible but in early modern England had not yet been differentiated: the state of equipoise and the act of restraint that produced it. This was the rule of moderation.

The result was that discussions of moderation and the middle way in early modern England often bore powerful connotations of coercion and control that have been lost over subsequent centuries, leaving behind only cosy connotations of equanimity and reasonableness. This does not mean that moderation was always externalised to an equal degree or in the same way; a vast range of nuances was available for contemporaries to describe the capacity of different actors for internal self-control, while options for external moderation ranged from polite admonition to public execution. I would not want to flatten these differences or argue that early modern English people were incapable of genuine accommodation; in early modern England, as in most times and places, most people just wanted to get along.[3] But nonetheless, moderation meant government, and the routine alliance of internal and external moderation, the stark absence of any ethics that was not at heart about the maintenance of public order, meant that it took rare effort to suppress the more aggressive side of moderation altogether. Historians who have analysed early modern discussions of moderation, however, have for the most part missed their coercive qualities, seeing in them only their modern meanings; given the pervasiveness of moderation and the middle way in early modern English historiography, the consequences of this omission are significant.

The most noteworthy context in which early modern English subjects and their modern historians have discussed moderation is the English Reformation, especially the development of an eccentric new institution called the Church of England. A central argument of this book, then, is that the English Reformation was understood as moderate, and its Church was defended as a *via media*, not so much because it was limited, compromised or reasonable, but because it was so very governmental. It was moderate not only in its restraint but insofar as it restrained, not only because it was reasonable but because it moulded reasonable subjects. Internal and external moderation produced one another; moderation was simultaneously peace and coercion, a state of equipoise and an act of control. In other words, in order to understand the *via media* of the developing Anglican Church, we need to understand that the Reformation

---

[3] Jeffrey Knapp has suggested, for instance, that accommodation was particularly suitable to theatre people because of their professional investment in fellowship predicated on simulation, while Linda Pollock has suggested that women played a vital role in facilitating accommodation in elite society: Jeffrey Knapp, *Shakespeare's Tribe: Church, Nation, and Theater in Renaissance England* (Chicago, 2002); Linda Pollock, 'Honor, Gender, and Reconciliation in Elite Culture, 1570–1700', *JBS* 46 (January 2007), pp. 3–29.

in England, arguably more than anywhere else, was always at heart about governance, and governance was moderation.

But while part of this book is about religion, much of it also concerns broader ideologies of governance in state and society. As such, the violent moderation of the English Reformation is both foundational to, and is the most baroque example of, the more general thesis of this book: that the quintessentially English quality of moderation, as it developed in the early modern period, was at heart an ideology of control. The various iterations of aggressive moderation analysed in this book were central to the emergence of a peculiarly English modernity in which the precocious development of the state was linked to its restraint, a Leviathan not of absolutism but of moderation. In the broadest sense, then, this book is a contribution to understanding one of the central puzzles of English history: how England came to represent reason, civility and moderation to a world it slowly conquered.

At the risk of appearing jejune and undergraduate, let us begin with dictionaries as rough indicators of the relationship between moderation and government. Within the new genre of English language dictionaries that appeared in the early seventeenth century, some offered definitions of moderation that would not seem out of place today. Robert Cawdrey's *A Table Alphabetical* (1604), for instance, defined moderation as 'keeping due order and proportion'.[4] But because this definition described moderation as an action rather than a condition, we must be careful to note its ambiguity: did it mean keeping yourself in due order and proportion, or keeping others? This ambiguity was made more explicit a decade later in John Bullokar's *An English Expositor* (1616), which defined the verb 'moderate' and the adjective 'moderate' in the same entry: 'Measurable, temperate, also to govern or temper with discretion'.[5] Soon afterwards, Henry Cockeram's *The English Dictionarie: or, an Interpreter of Hard English Words* (1623) was yet more blunt, defining the verb 'moderate' simply as 'to govern', and hence defining a 'moderator' as 'a discreet governor'.[6] Moreover, while Cockeram's 1623 edition defined the noun 'moderation' as 'temperance, good discretion' without explicit connotations of governance, in the 1670 edition this was changed to 'temperance, discretion, government'.[7] This change may have been in response

---

[4] Robert Cawdrey, *A Table Alphabetical* (London, 1604).
[5] J. B. [John Bullokar], *An English Expositor* (London, 1616).
[6] Henry Cockeram, *The English Dictionarie: or, an Interpreter of Hard English Words* (London, 1623).
[7] Henry Cockeram, *The English Dictionary: or, an Expositor of Hard English Words* (London, 1670).

to another great seventeenth-century dictionary, Edward Phillips's *The New World of English Words* (1658), which defined 'moderation' as 'temperance, government, discretion', and defined 'moderator' as 'a discrete governor, a decider of any controversy'.[8] Elisha Coles's *An English Dictionary* (1684) followed suit, defining 'moderation' as 'temperance, discretion, government'.[9]

In these examples, 'moderation' and 'moderate' carried meanings much closer to their Latin roots than to modern English usage. The first Latin dictionary printed in England, based upon Anglicus Galfridus's work of the 1440s, defined the verb *moderor* as 'measure or govern'.[10] Thomas Elyot's dictionary likewise defined a *moderator* as 'a governor' – a word of some significance to Elyot, and indeed on the first page of his classic *The Boke Named the Gouernour* (1531) he wrote, 'A public weal is a body living, compact or made of sundry estates and degrees of men, which is disposed by the order of equity, and governed by the rule and moderation of reason.'[11] Robert Estienne's *Dictionariolum Puerorum* (1552) defined *moderatio* as 'Rule, a measure, a moderation or governing' with the verb *moderari* as 'to set or give a measure, to govern, to moderate'. Estienne also described a *moderator* as 'a governor, a ruler, a master or pedagogue and tutor' and a *moderatrix* as 'a governess, a regent'.[12] By the time John Rider's influential dictionary appeared in its full form in 1606, the noun *moderatio* had acquired a series of meanings – 'moderation, temperance, moderate government, due measure and proportion, modesty, good disposition' – that would remain linked together for a century.[13] Moderation of the self and moderation of others were, linguistically speaking, two sides of the same coin, a point made particularly clear in Thomas Blount's *Glossographia* (1656), which defined *moderator* as 'a discreet governor or ruler; he that keeps both parties from running to extremes'.[14]

The alienness of these definitions to modern sensibilities only becomes fully apparent when we start looking at contemporary usages of these terms in contexts of authority and restraint where they would make no sense today. So, for instance, a 1559 translation of Johannes Ferrarius's *De Republica Instituenda* stressed the role of the prince, 'in whose

---

[8]  Edward Phillips, *The New World of English Words* (London, 1658).
[9]  Elisha Coles, *An English Dictionary* (London, 1684).
[10]  Anglicus Galfridus, *Ortus Vocabularum Alphabetico* (London, 1509).
[11]  Thomas Elyot, *Bibliotheca Eliotae* (London, 1542); Thomas Elyot, *The Boke Named the Gouernour* (London, 1531), fo. 1r.
[12]  Robert Estienne, *Dictionariolum Puerorum, Tribus Linguis Latina, Anglica & Gallica Conscriptum* (London, 1552).
[13]  John Rider, *Riders Dictionary Corrected and Augmented* (London, 1606).
[14]  Thomas Blount, *Glossographia: or, a dictionary* (London, 1656).

government the whole moderation of the common weal consisteth'.[15] Edward Forset in 1606 described how sovereigns 'uphold their government in a strict steadiness, tempering all extremities with an evenness of moderation'.[16] In the same year, Barnabe Barnes described how in the Roman Republic the authority of the people was 'atempered with the moderation of the authorities royal, and with the patricians'.[17] In these examples, moderation means governance, but in particular it means appropriate and measured governance, 'to govern or temper with discretion', neither too strict nor too slack. Since government itself was a middle way between tyranny and anarchy, moderation was built into the idea of governance just as governance was built into the idea of moderation.[18]

The same phenomenon can be seen in discussions of religion, where claims about the 'moderation' of the Church could be arguments for its governance. Stephen Gardiner defined the royal supremacy over the Church as the authority 'to bear rule over all the people, to command, remit and sometimes to bear with all the members thereof as much as tendeth to the use of all the whole body, and so to order and moderate every thing that the glory of God and the profession of the faith may be advanced'.[19] The 1535 English translation of Marsilius of Padua's *Defensor Pacis* claimed that the office of the priesthood consists in 'all disciplines found out and devised by man's wit, both speculative and practive, which do moderate, temper and govern the acts of men as well the inward as the outward acts, proceeding of appetite and knowledge'.[20] For the Elizabethan bishop Thomas Bilson, episcopacy was the 'fatherly moderation' of the bishops over the ministry, for, 'Where no man doeth govern, what order can be kept? Where no man doeth moderate, what peace can be had?'[21] Thomas Nash advised moderation in the sense of

---

[15] Johannes Ferrarius, *A Woorke of Ioannes Ferrarius Montanus, Touchynge the Good Orderynge of a Common Weale*, trans. William Bavand (London, 1559), fo. 166v.

[16] Edward Forset, *A Comparatiue Discourse of the Bodies Natural and Politique* (London, 1606), 31.

[17] Barnabe Barnes, *Foure Bookes of Offices* (London, 1606), p. 65.

[18] Yet real violence was possible, insofar as subjects like passions could be rebellious. When Edward Randoll was appointed provost marshal of Ulster in 1566, for instance, he was authorised 'to invade, pursue, and plague those rebels and traitors with fire and sword . . . authorising him moreover by the tenor hereof to execute the martial law and government . . . on all other those countries in Ulster and people therein which the deputy should commit to his moderation': Thomas Colby (ed.), *Ordnance Survey of the County of Londonderry* (Dublin, 1837), p. 80.

[19] Stephen Gardiner, *De Vera Obedientia* (1553), sig. E5v.

[20] Marsilius of Padua, *The Defence of Peace* (London, 1535), fo. 18r–v.

[21] Thomas Bilson, *The Perpetual Gouernement of Christes Church* (London, 1593), preface sig. TT4r and 2.

coercive limitation in response to Martin Marprelate's puritan excesses: 'It is not the spirit of mildness that must moderate the heart of folly; dogs must be beaten with staves, and stubborn slaves controlled with stripes. Authority best knows how to diet these bedlamites.'[22] Here Nash's image of enforced 'dieting' to rebalance the humours of madmen suggests how easily moderation could become externalised: the spirit of mildness might moderate some things, but the heart of folly required much more aggressive restraint.

We can peer more deeply into the meanings of moderation if we look to the parallel language of the 'middle way' or 'mean between extremes'. While moderation and the middle way were not precisely synonyms in early modern England, they were symbiotic and inseparable in ways somewhat alien to the classical tradition from which they derived. In ancient Peripatetic ethics in particular, moderation or *sophrosyne* was the virtue of self-restraint, while quite separately the ethical mean or middle way was the state between excess and deficiency that characterised all virtues. Hence, for the Peripatetics, *sophrosyne* might in some cases produce a middle way by restraining excess; for instance, moderating the excess of recklessness produced the mean of courage. But just as often, vices of deficiency required augmentation rather than restraint; for instance, the deficiency of cowardice had to be augmented to reach the mean of courage. In this sense, moderation and the middle way intersected no more than half the time.[23] Within early modern Protestant ethics, however, there was only very rarely any conception that the will might require augmentation rather than restraint: so great was the Christian emphasis on the weight of original sin and the dangerous appetites of fallen humanity that virtually all transgressions, and indeed the whole postlapsarian world, could be imagined as excesses requiring moderation. So, for instance, cowardice was routinely redescribed as an excess of self-love rather than a deficiency of courage, while stinginess was redescribed as an excess of desire rather than a deficiency of generosity, and strict abstention from the flesh was redescribed as an excess of pride rather

---

[22] Thomas Nash, *An Almond for a Parrat, or Cutbert Curry-Knaues Almes Fit for the Knaue Martin* (London, 1589), fo. 16r.

[23] Here I enormously simplify one portion of Helen North's magisterial survey of the evolution of *sophrosyne* in Greek, Roman and Patristic thought: Helen North, *Sophrosyne: Self-Knowledge and Self-Restraint in Greek Literature* (Ithaca, 1966). North contrasts the Peripatetic de-emphasis of *sophrosyne* with the Hellenistic stress on *sophrosyne* as the limitation of heroism and individuality necessary for the emerging *polis* (p. 150). See also Adriaan Redemaker, *Sophrosyne and the Rhetoric of Self-Restraint: Polysemy and Persuasive Use of an Ancient Greek Value Term* (Leiden, 2005), where Rademaker argues that in Plato's era *sophrosyne* referred to 'control of desires' when applied to men but routinely referred to fidelity when applied to women and obedience when applied to children.

than a deficiency of desire. In the aggregate, then, moderation became virtually synonymous with the ethical mean.[24]

So, for instance, Joseph Hall, in his *Christian Moderation* (1640), wrote, 'In every defect there is an excess, and both are a transgression of measure . . . for what goodness can there be in the world without moderation.'[25] In *Epieikeia: or, a Treatise of Christian Equitie and Moderation* (1604), William Perkins wrote, 'Christian equity is a rare and excellent virtue, whereby men use a true mean and an equal moderation in all their affairs.'[26] Countless other early modern writers concurred: moderation both produced and was the product of the mean between extremes, while finding the middle way both required and resulted in moderation. As literary critic Joshua Scodel has summarised this material, 'Early modern Aristotelians . . . generally equated the mean with moderation tautologically.'[27]

The language of the ethical mean was thus also a language of government. This was most obvious, of course, when the mean in question was explicitly about authority and obedience, as when Joseph Hall wrote, 'You see then how requisite it is that you walk in a middle way betwixt that excessive power which flattering casuists have been wont to give to popes, emperors, kings and princes in their several jurisdictions, and a lawless neglect of lawful authority; for the orthodox, wise and just moderation whereof these last ages are much indebted.'[28] Charles I defended his Church as 'keeping the middle way between the pomp of superstitious tyranny and the meanness of fantastic anarchy'.[29] The Restoration

---

[24] I am indebted here to J. O. Urmson, 'Aristotle's Doctrine of the Mean', and David Pears, 'Courage as a Mean', both in Amélie Rorty (ed.), *Essays of Aristotle's Ethics* (Berkeley, 1980). Both essays also note that for Aristotle self-restraint was not the same as excellence but rather was a lesser condition, since the excellent man should not need to restrain himself but should always will the good. This suggests a fundamental difference from Christian ethics, where the doctrine of the Fall implies that restraint is always necessary. As Urmson puts it (p. 160), 'For Aristotle, having to make oneself behave properly, however admirable the deed, betrays a defect of character. Excellence of character is not the triumph of grace over the old Adam; it is that state of character which entitles a man to be called *eudaimon*.'

[25] Joseph Hall, *Christian Moderation in Two Books* (London, 1640), Book I, p. 3. See also Thomas Wright, *The Passions of the Minde* (London, 1601), p. 120.

[26] William Perkins, *Epieikeia: or, a Treatise of Christian Equitie and Moderation* (Cambridge, 1604), sig. A2r.

[27] Scodel, *Excess and the Mean*, p. 290. Urmson notes that this is far from Aristotle's position, in which, for instance, the doctrine of the mean and the doctrine of moderation might both hold that we should very rarely drink alcohol, yet the doctrine of the mean might suggest that we should drink a lot of alcohol once in a while, while the doctrine of moderation would suggest that we should never drink more than a reasonable amount: Urmson, 'Aristotle's Doctrine of the Mean', p. 162.

[28] Joseph Hall, *Cases of Conscience Practically Resolved* (London, 1654), p. 215.

[29] Quoted in Roger L'Estrange, *The State and Interest of the Nation* (London, 1680), pp. 26–7.

Bishop of Oxford, Samuel Parker, wrote against religious toleration in 1671: 'Some theological Empericks have so possessed the people's heads with this fond conceit, that they will see no middle way between spiritual tyranny and spiritual anarchy, and so brand all restraint of government in affairs of religion as if it were antichristian, and never think themselves far enough from Rome, till they are wandered as far as Münster.'[30]

Yet this language of anarchy, tyranny and good government was constitutive of claims about the middle way much more broadly, because all middle ways in human society depended upon the exercise of restraint that was neither deficient nor excessive. While in an external, political sense this meant governance of subjects, in an internal, ethical sense it meant governance of passions. This was why giving free rein to the appetites was ubiquitously referred to as 'lawlessness', 'licentiousness', or 'libertinism': it was the refusal of good government. On the opposite side, while the rule of the passions was often associated with tyranny, so likewise was the overzealous suppression of the passions, for instance in Robert Boyle's claim that Stoic self-abnegation was 'not unlike those tyrants, who to acquire an absolute command over their subjects, destroy those subjects that they are to command'.[31] Joseph Hall described both sides in his *Christian Moderation* (1640): 'Happy are we if we know how to use our blessings and have learned so to order our appetite as that we make it neither a slave nor a wanton.'[32] Thus, commonplace claims for the golden mean that might in the classical world have been straightforward descriptions of intermediate states – the middle ways between too much and too little sleep, food, drink, or sex, for instance – were in early modern England calls for *regulation*, the exercise of restraining power (whether internal or external) upon a treacherous will and a fallen world.

In the sixteenth and seventeenth centuries, then, governance, restraint, repression and control were built into the very language of moderation. Claims about the *via media* of the Church of England, for instance, were *ipso facto* claims about governance not only because the polity of that Church was one of the major issues in dispute; it was equally the case that every middle way was a middle way precisely insofar as it was governed, kept within measure, restrained from the excesses to which the sinful world is prone. The same was true of a middle way between abstinence and gluttony, or a middle way between avarice and prodigality: the golden mean was the product either of the internal governance of

---

[30] Samuel Parker, *A Discourse of Ecclesiastical Politie* (London, 1671), p. 24.
[31] Robert Boyle, *The Early Essays and Ethics of Robert Boyle*, ed. John Harwood (Carbondale, Ill., 1991), p. 18.
[32] Hall, *Christian Moderation*, Book I, p. 67.

passion by reason or the external governance of behaviour by authority, two processes which were extremely hard to separate.

Then, in the eighteenth century, such connotations of governance disappeared from dictionary definitions of moderation. While the person of the 'moderator' kept his role as a decider rather than simply a mediator for another half a century, the notion of moderation itself as synonymous with rule quickly became unsustainable. Already in 1704, *Cocker's English Dictionary* retreated to the succinct word 'discretion' as the definition of moderation.[33] In 1708, John Kersey's *Dictionarium Anglo-Britannicum* had 'moderation' as 'temperance, prudence, discretion'.[34] As English dictionaries became more substantial and discursive, earlier associations of moderation with governance were largely replaced by more comfortable associations of calm, equanimity and reasonableness. In Thomas Dyche's *A New General English Dictionary*, first published in 1735, 'moderation' was defined as 'that happy disposition of mind that sedately considers the reasonableness, justice and equity of a thing that a person does or forbears, and that makes proper allowances for the actor and action'. A 'moderator', too, had become a calming agent more than an agent of control, 'one who is appointed a judge or arbitrator between contending parties; also one that endeavors to persuade people that are quarrelling, to peace and love, by showing both sides their faults'.[35] Samuel Johnson's great dictionary, published in 1755, defined the noun 'moderation' in three senses: first, 'forbearance of extremity; the contrary temper to party violence; state of keeping a due mean betwixt extremes'; second, 'calmness of mind; equanimity'; and third, 'frugality in expense'.[36] Finally, John Ash's *The New and Complete Dictionary of the English Language* (1775) had the noun 'moderation' as 'a mitigation of rigor, calmness, equanimity, frugality'.[37] Moderation had sloughed off its early modern connotations of government, inaugurating and enabling the process by which generations of historians would misinterpret early modern authors as defenders of reasonable accommodation when they wrote in favour of strong restraining authority.

---

[33] Edward Cocker, *Cocker's English Dictionary* (London, 1704).

[34] John Kersey, *Dictionarium Anglo-Britannicum: or, a General English Dictionary* (London, 1708). There were certainly exceptions to this rule, like Benjamin Defoe's *A Compleat English Dictionary* (Westminster, 1735), which kept government in the definition. There had also been dictionaries in the seventeenth century that lacked these associations. My goal is not to suggest a perfectly smooth terrain but rather to map trends of meaning.

[35] Thomas Dyche, *A New General English Dictionary* (London, 1740).

[36] Samuel Johnson, *A Dictionary of the English Language*, 2nd edn (London, 1755–6).

[37] John Ash, *The New and Complete Dictionary of the English Language* (London, 1775).

This brings us to the role of moderation and the *via media* in our historical understanding of early modern England. The historiography of the field remains saturated with these concepts, both because our subjects used them with such frequency and also because, perhaps as a result, so many elements of England's national history are routinely described as restrained or domesticated versions of European norms. Even the many scholars who dispute this putative moderation are nonetheless bound within its terms, so that the question of *whether* particular persons, positions and institutions were really moderate recurs in a surprising number of debates within the field: the development of the Church of England, the origins of the Civil War, the participatory nature of the legal system, the relative absence of social conflict and so forth. The first point to be made, then, is that by challenging the notion that moderation was normatively peaceful, and by suggesting that the middle way could be a path of domination as much as a path of accommodation, this book does not merely take issue with some particular historiographical position but rather challenges the framework of our debates. That is, my intent is not so much to argue that particular historians have been wrong to identify specific instances of moderation in early modern England, but rather to suggest that the whole question of moderation and its discovery in our sources means quite different things than we assume, denoting conflict and coercion as much as peace and consensus.

Rather than interrogating a host of books and articles to make this point, let me just discuss one example that can stand for the rest, a widely read account of popular politics and the English Reformation published in the past decade and generally well received. There the author, while arguing that there was less moderation in the English Reformation than other historians had seen, nonetheless at several points took moderation and the *via media* to be more or less what they seemed: claims to peace and reconciliation. He described, for instance, how the polarisation of religious positions in the 1540s 'allowed decreasing latitude for public neutrality, regardless of people's private hopes for moderation and consensus'. He also wrote, eloquently but somewhat contradictorily, that Henry VIII's famous plea for a *via media* in his Christmas Eve 1545 speech was 'not a self-conscious programme of religious moderation but a Sisyphean task of reconciliation put to a rancorous and divided nation'. At times he also seemed to accept that the claim that the Church of England's *via media* was essentially neutral, an attempt to avoid the pitfalls of religious controversy.[38] The present argument renders all of this

---

[38] Ethan Shagan, *Popular Politics and the English Reformation* (Cambridge, 2003), pp. 224, 232, 30–1, 44–7.

not merely wrong but *mal posée*. In fact, there was no contradiction between conflict and moderation, nor between intolerance and moderation, nor between ideological rigour and moderation. Moderation, for early modern subjects, could mean the enforcement of obedience to the Church as much as it meant self-restraint; the *via media* was a path of peace not only in the sense that people restrained their enthusiasms or accommodated differences but also in the sense that those unwilling or unable to do so were moderated and restrained by power. In other words, the author of this account was wrong to deny that Henry VIII was really moderate because he was so coercive; he should instead have acknowledged the apparent paradox that Henry VIII was moderate precisely in and through that coercion, so that moderation was constitutive of the massively increased authority of the Tudor state. Similar analysis could hold true for countless other works of historical analysis that imagine calls for moderation or claims to the middle way as remedies for the endemic violence of the age.

One important example in a broader European context is Norbert Elias's classic analysis of the 'civilising process' through which early modern Europeans overcame the endemic interpersonal violence of the middle ages.[39] Elias attributed this transition to the psychosocial development of moderation based upon Weberian rationalisation: as states monopolised legitimate force and economies were differentiated to the point that individuals relied upon networks of strangers for their survival, self-control became vital for social success. The result was the invention of the Freudian superego, so that, in Elias's magisterial analysis, the decline of knife attacks in the streets was linked to such diverse phenomena as table manners, bathroom hygiene and sexual taboos. The present book does not dispute this thesis but rather suggests that there is a parallel story to be told about what was, in England at least, the other half of moderation's import: not its psychology but its public government. As numerous historians have shown, and as Elias (drawing on Freud) was well aware, the 'decline of violence' came with enormous costs; the present book suggests that those costs *also* fell within the compass of moderation, so that the 'civilising process' must take cognisance of the sorts of power structures generated, and the sorts of force applied, when self-restraint was ineluctably tied to external restraint. To put it bluntly, it takes violence to produce moderation, and while modern liberal regimes disguise that violence, early modern England wore it proudly through a discourse of moderation that only in later

---

[39] Norbert Elias, *The Civilizing Process: Sociogenetic and Psychogenetic Investigations*, revised edn, trans. Edmund Jephcott (Maldon, Mass., 1994).

generations lost its capacity to encompass both peace and the coercion that forged it.

Now, this does not mean that I am denying the heuristic utility for early modern historians of the terms 'moderate' or 'moderation' and their synonyms.[40] In many cases it is necessary for scholars, in the forensic process of differentiation, to use the adjective 'moderate' to draw finer distinctions within categories: moderate Calvinists, moderate royalists and so forth. This usage carries little normative content so long as it is taken to mean 'less royalist' rather than, as sometimes appears, 'reasonable royalist'. It is equally appropriate for historians to use 'moderate' as a verb: the king moderated his tone, the rebels moderated their demands. This usage very usefully describes change-over-time, again so long as it is taken to mean 'lessened' rather than 'became more reasonable'.

More problematic analytical usage occurs when historians use the noun 'moderation' to refer to acts of limitation, such as the moderation exercised by a judge in sentencing. Here we stray onto dangerous ground: this usage tends to carry more normative moral content, and it misses the fact that for contemporaries the 'moderation' of a judicial sentence referred simultaneously to the limitation of the sentence, to the judge's self-restraint in issuing the sentence and to the judge's restraint of the person being sentenced. Likewise, historians get themselves into trouble when they refer to people as moderates: Erasmus was a moderate, Latitudinarians were moderates. These nominative usages are filled with normative moral content with little forensic value; they are acts of praise as much as analysis. Since 'moderate' in this nominative sense means 'reasonable person', the claim that a certain historical actor was moderate or practised moderation becomes little more than a way for historians to pass judgement or choose sides.

The real danger, however, is for historians to adopt categories of excess, deficiency and moderation from their subjects, allowing historical categories of debate to masquerade as scholarly categories of analysis. It is one thing for me to call someone a moderate royalist; it is quite another thing for me to quote a royalist calling himself moderate and then proceed to delineate a category of moderate royalism. This latter usage normalises and naturalises one position in early modern debates over the location of moderation, in the process defining as excessive someone who, for instance, believed our allegedly moderate royalist to

---

[40] On this issue, see the valuable critiques of the historiographical language of radicalism, moderation and conservatism in Conal Condren, *The Language of Politics in Seventeenth-Century England* (Basingstoke, 1994); Glenn Burgess and Matthew Festenstein (eds.), *English Radicalism, 1550–1850* (Cambridge, 2007).

be deficient in zeal, or believed all royalism to be dangerously excessive. It also, crucially, neglects the fact that when someone described his own royalism as moderate, this was a claim not just about extent but about content: his self-governance, his status as a well-governed subject of the crown and his capacity to govern others. The danger of the category of moderation in our scholarship, then, is not that it is empty but that it is filled with so much more than its simple, naturalistic usage implies. Claims to moderation *for* historical subjects, when they reproduce claims to moderation *by* historical subjects, fill the term with meaning while claiming simply to recognise natural meanings, ignoring the connotations of coercion and control which even a cursory glance at dictionaries, much less complex analysis of politics, reveals the concept to have carried in early modern England.

Thus, this book makes a general historiographical intervention: historians have minimised or ignored a great deal of aggression and violence in English history because it was justified through a language of moderation whose echoes remain fundamental to, but largely unexamined in, modern scholarship. Yet within this generality, I nonetheless want to take special issue with particular scholarly traditions that have emphasised the desire for, and production of, peace and consensus at the heart of England's experience of early modernity. This emphasis is very old, going back at least as far as the 'establishment Whig' tradition that justified the Glorious Revolution.[41] But within modern, academic historiography, a series of seminal works from the 1940s to the 1970s shaped our view of what used to be called the 'Elizabethan World Picture', a culture built around ideals of order, mutual interdependence and the harmonic affinity between humanity and the cosmos.[42] In these mid twentieth-century works, moderation – a desire for peace over conflict, an acceptance of compromise over ideology, a belief that virtue lay in the middle way between extremes – resonated with what was still widely described as England's innate national character. A. G. Dickens, for instance, wrote in *The English Reformation* (1964) that 'modest and mundane reforms sprung naturally from our Tudor age, with its deep aspirations to good order in Church, commonwealth and society', and he described how Englishmen 'were groping their way toward a Reformation of compromise and detachment, partly because these attitudes came

---

[41] Steve Pincus, *1688: The First Modern Revolution* (New Haven, 2009), ch. 1.

[42] See E. M. W. Tillyard, *The Elizabethan World Picture* (London, 1958); Arthur Lovejoy, *The Great Chain of Being: A Study of the History of an Idea* (Cambridge, Mass., 1936); Arthur Ferguson, *The Articulate Citizen and the English Renaissance* (Durham, N.C., 1965); James Daly, *Cosmic Harmony and Political Thinking in Early Stuart England*, printed in *Transactions of the American Philosophical Society* 69 (Philadelphia, 1979).

naturally to the English temperament'.[43] Sir John Neale, in his 1955 article 'The *Via Media* in Politics: A Historical Parallel', offered moderation as the antithesis of fanatical communism, suggesting parallels between the Cold War of the 1950s and Elizabeth I's battles against 'puritan extremists'. He ended with a rousing cheer: 'The name "Gloriana" and the phrase "*via media*" seem odd companions. But the liberal way of life is richest and fullest, and it was well for England that when men's passions led them from it, Queen Elizabeth preserved the tradition.'[44] Charles and Katherine George, in their classic *The Protestant Mind of the English Reformation* (1961), identified the moral authority of the *via media* as the great defining feature of the English Renaissance – an era whose unique genius 'cannot be explained, only admired and loved' – and argued for the essential unity of all English Protestants from Richard Hooker to William Walwyn: 'Between Roman Catholicism and Anabaptism, two chasms of profound error on the right and left, extends the wide and relatively level plateau of valid Protestantism.'[45]

Even as this sort of cultural essentialism was eroded in the late twentieth century, moderation ironically found its next generation of champions in the so-called revisionist historians, who so ably challenged the teleological assumptions of this earlier scholarship. Revisionism arose in reaction to liberal, Marxist and Protestant models of historical progress in which events marched resolutely towards predetermined outcomes. For revisionists, on the contrary, historical change occurred haphazardly if at all, and where earlier historians had seen conflict revisionists often found consensus. Hence the idea of moderation, while no longer explicitly described in outmoded terms of national character, became profoundly useful to argue that revolutionary moments were exceptions to, rather than fulfilments of, English history. Revisionists stressed the degree to which English society was normatively peaceful, gentlemanly, decorous and polite, and while they did not suggest that English society *always was* consensual, by emphasising that at some deep level it was *supposed* to be so, they portrayed outbreaks of conflict, whether physical or ideological, as aberrations in English history.

---

[43] A. G. Dickens, *The English Reformation* (New York, 1964), pp. 181–2. I owe this reference to Karl Gunther. See also p. 254: 'In their conscious attempt at a shrewd balance between the extremes of an unbalanced age, they are intensely English.'

[44] John Neale, 'The *Via Media* in Politics: A Historical Parallel', in his *Essays in Elizabethan History* (London, 1958), p. 124. This essay was originally published in the *Saturday Review* in 1955 under the title 'Elizabeth I and Her Cold War'.

[45] Charles George and Katherine George, *The Protestant Mind of the English Reformation 1570–1640* (Princeton, 1961), pp. 13, 16, 394.

Revisionist historians of politics, for instance, have seen the Civil War as resulting from the collapse of a genuinely moderate centre under prodding from small groups of extremists on both sides. Glenn Burgess summarised pre-1640 political theory as a moderate middle way: 'Instead of two ideologically opposed groups we have a broad consensus, with eccentric extremes sparsely inhabited. The consensus was real.'[46] David Smith, likewise, analysed why 'moderate Royalists and moderate Parliamentarians were unable to coalesce and form a united middle ground during the summer of 1642'. The 'spirit of moderate constitutionalism' on which this middle ground lay was 'guided by a temperate spirit which saw unity and reciprocity as the normative relationship between monarch and people'.[47] John Morrill analysed the phenomenon of 'neutralism' in the Civil War, particularly the 'totally committed efforts of moderate men' to keep both royalist and parliamentary armies out of their localities. For Morrill, their neutrality was not only practical but ontological; unlike earlier historians who saw 'neutrals and moderates' as apathetic, for Morrill their moderation was 'positive, clearsighted, principled'.[48] Revisionist historians of later Stuart politics have also stressed moderation, describing the equanimity that remained possible even in the face of the Exclusion Crisis and the Glorious Revolution. For instance, in a study of local politics John Miller followed his subjects in identifying 'three parties in Norwich – violent Tories, violent Whigs and moderate men, loyal to the existing government in church and state and committed to proceeding soberly and quietly'.[49]

---

[46] Glenn Burgess, *Absolute Monarchy and the Stuart Constitution* (New Haven, 1996), p. 209.

[47] David Smith, *Constitutional Royalism and the Search for Settlement, c.1640–1649* (Cambridge, 1994), pp. 7, 318–19. See also Mark Kishlansky, *The Rise of the New Model Army* (Cambridge, 1979), ch. 1; John Morrill, 'The Religious Context of the English Civil War', *TRHS* fifth series 34 (1984), pp. 155–78.

[48] John Morrill, *Revolt in the Provinces: The People of England and the Tragedies of War, 1634–48* (London, 1999), pp. 54–5, 60, 132–3. These passages survived unchanged from the 1976 edition, *The Revolt of the Provinces*. See also Martyn Bennett, 'Between Scylla and Charybdis: The Creation of Rival Administrations at the Beginning of the English Civil War', reprinted in Peter Gaunt (ed.), *The English Civil War* (Oxford, 2000). Against these arguments, one minority report was Gerald Aylmer's humourous suggestion that the idea of a 'moderate, irenic, ecumenical tradition' in the seventeenth century emerged from the self-image of historians rather than their sources, since 'most historians today are middle-of-the-road, as well as being middle-aged and middle class. And most of us would no doubt like to regard ourselves as irenic and ecumenical.' Nonetheless, Aylmer was locked into precisely the assumptions he critiqued; he accepted the equation of moderation with peace but merely argued that it was not as widespread as others had suggested: G. E. Aylmer, 'Presidential Address: Collective Mentalities in Mid Seventeenth-Century England: IV. Cross Currents: Neutrals, Trimmers, and Others', *TRHS* fifth series 39 (1989), pp. 1–22.

[49] John Miller, 'Containing Division in Restoration Norwich', *EHR* 121, no. 493 (September 2006), pp. 1019–47, quotes at pp. 1032 and 1046. See also John Miller,

Within revisionist studies of English religion, moderation likewise plays a crucial role. While historians have largely rejected the idea that England's early modern Reformations produced an authentically 'Anglican' middle way between Rome and Geneva, nonetheless revisionists continue to stress the overwhelmingly moderate mindset of English religion. If we begin with the sixteenth century, George Bernard argued that Henry VIII was profoundly motivated by a desire for a 'middle way' based upon religious peace and unity: 'Henry VIII sought unity and concord. Of course, that very search is itself evidence of religious divisions, but that in no way calls into question the king's purpose, however unrealistic or totalitarian it was.'[50] Bernard unfortunately left the issue of totalitarian moderation unexplored. Muriel McClendon stressed how the desire for civil peace trumped theology among the city elite of Norwich, whose moderation – 'the quiet Reformation' – restrained ideologues on both sides.[51] Lucy Wooding argued for a 'broad middle ground, in many ways the ground on which the English Reformation was constructed', which included both most Catholics and most Protestants; this Erasmian framework – 'scriptural, reforming, yet moderate' – excluded only the 'extreme positions' of 'more radical Protestants' and 'more traditional Catholics'.[52]

If we move into the seventeenth century, W. B. Patterson's *James VI and I and the Reunion of Christendom* identified James as a genuine centrist whose 'ecumenical and irenic' activities, intended to find a middle way between Protestants and Catholics, rendered him a moderate antidote to ideology rather than an ideologue himself.[53] Peter White structured his *Predestination, Policy and Polemic* entirely around the idea of moderation and the *via media*, arguing that there was far more middle ground in English religion than meets the eye and suggesting that 'the essence of theology' itself, as opposed to polemic, is 'a search for equipoise, the pursuit of the middle way'.[54] Joseph Levine noted in his study of Latitudinarians, 'It took a long time in the England of rebellion and civil war for the still small voice of Anglican moderation to be heard. Even after the Restoration the violence of religious and political debate

'A Moderate in the First Age of Party: The Dilemmas of Sir John Holland, 1675–85', *EHR* 114, no. 458 (September 1999), pp. 844–74.

[50] George Bernard, *The King's Reformation: Henry VIII and the Remaking of the English Church* (New Haven, 2005), p. 498.

[51] Muriel McClendon, *The Quiet Reformation: Magistrates and the Emergence of Protestantism in Tudor Norwich* (Stanford, 1999).

[52] Lucy Wooding, *Rethinking Catholicism in Reformation England* (Oxford, 2000), p. 89.

[53] W. B. Patterson, *King James VI and I and the Reunion of Christendom* (Cambridge, 1997), p. 362.

[54] Peter White, *Predestination, Policy, and Polemic: Conflict and Consensus in the English Church from the Reformation to the Civil War* (Cambridge, 1992), pp. 12, 5–6.

continued to obscure the call to reason and the growing desire for peace among Protestants.'[55]

These examples are the tip of a very large iceberg: a broad tendency among revisionist historians to accept their sources' claims to moderation even while critiquing other sorts of claims those sources make. In seeking to replace older teleologies, revisionists have unwittingly produced a teleology of their own: what we might call the historical development of Englishmen waiting patiently in queues. Of course, these scholars know very well that English culture was at times violent and repressive despite their subjects' claims to moderation, yet somehow moderation is never implicated in that violence even though in case after case these very historians cite examples of aggressive, coercive and sometimes bloodthirsty moderation. Claims for a middle way are interpreted as genuine attempts to preserve a normatively consensual culture rather than as bids for control over that culture.

Rowing against this revisionist tide, a growing number of scholars have noted, in particular moments and ideological contexts, ways that the discourse of moderation was turned to violent and exclusionary ends. The trailblazer is Peter Lake, who has argued that the debates between puritans and conformists from the Elizabethan accession to the Civil War were precisely battles over moderation. So, for instance, 'there was a discourse of moderation and consensus at or near the centre of religious debate at the early Stuart court. The ability to control that discourse and to type one's opponents as extreme, innovative subversives was a very valuable political commodity.'[56] Lori Anne Ferrell has argued that within the religious texts of James I's reign 'carefully crafted rhetorics – aimed at unifying the Church by promoting "moderation" – in actuality

---

[55] Joseph Levine, 'Latitudinarians, Neoplatonists and Ancient Wisdom', in Richard Kroll, Richard Ashcraft, and Perez Zagroin (eds.), *Philosophy, Science, and Religion in England 1640–1700* (Cambridge, 1992), p. 85.

[56] Peter Lake, 'The Moderate and Irenic Case for Religious War: Joseph Hall's *Via Media* in Context', in Susan Amussen and Mark Kishlansky (eds.), *Political Cultures and Cultural Politics in Early Modern England: Essays Presented to David Underdown* (Manchester, 1995), p. 57; Peter Lake, 'Joseph Hall, Robert Skinner and the Rhetoric of Moderation at the Early Stuart Court', in Lori Anne Ferrell and Peter McCullough (eds.), *The English Sermon Revised: Religion, Literature and History 1600–1750* (Manchester, 2001); Peter Lake, 'Order, Orthodoxy and Resistance: The Ambiguous Legacy of English Puritanism or Just How Moderate Was Stephen Denison?' in Michael Braddick and John Walter (eds.), *Negotiating Power in Early Modern Society: Order, Hierarchy and Subordination in Britain and Ireland* (Cambridge, 2001); Peter Lake, *Anglicans and Puritans? Presbyterianism and English Conformist Thought from Whitgift to Hooker* (London, 1988), e.g. 24; Peter Lake, *Moderate Puritans and the Elizabethan Church* (Cambridge, 1982), *passim* but esp. pp. 145–50, where he subtly argues that puritan claims to ethical moderation represented a sort of zeal against the flesh, a middle way between withdrawal from the reprobate world and submergence in it.

constructed the stereotype of "puritanism" that destroyed the political
coherence of the early Stuart Church'. Richard Strier has found in John
Donne's moderation the anti-puritan vitriol of the Arminians, while Gregory Dodds has shown how Laudian appropriations of moderation were
at the heart of Arminian attacks on predestination.[57] Stephen Greenblatt, discussing the destruction of the Bower of Bliss by the Knight of
Temperance in Spenser's *Faerie Queene*, has noted that 'Temperance –
the avoidance of extremes, the "sober government" of the body, the
achievement of the golden mean – must be constituted paradoxically
by a supreme act of destructive excess'.[58] Richard Ashcraft has shown
that claims to moderation by so-called Latitudinarians in the Restoration
were coded arguments that nonconformists could never be 'rational'.[59]
Mark Knights has traced how demands for religious moderation were
co-opted by Whigs and turned against High Church Anglicans in the
decades after the Glorious Revolution.[60] Steven Shapin has argued that
later Stuart science forged a self-conscious middle way between scepticism and credulity, ostensibly restoring moderation by basing 'epistemological decorum' upon gentlemanly norms of honour but in the process constituting 'a massively consequential system of exclusion'.[61] Steve
Hindle has critiqued the tendency of social historians to construct an
'optimistic "consensual" paradigm of social relations', noting the paradox that 'keeping of the peace might involve public processes of constraint
or coercion'.[62] The goal of this book, then, is to expand upon the work

[57] Lori Anne Ferrell, *Government by Polemic: James I, the King's Preachers, and the Rhetorics of Conformity, 1603–1625* (Stanford, 1998), p. 5; Richard Strier, 'Donne and the Politics of Devotion', in Donna Hamilton and Richard Strier (eds.), *Religion, Literature and Politics in Post-Reformation England 1540–1688* (Cambridge, 1996); Gregory Dodds, *Exploiting Erasmus: The Erasmian Legacy and Religious Change in Early Modern England* (Toronto, 2009), esp. ch. 6.
[58] Stephen Greenblatt, *Renaissance Self-Fashioning: From More to Shakespeare* (Chicago, 1980), p. 172. An important recognition of the interconnectedness of temperance and control can also be found in Malcolm Smuts, 'Force, Love and Authority in Caroline Political Culture', in Ian Atherton and Julie Sanders (eds.), *The 1630s: Interdisciplinary Essays on Culture and Politics in the Caroline Era* (Manchester, 2006), pp. 29–30 and 44–5.
[59] Richard Ashcraft, 'Latitudinarianism and Toleration: Historical Myth Versus Political History', in Richard Kroll, Richard Ashcraft and Perez Zagroin (eds.), *Philosophy, Science and Religion in England 1640–1700* (Cambridge, 1992). See also Richard Kroll's 'Introduction' to the same volume, pp. 16–24, for trenchant comments along the same lines.
[60] Mark Knights, 'Occasional Conformity and the Representation of Dissent: Hypocrisy, Sincerity, Moderation and Zeal', *Parliamentary History* 24, no. 1 (2005), pp. 41–57.
[61] Steven Shapin, *A Social History of Truth: Civility and Science in Seventeenth-Century England* (Chicago, 1994), p. 87 and ch. 3 *passim*.
[62] Steve Hindle, *The State and Social Change in Early Modern England, c.1550–1640* (New York, 2000), pp. 232, 94, 110–11.

of these and other scholars and suggest that these specific moments were examples or iterations of an entire system of thought whose contours have never before been explored, a broad politics of restraint in which moderation was simultaneously the harmony that subjects sought and the hammer with which they forged it.

A book like this one, on a topic so capacious, cannot possibly be comprehensive; instead it beats a particular path through the thickets of its subject, mapping territory along the way but inevitably leaving a great deal unexplored. As such, each chapter focuses on a particular case study of moderation, some defined thematically and others structured around particular events or debates, using a variety of historical methodologies from political history to cultural history to intellectual history, with the hope that together they will add up to more than the sum of their parts. I am painfully aware, however, of the many potential topics I have omitted. Just to name a few, I might have included chapters on: appropriations of moderation by the common people; moderation in the Elizabethan religious settlement; the debate over 'trimmers' in the 1680s; duelling as aggressive moderation; competing claims to moderation in the Civil War; Catholic claims to moderation; the moderation of Arminianism; and many others. That I have not written these chapters is not a commentary on their intrinsic importance but only a byproduct of my own scholarly instincts and the limitations of time and a publisher's patience. I would hope that the inclusion of these alternative topics would not have changed the overall argument, but that is certainly a discussion I am happy to have if this book sparks debate and encourages other scholars to consider its subject from different perspectives.

While my choice of topics is idiosyncratic, however, it is far from arbitrary: the architecture of this book is intended to argue for a particular trajectory of moderation in English history. Part I, 'Moderate foundations', including this Introduction and the first chapter, defines the themes and issues at the heart of this book. Chapter 1 explores the ideological work of moderation in early modern England, both in its more formal constructions and in its political uses, demonstrating how contemporaries understood moderation and the *via media* as activities of government that might include external and coercive interventions alongside internal and ethical ones. It first maps the meanings of moderation in the new vernacular culture of the period, then examines a series of representative sites where externalised moderation underwrote exclusion, coercion and violence in English society, culminating in the paradigmatic site of the moderation of women.

Part II, 'Moderate churches', analyses religious moderation and the *via media* of the Church of England from the reign of Henry VIII to the reign of James I. Chapter 2 offers an intensive case study of the first great assertion of the English religious *via media* – Henry VIII's simultaneous execution of three Protestants and three Catholics in July 1540 – showing how the identification of moderation with obedience was planted at the root of the Church of England. Chapter 3 demonstrates that subsequent conformist claims for moderation were in part based upon this Henrician model, requiring the external moderation of the Church by bishops, civil magistrates and the law to bridle its passions and reduce them to a virtuous mean. Yet at the same time, in a Protestant Church such government always had to be restrained to differentiate it from the perceived tyranny of unbounded papal primacy, so power came increasingly to be authorised by its moderation. Chapter 4 then analyses puritan claims for moderation in their own schemes for Church government, built around the argument that churches were capable of self-control through godly discipline, a form of authority that was entirely predicated on its restraint. On the whole, then, Part II suggests that the rule of moderation, with all its seemingly contradictory impulses of ethical self-government and coercive external authority, developed first and most influentially in the crucible of the English Reformation.

Part III, 'Moderate subjects', then expands outwards and explores how ideas which had developed in the Reformations of the sixteenth century permeated the social, cultural and political debates of the seventeenth century. In particular, its four chapters are organised around four sites that are not only central to Tudor-Stuart historiography but are widely taken as fundamental to English modernity. Chapter 5 explores the role of moderation in empire, showing how imperial promoters argued that England's colonies were sites of restraint, moderating the unruly impulses of social, religious and political extremists; they thus stumbled upon an argument that could justify virtually limitless expansion on the grounds of its limitation. Chapter 6 argues that the new, seventeenth-century idea of a 'middle sort of people' was as much a political as a social claim, recognising the authority of the middling sort in the public life of the commonwealth. Chapter 7 analyses the concept of political liberty in the 1640s and 1650s, showing how contemporaries typically identified liberty as a middle way between tyranny and anarchy, so that every claim for liberty was concomitantly a call for its restraint. Chapter 8 considers how religious toleration, long associated with extremism, became moderate in the second half of the seventeenth century. For liberty of conscience to become moderate, it paradoxically had to become a force of restraint, bridling sin in English society. In each of these four areas, then, new sorts of governance were authorised and the rule of moderation was inscribed in English modernity.

Two things remain to be stated explicitly. First is the extent to which this book posits English exceptionalism. A number of scholars have explored the issue of moderation in other early modern European contexts.[63] Most recently, Mark Greengrass has argued that moderation, or the 'government of the passions', acquired distinctive significance in the middle years of the French Wars of Religion as elites came to the conclusion that the passions of the kingdom had run amok and wholesale public reformation was necessary.[64] These historians, while acknowledging that discourses of moderation were never entirely transparent or apolitical, have nonetheless on the whole found peace and ecumenism rather than authority and coercion in their subject. Thus, if these historians are correct in their assessments – and the rest of this book provisionally assumes that they are – then this book tells a tale of English exceptionalism with profound implications for England's place in the modern world. This is not to claim that aggressive moderation was unique to England; undoubtedly versions of it can be found elsewhere, whether in the *politiques* of the Valois court or the anti-Anabaptist diatribes of Luther and Calvin. Rather, it suggests that the unique circumstances of the English Reformation, by explicitly structuring moderation around external governance, activated a fault line between ethical and political restraint that usually lay dormant, creating a much more capacious rule of moderation than can be found elsewhere.

It is also possible, however, that these European historians are wrong, and that like so many scholars of English moderation they have accepted their subjects' claims at face value rather than probing the politics of restraint embedded in them.[65] This would also be interesting, suggesting that perhaps England's local version of aggressive moderation was merely

---

[63] See, for instance, Luc Racault and Alec Ryrie (eds.), *Moderate Voices in the European Reformation* (Aldershot, 2005); Zdenek David, *Finding the Middle Way: The Utraquists' Liberal Challenge to Rome and Luther* (Washington, D.C., 2003); Howard Louthan and Randall Zachman (eds.), *Conciliation and Confession: The Struggle for Unity in the Age of Reform* (Notre Dame, 2004); Stéphane Gal, 'Malaise et Utopie Parlementaires au Temps de la Ligue: Les 'Moyenneurs' du Parlement de Dauphiné', *Revue Historique* 303 (2001), 403–31. For an older example, see Donald Nugent, *Ecumenism in the Age of Reformation: The Colloquy of Poissy* (Cambridge, Mass., 1974).

[64] Mark Greengrass, *Governing Passions: Peace and Reform in the French Kingdom, 1576– 1585* (Oxford, 2007). These discussions undeniably looked very different in France than they did in England. French elites regularly contrasted 'noble passions' in need of encouragement with 'ignoble passions' in need of restraint in ways that English writers rarely did; French debates were 'laicised' in ways English debates were not; and French writers reacting to the civil wars stressed the issue of 'pacification' in ways that were largely alien to English discussions.

[65] For intriguing comments along these lines, see Penny Roberts, 'The Languages of Peace during the French Religious Wars', *Cultural and Social History* 4, no. 3 (September 2007), pp. 297–315.

one thread in a broader strand of Renaissance culture that has hitherto gone unnoticed. I am not prepared to make this argument or to argue with any historian of the wider European context; at the end of the day this is not a comparative book and I must remain bound by the insular nature of my evidence. But I am aware that the possibility exists, and I hope that others will choose to explore it.

The second thing to be made explicit is the relationship between moderation and violence. As should be clear from this discussion, the word 'violence' in my subtitle is deliberately provocative: some examples of moderation in this book are plainly violent, others would seem to deserve softer words like restraint or coercion, while others seem like irenic accommodations of difference. Moderation and violence thus appear to run the gamut from nearly synonyms to nearly antonyms. My point is not to elide these distinctions but to put them into dialogue and notice how they relied upon the same ideological resources and slipped promiscuously between registers depending upon circumstances and perspectives. The dynamics of this relationship, the problem of how antonyms could also be synonyms, is the subject of this book. The politics of restraint was precisely the process that determined whether a given claim to moderation would be violent or not, and as such this book takes cognisance both of acts of bloodshed and of the more subtle assertions of power that prevented them. While moderation was not always violent, then, it was at heart a tool of social, religious and political power. England's ruling elite asserted their authority, fought their internal battles and expanded the power of the state not through *unmitigated* violence but through the rule of moderation, and this may help us in turn to understand the subtle violence of English history.

# 1    The bridle of moderation

## Introduction: the bridle and the square

George Wither was a terrible poet. According to a seventeenth-century anecdote, Wither's writing was so infamous that when he was captured by royalists in the Civil War, the royalist gentleman Sir John Denham 'went to the king and desired his majesty not to hang him', on the grounds that as long as Wither lived Denham himself 'should not be the worst poet in England'.[1] Yet bad poetry is sometimes just blunt enough to make good history, so we begin with an emblem taken from Wither's *Collection of emblems, ancient and moderne* (1635). Here, under the words 'Do not the golden mean exceed / in word, in passion nor in deed', we see the allegorical figure of moderation holding a horse's bridle in one hand and a carpenter's square in the other. The poem beneath tells us that, like a headstrong horse or mule, our nature is immoderate until 'grace and reason come to govern us'. Then, explicating the emblem's imagery, Wither explains:

> The square (which is an useful instrument,
> To shape forth senseless forms) may represent
> The Law: because mankind (which is by Nature,
> Almost as dull, as is the senseless creature)
> Is thereby, from the native-rudeness, wrought;
> And, in the way of honest-living taught.
> The bridle (which invention did contrive,
> To rule and guide the creature-sensitive)
> May type forth Discipline; which, when the law
> Hath schooled the wit, must keep the will in awe.
> And he that can by these his passions bound,
> This emblem's meaning usefully hath found.

Here, moderation is anything but peaceful; it is an active force of both moral and legal control. The alliance of internal and external

---

[1] Andrew Clark, ed., *'Brief Lives', Chiefly of Contemporaries, Set Down by John Aubrey, between the Years 1669 & 1696* (Oxford, 2 vols., 1898), I, p. 221.

Figure 1. George Wither, *A Collection of Emblemes, Ancient and Moderne* (London, 1635), p. 169.

moderation – between the ethical moderation of reason and grace to keep the 'passions bound' and the external moderation of law to restrain and civilise human beings in their words and deeds – is precisely the point of the emblem. They are symbiotic: once law has schooled the wit, discipline keeps the will in awe.[2]

---

[2] George Wither, *A Collection of Emblemes, Ancient and Moderne* (London, 1635), p. 169. The engravings for this book, including *Serva Modum*, had been created by Crispijn van de Passe for Gabriel Rollenhagen's *Nucleus Emblematum Selectissimorum* (misnamed *Nucleus Emblematorum* in the English STC and EEBO), first printed in 1611 and available in German, French and Dutch before the publication of Wither's English edition. Nonetheless, Wither's poetic emblem is an original composition.

This association of moderation with the bridle, with all its connotations of compulsion and control, was ubiquitous in early modern sources. Another emblem book, Henry Peacham's *Minerva Britanna* (1612), shows Temperance, queen of virtues, offering to 'moderate all human vain desires / Wherefore a bridle in my hand is seen / To curb affection, that too far aspires'.[3] The dissenting minister John Flavell, in his *Husbandry Spiritualized: or, the Heavenly Use of Earthly Things* (1669), wrote, 'Tis hard, in the midst of so many tempting objects, to keep the golden bridle of moderation upon the affections.'[4] Joseph Hall wrote, 'The chief employment of moderation is in the matter of pleasure, which like an unruly and headstrong horse is ready to run away with the rider, if the strict curb of moderation doe not hold it in.'[5] The Presbyterian Thomas Thorowgood argued in his *Moderation Iustified* (1645) that moderation 'stops the violence of a man's own passions, guiding them to their due ends, therefore in the hieroglyphic the bridle and helm are the emblems of moderation'. Yet if the bridle of moderation in one sense limited violence, in another sense it represented violence, as Thorowgood admitted two pages later: 'Moderation is a gracious and an acceptable virtue ... it offers a kind of violence upon men's affections before they be aware.'[6]

---

[3] Henry Peacham, *Minerva Britanna or a Garden of Heroical Deuises* (London, 1612), p. 93. Temperance and moderation were always closely related in early modern England but their precise relationship was not fixed. Temperance was sometimes understood simply as a synonym for moderation. More often, following Thomas Aquinas interpreting Aristotle, temperance was understood as a subset of moderation dealing particularly with the restraint of bodily appetites, whereas moderation might deal with any form of restraint. 'Temperance, which denotes a kind of moderation, is chiefly concerned with those passions that tend towards sensible goods, viz. desire and pleasure': St Thomas Aquinas, *Summa Theologica*, translated by the Fathers of the English Dominican Province (New York, 5 vols., 2007), III, p. 1761 (II.ii.Q.141.3). For a representative English example, William Perkins defined 'temperance' as 'the moderation of lust and appetite in the use of the gifts and creatures of God': William Perkins, *A Commentarie or Exposition, Vpon the Fiue First Chapters of the Epistle to the Galatians* (Cambridge, 1604), p. 448. Thomas Elyot, by contrast, rejected this framework, defining temperance broadly as 'not to excede the bounds of mediocrity, and to keep desire under the yoke of reason', while defining moderation narrowly as 'the limits and bounds which honesty hath appointed in speaking and doing': Elyot, *The Boke Named the Gouernour*, fos. 226–30. Some of this confusion was generated by the fact that, as Cicero pointed out, both *temperantia* and *moderatio*, along with *modestia* and even *frugalitas*, were appropriate Latin translations of the Greek word *sophrosyne*: North, *Sophrosyne*, p. 268. In this book I occasionally refer to examples of 'temperance' when it is clearly understood as a form of moderation, but I generally focus on 'moderation' itself, both because it was more explicitly linked to the idea of the 'middle way' and because it was more prevalent in public/political commentary.

[4] John Flavell, *Husbandry Spiritualized: or, the Heavenly Use of Earthly Things* (London, 1669), p. 38.

[5] Joseph Hall, *Christian Moderation in Two Books* (London, 1640), I, p. 8.

[6] Thomas Thorowgood, *Moderation Iustified, and the Lords Being at Hand Emproved* (London, 1644), pp. 5 and 7. And see the violent rhetoric of William Perkins: 'Put

Peter Paul Rubens's ceiling in the Banqueting House at Whitehall shows Temperance, with the bridle of moderation in her hand, stomping on the agonised figure of Wantonness or Intemperance; a nineteenth-century curator who made a key plan to the ceiling could not believe such a violent image represented Temperance, so instead he called it 'Government with a Bridle Trampling Rebellion Underfoot'.[7] The nearly limitless examples suggest not only a very deep connection between the metaphor of the bridle and the idea of moderation, but also the fact that when early moderns talked about 'unbridled' anger, zeal, love or despair, they were making far more specific charges of immorality than when we use the same vestigial metaphor today.[8]

Significantly, the source of this iconographic tradition was Nemesis, the goddess of retribution; in Roman antiquity she was closely associated with ideas of balance and was habitually depicted bearing the bridle. Helping to revive this tradition in the Renaissance, Erasmus's *Adages* contained a pen portrait of Nemesis which followed Martial's *Epigrams* in imagining her as an avatar of restraint as much as punishment: 'I, Nemesis, carry a bridle, and if you ask me why, my warning to all men is to do nothing beyond the mean.'[9] The emblem of Nemesis in Andrea Alciati's seminal *Emblemata* (1531) depicted her with a bridle and a ruler – the rule of moderation – commanding men in all things to keep within measure (*iubet in cunctis rebus adesse modum*). This model was followed in Geffrey Whitney's great English emblem book, *A Choice of Emblemes* (1586), where in addition to a bridle Nemesis now carried a carpenter's square – probably a slavishly literal rendering of Alciati's term *cubitus*, which can be translated both as ruler and as elbow. For Whitney, Nemesis's role was both to 'measure all our ways' and to bridle 'the lewd' with her retribution. In the sixteenth century, as David Greene has noted, this Nemesis tradition merged with a well-known early Renaissance

---

the knife to thy throat, that is, bridle thine appetite; have respect not to pass the limits of sobriety, temperance and moderation.' William Perkins, *A Godlie and Learned Exposition upon the Whole Epistle of Iude* (London, 1606), pp. 102–3.

[7] Arnout Balis (ed.), *The Ceiling Decoration of the Banqueting House*, part XV of the *Corpus Rubenianum* (London, 2 vols., 2005), vol. 2, plates 9 and 116–22. See also Vaughan Hart and Richard Tucker, 'Imaginacy Set Free: Aristotelian Ethics and Inigo Jones's Banqueting House at Whitehall', *RES: Anthropology and Aesthetics* 39 (Spring 2001), pp. 151–67.

[8] The association between passions and horses requiring restraint is a classical commonplace at least as old as Plato, *Phaedrus*, 253c–256b. For a thorough survey of classical antecedents, see North, *Sophrosyne*, 'Appendix: Imagery Related to *Sophrosyne*'.

[9] Desiderius Erasmus, *Collected Works of Erasmus: Adages II.i.1 to II.vi.100*, trans. R. A. B. Mynors (Toronto, 1991), volume 33 of the *Collected Works of Erasmus*, pp. 310–12 (II.vi.38). The most famous Renaissance image of Nemesis with her bridle was the *c.*1502 woodcut by Albrecht Dürer.

iconography – most famously depicted by Giotto in the Arena Chapel in Padua – in which Temperance wears a bridle with a bit in her mouth to keep her from speaking. The result by the seventeenth century was a tradition of representation that combined the external restraint of Nemesis's punishment with the internal restraint of Temperance's reason, producing, among other things, George Wither's tortured verse.[10]

The idea of moderation as *restraint* encoded in the image of a bridle – the instrument of civilised power upon unruly and uncivilised nature – elaborated the classical commonplace that moderation signified control of the passions.[11] Yet in a Christian and especially a Protestant religious context, where original sin cast such a long shadow upon human morality, this restraint was normally externalised: human beings naturally tended to sinful excesses and ordinarily could not be entrusted to moderate themselves, hence the *via media* required the external, coercive power of ministers and magistrates. This chapter, then, explores the dynamic relationship between internal and external moderation in early modern England, to establish a foundation on which subsequent chapters can be built. It demonstrates what was merely suggested in the introduction: that the interdependence of internal and external moderation found in Wither's emblem in fact characterised the discourse of moderation far more broadly. In a pre-Cartesian world, where there was as yet no clear boundary between self and other, ethical claims routinely contained and implied claims of authority and control, just as authority and control contained and implied claims to ethical moderation.

## Moderating the passions

*The Ethiques of Atistotle* (1547), an unfaithful, abridged and frankly atrocious translation that served the expanding vernacular market in Tudor England, told its readers unequivocally that 'virtue is gotten and kept by holding of the mean'.[12] Or, in slightly more elaborate terms, 'Virtues be found in things that have a mean between extremities, which are either

---

[10] Much of this paragraph is adapted from material in David Greene, 'The Identity of the Emblematic Nemesis', *Studies in the Renaissance* 10 (1963), pp. 25–43. I owe enormous thanks to Robert Harkins for bringing this to my attention.

[11] On Renaissance reception of this framework, see Scodel, *Excess and the Mean*; Gail Paster, Katherine Rowe and Mary Floyd-Wilson (eds.), *Reading the Early Modern Passions: Essays in the Cultural History of Emotion* (Philadelphia, 2004). See also Michel Foucault, *The Use of Pleasure: Volume 2 of the History of Sexualtiy*, trans. Robert Hurley (New York, 1990), e.g. pp. 55–88, 167–83, 251–2.

[12] Aristotle, *The Ethiques of Aristotle, That Is to Saye, Preceptes of Good Behauoute [sic] and Perfighte Honestie, Now Newly Tra[n]slated into English*, trans. John Wilkinson (London, 1547), sig. B6r.

too much or too little.'[13] This mean was ordinarily produced through the use of reason, whose superiority over the will produced 'right measure in delectation'; the mean was achieved when the 'concupiscable' part of the soul was 'obedient and under the power of that which is very reasonable, as the good child unto the father which receiveth his correction'.[14] This rational mean between extremes, the obedience of the passions to reason, was largely synonymous with the quality of 'moderation'. For instance, 'the continent man that hath understanding affirmeth himself and continueth in very reason and wholesome election, and departeth not from the right moderation'.[15] Likewise, 'a man that is of good understanding demandeth the pleasures of the body but moderately'.[16] 'Happiness' consists in 'moderate conducting in outward things'.[17] Here, then, in the first, simplified translation of Aristotle's *Nicomachean Ethics* for England's emergent chattering classes, we have a succinct distillation of an ancient conceit that was at the centre of virtually all ethical writings in early modern England: worldly virtue was achieved when the moderation of people's urges, passions or appetites produced a middle way between excess and deficiency.

It is an essential foundation for the rest of this book to explore this intellectual framework, to understand areas of conflict and consensus within its borders and to map some of its edges as competing frameworks emerged in the second half of the seventeenth century. I want to suggest that despite significant differences between the philosophical positions canvassed in many formal and self-consciously literary works in Tudor-Stuart England – Stoic, Peripatetic, Augustinian and so forth – at an informal or vernacular level these differences were largely flattened, and we can identify a series of widely held assumptions about the proper place of moderation and the sorts of work it should do.[18] But I want to stress

---

[13] *Ibid.*, sig. C1r    [14] *Ibid.*, sigs. B7r, B3r–v.

[15] *Ibid.*, sig. G8r.    [16] *Ibid.*, sig. G8v.    [17] *Ibid.*, sig. K8r.

[18] For both the differences between classical traditions in the Renaissance and their utter inseparability, see William Bouwsma, 'The Two Faces of Humanism', in his *A Usable Past: Essays in European Cultural History* (Berkeley, 1990), pp. 19–73. Bouwsma writes, p. 58, 'Neither pure Stoics nor pure Augustinians are easy to find among the humanists.' Margo Todd has described the commonplace books of Cambridge undergraduates containing both Ramist diagrams and Stoic morals: Margo Todd, 'Seneca and the Protestant Mind: The Influence of Stoicism on Puritan Ethics', *Archiv für Reformationgeschichte* 74 (1983), pp. 182–99. Mark Greengrass has written that 'given the overwhelming intellectual tendency towards the syncretic enrichment of traditions in the Renaissance', writers did not belong to particular 'schools' but expressed imaginative practical amalgams: Greengrass, *Governing Passions*, p. 44. Reid Barbour has argued that the Stuarts inherited from the Stoics 'a provocative set of contradictions as much as a cohesive set of beliefs': Reid Barbour, *English Epicures and Stoics: Ancient Legacies in Early Stuart Culture* (Amherst, 1998), p. 144.

that a comprehensive account of early modern English ethics is beyond the scope of this book. Instead I want to offer an account of moderation as an early modern cultural norm, intended to overcome our modern intuition of what it might mean.

The first point to be made is that, whereas late modern conceptions of ethical moderation tend to stress its passivity, for early modern writers moderation was by definition *active*.[19] Moderation was something you *did* to keep the passions under control. So, for instance, Richard Brathwaite's *The English Gentleman* (1630) defined moderation as 'a subduer of our desires to the obedience of reason, and a temperate conformer of all our affections, freeing them from the too much subjection either of desires or fears'.[20] In 'The Aretology or Ethicall Elements of Robert Boyle', written in 1645, 'The principal office of virtue is to regulate the passions of the mind and make them conformable to the laws of moderation.'[21] For Matthew Hale, moderation was 'the sovereignty and government of our passions', and he wrote, 'That man that keep his passions under that discipline as a man would keep an unruly creature, not to let him go without nor beyond his line, such a man can alone exercise moderation.'[22] And while the condition of moderation that resulted from such activity was ideally tranquil, it was also vigilant; being a moderate person both was the result of moderation and made further moderation possible. As a 1683 translation of Cicero put it, the peace of mind that resulted from 'moderation and constancy' is 'the virtue of the soul which some call temperance itself; others a quality obeying the rules of temperance'.[23] Moderation and its object collapsed onto one another.

Within this consensual framework of active ethical moderation, there was of course a great deal of disagreement about the precise goal of that project. The most significant difference of opinion, tracing an ancient debate, concerned whether virtue entailed the mere limitation of the passions through reason, as the Peripatetic (Aristotelian) philosophers had argued, or the eradication of the passions, as the Stoics had argued.

---

[19] As Susan James has shown, this sense of active moderation was dependent upon the Aristotelian philosophical framework of activity and passivity that came under fire in the seventeenth century, but James has stressed significant continuities on this issue even among critics of Aristotle: James, *Passion and Action*, esp. ch. 4.

[20] Richard Brathwaite, *The English Gentleman* (London, 1630), p. 306.

[21] Boyle, *The Early Essays and Ethics*, pp. 12–13. See also p. 80.

[22] From Hale's unfinished manuscript treatise 'Of Moderation': LPL MS 3497, fos. 121–35, at fo. 126v.

[23] Cicero, *The Five Days Debate at Cicero's House in Tusculum*, trans. Christopher Wase (London, 1683), pp. 228–33. See in this regard Helen North's characterisation of *sophrosyne* as 'the harmonious product of intense passion under perfect control': North, *Sophrosyne*, preface pp. ix–x.

Yet the existence of this debate does not imply significant divergence in practical understandings of moderation in early modern England. For one thing, despite the emergence of Neostoicism and the new prominence of Seneca and Tacitus in the later sixteenth century, it is virtually impossible to find any Renaissance writer advocating anything close to a thoroughgoing Stoic position on moderation of the passions. This was perhaps because, as Joshua Scodel has noted, Seneca himself was inconsistent on the issue, at times calling for the very middle way he was ostensibly attacking; Stoicism always contained an impulse to incorporate other philosophies into a great tradition of common wisdom, a tendency Renaissance humanism conspicuously shared.[24] Moreover, the necessity of emotions like compassion within a Christian moral system, and the fact that God often showed anger and love in the Bible, meant that at best early modern Christians who flirted with Stoicism had to argue that these were not passions at all – a manoeuvre which, whatever its philosophical import, in vernacular terms gave away the whole game.[25] Thus, even the great English Neostoic Joseph Hall, 'our English Seneca' as Thomas Fuller called him, wrote in his 1605 *Meditations and Vowes*,

I would not be a Stoic to have no passions, for that were to overthrow this inward government God hath erected in me; but a Christian, to order those I have. And for that I see that as in commotions, one mutinous person draws on more, so in passions that one makes way for the extremity of another (as excess of love causes excess of grief, upon the loss of what we loved). I will do as wise princes use, to those they misdoubt for faction: so hold them down, and keep them bare, that their very impotency and remissness shall afford me security.[26]

Besides the lack of committed arguments for the eradication rather than moderation of the passions, another salient feature of this debate was that the Stoic position was not as far from the Aristotelian one as it seems. As Cicero had pointed out in his *Tusculanae Disputationes*, while the Peripatetics argued that affections should be moderated rather than

---

[24] For Seneca, while the eradication of passions was a philosophical goal, the moderation of those passions was often acknowledged as a lesser but significant virtue: see Seneca, *Moral and Political Essays*, ed. John Cooper and J. F. Procopé (Cambridge, 1995), pp. 76 and 110. Scodel, *Excess and the Mean*, p. 2; Bouwsma, 'The Two Faces of Humanism', pp. 22–3; Todd, 'Seneca and the Protestant Mind'.

[25] It was also a powerful influence on all later Christians that St Augustine wrote against the Stoics in praise of moderated passions in his *City of God*: 'Scripture . . . places the mind itself under the governance and help of God, and the passions under the mind, so that they may be moderated and bridled and turned to righteous use.' St Augustine, *The City of God against the Pagans*, ed. R. W. Dyson (Cambridge, 1998), p. 365.

[26] Joseph Hall, *Meditations and Vowes, Divine and Morall* (London, 1605), pp. 98–9. Book I of Hall's *Christian Moderation* was also largely devoted to the virtuous use of moderated passions. On Hall's Stoicism, see Andrea McCrea, *Constant Minds: Political Virtue and the Lipsian Paradigm in England 1584–1650* (Toronto, 1997), ch. 5.

eradicated because a mean is best, the Stoics defined a passion as an 'over-vehement affection', hence passions were always already immoderate, but affections might indeed be moderated rather than eliminated.[27] This claim that the difference between Stoics and Peripatetics was merely semantic became a rallying cry for countless Christians: Augustine wrote that the difference was 'in words only and not in substance' while Aquinas wrote that 'this difference, although it appears great in words, is nevertheless in reality none at all or but little'.[28] This sleight-of-hand between passions and affections was useful to many early modern authors who wanted to defend moderation while partaking of fashionable late Renaissance Neostoicism. Edward Reynolds wrote in his *A Treatise of the Passions and Faculties of the Souls of Man* (1640), for instance, 'This controversy between the Peripatetics and Stoics was rather a strife of words than a difference of judgments, because they did not agree on the subject in question.'[29] Robert Boyle wrote that both sides agreed that 'no impulsions of the sensitive appetite should be able to make wander from the dictates of reason', so the 'difference here seems to be but nominally'.[30] The French philosopher Jean-François Senault, whose *The Use of the Passions* appeared in English in 1649, cited the authority of Augustine to argue that 'Stoics differed from other philosophers only in their manner of speech . . . for they blame not all passions, but only their excess.'[31] All of this was complicated by the fact that, as Gail Paster, Katherine Rowe and Mary Floyd-Wilson have noted, at the vernacular level 'some early modern writers treated "passions" and "affections" as synonyms, whereas others drew careful distinctions between the two terms'.[32] Hence, while the rise of Neostoicism had very real significance for English thought in this period, notably in the development of reason of state theories and in the developing notion that dissimulation could be an appropriate form of moderation, the debate between Stoic and

---

[27] Cicero, *The Five Days Debate*, pp. 239, 249. But on the other side, see Coluccio Salutati's claim in early Renaissance Florence, 'To harmonise Aristotle with Cicero and Seneca, that is the Peripatetics with the Stoics, is a great deal more difficult than you think': quoted in Bouwsma, 'The Two Faces of Humanism', p. 59.

[28] St Augustine, *The City of God*, p. 362; Aquinas, *Summa Theologica*, vol. II, p. 698 (II.i.Q.22).

[29] Edward Reynolds, *A Treatise of the Passions and Faculties of the Soul* (London, 1640), p. 49.

[30] Boyle, *The Early Essays and Ethics of Robert Boyle*, p. 17.

[31] Jean-François Senault, *The Use of the Passions*, trans. Henry, Earl of Monmouth (London, 1649), p. 5. See also Justus Lipsius, *Six Bookes of Politickes or Ciuil Doctrine*, trans. William Jones (London, 1594), pp. 32–3.

[32] Paster *et al.*, 'Introduction', in their *Reading the Early Modern Passions*, p. 2. See Thomas Cooper, *The Mysterie of the Holy Government of Our Affections* (London, 1620), fo. 2r; Wright, *The Passions of the Minde*, p. 13.

Peripatetic ethics left virtually unchallenged the fundamental principle at the centre of the current discussion: that moderation meant suppressing the unruly impulses to which human beings are prone.

The same can be said of the impact of Epicureanism on English Renaissance thought. There were certainly elements of classical Epicureanism that could be taken to contradict the idea that virtue resulted from the restraint of appetites and passions. But for the most part, as Reid Barbour has shown, English writers intent upon recuperating Epicureanism for Christians chose not to invoke those controversial elements but rather to envelop them within a larger syncretism. For Robert Burton, for instance, the essence of Epicureanism was that true pleasure depends upon virtuous austerity: 'He that is not satisfied with a little, will never have enough.' Henry Hammond likewise wrote, 'Temperance is the only Epicurism.' While the influx of Epicurean atomism did inform political debates and theories of absolute monarchy in the seventeenth century, then, it did not much impact the ideal of moderation.[33]

Other ethical debates involved what faculty actually did the moderating. So, for instance, there was disagreement over the role of the will. Many writers claimed that virtue lies in controlling the passions solely through reason, thereby limiting the role of individual volition; others, by contrast, argued that virtue lies in controlling the passions through the will itself, since freedom of will is the essence of moral choice.[34] A much more significant debate, however, concerned the role of religion, for while classical philosophers had stressed the capacity of reason to moderate the passions, Christians necessarily questioned the efficacy of fallen reason as a reliable ethical guide.[35] All early modern writers thus established some sort of framework through which religion or grace acted as moderators, and virtually all commented upon the failure of the classical world to produce a fully realised ethics: while the problems of human morality were clear to pagans through nature, their solution required revelation. This essential role of religion as moderator was made visually explicit in the 1649 English translation of Jean-François Senault's *The Use of the*

---

[33] Barbour, *English Epicures and Stoics*, pp. 65 and 98.

[34] Susan James, 'Reason, the Passions and the Good Life', in Daniel Garber and Michael Ayers (eds.), *The Cambridge History of Seventeenth-Century Philosophy* (Cambridge, 2 vols., 2003), II, pp. 1368–70; Bouwsma, 'The Two Faces of Humanism', p. 46.

[35] See Bouwsma, 'The Two Faces of Humanism', p. 25. Martha Nussbaum argues, against Foucault, that for stoics 'reason stands apart, resisting all domination, the authentic and free core of one's life'; in this sense, classical Stoicism would resist the blending of internal and external moderation that is at the heart of the present argument. My point, however, is that this autonomy of reason was necessarily effaced by Christian ethics, which radically attenuated the therapeutic effects of reason. See Martha Nussbaum, *The Therapy of Desire: Theory and Practice in Hellenistic Ethics* (Princeton, 1994), p. 354.

Figure 2. Jean-François Senault, *The Use of Passions. Written in French by J. F. Senault. And Put into English by Henry Earl of Monmouth. An. Dom. 1649.* (London, 1649), interior title page at sig. a2r.

*Passions*, where 'Divine Grace' stands behind enthroned 'Reason', guiding and advising her use of the shackled passions.[36]

Within this consensus, there was significant controversy about the details of how, when and for whom grace repaired reason and produced moderation. The Catholic position, elaborated in Senault's work, stressed the moderation of the sacraments and monasticism, as well as moderation as a work of supererogation.[37] Puritans, by contrast, stressed the moderation of the elect through their regeneration. As Richard Sibbes put it, 'None but a true Christian can carry himself moderately in the things of this world.'[38] The much-expanded 1655 edition of Edward Reyner's *Precepts for Christian Practice* claimed, 'Holiness of will is an effectual preparative to the government of the affections, seeing they are motions of the will; and if the will be sanctified, the affections will be holy.'[39] The radical potential of this puritan position generated a significant backlash. Thomas Cooper, for instance, in his anti-puritan diatribe *The Mysterie of the Holy Government of Our Affections* (*c*.1620) repeatedly mocked the hypocritical puritan claim that independence from lawful authority could constitute moderation, and he noted that 'in the godly, being but partly regenerate, the purest affections want not their mixture, as of corruption, so of temptation arising thereupon'.[40]

Yet there was no disagreement that all human passions, even zeal and love of God, required some sort of moderation in their expression. The anti-puritan Cooper made this a major theme, stressing that even though affections must be proportionate to their objects (hence there could not be too much love for an infinite God), nonetheless 'affections are good servants but bad masters' and even religious zeal must 'be in subjection' to the 'limitations of the Word, our callings, the common good'. Our affections must not 'exceed our judgment and knowledge of the truth', nor must they exceed our 'several offices and duties' in Church and commonwealth.[41] More broadly, the restraint of excessive zeal was such

---

[36] As Margo Todd has noted, this attitude might in some moods function as a critique of classical Stoicism, but it might also claim affinity with Stoic ideals insofar as Seneca was inconsistent on the relationship between reason and grace: Todd, 'Seneca and the Protestant Mind', pp. 190–1.

[37] Senault, *The Use of the Passions*, pp. 68, 91–2.

[38] Richard Sibbes, *The Spirituall-Mans Aime* (London, 1637), p. 5.

[39] Edward Reyner, *Precepts for Christian Practice, or, the Rule of the New Creature New Model'd* (London, 1655), sigs. AA4r, FF4v. At one point, the influential puritan theologian William Perkins even suggested that philosophy put too much emphasis on the 'restraint or moderation of affections' since theology also taught 'the renovation of them by regeneration': Perkins, *A Commentarie or Exposition*, p. 434.

[40] Cooper, *The Mysterie of the Holy Government*, fo. 29r–v.

[41] *Ibid.*, fos. 20v, 22r, 23r–24v.

a commonplace in Tudor-Stuart writing that it acquired its own special metaphor: the golden bridle. As Thomas Playfere put it in a much-quoted passage of his *The Pathway to Perfection* (1596), 'All blind zeal is a blind offering, which God will never accept. So that as Minerva is said to put a golden bridle upon Pegasus, that he should not fly too fast, in like sort our Minerva, that is our Christian discretion, must put a golden bridle upon Pegasus, that is our earnest zeal, lest if our zeal be unbridled it make us follow too fast.'[42]

It may be surprising to find that such claims were equally common in puritan texts: the outward expression of zeal must be tempered by the necessity of Christians living in the fallen world. Samuel Ward, the great puritan minister of Ipswich, borrowed from Playfere in his *A Coal from the Altar* (1615):

> The third kind, is turbulent zeal, called by James bitter zeal, a kind of wild-fire transporting men beyond all bounds and compass of moderation; proceeding sometimes of a weakness of nature in men, that have no stay of their passion, like to clocks whose springs are broken, and cities whose walls are down. Zeal is a good servant, but an ill master: metal is dangerous in a headstrong horse. And so the poets (which were the heathens' prophets) shadowed out the cure of this, in Minerva's golden bridle, wherewith she managed her winged Pegasus.[43]

Likewise, Edward Reyner warned that 'distempered zeal is a wrathful affection, and the wrath of man worketh not the righteousness of God . . . Zeal without knowledge is like a ship without a pilot, a horse without a rider.'[44] The great puritan theologian William Perkins, following Aquinas, had provided the theological rationale for this position in his posthumously published *Epieikeia: or, a Treatise of Christian Equitie and Moderation* (1604). There he made the key distinction that moderation is a virtue of men towards men, not of men towards God, hence zeal cannot be too great when directed towards God but nonetheless must be moderated with respect to human 'society and fellowship'.[45]

The point of this discussion is that despite considerable debate over the details, from the beginning of the English Renaissance to the beginning of the English Enlightenment we can see something like a consensus that virtuous human conduct depended upon moderation, bridling or governing the unruly passions and carnal concupiscence to which human

---

[42] Thomas Playfere, *The Pathway to Perfection* (London, 1596), pp. 42–3. For quotations, see Francis Meres, *Wits Common Wealth the Second Part* (London, 1634), p. 571; George Swinnock, *The Works of George Swinnock* (London, 1665), p. 169.

[43] Samuel Ward, *A Coal from the Altar* (London, 1615), pp. 21–2.

[44] Reyner, *Precepts for Christian Practice*, sig. II3r–v.

[45] William Perkins, *Epieikeia*, pp. 4–5. For Aquinas, see Aquinas, *Summa Theologica*, II, pp. 857–60 (II.i.Q.64, art.4).

beings are prone. But beginning around 1650, a number of different strands of thought emerged to challenge this consensus. These were only minority reports, and the vast majority of writers continued to rely upon the old framework until the end of the seventeenth century. But it is nonetheless important to outline these new approaches to ethics, moderation and the passions, if only to show that the framework which forms the foundation of this book did have contours and limits rather than being an undifferentiated cultural space.[46]

The first significant challenge in England to the traditional framework of moderation came, conveniently enough, at precisely mid century, with the English translation of René Descartes's *The Passions of the Soule* (1650). Descartes's treatise began with the remarkable premise that since nothing the classical world had to say on the subject was of any use whatsoever, he would simply invent his own theory *ex nihilo*. The result was an argument that human beings become habituated to conjoining certain actions with certain thoughts, such as running away when they are afraid, but that there is no intrinsic connection between particular thoughts and actions. As such, virtue does not consist in the moderation of particular responses but in educating and training ourselves how to respond to particular thoughts, and indeed virtue lies in exciting the correct passions for the occasion.[47] Now, Descartes did not escape from the ethical framework of moderation altogether: desire still required moderation in order for human beings to discern the correct passions to incite, and Descartes advised readers not to 'addict ourselves to anything excessively'.[48] But nonetheless, we have here a genuinely original framework that questioned the link between virtue and restraint.

Thomas Hobbes, another writer with little time for classical ethics, was yet more radical in eliding any distinction between passions, reason and the will. In Hobbes's *Leviathan* (1651), human thought is regulated by passion or desire, which leads people to follow one thought with another towards some specific goal. As such, 'whatsoever is the object of any man's appetite or desire, that is it which he for his part calleth good, and the object of his hate and aversion, evil'. This relativising of the passions and their complicity in ethics was completed by Hobbes's claim that, instead of the will being a rational faculty which controls the passions, will is simply the word we give to 'the last appetite or aversion immediately

---

[46] See especially James, *Passion and Action*, who stresses that, despite the enormous creativity of new, anti-Aristotelian intellectuals like Descartes and Hobbes, the Renaissance project of intellectual synthesis continued to incorporate their new ideas rather than producing a sharp break.

[47] René Descartes, *The Passions of the Soule* (London, 1650), pp. 107, 115, 121, 134.

[48] *Ibid.*, pp. 110, 112–13. See also pp. 136–7.

adhering to action'. For Hobbes, then, all talk of excess and deficiency was merely subjective, and the only difference between a moderate and an immoderate act was its utility; virtue consists not in the golden mean but in action conducive to peace.[49] Here, there is no possibility of an ethics built around the moderation of the passions, only an ethics built around the pursuit of individual goals arbitrated by lawful authority.

The ethics of Henry More, first published in Latin in 1667 and translated into English as *An Account of Virtue* (1690), minced no words in denouncing Aristotelianism: 'That virtue lies in a mediocrity is not quite untrue, if rightly understood; yet as some introduce virtue attended on each hand with opposite vices, and just as it were a rose placed between two nettles, this we do confess were a pretty show but it cannot possibly hold in every case.' This did not mean that More rejected all aspects of moderation; he was happy to confess that 'finding and electing a medium' rather than the medium itself was virtuous. But in his Platonist framework, this medium was to be found through what he called 'intellectual love', an emotional reaction which, for all More's claims that it was not properly a passion at all, nonetheless effaced the distinction between reason and passion that had been at the heart of earlier claims. Like his contemporary Blaise Pascal in France, More saw immorality flowing not from an excess of passion but from improper passion.[50]

Other examples could be explored as well. As Albert Hirschman wrote in his classic essay *The Passions and the Interests*, in the later seventeenth and eighteenth centuries 'interest' came to be seen as a mediating force between passion and reason, with the interests of the commonwealth served by balancing passions rather than subduing them, paving the way for self-interest to restrain the passions rather than being itself in need of restraint.[51] At roughly the same time, Libertine critiques of

---

[49] Thomas Hobbes, *Leviathan*, revised student edition, ed. Richard Tuck (Cambridge, 1996), pp. 20–2, 39–45, 111. *Leviathan* is a complicated text for the argument of this book. On the one hand, Hobbes's rejection of the classical association of reason with moderation and his radical separation of ethics from politics clearly point away from the Renaissance model described here. On the other hand, Hobbes's conclusion that all moderation depends upon sovereign authority makes him look like the epitome of that model.

[50] Henry More, *An Account of Virtue: or, Dr. Henry More's Abridgment of Morals, Put into English* (London, 1690), pp. 146–7, 149–51, 156–60.

[51] Albert Hirschman, *The Passions and the Interests: Political Arguments for Capitalism before Its Triumph* (Princeton, 1977), Part I. For Hirschman, this claim was an elaboration of Machiavelli's reason of state; for an argument that it emerged from rhetoric rather than politics, see Victoria Kahn, 'The Passions and the Interests in Early Modern Europe: The Case of Guarini's *Il Pastor fido*', in Gail Paster, Katherine Rowe and Mary Floyd-Wilson (eds.), *Reading the Early Modern Passions: Essays in the Cultural History of Emotion* (Philadelphia, 2004).

traditional Christian morality proposed that some people, usually the nobility, might ethically enact their freedom from restraint.[52] These new developments all chipped away from different directions at the broad Renaissance framework explored here, and while none of them had chipped very far by the time of the Glorious Revolution, they at least point the way towards an eighteenth century when David Hume could write, 'Reason is and ought to be only the slave of the passions,' and William Blake could write, 'The road of excess leads to the palace of wisdom.'

## Government and the failure of ethics

The discussion so far frames the ethical necessity of moderation for early modern English writers: a diversity of opinions over the details, but a consensual core in which active moderation bridles or governs the unruly passions and carnal concupiscence to which human beings are prone. The next crucial point, then, is that English writers were nearly as unanimous in stressing the extraordinary difficulty of moderation and the great rarity of its achievement. While there were certainly philosophical and theological differences over the nature of this difficulty, at a vernacular level a wide array of positions converged on the intrinsic immoderation of the majority and the need to organise society to moderate them. Moderation was thus near the heart of the ideological system by which early modern elites authorised their governance.

As Alexandra Shepard noted in her path-breaking work on masculinity, for early modern writers 'man's estate was not characterised simply by rational moderation . . . but by the repeated failure to live up to that ideal'.[53] Most people simply could not bridle their passions, and none could do so absolutely; human passions and appetites were so wild, and the human will so fallen, that only in rare circumstances was moderation possible. William Fulbecke, for instance, wrote, 'There is not one amongst a thousand that doth these things which he knoweth are to be practised, but we cleave as yet to the dirt, wallow in the mire, and though the loathsome satiety of pleasures do breed a surfeit in us, yet cure we the poison of pleasures with the hemlock of obstinacy.'[54] Robert Burton wrote, 'All men are subject to passions . . . the wisest men,

---

[52] James Turner, *Libertines and Radicals in Early Modern London: Sexuality, Politics, and Literary Culture, 1630–1685* (Cambridge, 2002); Scodel, *Excess and the Mean*, chs. 6 and 8.

[53] Alexandra Shepard, *Meanings of Manhood in Early Modern England* (Oxford, 2003), p. 68.

[54] William Fulbecke, *A Booke of Christian Ethicks* (London, 1587), sig. C4r.

greatest philosophers of most excellent wit, reason, judgment, divine spirits, cannot moderate themselves in this behalf; such as are sound in body and mind, Stoics, heroes, Homer's gods, all are passionate and furiously carried sometimes.'[55] The limit case of this argument appeared in a 1576 translation of Levinus Lemnius's *The Touchstone of Complexions*, which came close to claiming that Jesus had been the only moderate man: 'In this frail and transitory life of man, in this so great corruption and inclination of nature, I do not see to whom these things ought more aptly to be applied than to Christ himself.'[56] Unlike in classical antiquity, where the possibility for perfect moderation was at least normatively available and crucial for the theoretical construction of ethics, for early modern Christians perfect moderation was unavailable as anything more than a prelapsarian state whose moral requirements mirrored human fallibility.

What matters for our purposes, however, is not just that all these writers saw ethical moderation as an ultimately unattainable goal, beyond the capacities of most people even to approach, but that so many writers differentiated starkly between the capacities of different sorts of people. Gentlemen were commonly identified by their constant striving for self-control, even if most authors admitted at more pious or reflective moments that such self-control was always incomplete. But women, servants and other subordinate ranks were virtually incapable of self-restraint and required exterior restraint by definition. We will return to the issue of women's moderation below, but it is worth noting here in passing that, for instance, Edward Reyner wrote, 'The affections are headstrong and cannot be held but by a strong hand. The weaker the person is in understanding and parts, the stronger are the passions, as in women, because they are the weaker vessels.'[57] Class-based judgements were ubiquitous: Edward Reynolds, for instance, stressed that 'silly and unstable minds', that is to say 'weak and simple people', cannot keep their understanding from being invaded by passion.[58]

As we have seen, the puritan position on this issue stressed that moderation was available only to the small minority of elect saints through their regeneration, so that the vast, reprobate majority were irredeemably immoderate. As Thomas Taylor put it in 1612, 'such men as have not received grace to moderate themselves and their affections in their

---

[55] Robert Burton, *The Anatomy of Melancholy* (Oxford, 1621), pp. 360–1. See also p. 711.
[56] Levinus Lemnius, *The Touchstone of Complexions*, trans. Thomas Newton (London, 1576), p. 37.
[57] Reyner, *Precepts for Christian Practice*, sig. BB6v.
[58] Reynolds, *A Treatise of the Passions*, pp. 65–6.

pleasures are not yet regenerate'.[59] William Perkins claimed that sanctification 'tempereth the affections to such moderation as becommeth holiness'.[60] All but the most radical puritans would have denied the antinomian or perfectionist potential of these claims and admitted that in this world true or absolute moderation is impossible. Puritans were pure not because they always restrained their own appetites but because when they occasionally failed to do so God's grace gave them the capacity for genuine repentance so that they willfully submitted themselves to correction. Nonetheless, this rhetoric, like the rhetoric of gentlemanly moderation, tended to support the independence of the godly and reduced those outside the golden circle to the status of habitual objects of moderation.

An example that brings together many of these themes is Robert Boyle's 1645 'Aretology'. Boyle wrote that 'the most part of men' take for pleasure that which is 'lawless and excessive' rather than the true pleasure of virtuous moderation. The rational part of man is naturally inclined to good and the animal part inclined to evil as a result of the Fall, but 'in the most part of men the pusillanimity of the reasonable part gives leave, as it were, to the unruly affections, to snatch out of its hand the sceptre of power whereby Nature had enabled it to keep them in awe'. While this was true in 'most men', nonetheless 'in sundry persons, the natural clearness and strength of their reason, good education, or the divine assistance do over-sway the bent of the affections and make a man less inclinable to evil than to good'. Here, then, were three exceptions to the rule, three ways that individuals might sometimes achieve moderation despite the immoderate affections of the multitude. One of these, befitting Boyle's godly sensibilities, was 'divine assistance', while another, befitting his high birth, was natural virtue. The third and most important was education. At some moments in the treatise, this claim seemed theoretically to open virtue to a broader public; but in other moments it underwrote claims for the moral superiority of the learned over the 'vulgar', or over 'women, young men and fools' who were unfit for education, or over inferior categories defined by 'the nation, as in times past amongst the Persians; or the age, as in children; or the sex, as in women; or, lastly, from diseases and the like'.[61]

---

[59] Thomas Taylor, *A Commentarie vpon the Epistle of S. Paul Written to Titus* (Cambridge, 1612), p. 615.

[60] Perkins, *A Godlie and Learned Exposition*, p. 8.

[61] Boyle, *The Early Essays and Ethics*, pp. 31, 49–50, 57, 64, 115, 129. The ambivalences of this argument neatly distil the aristocratic exclusivity that William Bouwsma identified with the 'Stoic' side of the Renaissance: Bouwsma, 'The Two Faces of Humanism', p. 41.

If most people in most circumstances were incapable of virtuous moderation in its internal, ethical sense, yet moderation of the passions remained the basis of civil society, then that left only one alternative: external moderation. That is, if moderation meant government, yet self-government in most cases was proper to angels rather than men, then the solution was government by external authorities to prevent the fallen wills of subjects from resulting in sinful or dangerous behaviour. The Catholic Thomas Wright, in *The Passions of the Minde* (1601), wrote, 'If a superior or a magistrate see his inferior or subject vehemently carried in any passion, he may threaten or reprehend him, because one passion often cureth another, so here the passion of fear may expel the passion of anger, lust or what else soever tempteth either to the passionate's evil, or any disorder in the commonweal.' Since most men are 'more guided by passions than ruled by reason, therefore the wiser ought to provide a salve proportioned to the sore, and means to prevent malice, lest the children of darkness in prudence surpass the children of light'.[62] As the appalling mid-Tudor translation of Aristotle's *Ethics* put it, 'A man that cannot come to the perfection of this life ought to choose a way to live according to the common laws'; while some men can be made good by teaching and fair words, there are others 'that cannot be by words but by pain'.[63]

Depending upon the agenda and ideological position of the author, this external moderation could take various forms. For Robert Boyle, following Cicero, shame was 'the principal bridle that restrains the wicked from the most abominable offences'; hence he advised schoolmasters to shame students through moderate beatings: 'To beat people without first teaching them is to use them worse than dogs. Instruction must be first premised; and then correction put home. Instruction without any correction makes us impudently bold; and correction without instruction makes us slavishly fearful.'[64] The puritan Richard Sibbes, by contrast, described how a 'carnal man' – that is, not one of the godly – 'hath no

---

[62] Wright, *The Passions of the Minde*, pp. 154–5, 132–3, 147.

[63] Aristotle, *The Ethiques of Aristotle*, sigs. K7v, L2r–v.

[64] Boyle, *The Early Essays and Ethics*, pp. 81–2. Unlike Seneca, who had advocated shame as an alternative to corporal punishment, Boyle argued for their collaboration: see Todd, 'Seneca and the Protestant Mind', p. 195. The link between shame and moderation is elaborated in detail in Book I of Cicero's *De Officiis*. Boyle's version of education fits well within the paradigm described by Rebecca Bushnell, who found that English Renaissance authors understood the schoolmaster ideally as a moderate ruler rather than a tyrant, using reason to moderate his own passions and making his pupils subjects rather than slaves through carefully measured violence: Rebecca Bushnell, *A Culture of Teaching: Early Modern Humanism in Theory and Practice* (Ithaca, 1996), ch. 2. I owe this reference to Aysha Pollnitz.

bounds' in either his merrymaking or his sorrow 'if someone restrain him not', an idea clearly tied to the puritan programme for the reformation of manners.[65] In a different context, Robert Burton argued that moderation required the help of physicians. Sometimes this figure of the physician was collapsed onto the 'friend' to whom we ought to impart our miseries when 'our judgment be so depraved' that we cannot 'moderate ourselves'. Sometimes there was an element of coercion mixed in, as when Burton wrote that the friend or physician 'must be ready to supply what is wanting' in the immoderate melancholic and may use 'fair or foul means to alienate his mind by some artificial invention'. But at other times this framework carried a downright violent edge: 'Voluntarily thou wilt not do this or that which thou oughtest to do, or refrain, etc. But when thou art lashed like a dull jade, thou wilt reform it, fear of a whip will make thee do or not do. Do that voluntarily, then, which thou canst do and must do by compulsion.'[66]

By far the most important agent of external moderation, however, was the state. As Albert Hirschman put it, the 'appeal to coercion and repression' was always the most obvious way to moderate the passions: 'The task of holding back, by force if necessary, the worst manifestations and the most dangerous consequences of the passions is entrusted to the state.'[67] The *locus classicus* for this principle was Plato's *Republic*, with its extended analogy between moderation of the *polis* and moderation of the soul, and even though there was no English Renaissance edition of the *Republic* there can be little doubt that this was the source for at least the more learned versions of the theory in England. As Plato put it, moderation in the city consists in 'the desires of the inferior being controlled by the superior few, just as the better part of the soul controls the worse part'. Or elsewhere: 'It is better for everyone to be ruled by divine reason, preferably within himself and his own, otherwise imposed from without.'[68]

So, in an English context, Walter Charleton's *Natural History of the Passions* (1673) claimed under the heading 'General Remedies against Immoderate Passions' that, 'Among us men, if any hath power to hinder this or that evil, and yet doth not hinder it, we accuse him as cause of it; and justly, too, because the power that men have one over others was instituted and committed to them to that end that they should use it to the

[65] Sibbes, *The Spirituall-Mans Aime*, p. 41.
[66] Burton, *The Anatomy of Melancholy*, pp. 359–71.
[67] Hirschman, *The Passions and the Interests*, p. 15.
[68] Plato, *Republic*, trans. G. M. A. Grube and C. D. C. Reeve (Indianapolis, 1992), pp. 106–7, 262–3 (431c–d, 590d–591b).

restraining of others from evil.'[69] Thomas Hobbes, whose *Leviathan* was first and foremost a discourse on peace, argued that strong state authority was necessary 'because the bonds of words are too weak to bridle men's ambition, avarice, anger and other passions, without the fear of some coercive power'. Or, as he put it later, 'As for the passions of hate, lust, ambition and covetousness, what crimes they are apt to produce is so obvious . . . as there needeth nothing to be said of them, saving that they are infirmities so annexed to the nature, both of man and all other living creatures, as that their effects cannot be hindered but by extraordinary use of reason, or a constant severity in punishing them.'[70] A republican play from 1680, Nathaniel Lee's *Lucius Junius Brutus*, described how the glory of the state was built upon its capacity for external moderation:

> Vagabonds, walkers, drones and swarming braves,
> The froth of states, scum'd from the commonwealth;
> Idleness banish'd all excess repressed,
> And riots check'd by sumptuary laws,
> O, Conscript Fathers, 'tis on these foundations
> That Rome shall build her empire to the stars,
> Send her commanders with their armies forth,
> To tame the world and give the nations law.[71]

### Internal and external moderation

So let us explore some examples of this reciprocal and reinforcing relationship between internal and external moderation and the resulting politics of restraint. I want to stress that the point of this discussion is not to 'catch' my sources or to accuse them of hypocrisy, but only to reveal a dynamic relationship between ethics and authority that has largely been forgotten. When modern commentators or politicians justify coercion on the grounds of moderation, they are rightly accused of duplicity; when early moderns did so, they were expressing ideas that seemed to them to snap together in a virtually seamless whole. On the rare occasion that they acknowledged some potential incongruity or awkwardness in this construction, as we shall see sporadically throughout this book, rather than backpedalling or denying they fulsomely defended its legitimacy.

---

[69] Walter Charleton, *Natural History of the Passions* (London, 1673), p. 171.
[70] Hobbes, *Leviathan*, pp. 96, 206.
[71] Cited in Jonathan Scott, *Commonwealth Principles: Republican Writings of the English Revolution* (Cambridge, 2004), pp. 331–2.

To begin with one rather simple example: it was a mainstay of early modern English religious writing that *grief* must be moderate.[72] Excessive grief over the death of loved-ones was symptomatic of insufficient faith in the righteousness of God and represented a potentially dangerous attachment to worldly things. We can find these sentiments in Christian writings of all persuasions – the most elaborate example is *The Meane in Mourning* (1596) by the non-puritan Calvinist Thomas Playfere – but they occur particularly often in the works of puritans. So, for instance, Richard Greenham wrote that while grief in itself is indifferent, 'to be grieved out of time, measure or place is fault-worthy'.[73] Richard Sibbes condemned immoderate grief 'for the loss of father, or of wife, or of child' and told readers that 'the best grief of all must be moderate, much more grief for any earthly thing'.[74] These comments partake of an ancient commonplace, with firm precedents in Scripture, the Church Fathers and (in more secular form) Aristotle, and they do not seem on the surface to carry connotations of external authority. Yet more is going on here. In fact, these comments were part of a long debate between puritans and conformists, going back to 1570s, over 'mourning apparel' and other traditional customs of grieving approved in the Book of Common Prayer but condemned by puritans as dregs of popery. John Whitgift, for instance, wrote in response to puritan attacks on mourning apparel, 'It is the affection of the mind that is to be moderated and bridled, and not the lawful use of decent and civil orders.'[75] Richard Hooker wrote, like Richard Greenham, that grief in itself was indifferent, but he meant that customs of grief, even those specifically condemned in Scripture like those practised by 'the Canaanites or the Egyptians', were in fact lawful except when 'used as signs of immoderate and hopeless lamentation for the dead'.[76] Here, then, within a seemingly uncontroversial ethical argument against immoderate grieving, we have a debate over whether government ought to moderate grief or whether the government's attempts at moderation in fact needed to be restrained. Moderation could be made to support very different agendas; as a language of control, it was an enormously useful tool for early modern elites to defend and naturalise their various and sometimes contradictory ideological programmes.

---

[72] See Ralph Houlbrooke, 'Civility and Civil Observances in the Early Modern English Funeral', in Peter Burke, Brian Harrison and Paul Slack (eds.), *Civil Histories: Essays Presented to Sir Keith Thomas* (Oxford, 2000).

[73] Richard Greenham, *The Workes of the Reverend and Faithfull Servant of Iesus Christ M. Richard Greenham* (London, 1601), pp. 390–1.

[74] Sibbes, *The Spirituall-Mans Aime*, pp. 32–5.

[75] *WJW*, III, p. 370.      [76] *WRH*, 1, p. 291 (Book IV, 6.3).

This context becomes altogether more violent when we turn to Ireland, where Edmund Spenser, a man with strong puritan leanings, condemned the Gaelic Irish 'lamentations at their burials, with despairful outcries and immoderate wailings'. Spenser was aware that Scripture condemned Egyptian practices of immoderate grieving, and he suggested with tongue in cheek that Irish immoderation could be used by his contemporary Richard Stanihurst as evidence in his attempt to prove that the Irish were descended from Egyptians. But in fact, Spenser argued, the specifics of their 'heathenish' immoderation clearly showed their descent from the ancient Scythians, since their immoderate wailings 'savour greatly of the Scythian barbarism' described by the ancient Greek historian Diodorus Siculus. This, then, became central to Spenser's claim that the Irish were not merely popish but wholly unchristian, 'for it is the manner of all pagans and infidels to be intemperate in their wailings of the dead, for that they had no faith nor hope of salvation'. And it was on these grounds that Spenser explained, in a famous passage, that since the Irish refused all spiritual comfort, the first course of action must not be the reformation of their religion but 'to settle such a course of government there as thereby both civil disorders and ecclesiastical abuses may be reformed and amended'. Here moderation was the business of the imperial state.[77]

Another surprising example of externalised moderation was the aging process: male adulthood was deemed a virtuous golden mean between the excesses of youth and the deficiencies of age. Young men had too much energy, old men had too little. In Galenic terms, young men were too hot and moist, while old men were too cold and dry. Hence Tobias Whitaker wrote in *The Tree of Humane Life* (1638) that male adulthood is 'the constant *media*, between flourishing young age and old age; yet doth it not so participate of either, as that it is intemperate or infected thereby'.[78] Henry Cuff's *The Differences of the Ages of Mans Life* (1607) glossed Aristotle's division of men's lives into three ages with 'middle age' as the golden mean: 'The space between the two extremes is most temperate, forasmuch as nature never passeth from one extreme unto the other but by the mean.'[79] As Alexandra Shepard has summarised this material, 'Both youth and old age were frequently approached as periods of instability attributed either to a surfeit of vitality or to its absence . . . Manhood was designated the "firmest age", characterised by the ability to control youthful energies without yet being threatened by

---

[77] Edmund Spenser, *A View of the State of Ireland*, ed. Andrew Hadfield and Willy Maley (Oxford, 1997), pp. 61 and 85–6. Ralph Houlbrooke's 'Civility and Civil Observances' notes similar rhetoric used to describe the immoderate grief of American Indians.

[78] Tobias Whitaker, *The Tree of Humane Life* (London, 1638), p. 44.

[79] Henry Cuff, *The Differences of the Ages of Mans Life* (London, 1607), pp. 116–19.

their debilitating decline.'[80] This understanding was not ideologically neutral but, as Shepard has argued, served to justify patriarchal control of youth. Hence countless texts emphasised the need to 'bridle', 'tame' and 'discipline' youth – and those subsumed within that category because they lacked financial independence – in the name of moderation. Hence William Guild described youth as an 'untamed or wild colt [who] can hardly hear or will obey the straight bridle that restraineth liberty'.[81] The anonymous author of *The Discoverie of Youth and Old Age* (1612) complained that 'unbridled youth will run itself forth' and described the need for strict adult control: 'The heat of blood is loath to admit of any qualification, or reducing to a mediocrity, so long as years grant a dispensation for the contrary and the laws of the commonwealth will become indulgent.'[82] Gerrard Winstanley claimed that fathers must whip children who offend because 'the rod is prepared to bring the unreasonable ones to experience and moderation'.[83]

A more baroque example of externalised moderation concerns bodily consumption. Within traditional Galenic medicine, disease flowed either from a deficiency or superfluity of one of the body's humours, or from excess or deficiency of heat. Food and drink were to be consumed precisely so far as was necessary to restore equilibrium and no further. So, for instance, Thomas Paynell summarised millennia of Galenic medical tradition in his preface to a 1528 translation of Johannes de Mediolano's *Regimen Sanitatis Salerni*: 'A temperate and moderate diet prolongeth man's life and saveth him from all such painful diseases . . . O how wholesome is it then to use good diet, to live temperately, to eschew excess of meats and drinks.'[84] Among the more interesting particulars in this text, reprinted at least ten times before 1650, was 'one lesson touching the use of ale: that is, one ought to drink it moderately, so that the stomach be not hurt thereby, nor drunkenness caused. For it is worse to be drunk of ale than of wine, and endureth longer, and the fumes and vapors of ale that ascend to the head are gross, wherefore they be not so soon resolved.'[85] Hundreds of other texts of course stressed moderate alcohol consumption,

[80] Shepard, *Meanings of Manhood*, p. 23.
[81] William Guild, *A Yong Mans Inquisition, or Triall* (London, 1608), pp. 26–7.
[82] *The Discoverie of Youth and Old Age* is the second half of *A Two-Fold Treatise* (Oxford, 1612), quote at p. 6.
[83] Gerrard Winstanley, *The Law of Freedom in a Platform* (London, 1652), p. 40.
[84] Johannes de Mediolano, *Regimen Sanitatis Salerni*, trans. Thomas Paynell (London, 1528), sig. A3r. On links between health and moderation following Aristotle, Hippocrates and Galen, see, e.g., Thomas Elyot, *The Castel of Health* (London, 1539), fos. 43–63; William Bullein, *A New Booke Entituled the Government of Healthe* (London, 1558), sig. A6r.
[85] Mediolano, *Regimen Sanitatis Salerni*, fol. 39v.

and as new drugs became available in the era of colonisation, the ideal of moderation was adapted to them. The physician Tobias Venner recommended in 1621 that tobacco 'be taken with moderation, not (at the most) exceeding the quantity of a pipe full at a time; for everything which is superfluous, is very adverse to Nature, and nothing more than tobacco'.[86] Thomas Herbert wrote in 1634 that opium could be 'of great use and virtue ... [when] taken moderately'.[87]

Again, this would seem to be a more or less ideologically neutral framework, merely applying classical commonplaces to early modern conditions. But there is more to these discussions of alcohol than meets the eye, for Paynell's comparative discussion of beer and wine was not in fact in the original *Regimen Sanitatis Salerni* but was Paynell's own conceit, which became a mainstay of English medical writing for decades. Thomas Elyot's *The Castel of Health* (1539), for instance, agreed that both wine and beer were to be consumed in moderation but also concluded that beer and ale were much more intrinsically excessive than wine and nearly impossible to moderate: 'Neither ale nor beer is to be compared to wine, considering that in them do lack the heat and moisture which is in wine. For that, being moderately used, is most like to the natural heat and moisture of man's body. And also the liquor of ale and beer, being more gross, do engender more gross vapors, and corrupt humours, than wine doth, being drunk in like excess of quantity.'[88] William Bullein's *The Government of Health* (1558) agreed. God created wine 'for the great comfort of mankind, to be taken moderately', but when taken in excess it 'maketh men like unto monsters ... it dishonoureth noblemen, and beggereth poor men'. Beer and ale were likewise to be taken moderately, but the tone of Bullein's discussion was wholly reversed and moderation in these drinks was considered extremely unlikely. Bullein's discussion began, 'Ale doth engender gross humours in the body', and he described how 'to temperate bodies, it increaseth blood'. Beer was sometimes useful in cleansing the body 'if it be not very strong', but in general beer and ale had 'no such virtue nor goodness as wine have, and the surfeits which be taken of them through drunkenness be worse than the surfeits taken of wine'.[89]

---

[86] Tobias Venner, *A Briefe and Accurate Treatise, Concerning, the Taking of the Fume of Tobacco* (London, 1621), sig. C3r. See also Robert Hayman's 1628 poem, 'Since most preachers of our nation / Tobacco drink with moderation / Why should I fear profanation?': cited in Joyce Chaplin, *Subject Matter: Technology, the Body, and Science on the Anglo-American Frontier, 1500–1676* (Cambridge, Mass., 2001), p. 148.

[87] Cited in Brian Cowan, *The Social Life of Coffee: The Emergence of the British Coffeehouse* (New Haven, 2005), p. 39.

[88] Elyot, *The Castel of Health*, fos. 34v–37v.

[89] Bullein, *A New Booke Entituled the Government of Healthe*, fos. 109–12.

What gave teeth to these claims was that in England wine, a comparatively expensive import from the Continent, was paradigmatically the drink of the elite, while ale and (increasingly in the sixteenth century) beer were cheap domestic alternatives and paradigmatically the drinks of the poor. As such, comparative arguments about the moderation of wine and beer doubled as claims about social authority. As the literary critics Joshua Scodel and Stella Achilleos have described, the genre of drinking poetry known as the *anacreontea* and the symposiastic poetic tradition routinely portrayed moderate wine consumption as the lubricant of wit, poetry and civilised conversation; hence the elite drink of choice was imagined to be *moderately* alcoholic wine rather than beer, and the image of watered-down wine stood as figure of idealised self-control.[90] So, for instance, the *Leges Convivales* or drinking club laws written by Ben Jonson in the 1620s, later translated into English verse by Alexander Brome, stressed moderation:

> And let our only emulation be,
> Not drinking much, but talking wittily.
> Let it be voted lawful to stir up
> Each other with a moderate chirping cup;
> Let none of us be mute, or talk too much.[91]

This did not mean, of course, that the social elite did not get drunk, but rather that when they did so they became more like their subaltern neighbours: 'It dishonoureth noblemen.' The poor, by contrast, lacked self-control and their drinking was precisely excessive. As Steve Hindle has noted, for instance, the late Elizabethan parliamentary debates on drunkenness were 'both hysterical and class-specific', condemning the 'sins and enormities' that alcohol promoted in the poor.[92] A bill 'To Reform the Excess and Disorder Used in Inns and Victualing Houses', for instance, tried to create a complex licensing system for wholesalers of beer and ale, for the purpose of 'avoiding the great excess grown of late years in far more abundance amongst the inferior and baser sort of people than in times past, whereof infinite losses and inconveniences do grow to the commonwealth'.[93] Another bill, 'Against Excessive and Common Drunkenness', began with a moralising preamble:

---

[90] Scodel, *Excess and the Mean*, chs. 7–8; Stella Achilleos, 'The *Anacreontea* and a Tradition of Refined Male Sociability', in Adam Smyth (ed.), *A Pleasing Sinne: Drink and Conviviality in 17th-Century England* (Cambridge, 2004).
[91] Cited in Achilleos, 'The *Anacreontea*', p. 29.
[92] Hindle, *The State and Social Change*, pp. 181–2.
[93] PRO SP 12/282, fos. 77r–82v.

The said vice of drunkenness is . . . a vile and detestable thing in the abuse of God's good benefits, whereby both that is wasted by a few in excess, which being moderately used would nourish and suffice many, and the said drunken persons (the most part of them being of the worst and inferior sort of people) not only consume their substance (an occasion that often drives them to unlawful shifts, and become more like brute beasts than reasonable creatures) but also out of the said vice do spring diverse other enormities in the commonwealth.[94]

Yet another bill, this one against people drinking in alehouses within two miles of their homes, led the MP Edward Glasscock to comment that he hoped gentlemen would be exempted so they could still visit alehouses while hunting; the bill itself he described as 'a mere cobweb to catch poor flies in'.[95] For England's social elite, the alehouses of the poor were paradigmatically sites of prostitution and political disorder requiring constant government regulation, while the drunken poor themselves were reduced to the bestial state that best displayed their true nature. Such beasts required the bridle.

A final arena of interconnection between internal and external moderation was the state itself, not in the obvious sense that the state moderates its subjects, but in the sense that the body politic was analogous to a natural body whose different members – monarchy, aristocracy and democracy – moderated one another like the four humours in the human body.[96] This Polybian framework of mixed government was customarily described in early modern England as a species of moderation, for instance in the discussion of the need for proper 'proportion' in *Maxims of State* (1642), attributed (probably spuriously) to Sir Walter Raleigh:

Proportion is a just measure or mediocrity of the state, whereby it is framed and kept in that order, as that neither it exceed nor be defective in his kind, to wit, so that a monarch be not too monarchical, nor strict, or absolute, as the Russe Kings; nor aristocratical, that is over-mated or eclipsed by the nobility, as the Scottish kingdom, but ever respective to the other degrees . . . So a Free-State or Commonwealth that it be not over popular, *viz.* that it depress not too much the richer, wiser, nor learneder sort . . . The moderate states in their several kinds (as all other things that observe the mean) are best framed for their continuance.[97]

---

[94] PRO SP 12/282, fo. 91r–v.

[95] David Dean, *Law-Making and Society in Late Elizabethan England: The Parliament of England, 1584–1601* (Cambridge, 1996), p. 178.

[96] See Tuck, *Philosophy and Government*, introduction, p. xiv; Tully, *An Approach to Political Philosophy*, ch. 6.

[97] [Walter Raleigh?], *The Prince, or Maxims of State* (London, 1642), p. 6. Assuming that this was a 1642 forgery rather than really Raleigh's, a heavy dose of Civil War royalism emerges: displacing the sins of monarchy upon Russian (noticeably not French or Catholic) absolutism, denouncing Scots extremism, and imagining a mixed English constitution in the mould of the royalist propaganda masterwork, the *Answer to the xix Propositions*.

If different members of the state required 'moderation' just as did mankind's passions, then the same rigorous control, the same bridling of excesses, would be as necessary in the state as in society. Advocates of strengthened royal power, for instance, stressed that monarchy itself was a form of moderation, conveniently omitting the need to moderate monarchy. As we have seen, in 1606 Edward Forset wrote that the role of kings was to moderate their kingdoms: 'Right wisely do sovereigns hereof take this instruction, to uphold their government in a strict steadiness, tempering all extremities with an evenness of moderation, that none about them grow too violent or headstrong, which cannot but work as a disturbance to their persons, so a disproportion to their states.'[98] Half a century later, the poet William Davenant noted in his 1651 *Gondibert* that 'Extremes, from which a king would blushing shrink, / Unblushing Senates act as no excess.'[99] Another, anonymous royalist poem of the same era explained:

> And thus we see, the golden mean defied
> And how by two extremes 'tis crucified
> But 'tis no matter we see stranger things
> Kings must be subjects now, and subjects kings.[100]

John Arnway's *The Tablet or Moderation of Charles the First Martyr* (1649) noted that Charles I 'was of an even temper, steering beside extremes, excess and riot, cruelty and incontinency', yet it was the will of providence that 'the greatest president of moderation (called by Plato *amicus dei*) suffers violence by a heard of beasts, scrambling for each lock and mouthful within their power'.[101] Moderation was an argument for who should rule and who should be ruled.

Among those of a different persuasion, it was commonplace to argue that parliaments represented moderation. Fulke Greville, for instance, described in his *Treatise of Monarchy* (*c*.1611?), 'assemblies of estate / Which in great monarchies true glasses are / To show men's griefs, excesses to abate / Brave moulds for laws, a medium that in one / Joins with content a people to the throne'.[102] Thomas Scott wrote from exile in 1624,

A parliament therefore, where prince and people meet and join in consultation, is fit only for that weighty and important work in whose even balancing the weal of

---

[98] Forset, *A Comparatiue Discourse*, sig. E4r.
[99] William Davenant, *Gondibert an Heroick Poem* (London, 1651), p. 176.
[100] BL Harleian MS 2127, fo. 15r–v.
[101] John Arnway, *The Tablet or Moderation of Charles the First Martyr* (The Hague, 1649), pp. 11 and 30.
[102] Fulke Greville, *The Remains of Sir Fulk Grevill Lord Brooke Being Poems of Monarchy and Religion* (London, 1670), p. 78.

a state doth consist. And without this counsel, the greatest peer or officer, yea the greatest professed engineer in state stratagems, may easily err upon either hand, many degrees from good government, and so fall into an anarchy or tyranny.[103]

In a sermon before the Long Parliament, the Presbyterian Thomas Thorowgood argued that parliament's moderation consisted in their desire to 'confine and regulate the evil counselors about the king in religious and civil affairs'.[104]

In this tradition, apologists for the English Republic justified severing Charles Stuart's head from his shoulders by denouncing monarchy as *ipso facto* excess. A writer calling himself Veritie Victor argued that 'kings' courts are the fountains from whence the streams of excess do flow'.[105] Francis Osborne, in his *Perswasive to a Mutuall Compliance under the Present Government* (1652), called the revolutionary regime 'as admirable for moderation, as success hath proclaimed them famous for valour', arguing that monarchy was intrinsically excessive, 'a sacrilegious over-charging a single person with more honour and power than so frail a creature is able to bear without falling into the distempers of excess'.[106] Marchamont Nedham argued in 1650 that 'this present combination of royalists and presbyters . . . must of necessity put the nation in hazard between Scylla and Charybdis, that we cannot choose but fall into one of the pernicious gulfs, either of Presbyterian or Monarchical tyranny'.[107] Six years later, with political circumstances altered, Nedham altered his middle way. Now, in *The Excellencie of a Free-State* (1656), Nedham responded to the excesses of Cromwellian parliaments by arguing that Solon the lawgiver had forged a middle way that avoided 'kingly tyranny on the one side, and senatical encroachments on the other'. In this scheme, just as tyrants had to be moderated, so too representatives of the people 'were as bridles to restrain the power and ambition of the senate'.[108]

I want to stress that in none of these different areas was it simply the case that those unable to moderate themselves required external moderation; it was equally the case that government itself was authorised by its own limitation. Moderation contained a transitive principle, governing and governed, so that just as no one was capable of perfect self-control,

[103] Thomas Scott, *Vox Regis* (Utrecht, 1624), p. 68.

[104] Thorowgood, *Moderation Iustified*, p. 14.

[105] Veritie Victor, *A Plea for Moderation in the Transactions of the Army* (London, 1648), sig. A2r.

[106] Francis Osborne, *A Perswasive to a Mutuall Compliance under the Present Government* (Oxford, 1652), pp. 2, 24.

[107] Marchamont Nedham, *The Case of the Common-Wealth of England Stated* (London, 1650), p. 55.

[108] Marchamont Nedham, *The Excellencie of a Free-State* (London, 1656), pp. 8, 15–16.

so likewise those whose self-control was imperfect might nonetheless be qualified through external restraints to participate in the control of others. At its most expansive moments, this dynamic tension created a vision of balance and harmony in which every part of society was both restraining and restrained; at its most perverse, it paradoxically used the depravity of all mankind to justify the authority of a small minority over the rest.

### The moderation of women

We have so far seen a variety of contexts in which claims to the bridle of moderation authorised particular assertions of social and political power. We have also seen hints of how such arguments could underwrite substantial violence. In this final section, then, I want to push more deeply into one particular example of moderation – the moderation of women – where these connections between rhetoric and reality can be more securely established.

Ethical writings for and about early modern women clearly stated that women were supposed to be moderate, governing their passions with reason in order to produce middle ways in every aspect of their lives. Let us take, for example, a tract entitled *The Mothers Counsell or, Live Within Compasse* (1630). Its title page provided a visual metaphor for the female middle way: mother and daughter stand safely within a circle defined by the feminine virtues of temperance, chastity, humility and (moral) beauty, while outside the circle lurk the feminine sins of madness, wantonness, pride and odiousness. To live 'within compass', then, was a radial image (as opposed to the more usual lineal image) for moderation.[109] So, for instance, in its discussion of health it claimed women should not seek 'an over-weaning ability of strength' but rather should good-naturedly 'groan under the hand of sickness', since 'there is no perfect health in this world, but a neutrality between sickness and health'. Too much strength in a woman threatened to release her carnal excesses. Beauty, too, was defined by mediocrity: since physical beauty was a 'seemly composition of all the members', a woman should not 'strive to excel in beauty, but hold the golden mean, which is the true mediocrity and best part of any action'. To exceed one's 'nature or condition' in beauty was an act of sinful pride, so women should not attempt to beautify themselves artificially; as the author put it, 'a painted woman's face is a liver smeared with carrion'.[110]

---

[109] M. R., *The Mothers Counsell or, Live Within Compasse. Being the Last Will and Testament to Her Dearest Daughter* (London, 1630). This text has been discussed in Shepard, *Meanings of Manhood*, ch. 1. It was a female version of John Trundle's popular didactic text *Keepe within Compasse* (London, 1619).

[110] M. R., *The Mothers Counsell*, sigs. B7r–B8r, C1r–C2v, A7r.

Figure 3. M. R., *The Mothers Counsell or, Liue within Compasse Being the Last Will and Testament to Her Dearest Daughter* (London, 1630), title page.

Another example was a 1627 sermon preached by John Donne in commemoration of the late Lady Magdalen Danvers, mother of the poet George Herbert. The centrepiece of Donne's panegyric for Lady Danvers was that 'her rule was mediocrity'.[111] Just as the 'rule of all her civil actions was religion', Donne claimed, 'so the rule of her religion was the scripture; and her rule for her particular understanding of the scripture was the Church. She never diverted towards the papist in undervaluing the scripture, nor towards the separatist in undervaluing the Church.'[112] Here we have a textbook argument for the Church of England's middle way, suggesting that moderation in life was synonymous with moderation in religion. Yet this argument must not be lifted out of context and seen as just one more example in an endless series of illustrations of how to lead a moderate life in the Church of England. Instead, it was highly significant that Lady Danvers was a woman, since her gender made the particular features of her 'mediocrity' distinctive. Donne took unusual note, for instance, of her moodiness. Earlier in her life she was 'naturally cheerful', yet not so cheerful that she approved of 'wit to the prejudice of godliness'; later in her life she suffered from an 'overflowing of melancholy', yet never so much that it caused her to 'dispute upon any of God's proceedings or to lodge a jealousy or suspicion of his mercy'.[113] Donne also took unusual note of her physical appearance: 'God gave her such a comeliness as, though she were not proud of it, yet she was so content with it as not to go about to mend it by any art.' Her clothing, likewise, was 'never sumptuous' yet also 'never sordid'.[114] Perhaps most conspicuously, Donne emphasised Lady Danvers's moderate charity. While some people had too much sympathy and others had too little, Lady Danvers 'never turned her face from those who in a strict inquisition might be called idle and vagrant beggars, yet she ever looked first upon them who laboured'.[115]

Even these sources praising moderate women, then, left no doubt that such women were the exception, and that the natural excesses of women made their moderation difficult and precarious. As such, in most early modern sources women were routinely described as creatures of extremes, wholly virtuous or wholly fallen, virtually incapable of native moderation. As the Scotsman George Buchanan glossed this classical commonplace in his diatribe against Mary Stuart, women 'have vehement affections both ways; they love with excess and hate without measure; and

---

[111] John Donne, *A Sermon of Commemoration of the Lady Danvers, Late Wife of Sir John Danvers* (London, 1627), p. 147. I owe this reference to Michelle Wolfe.
[112] *Ibid.*, pp. 156–7.      [113] *Ibid.*, pp. 131 and 135–6.
[114] *Ibid.*, pp. 145–7.      [115] *Ibid.*, pp. 148–51.

to what side soever they bend, they are not governed by advised reason, but carried by violent motion'.[116] The revolutionary writer John Rogers said of women, 'Where they are bad, they are extreme bad, but where they are good, they are exceeding good.'[117] For the author of *A Strange Wonder or a Wonder in a Woman* (1642), 'Women are admirable angels, if they would not be drawn with angels to become devils.'[118] Women lacked self-control; they were slaves to their bodies and unable to moderate their behaviour. It was for this reason, according to William Tyndale, that God had put woman under obedience to her husband, 'to rule her lusts and wanton appetites'.[119] To a worried observer of female preachers in Civil War London, women were 'passionate and vainglorious, indiscreet, easily led into extremes either good or evil', and it was for that lack of self-governance that woman was 'made subject unto man's government'.[120] According to Joseph Swetnam, the most famous misogynist of his age, virtuous mediocrity was nearly impossible for women: 'Plato saith that women are either angels or devils, and that they either love dearly or hate bitterly, for a woman hath no mean in her love, nor mercy in her hate; no pity in revenge nor patience in her anger.'[121]

Such views came naturally to Swetnam, but virtually identical assumptions appeared in texts intended to defend women. So, for example, the 1617 reply to Swetnam, *The Worming of a Mad Dogge*, praised some women as 'the end, crown and perfection of the never-sufficiently glorified creation', yet the author divided women into Madonnas and whores in terms worthy of Swetnam himself: 'A private abuse of your own familiar doxies should not break out into open slanders of the religious matron together with the prostitute strumpet; of the nobly-descended ladies as the obscure, base vermin that have bitten you; of the chaste, modest virgins as well as the dissolute and impudent harlot.'[122] A 1588 puritan sermon admitted that women's inability to keep secrets was 'an infirmity incident to the greater part of this sex' but argued that 'godly and virtuous women' – that is, puritans by virtue of their regeneration – 'are

---

[116] Cited in J. E. Lewis, *The Trial of Mary Queen of Scots: A Brief History with Documents* (Boston, 1999), p. 14.

[117] Cited in James Holstun, *Ehud's Dagger: Class Struggle in the English Revolution* (London, 2000), p. 261.

[118] I. H., Gentleman, *A Strange Wonder or a Wonder in a Woman* (London, 1642), p. 1.

[119] William Tyndale, *The Obedience of a Christian Man*, ed. David Daniell (London, 2000), pp. 34, 42.

[120] *A Spirit Moving in the Women-Preachers* (London, 1646), p. 4.

[121] Joseph Swetnam, *The Araignment of Lewde, Idle, Froward, and Unconstant Women: Or the Vanitie of Them, Choose You Whether* (London, 1615), sig. D1v. See also sig. E2v.

[122] Constantia Munda, *The Worming of a Mad Dogge: Or, a Soppe for Cerberus the Iaylor of Hell No Confutation but a Sharpe Redargution of the Bayter of Women* (London, 1617), sigs. B3r, C4v, C2r. It is unknown whether this tract was actually written by a woman, although other replies to Swetnam certainly were.

able . . . to temper their tongues and to bridle their affections which move them to reveal secrets'.[123] A more shocking example comes from Thomas Wright, whose *The Passions of the Minde* (1601) took issue with Seneca's opinion that women either love or hate with nothing in between, saying that this was only true of dark-skinned women:

For although in some sort of women I hold it very probable, yet I cannot allow it to be common to all, for only women that be of a hot complexion, and for the most part those that be black or brown, I take to be of that constitution and indeed those have their affections most vehement.[124]

Moderation was thus routinely described as quintessentially masculine, and masculinity as quintessentially moderate, since, as Alexandra Shepard and Elizabeth Foyster have shown, both were ideally defined by self-control.[125] In William Loe's sermon on marital relations *The Incomparable Jewell* (1632), for instance, he referred to the 'medium or mean wherein this masculine virtue is to be sought and found' and described how 'the affections' of the virtuous man are 'the object of virtue, in the moderation and subjection whereof his masculine virtue is chiefly busied'.[126] Joseph Hall, author of *Christian Moderation* (1640), wrote, 'Our pleasures should be like ourselves, masculine and temperate' and he asked rhetorically, 'How many brave hopes have we known dashed with youthly excess? How many high and gallant spirits effeminated?'[127] For the Anglican royalist minister Anthony Farindon, to moderate the passions was precisely to discipline the feminine:

Our passions which have *quondam mulieritatem*, a kind of womanishness in them, and are many times as froward and perverse as any of that sex, yet may be made useful and serviceable . . . by turning their effeminacy into true manhood; by making my fear a sentinel to warn me of danger, my anger a magistrate to punish my sin, and my sorrow a penitentiary to water my couch with tears . . . by making that divine which was bestial and brutish in them.[128]

---

[123]  E. R., *Two Fruitfull Exercises* (London, 1588), p. 77.

[124]  Wright, *The Passions of the Minde*, pp. 77–8.

[125]  See Shepard, *Meanings of Manhood*, ch. 1 and *passim*; Elizabeth Foyster, 'Male Honour, Social Control and Wife Beating in Late Stuart England', *TRHS* sixth series, 6 (1996), pp. 215–24.

[126]  William Loe, *The Incomparable Jewell Shewed in a Sermon* (London, 1632), pp. 31–3.

[127]  Hall, *Christian Moderation*, Book I, pp. 62 and 90. See also examples on pp. 96 and 129.

[128]  Anthony Farindon, *Fifty Sermons Preached at the Parish-Church of St. Mary Magdalene Milk-Street, London, and Elsewhere* (London, 1674), pp. 176–8. Classical antecedents for these ideas are not hard to find. See, for instance, Seneca, *De Ira*, where he refers to anger as a 'particularly feminine and childish failing' but argues that even men can have feminine and childish characters: Seneca, *Moral and Political Essays*, p. 39. Aristotle made a correspondence between 'reason and appetite' in the soul and 'a man and a woman' in the family: Aristotle, *Aristotles politiques*, trans. I. D. (London, 1598), p. 144.

Female moderation was thus inevitably embodied in the external moderation *of* women as much as internal moderation *by* women, while the enactment of such moderation by men proved and constituted their manhood.

The point of all this is not just that women were rhetorically framed as requiring moderation, but that this rhetoric authorised material violence. So, for instance, the beating of wives, when virtuously limited in magnitude and undertaken rationally rather than precipitously, was justified as 'moderate correction' rather than excessive force. Laura Gowing cites a representative case from 1588 in which Simon White 'did upon just occasion chastise and correct the said Elizabeth [his wife] with a small beechen wand for her misusage and intolerable misbehavior towards him, which he did in honest, reasonable and moderate sort'.[129] According to Blackstone's *Commentaries* (1765), 'the husband also (by the old law) might give his wife moderate correction. For, as he is to answer for her misbehaviour, the law thought it reasonable to entrust him with this power of restraining her, by domestic chastisement, in the same moderation that a man is allowed to correct his apprentices or children.' Blackstone noted that in the reign of Charles II, 'this power of correction began to be doubted, and a wife may now have security of the peace against her husband'; nonetheless, 'the lower rank of people, who were always fond of the old common law, still claim and exert their ancient privilege, and the courts of law will still permit a husband to restrain a wife of her liberty'.[130] The later Stuart alteration Blackstone had in mind was probably a report by Sir Matthew Hale in 1675 in which he wrote, 'The *salva moderata castigatione* in the register is not meant of beating, but only of admonition and confinement in the house in case of her extravagance; which the court agreed.'[131] There was in fact considerable debate in early modern England over the limits of moderate correction, as Susan Amussen and Elizabeth Foyster have shown, and there were as many cases of public outcry against immoderate violence as there were defences of moderate correction.[132] But this is precisely the point, for

---

[129] Laura Gowing, *Domestic Dangers: Women, Words, and Sex in Early Modern London* (Oxford, 1996), p. 219.

[130] William Blackstone, *Commentaries on the Laws of England* (Oxford, 4 vols., 1765–9), I, pp. 432–3.

[131] *The English Reports* (Edinburgh, 176 vols., 1900–30), LXXXIV, King's Bench Division 13, Lord Leigh's Case, p. 807.

[132] Susan Amussen, *An Ordered Society: Gender and Class in Early Modern England* (Oxford, 1988); Susan Amussen, 'Being Stirred to Much Unquietness: Violence and Domestic Violence in Early Modern England', *Journal of Women's History* 6, no. 2 (Summer 1994), pp. 70–89; Elizabeth Foyster, *Marital Violence: An English Family History, 1660–1875* (Cambridge, 2005). William Perkins denounced all physical 'correction' of spouses:

moderate correction was moderate both in the sense that it restrained the feminine and in the sense that it was restrained by masculine reason and judgement. These two meanings contained and implied one another, so that the lesser penalty – '*only , , , admonition and confinement*' – could be defined as moderate rather than extreme: the limitation of government paradoxically authorised government.

Moreover, when this idea of moderate correction was crossed with the ubiquitous metaphor of moderation as a bridle, the results were horrific. At first this was merely rhetorical: the image of women as horses requiring bridles had a long pedigree in England. As William Baldwin put it in his runaway bestseller *A Treatise of Morall Phylosophie* (1547), 'Like as to a shrewd horse belongeth a sharp bridle: so ought a shrewd wife to be sharply handled.'[133] Anthony Fitzherbert's *Book of Husbandry*, first published in 1523, claimed that horses were like women, 'ever to be chewing on the bridle'.[134] *The Mothers Counsell* argued that 'a mad woman is like a rough stirring horse, and as he must have a sharp bit, so must she have a sharp restraint'.[135] But in the early seventeenth century, reality followed rhetoric as a Scottish instrument of torture known as 'the branks' was adapted into England, where it was renamed the 'scold's bridle' and became a commonplace, although never officially sanctioned, punishment for unruly women. Scold's bridles were iron cages placed over women's heads, fitted with long metal spikes or plates to be inserted into their mouths to keep them from speaking, like a horse's bridle with a bit. Their use can be documented in at least five English counties in the seventeenth century, such as in Worcestershire, where the city of Worcester paid four shillings 'for mending the bridle for bridling of scolds'.[136]

In a more detailed example, Robert Plot's *The Natural History of Stafford-Shire* (1686) offered voyeuristic readers a labelled illustration of a scold's bridle at Newcastle-under-Lyme and described how it provided

for correcting of scolds...such a bridle for the tongue, as not only quite deprives them of speech, but brings shame for the transgression and humility

William Perkins, *Christian Oeconomie: or, a Short Survey of the Right Manner of Erecting and Ordering a Familie* (London, 1609), pp. 126–9.

[133] William Baldwin, *A Treatise of Morall Phylosophie* (London, 1547), sig. Q2v.

[134] Joan Hartwig, 'Horses and Women in *The Taming of the Shrew*', *Huntington Library Quarterly* 45, no. 4 (Autumn 1982), pp. 285–94, quoted at p. 286.

[135] M. R., *The Mothers Counsell*, p. 15. As Laura Gowing has pointed out, the image of wives keeping their husbands in bridles was also commonplace in the popular culture of social inversion and female misconduct: Gowing, *Domestic Dangers*, p. 84.

[136] Lynda Boose, 'Scolding Brides and Bridling Scolds: Taming the Woman's Unruly Member', *Shakespeare Quarterly* 42, no. 2 (Summer 1991), pp. 179–213, at p. 197. See also Stevie Davis, *Unbridled Spirits: Women of the English Revolution: 1640–1660* (London, 1998).

Figure 4. Ann Bidlestone wears the scold's bridle, from Ralph Gardiner, *Englands Grievance Discovered, in Relation to the Coal-Trade* (London, 1655), p. 110.

thereupon . . . which being put upon the offender by order of the magistrates, and fastened with a padlock behind, she is lead round the town by an officer to her shame, nor is it taken off till after the party begins to show all external signs imaginable of humiliation and amendment.[137]

The most harrowing evidence comes from a first-person account by a Quaker woman named Dorothy Waugh. In 1656, Waugh described how the mayor of Carlisle

[137] Robert Plot, *The Natural History of Stafford-Shire* (Oxford, 1686), p. 389.

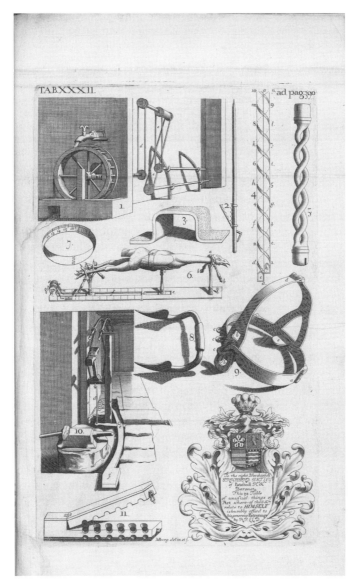

Figure 5. The scold's bridle, from Robert Plot's *The Natural History of Stafford-Shire* (Oxford, 1686), unpaginated illustration facing p. 390.

was so violent and full of passion he scarce asked me any more questions, but called to one of his followers to bring the bridle, as he called it, to put upon me, and was to be on three hours, and that which they called so was like a steel cap, and my hat being violently plucked off which was pinned to my head whereby they tare my clothes to put on the bridle, as they called it, which was a stone weight of iron . . . and a piece of it was put in my mouth, which was so unreasonable big a thing for that place as cannot be well related, which was locked to my head, and so I stood their time with my hands bound behind me with the stone weight of iron upon my head and the bit in my mouth to keep me from speaking.[138]

Such was the logic of moderation: the bridle that restrains excess, the exercise of power to produce a virtuous middle way. But early modern England was filled with dangerous excesses: women, youths, the poor, Catholics, puritans and many others. Indeed, given contemporary pessimism about the human condition, we might profitably interpret the vicious moderation of the scold's bridle not simply as a distasteful episode in the history of women but as a particularly vivid illustration of a much more general phenomenon. While violence was shunned as uncivilised, restraint was the essence of moderation; the politics of restraint was the process of drawing the line between them.

## Conclusion

We have seen, then, how the bridle of moderation – the restraint of excess to reduce it to a mean – combined ethical and political ideals in ways both subtle and powerful. Moderation was, at heart, directed towards peace and tranquillity, but achieving that peace and tranquillity required the exercise of coercive authority. The rule of moderation thus naturalised the exercise of power through the language of ethical restraint. Yet there were often multiple claimants to the role of moderator and contradictory versions of just when, how and in what sense moderation should be applied. In the chapters that follow, we will examine a variety of arenas where moderation was deployed and contested; these conflicts over moderation went a long way towards constituting the structure of English governance.

[138] *The Lambs Defence against Lyes* (London, 1656), p. 30.

*Part II*

# Moderate churches

We have seen in Part I, in general and synchronic terms, how the ideal of moderation in early modern England combined ethical restraint and political authority. This did not simply mean, as has often been stated, that self-control authorised external government; this was partly true, as in the paradigmatic cases of idealised manhood and idealised godliness, but at the same time claims for self-government were always at least partially attenuated by the weight of original sin. The point, then, is that at one higher level of abstraction the concept of moderation subsumed and combined internal and external moderation in a dialectical relationship: the moderation of individuals always depended upon them being restrained from the outside, but that external restraint was authorised by the moderation of the individuals who performed it. In a public or political context, this tension produced a suspicion of worldly power as sinful, fallen and in need of restraint, even as it nominated such worldly power as the proper agent of restraint upon a sinful and fallen world.

Part II turns to the diachronic development of this model in English history. For while this *intellectual* tension was built into English thought from the second quarter of the sixteenth century onwards, as the Renaissance emphasis on social improvement was crossed with the Reformation emphasis on human depravity, its actualisation as a *political* phenomenon, with real implications for English governance, depended upon tangible institutions and substantive policy debates. Part II argues that the politics of restraint developed first and most influentially in *religious* debates, not because moderation was simply or necessarily a religious ideal, but because the unique institutional configuration of the Church of England as a branch of the state subsumed religious debates under questions of governance. Moderation, after all, was fundamentally a constitutional ideal: by delimiting and regulating the excesses and deficiencies of a fallen human order, by drawing boundaries to constitute communities, it conjured government out of chaos. And the English Reformation, with its miraculous conjuring by parliamentary statute and royal fiat of a new ecclesiastical polity called the Church of England, was early modern England's quintessential constitutional moment.

The result was the *ecclesiological* Reformation, obsessed with constitutional debates over the precise structure, powers and limits of this new and unique Church-state. The Church of England was founded as a solution to a constitutional rather than a theological problem, and in the decades that followed, as developing factions in the Church fought over its future, they almost always claimed (if sometimes disingenuously) that they did not differ one iota in their theology but only in matters of external government. The ideal of moderation was thus perfectly suited to the conflicts of England's long Reformation, allowing all sides to offer models of Church government that were neither tyrannous nor anarchic, neither excessive nor deficient, neither unreformed nor reformed to the detriment of order, preserving Christian liberty while producing government that restrained the passions of the worldly church and its sinful members. It is no exaggeration to say that England's great constitutional debates of the seventeenth century were elaborations for the civil polity of ideas that had been debated and canvassed in the ecclesiastical polity for generations.

Part II examines these debates from the break with Rome to the early seventeenth century. Its chapters analyse the development of three constellations of arguments for the moderation of the Church and show the growth and development of the notion that power was authorised by its limitation. First, we will examine the foundational *via media* of Henry VIII's royal supremacy, in which moderation was associated strictly with authority and obedience; moderation was government, authorised by its limitation only in the narrow sense that it was limited to so-called *adiaphora* or 'things indifferent'. Second, we will examine the arguments of Elizabethan and early Stuart 'conformists' who sought moderation through strong central authority over the Church; alongside the absolutist potential of these arguments, there was also a constitutionalist potential that sought to authorise the massive expansion of state power through the moderation of law. Third, we will examine the arguments of puritans who claimed the authority of the godly to moderate the Church from within; here power was authorised by its moderation through the mechanics of discipline. These positions all claimed to be middle ways between excessive and deficient ecclesiastical government, and the result was a politics of restraint in the Church that produced, at different moments under different regimes, forms of moderation ranging from political exclusion to judicial murder.

The chapters in Part II are by far the most tightly wound and technical in this book, engaging at a detailed level with sometimes arcane religious debates over the proper location and extent of authority in and over Christian Churches. It could not be otherwise, for it was in the technical details of these debates that the rule of moderation emerged as a coherent approach to the problem of government. The positions canvassed in these three chapters, and the styles of argumentation they developed, were the ideological foundation and wellspring for the much broader social, cultural and political developments we will explore in Part III.

# 2 Violence and the *via media* in the reign of Henry VIII

### Introduction: six characters in search of a scaffold

On 30 July 1540, a peculiar procession ambled its way from the Tower of London to the gallows at Smithfield. In the centre, surrounded by soldiers, sheriffs and royal officials, six priests were carried on 'hurdles' – wooden sledges upon which, under English law, condemned felons were paraded through the streets to spare them 'the extreme torment of being dragged on the ground'.[1] Three of these priests – Robert Barnes, Thomas Garret and William Jerome – were evangelical reformers (soon to be known as Protestants) who had been condemned by parliament for heresy. The other three – Edward Powell, Richard Fetherston and Thomas Abel – were Roman Catholics who had been condemned by parliament for treason. Upon each hurdle two men were tied, one evangelical and one Catholic, in a grisly and calculated display of symmetry. When they reached Smithfield, the prisoners found a unique and ghastly sight awaiting them: two adjacent instruments of execution built within view of one another. On one side were three stakes surrounded by kindling, intended to burn men to death, the traditional penalty for heresy; on the other side was a large scaffold and three ropes, with knives close at hand to hack the strangled bodies to pieces, the traditional penalty for treason. Thus did six priests watch each other die, along with the throngs who gathered to observe the epitome of royal justice. The Tudor regime not only inflicted the law upon the bodies of its victims but viscerally imprinted it upon the senses of the crowd: smoke stinging their eyes, blood staining their clothes, the smell of burning flesh, the screams of dying men.[2]

---

[1] OED, citing Blackstone's *Commentaries*.

[2] Edward Hall, *The Vnion of the Two Noble and Illustre Famelies of Lancastre [and] Yorke* (London, 1548), sig. SSS3r–v; Raphael Holinshed, *The Firste Volume of the Chronicles* (London, 1577), p. 1580; John Foxe, *Acts and Monuments* (London, 1563), pp. 616–17 (wrongly paginated as pp. 612–13), available at www.hrionline.shef.ac.uk/foxe/. Foxe has a woodcut of the three Protestant martyrs, and Holinshed has a woodcut of the three Catholic martyrs, but there is no image of the entire scene.

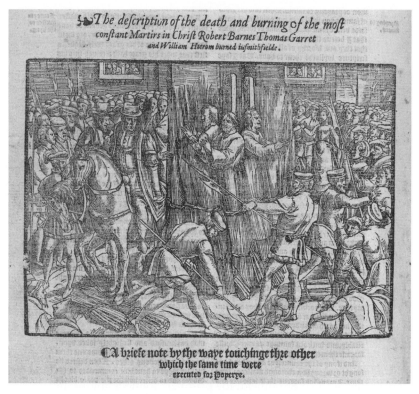

Figure 6. John Foxe, *Actes and Monuments of These Latter and Perillous Dayes* (London, 1563), p. 612. Below this image of the burning of Barnes, Garret and Jerome begins a section entitled 'A brief note by the way touching three other which the same time were executed for popery'.

This event was undoubtedly a crucial, founding moment of the Church of England's self-proclaimed 'middle way' in the Reformation. In a public display of enormous symbolic significance, Henry VIII and his government defined the boundaries of acceptable religion and declared a whole series of beliefs and practices – on both sides of the emerging Reformation divide – beyond the pale of judicious, temperate English religion. Yet if this elaborate, six-way execution was the founding moment of the Anglican *via media*, it is worth noticing that it was not by every standard a particularly *moderate* way to behave. Even by the standards of Henry VIII, this was a bloodbath. Moreover, because the victims were condemned by bills of attainder rather than by juries of their peers, the whole process stank of extra-legality and arbitrary rule. So how can we understand this extraordinary incident? How should we interpret an act of self-conscious religious moderation based upon the public burning and dismembering of human beings?

This chapter will argue that the executions of 30 July 1540 ensconced a particularly aggressive vision of moderation near the heart of the nascent Church of England. By explaining why and how these executions occurred – something which, rather remarkably, has never been considered in depth before – I want to suggest that it is no coincidence that the *via media* was constituted through violence. The peculiar version of moderation that underwrote Henry VIII's policies and led six clerics to the gallows defined the *via media* through the power of the king to moderate his subjects, thereby establishing government control of religion and absolute obedience to authority as the essence of moderation. Of course, it is no novelty to claim that Henry VIII was motivated by a desire for obedience; all early modern governors were, and none more so than a man who forced his people to follow him into schism from the Roman Catholic Church.[3] But it has never been appreciated how thoroughly Henry VIII's government defined religious moderation, and its much-vaunted *via media*, as the enforcement of a state monopoly on conscience; in this sense, the executions of the six priests did not merely delineate a middle way but actually embodied it, since that middle way was precisely the path of restraint. The Church of England defined obedience to the state – and the state's use of terror to enforce that obedience – as the only safe path between superstition and error. Even if this definition never completely won the field and competing discourses soon emerged, nonetheless it constituted a crucial starting point for a century and a half of debates over the moderation of the Church of England.

## The moderation of things indifferent

The first question to be asked is an ideological one: just what sort of a *via media* did Henry VIII and his government think they were claiming on 30 July 1540? That is, if we begin not with politics or personalities but with ideas, can we locate a core ideology that the executions were supposed to promote or sustain? This question immediately leads us to one of the great enigmas of English history: what did Henry VIII think he was doing when he broke with the Church of Rome and promulgated

---

[3] See Richard Rex, 'The Crisis of Obedience: God's Word and Henry's Reformation', *HJ* 39, no. 4 (1996), pp. 863–94; Daniel Eppley, *Defending Royal Supremacy and Discerning God's Will in Tudor England* (Aldershot, 2007).

a series of baffling religious settlements upon his people? Was there some guiding principle that held the centre together and was worth killing for?

It has sometimes been claimed that this guiding principle was 'Catholicism without the pope', or even a 'reformed Catholicism' on the model of Erasmus of Rotterdam. Indeed, some historians have recently argued that Henry VIII's seemingly capricious reversals actually had their own internal logic: a self-conscious and consistent quest for a moderate, humanist middle way.[4] Yet it is very difficult to sustain these arguments, not only because both Catholics and humanists found Henry VIII insufferable, but also because Henry VIII famously promoted men of contradictory doctrinal stances when it fit his political needs. Even hardcore evangelicals like Archbishop Thomas Cranmer and the Earl of Hertford, Edward Seymour, survived the *auto de fé* of 1540; they were no less Protestant than Robert Barnes, William Jerome or Thomas Garret, but they remained at the heart of Henry VIII's government. Moreover, if Henry VIII remained throughout his life in some sense a Catholic, he was a remarkably atavistic one, dismantling vast chunks of traditional orthodoxy and stealing vast chunks of the Church's wealth without providing anything to replace them. Thus, if we want to understand the Henrician *via media*, we must seek an ideology more concerned with the *process* of defining orthodoxy than with the result of that process. We must seek, in other words, claims to religious legitimacy that were 'moderate' by virtue of their authorisation rather than their divinity. Luckily, just such a model was available to English thinkers in the 1530s: the concept of *adiaphora* or 'things indifferent'.

The idea of 'things indifferent', whose development has been studied by Bernard Verkamp, had its roots in Greek philosophy, where it referred to external actions that were irrelevant to the morality of human beings, or, more broadly, external actions that were neither intrinsically good nor intrinsically evil but could be directed to either end. In a Christian context, this concept was modified to refer to its most obvious New Testament parallel: St Paul's discussion of the freedom of Christians from the burden of Jewish ceremonial law. Many Fathers of the Church interpreted Paul's epistles to argue that human actions like eating and drinking were morally indifferent for Christians unless they were imbued with particular moral intent – in contrast to the Jews, for whom certain foods were absolutely prohibited and others absolutely required at particular times. This position was refined and debated in the middle ages, when theologians questioned whether human morality depended upon outward actions at all. Peter Abelard, for instance, expanded the

---

[4] Bernard, *The King's Reformation*; Wooding, *Rethinking Catholicism*.

category of *adiaphora* almost indefinitely, arguing that, considered in themselves, without reference to the morality of the actor, all human actions were indifferent; even violations of the Decalogue might have mitigating circumstances. At the opposite end of the spectrum, Thomas Aquinas contracted the category of *adiaphora* almost indefinitely, allowing it only to include genuinely neutral and amoral actions like picking blades of grass. But by far the most common position was that some actions were good in themselves, others were evil in themselves, and in between was a large category of 'middle things' which could be good or evil depending upon the circumstances.[5]

Beginning with John Wyclif in the fourteenth century, but expanding considerably with Christian humanists like Erasmus in the early sixteenth century, it became commonplace for religious reformers to use the idea of *adiaphora* to attack the ceremonial 'yoke' of the Roman Catholic Church, which bound Christians to perform actions that were in themselves indifferent. St Paul had attempted to free Christians from the Jewish law, but under the Roman Catholic Church, reformers claimed, there were more fast days and more required prayers than there had ever been within Judaism.[6] Then, with the Reformation and the new Protestant argument that the Bible alone contained all that was necessary for salvation, the idea of 'things indifferent' took on a potent new meaning: they were things neither required nor forbidden by scripture. Anything required by scripture was good in itself and could not be forbidden by any human authority. Anything forbidden by scripture was evil in itself and could not be required by any human authority. But things neither required nor forbidden – and of course this category expanded and contracted depending upon the biblical hermeneutics employed – were indifferent, and thus in some sense left within human discretion. This included, most notably, the vast majority of outward religious ceremonies.

Protestants thus all agreed that *adiaphora* were left in some sense within human discretion: whether to perform an indifferent ceremony was not intrinsically binding on Christian consciences, but rather depended upon the circumstances. But the question remained, *who* had discretion to interpret the requirements of the circumstances? Was it the individual, the corporate Church, or civil magistrates? Likewise, there remained the question of what *criteria* should be used when deciding whether to perform indifferent ceremonies: was it the orderliness of the ceremonies themselves, the likelihood of the ceremonies to cause offence, or the laws

---

[5] For this paragraph, see Bernard Verkamp, *The Indifferent Mean: Adiaphorism in the English Reformation to 1554* (Athens, Ohio, 1977), pp. 10–12, 20–4.

[6] *Ibid.*, pp. 9–11.

of the civil polity? In practice, very few reformers used the concept of *adiaphora* to argue for radical individualism or to suggest that Christians were left completely to their own conscience in religious observance. Luther and Zwingli flirted with these ideas early in the 1520s but rapidly withdrew from them after the Peasants' War in 1525. Instead, most Protestants focused on the Pauline injunctions that ceremonies should 'edify', that they should be performed 'decently and in order' and that care should be taken not to offend 'weaker brethren'. These criteria, generally speaking, were social and corporate rather than individual, and thus properly constituted authorities – civil authorities rather than clerics – were given power to require ceremonies in Protestant lands. But it was always stressed that they should require the *minimum* necessary to preserve order, and that the requirement never implied that the ceremonies were intrinsically necessary; what was necessary was obedience to the authorities who required them, according to the language of Romans 13: 'Let every soul be subject unto the higher powers . . . not only for wrath, but also for conscience sake.' Hence, while in *theory* the Protestant Churches of Europe claimed that their ceremonies were indifferent and not binding on the conscience, in *practice* they were generally just as strict as the Roman Catholic Church in their requirements of outward conformity. The main difference was that those ceremonies were not authorised by Church authorities but by civil magistrates acting through law.

We can see this system at work in one of the earliest texts of Reformation adiaphoristic thought: Philip Melanchthon's *Loci Communes*, first published in 1521 and then regularly revised and expanded until the author's death in 1560. The 1521 edition of the *Loci* sought to create a new, Lutheran solution to the problem of overlapping jurisdictions between Church and state that had plagued Europe since the eleventh century. In essence, it redefined ecclesiastical power as wholly spiritual, with no worldly jurisdiction; priests existed solely to minister the gospel. Whereas human laws had traditionally been divided into two sorts, called the 'pontifical' and the 'civil', Melanchthon argued that clerics had no authority to make laws but rather lived entirely within civil jurisdiction: 'What now about pontifical laws? As far as pontiffs decide litigations and judgments, they are plainly worldly princes. Moreover, divine law has made subject to civil magistrates, kings and princes, both that which pertains to litigations and judgments and the priests themselves as well.'[7] The Church was thus empowered to promote the divine order set forth in

[7] Philip Melanchthon, *The Loci Communes of Philip Melanchthon*, trans. Charles Leander Hill (Boston, 1944), p. 131.

scripture but had no power to create laws: 'It is not permitted bishops to order anything that is not contained in the scripture.'[8] Most importantly for our purposes, Melanchthon specifically called upon people to *disobey* clerical authorities, not only when they commanded behaviour contrary to divine law, but even when they commanded obedience in things indifferent: if bishops teach scripture 'they are to be heard as Christ'; if they teach contrary to scripture 'they are not to be heard'; and if they teach 'anything outside of scripture with a view to binding consciences, they are not to be heard. For nothing binds the conscience save the divine law.'[9]

On civil authorities, however, the *Loci* took an opposite line, stressing that magistrates could indeed command obedience in *adiaphora*, as long as it was commanded for obedience's sake and not for the sake of the ceremonies themselves. As Melanchthon put it, 'Christ has dispensed with Pharisaic traditions . . . but he has not dispensed with civil laws.'[10] Magistrates, of course, could not lawfully command anything contrary to divine law, but on indifferent matters, even the most tyrannical orders are to be obeyed: 'If they shall have ordered anything that is tyrannical, the magistrate is here also to be suffered for the sake of love, where nothing can be changed without public disturbance and without sedition.'[11] The point here is not that the prince can bind the conscience *per se*; it remains the case that 'consciences are not to be bound by human traditions; and he does no sin who violates them unless he falls into the misfortune of giving offence'.[12] The point, however, is that 'giving offence' most definitely includes civil disobedience, hence in practice civil laws on *adiaphora* must be obeyed – even if, according to Melanchthon, those laws generally should not be made in the first place.

Protestant theories of *adiaphora* obviously had enormous potential utility for the not-yet-Protestant Church of England in the 1530s, because Henry VIII needed an intellectual framework with which to discard Roman Catholic jurisdiction in theory while maintaining 'order' and 'decency' in practice. Yet in fact, the interpretation of *adiaphora* employed by Henry VIII and his advisors was very different and throws into sharp relief the genuine novelty of the English Reformation. The primary theorist who rose to the task of translating adiaphorist thought for the English crown was not a Protestant at all, but rather Thomas Starkey, an Italian-trained humanist who published his great analysis of *adiaphora*, *An Exhortation to the People, Instructynge Theym to Vnitie and Obedience*, in 1536. This text has long been known to historians as a blueprint for the *via*

<hr>

[8] *Ibid.*, p. 138.    [9] *Ibid.*, pp. 263–4.
[10] *Ibid.*, p. 264.    [11] *Ibid.*, p. 262.    [12] *Ibid.*, p. 140.

*media* of Henry VIII, rejecting both the Romanism of Reginald Pole and the evangelism of Thomas Cranmer in favour of a moderate middle way. It is therefore significant that Starkey's understanding of *adiaphora* led him not towards an elucidation of 'Christian liberty' but rather in political directions that can only be described as authoritarian. Starkey's curiously expansive definition of 'things indifferent' led him to argue for a virtually omnipotent Church-state that subordinated every aspect of personal morality and conscience to its own needs. By reducing the whole Protestant Reformation to a quibble over indifferent matters, Starkey's *via media* made the state uniquely competent to choose amongst rival practices and doctrines on behalf of its people – a singularly aggressive vision of religious moderation.

In his *Exhortation*, Starkey claimed repeatedly that the solution to the factional and ideological struggles of the Reformation was an Aristotelian golden mean:

> By a certain mean, the harmony of this whole world is contained in this natural order and beauty. By a mean, all civil order and policy is maintained in cities and towns with good civility. By a mean, man's mind with all kinds of virtue is garnished, is brought to his natural perfection and light. And by a mean, all true religion, without impiety or superstition, is established and set forth to God's honour and glory in all Christian nations and countries. Yea, and so by a mean, we shall, most Christian people, chiefly avoid this dangerous division grown in among us, by the reason whereof some are judged to be of the new fashion and some of the old.[13]

Already we can see here a potent brew of inward and outward moderation, the mean simultaneously as ethical behaviour and as 'civil order and policy'. The particular 'middle way' Starkey identified was quite specific. He argued that the Scylla and Charybdis between which the Church of England sailed were the twin extremes of 'superstition' on one side and 'impiety' or 'contempt of religion' on the other. 'Superstition' for Starkey had a particular meaning: attributing spiritual necessity to things not required by God's law, for instance pilgrimages or images in churches. On the opposite side, 'contempt of religion' meant the rejection of all ceremonies, laws and traditions that were not explicitly required by scripture. Starkey denounced those who, under pretence of 'the liberty of a Christian', denounced all ceremonies as merely 'snares and stays unto weak minds'.[14] Again, pilgrimages and images in churches made good examples: while not required by God's law, neither were they

---

[13] Thomas Starkey, *An Exhortation to the People, Instructynge Theym to Vnitie and Obedience* (London, 1536), sig. Y4r.

[14] *Ibid.*, sig. F3v.

intrinsically forbidden. The golden mean, then, was constituted through a proper understanding of *adiaphora*.

Yet Starkey's understanding of 'indifference' was subtly but crucially different than the versions produced by Philip Melanchthon, for Starkey elaborated an extraordinarily difficult standard for something to be 'required': the only things required rather than indifferent were those 'necessary to man's salvation'.[15] This conception of 'necessity' was based on the humanist ideal of the *philosophia Christi*, a theory of Christian simplicity that had been advocated by Erasmus since the 1510s and which Starkey echoed throughout his tract. According to this view, laypeople should be encouraged to read the scripture without the mediation of priests, because Christianity was, when stripped of scholastic philosophy and ceremonial hocus pocus, essentially *simple*. It could be boiled down to a few basic messages which anyone could understand and transcended theological debate. As Starkey put it, the things required by scripture 'are but few in number and open to every man's eye'. Everything else – even things praised in scripture but not expressly commanded – should be seen as 'of no necessity, but as things indifferent'.[16]

This meant not only that the category of *adiaphora* expanded exponentially for Starkey, but also that *adiaphora* included beliefs as well as actions. Any idea without which human beings could be saved – or without which any human being *had* ever been saved – was suddenly up for grabs. Of course, most crucially this meant the primacy of the pope: there were many Christians in the early Church and in the Greek Church who did not accept the papal primacy but were still saved, therefore papal primacy was indifferent. It also referred to vernacular Bibles – which Protestants would never have classed as indifferent! – without which many Christians had undoubtedly been saved.[17] Another obvious candidate was monasticism. Starkey might agree with Roman Catholics that monasteries were theoretically spiritually uplifting, and he might agree with Protestants that monasteries had long been centres of abuse, but could anyone seriously suggest that monasticism was necessary for salvation?[18] More controversially, Starkey was also prepared to argue that the sacraments were indifferent. He suggested that the core of each sacrament was its 'inward and heavenly mystery', and that it was a 'very foolish and superstitious opinion' to place spiritual importance in the 'outward sign and ceremony'. These ceremonies, then, were not essential for salvation and might be altered by 'common authority'.[19] Starkey made a similar argument about the liturgy of the Church, which had

---

[15] *Ibid.*, sig. C2r, sig. B2v, sig. Z4r, and elsewhere.     [16] *Ibid.*, sig. Z4v.
[17] *Ibid.*, sig. L3v.     [18] *Ibid.*, sigs. E4r–F1r.     [19] *Ibid.*, sig. F2r–v.

clearly evolved over the centuries, and was thus by definition indifferent. He condemned the superstition of people who would object if 'the prayers commonly said among us in temples in a strange tongue, of the people not understood, should openly be rehearsed in the mother tongue'.[20]

In case this is starting to sound too Protestant, Starkey's broad concept of indifference also allowed the *continuation* of many practices that reformers wanted to ban. He suggested that there was no clear biblical proof either for or against purgatory, hence it could be believed or disbelieved, and intercessory prayers for the dead remained indifferent.[21] Likewise, he argued that prayers to saints and the veneration of images were not idolatrous since they 'in no part doth derogate the honour of God'. Thus, these practices were 'agreeable' to scripture and 'conveniently received' in the Church, even though 'they be not of high necessity'.[22] Again, Starkey created his middle way through bilateral reasoning: indifferent things should neither be embraced as necessary components of Christianity nor condemned as necessarily anti-Christian.

The result was that Starkey effectively dismissed the entire Protestant Reformation as a huge misunderstanding, a series of fundamentally unnecessary disagreements that had got out of control because of people's unwillingness to accept the golden mean between superstition and irreligion. In Germany, he wrote, 'all their controversy and sedition' – a reference certainly to Lutheranism and possibly to the Peasants' War – 'rose of things in no point necessary to man's salvation'.[23] Catholic Germans wrongly 'took as God's law' certain things that were merely 'convenient to a certain policy' and 'of long time received'. Protestant Germans failed to accept ceremonies and traditions as 'things convenient to maintain unity'.[24] Transported into an English context, Starkey thus condemned Catholics who referred to their opponents as heretics, since those of the 'new faction' could be 'true and obedient persons both to God and their prince'.[25] On the opposite side, Starkey condemned Protestants who attacked their opponents as anti-Christian, since their errors were not 'of such moment and weight... wherefore we ought to condemn all antiquity and all our forefathers for the ignorance thereof'.[26] He thus advised Englishmen simply to ignore ministers who preached 'clean contrary to one another' since their debates seldom involved anything necessary for salvation: 'It is enough that they accord in the articles of our faith, and as for the rest, let them prove their wits after their own pleasure, mind and liberty.'[27] Here only the 'articles of our faith' (in other words the Creed) were necessary for salvation, and all other

---

[20] *Ibid.*, sig. F1v.     [21] *Ibid.*, sigs. X1r and X3v.     [22] *Ibid.*, sig. X2v.
[23] *Ibid.*, sig. A4r. A more specific reference to the German Peasants' War is on sig. H4v.
[24] *Ibid.*, sig. A4r–v.     [25] *Ibid.*, sig. H2r.     [26] *Ibid.*, sig. E1r.     [27] *Ibid.*, sig. B4r.

beliefs – whether about justification, the sacraments, predestination, or ecclesiology – were mere indifferent superstructures.

Thus far, it would seem, Starkey could make a claim to genuine tolerance in an age of persecution, based upon his profound belief that the peace of the Church should trump virtually all theological disagreement. Yet in practice Starkey's arguments for unity in *adiaphora* led him to reject any inconsistency or variation in religion and to argue for absolute uniformity in those indifferent matters. At the root of this claim was Starkey's doctrine of the 'two polities', a variation on a common theme among sixteenth-century intellectuals. Starkey suggested that for 'man here in earth . . . there be as it were two politics, two diverse manners of living, two diverse ways and fashions of passing this pilgrimage, of which the one is heavenly, spiritual and godly, the other civil, natural and worldly'. What defined *Christian* states was that these two polities were coterminous: 'In us Christian men they in one must perfectly agree, they must consent, and in the perfect coupling thereof resteth the conservation of this spiritual unity, the which of necessity doth require in common policy a certain consent and sure agreement.' Thus, just as the civil polity cannot be maintained 'separate from peace and unity', so the spiritual polity 'without respect of common policy, shortly by necessity shall fall to confusion'. The upshot was a theory of *adiaphora* in which obedience in indifferent things, despite not being necessary for the salvation of individuals, was absolutely indispensable for the well-being of the polity as a whole. As Starkey put it: 'This must be taken as a sure and common ground, that in all Christian civility of great and high necessity to all such things as by common authority are established and founded, without repugnancy to the spiritual unity and manifest doctrine of Christ, the people must ever be obedient to all such things, with glad heart they must ever agree and consent.'[28]

Here, then, was a doctrine that gave civil authorities virtually infinite discretion to set rules for 'indifferent' things, and gave them an abiding motivation to enforce those rules, despite Starkey's contention that those issues were hardly important at all. Moreover, indifferent matters included not just ceremonies but all *doctrinal* issues except the few necessary and indisputable rules of the *philosophia christi*. Now we can see why Starkey told his English readers to ignore the doctrinal debates flying at them from the pulpits: these arguments were not only irrelevant to their salvation, but too much knowledge might lead people to think for themselves about matters on which they should merely obey the king. This extended even to knowledge of the Bible itself: 'Scrupulous and exact knowledge of things contained in God's scriptures is nothing so necessary

---

[28] *Ibid.*, sigs. K3v–L1v.

to induce them to obedience, as is meekness and humility.'[29] The key word here was 'scrupulous'. Certainly Starkey accepted that laypeople could read the Bible if it were authorised by civil authorities, but only because the basic message of the Bible was so simple that anyone could understand it. Those lay readers were on no account to acquire 'scruples' from their reading, because on all but the most simple and indisputable messages of Christ, obedience to authority trumped whatever they might believe.

Indeed, one of the most remarkable things about Starkey's understanding of *adiaphora* is its implication for the concept of individual conscience and responsibility before God. In matters essential to salvation, of course, individuals remained responsible for their own souls, and if the authorities decreed anything contrary to the 'word of God' they must be 'boldly disobeyed'. On indifferent matters, however – and of course for Starkey this meant virtually everything, including even the sacraments or belief in purgatory – there could be no private conscience; any supposed pangs of conscience on these issues were the result of either superstition or irreligion. As Starkey put it, the moral standing of *adiaphora* were 'left to worldly policy, whereof they take their full authority, by the which . . . they are sometimes good and sometimes ill'. The state, in other words, had authority to make an indifferent thing either good or evil by fiat.[30] Hence, according to Starkey, 'if any private person' were 'moved by any scruple of conscience' on any indifferent matter and consequently made his objection public, 'if he may neither be brought to knowledge by good instruction, nor yet to just obedience with due admonition, he is not worthy to live in that common policy'. Starkey thus suggested that 'every man learned in scripture, whose conscience is troubled with any scrupulosity conceived by anything decreed by common authority' had only one lawful remedy: 'to give obedience to such things as be decreed by common authority' so that 'all such division as hangeth over our heads, which might bring in confusion into this our country and policy, we shall right well avoid and eschew, living together in due obedience and perfect unity'.[31]

On the crucial issue of ceremonies in the Church, Starkey thus remained remarkably conservative. Melanchthon had argued that non-scriptural ceremonies were dangerous even when they were allowable; he described 'human inventions' in the Church as 'vile puke' and wrote that throughout history 'there has been no tradition, however so pious in appearance, but what has been a great evil to the Christian cause'.[32] For Melanchthon, then, the purpose of *adiaphora* was to promote Christian

---

[29] *Ibid.*, sig. B3r.     [30] *Ibid.*, sig. B2v.     [31] *Ibid.*, sigs. B4v–C3r.
[32] Melanchthon, *The Loci Communes*, pp. 139–43.

liberty and the primacy of scripture. For Starkey, however, the purpose of *adiaphora* was to promote *unity*, and it was not particularly unified for everyone *not* to perform ceremonies. Since the whole point of the Christian polity was to bring people to Christ who were separated from him by the Fall of Adam, that polity had to actually *do* something to bring people to Christ rather than simply doing nothing: moderation was regulation. The result, then, was that according to Starkey all ceremonies and other traditions used by the Catholic Church remained compulsory unless specifically removed by the magistrate.[33]

The sum of Starkey's *via media*, then, was a system that equated moderation with the dyad of government and obedience. Now, of course, this is not to claim that Starkey's *Exhortation* can be read as a simple blueprint for Henry VIII's views and policies. There were other versions of *adiaphora* floated in the 1530s – including the 1535 edition of Melanchthon's *Loci Communes*, dedicated to none other than Henry VIII – which did not define the category so broadly or use it for such centralising and authoritarian purposes. But because Starkey's version represented such a powerful *reductio ad absurdum*, giving virtually unlimited authority to the king to control and remodel religious behaviour and even religious doctrine while still remaining fundamentally *moderate*, Starkey's system was the one towards which royal policies naturally gravitated. Starkey's version of *adiaphora* could accommodate virtually anything that Henry VIII chose to do, even if Henry himself did not always have Starkey in mind when he did it. As such, it proved an irresistible lure for a capricious king who, at the end of the day, often found himself excusing greed and lust as matters of religious principle.

### Conscience and authority in the Henrician Reformation

With the Henrician ideology of moderate obedience established, we can now turn to the six priests who were executed on 30 July 1540. What had they done to earn their fate? The parallelism of their deaths clearly delineated some sort of 'middle way', but if it was supposed to represent the boundaries of acceptable religiosity it was a stunning failure, because observers consistently complained that they had no idea why these six men were executed. The French ambassador in England, for instance, noted that the victims on both sides complained that they did not even 'know the cause for which they had been condemned'.[34] These claims might be dismissed as self-serving were it not that so many of their

---

[33] Starkey, *An Exhortation*, sigs. G4r–v and Y3r.
[34] Jean Kaulek (ed.), *Correspondance politique de MM. de Castillon et de Marillac, Ambassadeurs de France en Angleterre (1537–1542)* (Paris, 1885), p. 209. 'Ilz affermoient n'avoir

contemporaries seemed equally baffled. On the Protestant side, this confusion was generated by the fact that the parliamentary bill of attainder against them refused to state the crimes for which they were condemned; it simply noted that they were guilty of so many heresies that it would be tedious to mention any of them in particular. Thus Protestants were left to guess the real reason for the deaths of Barnes, Garret and Jerome. Martin Luther wrote in 1540, 'The cause why Barnes was martyred is still hidden, because Henry must be ashamed of it,' and he hypothesised that it was because Barnes had opposed the king's recent annulment of his marriage to Anne of Cleves.[35] The chronicler Edward Hall wrote of the Protestant martyrs that 'wherefore they were now thus cruelly executed I know not, although I have searched to know the truth'. He claimed that at their deaths they 'asked the sheriffs wherefore they were condemned, who answered [that] they could not tell'. Hall hypothesised that it might be because they had dared to preach against Stephen Gardiner, Bishop of Winchester.[36] On the Catholic side, moreover, while the political opposition of Powell, Fetherston and Abel was more clear – they had all supported papal authority and opposed the royal supremacy – the three victims had all been in custody for many years, and none of them had apparently done anything new to warrant their execution. On the contrary, Thomas Abel had written from prison to Thomas Cromwell as early as 1537, protesting that he had never been interrogated concerning any alleged offences and reminding Cromwell that other priests who had been imprisoned with him for similar reasons had long since been released.[37]

So to understand the executions of 30 July 1540, and the *via media* that it represented, clearly we need to understand something more about these six men, something which was not obvious to contemporaries and which the Tudor regime was interested in obscuring rather than advertising. What we will find is that the ostensible symmetry of their executions – three for heresy, three for treason – is a thoroughly inadequate framework for understanding either their deaths or the more general dynamics of moderation in the English Reformation. Rather, all six men died because they questioned the king's authority to order the religious beliefs of his people. The precise *ideas* for which they died, then, were not only beside the point but were actually a distraction from the regime's message: that moderation lay in the enforcement of religious order, not in the

jamays esté appelez ne sçavoir la cause pour laquelle ilz avoient esté condamnez.' This and all other translations from Marillac are my own.
[35] Cited in *LP*, XVI, 106.
[36] Hall, *The Vnion of the Two Noble and Illustre Famelies*, sig. SSS3r.
[37] PRO SP 1/116, fo. 173r.

particular form of order that was enforced. Hence the regime's studied silence about the details of their crimes. Their unwillingness to specify what the six men had done suggests that this was not really an exercise in delineating the boundaries of acceptable religion so much as it was an attempt to blur those boundaries and declare them irrelevant. Thus, rather than representing two opposite offences, all six men died for essentially the same transgression: they were among the earliest victims of a version of the *via media* that defined conscience in the face of authority as immoderate.

If we begin with the three Roman Catholic priests, the remarkable thing is how disconnected they all were from the ecclesio-political debates of 1540, because they had all been locked away for more than five years at the time of their deaths. Each of them had been involved in the 1520s with Catherine of Aragon's defence against Henry VIII during his attempts to annul their marriage, and in that sense their transgressions were very real. But those transgressions were hopelessly outdated by 1540.

To briefly summarise their careers: Richard Fetherston had been Catherine of Aragon's chaplain, and he is said to have written a now-lost tract *Contra Divortium Henrici et Catherinae*. In 1529 he defended the queen in the divorce trial before the papal legates at Blackfriars, and in 1534 he was imprisoned for refusing to take the Oath of Supremacy. He entered the Tower of London in December 1534, was attainted of treason in January 1535, and did not surface again until the day of his execution in 1540. Thomas Abel was likewise a chaplain to Catherine of Aragon, and in 1532 he published *Invicta Veritas*, a treatise that 'by no manner of law it may be lawful for the most noble King of England . . . to be divorced from the queen's grace'.[38] This was a remarkably impolitic tract, repeatedly calling the views of the king's advisors 'suspect heretical'; it was immediately denounced as 'slanderous and seditious' by the king's supporters.[39] Abel was imprisoned first briefly in 1532 and then permanently (except for a brief period on bail) in 1533 after becoming involved in the conspiracies surrounding Elizabeth Barton, the so-called Holy Maid of Kent. Edward Powell, the most famous of the three, was a doctor of theology who had been commissioned by the king and Cardinal Wolsey in the early 1520s to write tracts against Martin Luther, and he continued his anti-Protestant activism into the 1530s, preaching against the evangelical firebrand Hugh Latimer in Bristol. More importantly for our purposes, Powell also advised Catherine of Aragon in her

---

[38] Thomas Abel, *Inuicta Veritas* (Antwerp, 1532), sig. f1r.
[39] *Ibid.*, sigs. F1v, H4r, I2v, etc. For government responses, see PRO SP 1/60, fo. 1r, the introduction to a manuscript entitled 'A Confutation of Abel's Babbling'.

legal defence and was one of the few English theologians who publicly opposed the king's divorce. He was attainted of treason for refusing to take the Oath of Succession in the same statute that condemned John Fisher in December 1534, and he too, besides a brief stint on bail, spent the rest of his life in prison.

Given these career trajectories, it is no surprise that these men were executed. What is surprising, however, is that they were executed in 1540 rather than five years earlier. After all, by 1540 both Catherine of Aragon and Anne Boleyn were long since dead and the king's divorce was ancient history. Moreover, in the five years before 1540, none of the three had published a word, nor earned more notoriety than a stray mention in the State Papers. If the regime had been content to let Fetherston, Abel and Powell rot in their cells for five years, why did they not just leave them there?

The first references we have to renewed government interest in Powell, Fetherston and Abel come from Thomas Cromwell's handwritten notes – undated, but internal evidence suggests April 1540 – in which he twice reminded himself to deal with Powell and Featherston and once reminded himself (somewhat enigmatically) to deal with 'Abell in the King's Bench'.[40] These notes, while no more than jottings, can at least tell us something about the *context* of Cromwell's consideration of the three men: they were filled with references to other Roman Catholics arrested in 1540, including Lord Lisle, the 'blind harper' William More, the king's chaplain Richard Manchester, the London grocer Richard Fermour and others. Powell, Fetherston and Abel were thus mentioned alongside these newly arrested men, as if they had somehow come back to the government's attention in the company of other Romanists whom they had never met.

The reason seems to be that, beginning early in 1540, prominent religious conservatives had begun manoeuvring to have Powell, Fetherston and Abel released from prison. We can see this first in a letter to Thomas Cromwell dated 4 June 1540 from the theologian Dr Nicholas Wilson. Wilson had been another leading supporter of Catherine of Aragon in the divorce case, and as late as 1533 he spoke in convocation on behalf of the papal supremacy. That same year, Wilson had joined his friend Edward Powell in preaching against Hugh Latimer in Bristol. Then, in 1534, Wilson was the only London priest to refuse to swear the Oath of Supremacy, and he was attainted for misprision of treason in the same Act of Parliament that attainted Thomas More, John Fisher and

---

[40] *LP*, XV, 598 and *LP*, XV, 615. I have been unable to find documents related to Abel in the records of the King's Bench.

Edward Powell. Unlike More, Fisher and Powell, however, Wilson chose to conform; he swore the oath under duress and was pardoned in 1537. Thereafter, the regime regarded him as something of a poster child for conformity to the royal supremacy, giving him significant preferment. Wilson's good favour with the regime came crashing down, however, in the last week of May 1540, when he was imprisoned once again for opposition to the royal supremacy. In his 4 June letter to Cromwell, then, Wilson apologised for having 'offended in procuring and giving Powell, Fetherstone and Abell relief in such sort as I did, for . . . God is my judge I intended but their relief till the king's highness should someway dispose on them, and no maintenance of their evil opinions, but wished their amendment and conformity'. He admitted that he had met with Powell at least once (he denied a charge that they had met a second time), and he also admitted that he had spoken 'to the bishop of Chichester for Doctor Powell, that he would be a suitor for him to have some ease of his imprisonment'.[41] It seems, then, that Wilson's conformity had been no more than skin-deep, and in 1540 he was trying to help the few remaining members of Catherine of Aragon's legal team who remained alive.

Moreover, the other man mentioned here as a 'suitor' for Powell – the Bishop of Chichester, Richard Sampson – had also been arrested the previous week on charges of opposing the royal supremacy. Sampson, unlike Nicholas Wilson, had been an early supporter of the royal supremacy, for which he was rewarded with his bishopric in 1536. But Sampson was also widely known as a religious conservative and an enemy of Thomas Cromwell, and he had many connections to the remaining supporters of Catherine of Aragon through his earlier career as ambassador to Spain in the 1520s. It is significant, then, that in addition to Sampson's support for Powell, a different letter identified Sampson as having sent alms to an imprisoned priest named Abel, undoubtedly Thomas Abel.[42] We start to get a sense, then, that there was a concerted effort in the spring of 1540 – 'conspiracy' would be too strong a word, since none of this was ostensibly illegal – to aid the surviving Aragonese faction or free them from prison.

The problem with this effort, however, was that it did not occur in a vacuum but rather was implicated in a series of far more dangerous criticisms of the king's religious policies. Most importantly, Nicholas Wilson was accused not only of trying to aid the three imprisoned priests but also of seditious communication with one Dr Richard Hilliard, formerly

[41] PRO SP 1/160, fo. 156r–v [*LP* XV, 747].
[42] *ODNB*, *sub nomine* Richard Sampson.

chaplain to the conservative Bishop Cuthbert Tunstall and now a fugitive in Scotland, who had counselled resistance to the dissolution of the monasteries.[43] Likewise, Richard Sampson was accused of opposing the king's alterations to the ceremonies of the Church of England. In a letter to Cromwell dated 7 June 1540, Sampson vehemently denied the charge that he and Bishop Tunstall had conspired to 'lean and stick to the old usages and traditions of the Church'.[44] The king, when told of Sampson's denials, thought they only made him sound more guilty.[45] We get the sense, then, that Powell, Fetherston and Abel were embroiled not merely in a five-year-old controversy over the royal supremacy, but in a brand new discussion among traditionalists about whether Henry VIII's *uses* of his supremacy over the Church had gone too far.

This is all we hear about the three Catholic priests until early July 1540, when parliament and the king negotiated the traditional royal pardon to be promulgated at the dissolution of parliament. This bill of pardon, unlike previous pardons from Henry VIII's reign, specifically exempted roughly forty people by name. On the one hand, the list exempted a wide array of evangelicals, including Barnes, Jerome and Garret. But on the other hand, it also exempted many Catholics, including Bishop Richard Sampson, Dr Nicholas Wilson and our three friends, Powell, Fetherston and Abel.[46] Nonetheless, in actuality, while Powell, Fetherston and Abel were all put to death within a month, Sampson and Wilson were pardoned in August and later regained the favour of the regime.[47] The implication is that *helping* Powell, Fetherston and Abel was a considerably less serious crime than actually *being* Powell, Fetherston and Abel – no doubt because they still refused to take the Oath of Supremacy, while Sampson and Wilson were willing to conform.

This is essentially all the information we have on the three Catholic victims of 30 July 1540. Admittedly, it does not amount to much. The overwhelming impression is that their deaths were only incidentally of their own making; they had done nothing new to deserve punishment for over five years. What they had done, however, was continue to defy the king even as political and religious circumstances changed and the

[43] For Hilliard's resistance and a denial that Wilson shared his opinions, see *LP*, XV, 125. The previous October, Hilliard had a public confrontation with Robert Barnes: *LP*, XV, 31.

[44] John Strype, *Ecclesiastical Memorials, Relating Chiefly to Religion* (Oxford, 3 vols., 1822), I, part 2, pp. 381–3.

[45] *State Papers Published under the Authority of Her Majesty's Commission, King Henry VIII* (London, 11 vols., 1830–52), I, p. 627.

[46] *SR*, vol. III, pp. 809–12 (32 Hen.VIII. c.49).

[47] Stanford Lehmberg, *The Later Parliaments of Henry VIII, 1536–1547* (Cambridge, 1977), p. 127.

old issue of the king's marriage faded to obscurity. When traditionalists within the government tried to connect their own growing concerns about government policy to the beliefs of the old Aragonese faction, then the king had to show that he had a long memory.

If we turn to the three Protestant martyrs, we find a very different sort of story, embedded in the ongoing attempts of reformers to dismantle England's religious past. The lives of Barnes, Garret and Jerome converged for the first time in February 1540, when all three were invited to preach sermons before the king at St Paul's Cross, the chief pulpit of the realm. They must have believed their ideas to be in royal favour; they were very wrong. On 3 April all three men were arrested and committed to the Tower, and four months later they were dead. Yet while their supposed crime was heresy, there is no evidence that any of the three ever supported, much less dared to preach before the king, the principal heresy for which most evangelicals in Henry VIII's reign were executed: denial of the Real Presence of Christ in the sacrament. If we want to understand the transgressions for which they died, then, we must look elsewhere.

It makes sense to begin with Robert Barnes, by far the most famous of the three. The outline of his career is well known. Barnes, an Augustinian friar and doctor of theology, flirted with reforming ideas as early as 1525, but his real career as an evangelical began in the late 1520s, when he fled from England, moved to Wittenberg and became close friends with Martin Luther. From 1530 onwards he wrote Lutheran tracts for both English and continental audiences, and as early as 1531, in the increasingly fraught context of the king's divorce case, he was embraced by Henry VIII's government as a possible link to the German Lutherans. Between 1531 and 1539, then, he was employed repeatedly by the Tudor regime as an ambassador to Lutheran governments, during which assignments he was active in the (failed) negotiations to convince Philip Melanchthon to come to England, and in the (temporarily successful) negotiations to marry Henry VIII to the German princess Anne of Cleves. Throughout this period, Barnes's Lutheran beliefs placed him in constant danger, and he was denounced as a heretic by Thomas More and others; however, as a Lutheran he always supported the Real Presence of Christ in the sacrament, which partially shielded him from prosecution.

The proximate cause of his arrest in April 1540, then, was not his Lutheranism but something quite specific: a public confrontation with Bishop Stephen Gardiner of Winchester, the realm's most powerful conservative cleric. In 1539, Gardiner had angrily attacked Thomas Cromwell in a Privy Council meeting for using Barnes, a known heretic, as an ambassador; Gardiner was temporarily excluded from the Council for his outburst.[48] In February 1540, then, when Barnes was scheduled to preach at St Paul's Cross, Gardiner inserted himself into the pulpit and preached an angry sermon against the Lutheran doctrine of justification by faith alone. Barnes took the bait and two weeks later preached a sermon from the same pulpit denouncing Gardiner and upholding the Lutheran doctrine of justification. This more or less guaranteed his arrest, although it took a series of bizarre recantations, withdrawals of recantations and half-apologies before he was actually committed to the Tower.[49]

So that explains why Barnes was troubled by the authorities. However, despite appearances, the theological question of justification and the debate with Gardiner were at best half the issue. In his formal recantation, recorded in the register of the Bishop of London, Barnes was forced to confess that good works were profitable for salvation. But he was also forced – much more unusually for a heresy recantation – to admit that 'laws and ordinances made by Christian rulers ought to be obeyed by the inferiors and subjects, not only for fear but also for conscience'.[50] This sounds like a recantation not of Lutheranism but of disobedience to the regime's interpretation of *adipahora*. Moreover, in the various diatribes against Barnes printed after his death, he was repeatedly accused of opposing or limiting obedience to civil authorities. One propagandist, for instance, wrote that Barnes 'Said certain / in words plain / it could not be found / that we were bound / to be obedient . . . / to the commandment / of the high powers / at any hours / on pain of sin'.[51] Likewise, a long confutation of Barnes's gallows speech by the Catholic propagandist John Standish repeatedly condemned Barnes for claiming liberty in *adiaphora*: 'Who hath not heard him preach against all the ordinance of Christ's Church, and erroneously rail and traitorously speak against the observing of days both fasting and praying? And contrary to Paul, Romans 13, denying godly ordinance to bind deadly sin? And that . . . the Church cannot restrain those things which are free by the gospel?'[52]

---

[48] *LP*, XIV, ii, 750. On the unclear dating of this event, see G. R. Elton, 'Thomas Cromwell's Decline and Fall', *Cambridge Historical Journal* 10, no. 2 (1951), pp. 150–85, at pp. 171–2.

[49] The most complete version of these events we have is Gardiner's self-serving reminiscence, printed in Stephen Gardiner, *The Letters of Stephen Gardiner*, ed. J. A. Muller (Cambridge, 1933), pp. 164–75. I have tried not to accept Gardiner's version at face value, especially his account of the king's views.

[50] This document from Bishop Bonner's Register is printed in Appendix VII of John Foxe, *The Acts and Monuments of John Foxe*, ed. G. Townshend and S. R. Cattley (London, 8 vols., 1837–41), V.

[51] Seymour Baker House, 'An Unknown Tudor Propaganda Poem c.1540', *Notes and Queries*, new series 39, no. 3 (September 1992), pp. 282–5, at p. 283.

[52] John Standish, *A Lytle Treatyse Composed by John Standysshe* (London, 1540), sig. A5r.

Standish also more bluntly accused Barnes of advocating opposition to royal commands:

What need we any other or stronger reproof in this matter than his own book printed about 10 years ago? There he, speaking of the Testament in English, sayth if the king would by tyranny take the book from them, that they should not suffer him. Be these your words, Master Barnes?[53]

This accusation was a reference to *A Supplication Made by Robert Barnes Doctor*, first published in 1531. In this book, on the subject of the Bible in English, Barnes had indeed used dangerous language questioning civil authority over religion. Using a clever but transparent rhetorical device, he claimed that Henry VIII had never prohibited vernacular scriptures, but he suggested that some day 'it may please God to take so great vengeance for our abominable sins that . . . he may send us such a tyrant that shall not only forbid the New Testament but also all things that may be to the honour of God'. In that *hypothetical* case, he advised the people to use passive disobedience, although not violent resistance: 'They shall keep their Testament with all other ordinance of Christ, and let the king exercise his tyranny (if they cannot flee). And in no wise under pain of damnation shall they withstand him with violence, but suffer patiently all the tyranny that he layeth on them.' To give up one's English bible, he wrote, was to 'deny Christ' – a claim which Thomas Starkey would directly deny in 1536, when he listed vernacular bibles among things indifferent.[54] Moreover, in responding to a sermon by the bishop of London against vernacular bibles, Barnes used unusually strong language: 'God is mightier than you, and I do reckon and faithfully believe that you are ten times worse than the Great Turk, for he regardeth no more but rule and dominion in this world, and you are not therewith content, but you will also rule over men's consciences, yea and oppress Christ and his holy word.'[55]

This last phrase brings us again to the subject that keeps reappearing in Catholic attacks on Barnes: conscience. In this case, of course, the people accused of binding the conscience were the clergy rather than the king, and this is a crucial distinction; there is no question that Barnes, like Melanchthon, believed that kings wielded lawful worldly authority while priests and bishops did not. Nonetheless, the centrepiece of Barnes's tract was the argument that 'men's constitutions, which be not grounded in scripture, bind not the conscience of man under pain of

---

[53] *Ibid.*, sig. G5r.
[54] Robert Barnes, *A Supplication Made by Robert Barnes* (Antwerp, 1531), sigs. P1v–P3v.
[55] *Ibid.*, sig. N6r.

deadly sin', and his approach to civil control over *adiaphora* was subtly more radical than Melanchthon's and considerably more radical than Starkey's.[56] Barnes chose to emphasise the fundamental Protestant doctrine of Christian liberty, the idea that, as he put it, 'we be not only by Christ made free from sin, but also made free in using all manner of things that be indifferent, and unto them we cannot be bound as unto things of necessity'. Christians generally should be obedient and promote the common peace by accepting the ceremonies and outward forms instituted by the state, and they should even obey the authorities in indifferent matters if those authorities tried to 'compel [them] by outward pains'. But this obedience was an act of 'brotherly charity' rather than a *moral* requirement of uniformity. The moment human authorities tried to compel such outward ceremonies 'under the pain of deadly sin', it became the Christian's *duty to disobey* in order to protect the liberty won by Christ: 'If man command anything to be done that may be done in time and place convenient, if he will bind us unto indifferent things as unto a thing of necessity, then shall we not do it, not because it is evil to do, but that it is damnable to be done as a thing of necessity.'[57]

The inevitable corollary of this doctrine was that, unlike Starkey, Barnes considered conscience very much at stake in ceremonial issues, since people had to determine whether their consciences were being bound. Barnes's text was thus peppered with phrases like 'let every Christian man judge in his conscience if this be right or lawful'.[58] Most importantly, Barnes stressed that any attempt to bind the Christian conscience in worldly matters was positively wicked: 'They do unright to bind our conscience in such things.'[59] Like Starkey, Barnes defined 'superstition' as the belief that something not essential for salvation was in fact a necessary part of Christian religion. But for Barnes this implied that the imposition of non-biblical ceremonies on pain of deadly sin was by definition superstitious, regardless of who was doing the binding, exactly because it tried to convert something intrinsically indifferent into a 'thing necessary'.[60]

We thus have strong evidence to suggest that Robert Barnes's principal offence was not his Lutheranism but his parsing of exactly when and how obedience was due to civil authorities in religious matters. If we turn from Barnes to his fellow martyr William Jerome, we again find substantial evidence that his ideological transgression was not about the nature of Christ but about the nature of government. In Jerome's case, this can be seen in the various extant versions of the confession and recantation

---

[56] *Ibid.*, sigs. O8v–P1r.    [57] *Ibid.*, sigs. P7v–Q2v.    [58] *Ibid.*, e.g. sigs. O1r and H8r
[59] *Ibid.*, sig. P8v.    [60] *Ibid.*, sigs. Q1r–Q2v.

sermon that he produced in March 1540 in an effort to save his life. What is notable first about these texts is that there is no suggestion that he had ever been accused of sacramental heresy. Rather, there were three main points that he abjured. First, he recanted a Paul's Cross sermon in which he had defended *sola fide*, having argued that 'Abraham's wife betokened the Church, and that like as she being a free woman had a free child without any condition, so were we justified by faith freely without any condition'. He now admitted that the sacraments were also efficacious and stressed the importance of genuine repentance for salvation. Second, he apologised for (or in some versions denied) genuine political radicalism, having allegedly 'used opprobrious words against the burgesses of the parliament, as calling them butterflies, dissemblers and knaves'. Third, and most interesting for our purposes, he recanted having preached that 'magistrates, as concerning things left indifferent by God's word, could not make any laws that should bind men's consciences'. He now admitted that this was not only 'contrary to the scriptures' but also tended to bring the people into 'disobedience, which should be the subversion of the public weal and breaketh all honest orders'.[61] Jerome had evidently attacked the Tudor government's notion of *adiaphora* just as Robert Barnes had, so it is no surprise that when John Standish posthumously attacked Robert Barnes, he threw a glancing blow at Jerome as well, accusing him of having believed that 'man's laws could not bind to deadly sin'.[62]

For further proof that the doctrine of *adiaphora* was indeed the crucial issue in Jerome's prosecution, we can turn to a government memorandum outlining 'the effect of certain erroneous doctrine' in Jerome's 7 March 1540 sermon at St Paul's Cross. The first argument attributed to Jerome was that 'no magistrate had power to make that thing which of itself is indifferent to be not indifferent'. In the margin beside this passage, someone has written, 'This article confirmeth Doctor Barnes's book where he teacheth that men's constitutions bind not the conscience.' Clearly, then, the Henrician authorities had linked Barnes to Jerome precisely on the issue of *adiaphora*. The second argument attributed to Jerome was his desire that 'honest men and good Christian men would observe and keep all laws and ceremonies that tend to the honour and glory of God'. This may seem uncontroversial and even anodyne, but the marginalia on the government memorandum describes it as an 'evasion'; the phrase 'all laws and ceremonies that tend to the honour and glory of God' was ambiguous

---

[61] PRO SP 1/158, fos. 124r–125v [*LP*, XV, 414]. See also Foxe, *The Acts and Monuments of John Foxe*, V, Appendix VIII.
[62] Standish, *A Lytle Treatyse*, sig. G5r.

at best to a government that wanted obedience to all things *not specifically forbidden* by God. Then at the end of the memorandum, the writer noted that Jerome's doctrine of justification by faith alone 'engendereth such an assured presumption and wantonness that we care not greatly whether we obey God or no'. Here, again, the danger of Lutheranism seems to be its potential for 'wantonness' and disregard for obedience. Finally, and perhaps most importantly, the writer summarised Jerome's views of *adiaphora* by noting that he 'maketh obedience to princes an outward behavior only, which is but a play either for fear or manners' sake'.[63] Here, then, we can see that despite the ostensible requirement of only outward obedience, nothing was scarier to the regime than the inward conscience lurking beneath.

This all explains the ideological context of the executions of Barnes and Jerome. But what of Thomas Garret, fellow of Magdalen College, Oxford, curate of Honey Lane, London and sometime chaplain to Bishop Hugh Latimer? His theological career was so obscure that all John Foxe could say for the period between his abjuration of heresy in 1528 and his execution in 1540 was that 'Master Garret, flying from place to place, escaped their tyranny until this present time that he was again apprehended and burned with Dr. Barnes'. This certainly did not make Garret a likely candidate for execution if the government wanted to send a clear signal of what constituted unacceptable religion. Moreover, the articles alleged against him in 1528 had included various sorts of Protestant activities, none of which seem particularly promising reasons to burn him more than a decade later. First and foremost Garret was a distributor of banned books, but he also was said to have preached salvation through faith alone and the impotency of pardons, images, pilgrimages and the veneration of saints – none of this would have made Garret a likely candidate for martyrdom twelve years later, and indeed much of it had in the meantime become central to Henry VIII's own policies. More to the point for our purposes, Garret also allegedly argued that 'the laws and constitutions of holy Church be not to be observed, nor ought to bind any man', and that 'every man may preach the word of God, and that no law to the contrary can be made'. These statements would tend to put Garret in the same camp as his fellow victims Barnes and Jerome, limiting the ability of human authorities to bind the consciences of Christians.[64]

The hint that something more significant was afoot in Garret's early career, however, was the final article alleged against him, which sticks

---

[63] Foxe, *The Acts and Monuments of John Foxe*, V, Appendix VIII.
[64] John Foxe, *Acts and Monuments* (London, 1563), p. 481, wrongly paginated as p. 477.

out like a sore thumb for its uniqueness is contemporary heresy proceedings: 'Item, that he fled away in a layman's apparel, from Oxford
to Bedminster, when he should have been attached for heresy.'[65] The
story behind this bizarre statement was in fact the only thing of any significance that Foxe could say about Thomas Garret, and saying it took
him something over 7,000 words; this suggests that it was of more than
passing importance. According to Foxe, Garret was visiting Oxford early
in 1528 when word was sent by Cardinal Wolsey to have him arrested
for heresy; he was subsequently taken into custody by two officers of the
university, one of whom was 'Mr Standish' – the same Standish who,
more than a decade later, would write a tract against Robert Barnes.
Garret was placed in the custody of Dr Cottisford, rector of Lincoln
College, who was also commissary of the university. Yet Cottisford was
less than vigilant: 'At evensong time, the commissary and all his company went to evensong and locked him alone in his chamber. When all
were gone and he heard nobody stirring in the college, he put back the
bar of the lock with his finger.' He sneaked to the rooms of a young
scholar, who gave him a sleeved coat to replace his academic hood and
gown. In these clothes, Garret escaped and made his way westward to
escape a massive manhunt; he was apprehended in Bedminster eight days
later.[66]

The importance of this event lay not merely in its intrinsic excitement,
but also in the ways it was discussed afterwards, most notably – and
not coincidentally – by Robert Barnes. For in Barnes's 1531 *Supplication*, the chapter entitled 'men's constitutions which be not grounded
in scripture bind not the consciences of man under pain of deadly sin'
actually began with a long argument, obviously referring to Garret, that
it was lawful for men arrested for spreading the gospel to escape from
prison. This was an unusual claim. While flight from persecution was
a well-established trope in patristic sources and was usually condoned,
escape from prison was something else altogether, since ordinary Protestant doctrine held that, like Christ himself, the godly should submit to
the persecution of lawful authorities, disobeying unlawful commands but
nonetheless meekly accepting the punishment for their disobedience.[67]
Barnes, however, argued that for those 'cast in prison wrongfully', if they

---

[65] *Ibid.* Robert Barnes used a similarly interesting ruse to flee England, faking his own
suicide and then disguising himself as a pauper. But because Barnes was not in custody
at the time, the relationship of this ruse to obedience doctrine was very different.

[66] Foxe, *Acts and Monuments* (1563), pp. 608–14, wrongly paginated as pp. 604–10. See
also Foxe, *The Acts and Monuments of John Foxe*, V, Appendix VI.

[67] Jonathan Wright, 'Marian Exiles and the Legitimacy of Flight from Persecution', *Journal
of Ecclesiastical History* 52, no. 2 (April 2001), pp. 220–43.

could 'save their self... without any sedition' they might lawfully do so 'and thy conscience is free so doing, and thou dost not sin nor offend the law of God'.[68]

Given that Garret's prison-break was the only thing that Foxe knew about him thirty years later, and given that the subject of prison-breaks was given such explicit treatment by one of his fellow martyrs, it seems almost certain that Garret was executed because this doctrine of lawful flight was antithetical to the sort of Church that Henry VIII was trying to establish. Moreover, another piece of evidence indicates that this unlikely issue was the subject of considerable debate within Protestant discussions of obedience, *adiaphora* and Christian liberty. The 1521 edition of Melanchthon's *Loci Communes* had argued explicitly in the section 'On Magistrates' that even though princes are to be obeyed for the sake of conscience, 'If you are thrown into prison without deserving any evil, and you can escape without public commotion, nothing prohibits your flight; as in 1 Cor. 7, "If you can make yourself free, do so instead."'[69] This is undoubtedly the authority on which Barnes (who knew Melanchthon well) based his 1531 claims about the legitimacy of Garret's flight. By the middle of the 1530s, however, Melanchthon had distanced himself considerably from this earlier radicalism, and in the 1535 revision of the *Loci Communes* – dedicated to Henry VIII – Melanchthon dropped the whole idea that flight was a lawful alternative to obedience. The idea that obedience was somehow separable from acceptance of punishment, then, was something that Henry VIII's government found unacceptable, and on 30 July 1540 Thomas Garret went to his punishment after all.

It is hard, then, to escape the conclusion that all six of these men, evangelicals as well as Catholics, died because of their views of royal authority rather than because of their views of Christian salvation. When the six were executed together, the symmetry of the event was by no means obvious but rather was itself a sort of statement of the king's authority. By claiming that three men died for treason and three others died for heresy – but then executing three for crimes committed six years earlier, and executing the other three for crimes never mentioned – the regime was essentially claiming that it could make both treason and heresy by fiat. The government's moderation of men's consciences was mirrored by the *via media* of their executions.

---

[68] Barnes, *Supplication*, sig. P1r–v.
[69] *Corpus Reformatorum* (Leipzig, 101 + vols., 1834–), XXI, p. 224. 'Si coniectus sis in carcerem nihil mali meritus, et effringere possis, sine publico motu, nit vetat fugere. Iuxta illud, primae Corinth. VII. [vs. 21] So potes liber fieri magis utere.'

## The politics of restraint in Henry VIII's Church

If we turn finally from ideology and biography to politics, we find a world in which Henry VIII was trying desperately to wring religious peace from a ruling elite comprised of ambitious, fractious and often obstinate men. Whether or not the king had a consistent theology in the years leading up to 1540 – an issue much debated by historians – certainly he had a consistent political goal: the creation of a religious peace that upheld his authority over the Church. Yet this was not as easy as it sounded. The king had very real *negative* power: he could enforce conformity through violent repression and thus keep public religious discourse within a fairly narrow spectrum. His *positive* power, however, was more limited; there was little that threats and swords could do to produce a lasting peaceful settlement. Nonetheless, Henry VIII seems to have believed that, because he had the power to enforce obedience upon the nation, he therefore had the power to effect genuine peaceful reconciliation, and throughout 1539–40 he tried to leverage his negative power into a positive religious peace. This repeatedly proved futile, and every time the king discovered his inability to create harmony by fiat, he fell back upon his power to silence dissent and enforce obedience. The executions of 30 July 1540, then, represent peace at the point of a sword, the very essence of external moderation.

Let us begin the story in June 1539, with the passage by parliament of the so-called Act of Six Articles, which confirmed significant aspects of Catholic orthodoxy and sought to halt the radicalisation of English Protestantism. The Act was, from a theological perspective, a piece of fairly straightforward boundary-drawing: it affirmed the Real Presence of Christ's body and blood in the sacrament, the illegality of clerical marriage, the necessity of auricular confession and other aspects of Roman Catholic theology. Moreover, it took the unprecedented step of imposing a special penalty for denying the Real Presence: violators were to be burned to death for heresy, even for a first offence, without any possibility of recantation. On one level, then, the purpose of the Act was to uphold Catholic orthodoxy and declare so-called 'sacramentarian' heresy beyond the pale. Yet from a political rather than a doctrinal viewpoint, what is most interesting about the Act is the process that produced it. The king appointed a committee in the House of Lords, announced by Lord Chancellor Thomas Audley on 5 May 1539, to create a religious settlement. He placed on that committee a perfect balance of reformers and conservatives – neatly represented by Archbishop Cranmer of Canterbury on one side and Archbishop Lee of York on the other – so that the settlement it produced would represent the genuine consent of the political nation to the king's policies. But in the event, the king's hope in this mixing of evangelical and conservative bishops proved disastrously misplaced. Within less than two weeks, their bickering proved so contrary to his intentions that he appointed another peer, the conservative Duke of Norfolk, to stand up in the House, denounce the committee as hopelessly impotent, and instead present them with the Act of Six Articles as a *fait accompli*. It was passed the following month with only minor emendations, as the king desired. He had got the bill he wanted, but not the process he wanted; he could enforce obedience but not legislate harmony.[70]

Yet despite the failure of Henry's peace process, he did not abandon hopes of using the Act of Six Articles to bring heretics to the table rather than bringing them to the fire. It is noteworthy that, despite the uniquely draconian penalties in the Act, its passage did not lead to the massive repression that conservatives desired and evangelicals feared; the only large-scale attack on heretics was in far-away Calais, and the origins of that attack predated the Act by several months. In practice, then, the Six Articles was not the blunt instrument of later Protestant mythology but rather was a tool of negotiation, and the king continued to support evangelicals in several respects. Most notably, in January 1540 the king married Anne of Cleves and seemingly cemented England's foreign policy connections with the German princes, many of whom (although not Cleves) were Protestants. Significantly, Henry decided to hold the nuptials on the feast day of the Epiphany, when marriages were traditionally banned by the Church; on indifferent matters, the king clearly believed in no power but his own.[71] Then in April 1540, Thomas Cromwell was made Earl of Essex and Great Chamberlain of England, a significant promotion for the realm's leading evangelical and a clear sign of the king's favour. Henry VIII, then, was playing a complicated game, offering both the carrot and the stick to convince reformers to subsume doctrinal niceties to royal power.

Yet Henry VIII's vision of the political 'centre', in which moderation was defined by the abandonment of doctrine in favour of obedience to the king, was not compatible with what many leaders on either side of the Reformation divide had in mind. They were willing to accept Henry VIII's authority over the Church – that was why they were still alive in 1540 – but they sought to persuade him to use that authority for particular doctrinal purposes. Hence the peace that the king had wanted to achieve through the Act of Six Articles – technically known, not coincidentally, as the 'Act Abolishing Diversity in Opinions' – was actually a recipe

---

[70] For this whole story, see Elton, 'Thomas Cromwell's Decline and Fall'.
[71] Retha Warnicke, *The Marrying of Anne of Cleves* (Cambridge, 2000), pp. 161–3.

for just the sort of divisive politics that the king despised. In the royal court and in the Privy Council, coups and counter-coups continued unabated. First, the conservative bishops John Stokesley and Stephen Gardiner were 'excluded from court and public business' by Cromwell's plotting in October 1539.[72] Significantly, Gardiner's alleged indiscretion was calling Robert Barnes a heretic.[73] Then, by 15 February, Gardiner was back in London, preaching vituperative, *ad hominem* sermons against Barnes; this time the king let him get away with it and had Barnes locked in the Tower.

It was in this fraught atmosphere, then, that Henry VIII reconvened parliament on 12 April 1540 – the same parliament he had prorogued in 1539 after they passed the Act of Six Articles – intending that they should now produce a religious settlement that would end ideological conflict. At the opening meeting of the session, Cromwell gave a long speech in which he spoke on the king's behalf:

The rashness and licentiousness of some, and the inveterate superstition and stiffness of others in the ancient corruptions, had raised great dissentions to the sad regret of all good Christians. Some were called papists, others heretics; which bitterness of spirit seemed the more strange, since now the holy scriptures, by the king's great care of his people, were in all their hands in a language which they understood. But these were grossly perverted by both sides, who studied rather to justify their passions out of them than to direct their belief by them. The king leaned neither to the right nor to the left hand, neither to the one nor the other party, but set the pure and sincere doctrine of the Christian faith only before his eyes, and therefore was now resolved to have this set forth to his subjects without any corrupt mixtures, and to have such decent ceremonies continued and the true use of them taught.[74]

External moderation was needed here precisely to restrain the 'passions' of both sides, a moderation inseparable from coercive violence. This was why the only solution to England's religious crisis was a settlement dictated by the government, refusing any 'corrupt mixtures' from either side: when Cromwell condemned the 'bitterness of spirit' with which people called each other 'heretic' and 'papist', he implied that the government's own continuing policy of condemning people to death for heresy and papistry was not excess but moderation. As a statement of the king's desire for a *via media*, then, it is worth noting how aggressive this statement was, managing in a brief paragraph to attack virtually

---

[72] *LP*, XIV, ii, 423.      [73] SP 1/155, fo. 156r [*LP*, XIV, ii, 750].

[74] Quoted in Lehmberg, *The Later Parliaments*, p. 90. This is a translation of the Latin in the *House of Lords Journal*, I, pp. 128–9, consulted online at www.british-history.ac.uk/report.aspx?compid=30888, accessed 24 August 2010. The extant text is probably not a verbatim transcript of the speech.

everyone in England as either licentious or superstitious. The middle
way, in this view, was only wide enough to encompass the king's own
rapidly expanding person.

After this aggressive opening salvo, Cromwell then explained that the
purpose of this session of parliament was to produce a lasting religious
peace. Cromwell told parliament that, since the king was resolved that
'the gospel of Christ and the truth should have the victory', he had
decided to name two committees of bishops and theologians: one 'to
draw up an exposition of those things that were necessary for the institution of a Christian man', and the other to 'examine what ceremonies
should be retained, and what was the true use of them'. Both committees, whose memberships were read out by Cromwell at the end of his
speech, were consciously balanced between reformers and conservatives
(although this time the committee on doctrine leaned a bit to the conservative side), making clear the king's desire that neither side would triumph
over the other. Neither of these committees, moreover, could have had
any illusions that they were supposed to produce genuinely independent
conclusions. On the issue of ceremonies, there was no question what they
were supposed to decide. In January 1539 the king had issued a proclamation ordering the continuation of all 'laudable ceremonies heretofore
used in the Church of England which as yet be not abolished nor taken
away by his highness', and commanding priests to 'instruct the people'
in the use of those ceremonies 'without superstition'. This proclamation
had included specific instructions on the proper use and meanings of
several controversial ceremonies, including the use of holy water, the use
of candles and 'creeping to the cross' on Good Friday.[75] Clearly the parliamentary committee on ceremonies was supposed to endorse this view.
While the parliamentary committee on doctrine may have had slightly
more leeway, the explication of 'necessary' doctrine – a phrase reminis-
cent of Thomas Starkey – had already received explicit treatment in the
Act of Six Articles. The king's strategy, then, was not to engender a new
settlement but to obtain the sort of support for the current settlement
that had been sorely lacking; all religious factions were to submit their
own 'passions' to the king's moderation.

It should be noted that at the time the 1540 parliament received
this brief, the six priests, Powell, Abel, Fetherston, Barnes, Jerome and
Garret, were all already locked in the Tower of London, and there was
a palpable sense among observers that the political process of creating
a religious settlement in parliament would settle the fate of these and

---

[75] Paul Hughes and James Larkin (eds.), *Tudor Royal Proclamations* (New Haven, 3 vols.,
1964–9), I, p. 279.

other political prisoners. On 23 June, the French ambassador Charles de Marrilac reported that the English government 'had decided to empty the Tower at this parliament'; the phrase is ominous but its meaning is ambiguous.[76] Later in the summer, on 10 July, Bishop John Clark of Bath told the Venetian ambassador in Bruges that Cromwell would soon be burned 'together with two other heretics, one of whom was a friar who preached Lutheranism'; this can only be a reference to Barnes and his compatriots.[77] But more remarkably, as early as 24 April, the French ambassador reported that the main purpose of the current parliament was to deal with 'some matters which have been left undecided', especially the fate of the 'prisoners who have been held since Easter because of questions concerning religion'. Some of these prisoners, he reported, had been released without punishment, but others – and here his mention of certain 'doctors' implies that he had Barnes and Powell in mind – 'have not yet seen trial because of the great contention into which the bishops of this country are entered, the one side wanting to maintain their doctrine as incontestably true, the other side reproving it as error and falsehood'.[78] Later, on 1 June, he again reported that parliament continued in session for the twin causes of religious disputes among the bishops and the '*affaire des prisonniers*'.[79]

As these latter quotes imply, from the very beginning of the 1540 parliament the two committees on religion bogged down in dispute and recrimination, a bitter mockery of the process of consensus building that Henry VIII desired. On 8 May, Marillac noted 'the contention in which the bishops are entered on some propositions concerning religion'.[80] By 21 May, he reported that parliament would have been dissolved already, since the king's financial needs had been met, were it not for religious affairs in which 'the bishops are not yet come together in conformity of

---

[76] Kaulek (ed.), *Correspondance politique*, p. 194: 'ainsi qu'il se pourra veoir dans peu de jours, attendu mesmement qu'on a délibéré de vuyder la Tour à ce parlement qui doibt finer avec ce moys'.

[77] *Calendar of State Papers Relating to English Affairs in the Archives of Venice* (London, 38 vols., 1864–1947), V, p. 85.

[78] Kaulek (ed.), *Correspondance politique*, p. 178: 'pour aucunes propositions qui avoient demeuré indécises, où mainctenant ilz font compte d'y mettre fin, et mesmement sur le faict des prisonniers qui depuis Pasques ont esté prins à cause des questions qui concernent la religion, ainsi que par mes précedantes, Sire, vostre bon plaisir aura esté entendre; desquelz aulcuns ont esté délivrez sans avoir porté aultre punition, des aultres, comme les docteurs, n'est encores vuidé le procès, pour la grand contention où les évesques de ce pays sont entréz, les ungs voullant mainctenir [leur] doctrine comme véritable, autres la réprouver comme erronée et false; sur quoy ilz sont encores'.

[79] *Ibid.*, p. 187.

[80] *Ibid.*, p. 181. 'La contention où les évesques sont entrez sur aucunes propositions qui concernent la religion.'

opinion, and would seem day by day to put things more in doubt, if it were not that the king holds them close, wanting to hear and examine their reasons and the grounds of their opposition and then adjusting and determining things as he sees fit'.[81] The general tenor of these reports is corroborated by the fact that the king temporarily prorogued parliament from 11 to 25 May, because, as Thomas Audley put it to them in the king's name, 'that great work' of the religious committees 'cannot so soon be perfected', hence it was necessary that 'these matters should be more maturely treated and discussed by himself, the bishops and clergy'.[82]

We get the sense, then, that the king was rapidly growing tired of this wrangling and the inability of his clergy to take the hint that too much ideology of any sort would not be tolerated. On 21 May, Marillac reported that certain unnamed 'ministers' had told him that parliament would adopt a religious settlement 'neither according to the doctrines of the Germans nor of the pope, but of the truth conforming to the ancient councils of the Church'.[83] This was more like what the king wanted, and indeed sounds suspiciously like the king's own propaganda. By 1 June, however, Marillac's sources had convinced him that the bishops in parliament were 'irreconcilable' and that the bishops of each party, 'to establish what they believe, want reciprocally to destroy those who sustain the contrary'. As he put it in another letter the same day, 'They are supposed to put an end to this parliament and make a middle way [*moyen chemyn*] that all must follow, but from what I can see it will come about like the diets of Germany, of which one begets more to follow, as the parliament first one then another, and the doubts instead of ending will expand.'[84]

It thus appeared that a religious settlement would once again elude the English government, but Henry VIII was not yet willing to give up. So instead of merely nudging parliament towards the desired goal, he gave them a more palpable jolt. His first significant manoeuvre to force a compromise occurred at the end of May, when Bishop

---

[81] *Ibid.*, p. 184. 'Les évesques ne se sont encore convenuz en conformité d'oppinion, ains semble de jour en jour ilz seroient pour mectre les choses en plus grand doubte, si n'estoit que ce roy leur tient de près, voulant oyr [et] examiner raisons et fondement de leur oppinion en y adjoustant et déterminant comme bon luy semble.'

[82] Cited in Lehmberg, *Later Parliaments*, p. 103.

[83] Kaulek (ed.), *Correspondance politique*, p. 184: 'non selon les doctrines des Allemans ny du pappe, mais de la vérité conforme aux conciles anciens de l'Église'.

[84] *Ibid.*, pp. 186–8: 'lesquelz pour establir ce qu'ilz maintiennent veullent réciproquement faire perdre ceulx qui soustiennent le contraire'. 'L'on debvoit mettre fin à ce parlement et prendre un moyen chemyn qu'on debvoit ensuyvre, mais à ce que je puis veoir il en adviendra comme les diettes d'Allemaigne dont une en engendre plusieurs suyvantes, aussi le parlement ung aultre, et les doubtes au lieu de prendre fin croistront.'

Richard Sampson of Chichester and the eminent theologian Dr Nicholas Wilson were both arrested for treason; Wilson was on the parliamentary committee for religion, Sampson was on the parliamentary committee for ceremonies. There can be no doubt that their removal was part of an attempt to remove bottlenecks in the two committees caused by overzealous conservatives.[85] The arrest of these two members of the parliamentary committees on religion naturally set the rumour mill churning. The French ambassador thought that things had come to a point where 'it is necessary that either the party of the said Cromwell succumbs or that of the bishop of Winchester with his adherents'; with Sampson and Wilson gone, he believed that Cromwell had the distinct advantage and, interestingly for our purposes, he used as evidence for this belief the rumour that 'le docteur Barnes' was 'soon to be released'.[86] Another rumour, probably from early June, claimed that Barnes had already been released and 'made the king's almoner'.[87]

Unfortunately for the evangelicals, however, they wrongly assumed that this upturn in their fortunes represented a genuine royal swing towards Protestantism, when in fact all it represented was the king's desire for peace on his own terms. Hence evangelicals overplayed their hand and furiously lobbied for the arrest of more conservatives. The French ambassador was told that Cromwell had been heard to say that 'there were still five bishops who ought so to be treated'.[88] Archbishop Cranmer likewise took the arrests of Wilson and Sampson as a sign of royal favour. Some time before 1 June he inserted himself in the place of the imprisoned Bishop Sampson to preach at St Paul's Cross, and according to the French ambassador, he 'began to advance propositions opposite to those which the bishop of Winchester preached in the same place at Lent'; in other words, he preached in favour of salvation by faith alone, against Stephen Gardiner, just as Robert Barnes had done.[89]

Yet this was not at all the outcome the king wanted. Cromwell's success in bringing the 'treasons' of Sampson and Wilson to the king's attention had been possible because Henry believed that these men were impediments to his 'middle way'. Yet by overreaching, Cranmer and Cromwell

---

[85] Strype, *Ecclesiastical Memorials*, I, part 2, pp. 381–3.

[86] Kaulek (ed.), *Correspondance politique*, pp. 187–8: 'Les choses sont réduites à ces termes qu'il fault ou que le party dudit Cramvel succumbe ou celuy de l'éveque d Hoyncester avec ses adhérans.'

[87] *LP* XV, 792.

[88] Kaulek (ed.), *Correspondance politique*, pp. 187–8: 'Ung personnaige digne d'estre creu m'a dict qu'il avoit entendu du seigneur Cramvel qu'il y avoit encores cinq évesques qui devoient estre ainsi traitez.'

[89] *Ibid.*, p. 188: 'Il a commencé à mettre en avant [propositions] toutes contraires à ce que a ledit de Hoincester au mesme lieu ce karesme presché.'

themselves became the new focus of the king's ire, and conservatives on the Privy Council pressed the advantage. The result was that the king took rapid action against his former favourite: on 10 June Cromwell was arrested and committed to the Tower on charges of treason and heresy. The charges against Cromwell were essentially a tissue of lies, except for the very legitimate claim that he had protected heretics from prosecution. But what is most interesting for our purposes is that, despite the fact that Cromwell was formally attainted of both heresy and treason, the religious charges against him were entirely subsumed within the civil charges. For instance, while accused of 'being a detestable heretic', Cromwell's actual offence was thereby sowing 'sedition and variance' among the king's loving subjects. When he was accused of freeing heretics from prison, the actual heresies he thereby abetted were omitted from the charges – being 'over tedious, long and of too great number here to be expressed' just like the heresies of Barnes, Jerome and Garret – and his real offence was falsely claiming to have had the king's consent for his actions. Most notably, the *pièce de résistance* was the allegation that Cromwell had publicly declared that he would support the theology of Robert Barnes and others, violently if necessary, even 'if the king would turn from it'.[90] Throughout the bill of attainder, then, the crown let it be known that disobedience, rather than any particular doctrinal error, was Cromwell's real crime.

While the fall of Cromwell was devastating for the evangelical cause, then, once again the king let it be known that his goal was not a conservative reaction but obedience. Yet nonetheless, conservatives again pressed their advantage too far, perhaps because it was at this very moment – between 5 and 9 July 1540 – that the king finally asked parliament and convocation to annul his marriage to Anne of Cleves. With the collapse of the Cleves marriage, the diplomatic advantage of English Protestantism suddenly disappeared and it seemed that there was a chance for religious conservatives to go back on the offensive. Thus in the parliamentary committee on religion, the reaction to Cromwell's arrest was that fence-sitters and even some evangelicals immediately turned against Archbishop Cranmer. As Cranmer's secretary later remembered it, 'the whole rabblement which he [Cranmer] took to be his friends, being commissioners with him, forsook him and his opinion in doctrine, and so, leaving his post alone, revolted altogether'.[91] Outside parliament as well,

---

[90] Quoted in Elton, 'Thomas Cromwell's Decline and Fall', pp. 178–9; for the text of the attainder, see Gilbert Burnet, *A History of the Reformation of the Church of England*, new edition (Oxford, 3 vols., 1816), I, pp. 504–6.

[91] J. G. Nichols (ed.), *Narratives of the Days of the Reformation*, Camden Society, old series 77 (Westminster, 1859), pp. 248–9.

conservatives were sure that the fall of Cromwell was a signal that their long-desired enforcement of the Act of Six Articles could now begin. In London, something like 500 evangelicals were rounded up and imprisoned within less than two weeks. But the conservatives had considerably overplayed their hand, and the 500 imprisoned Londoners were all freed without trial at the beginning of August, apparently by the king's own command.[92] When Cranmer's erstwhile friends tried to convince him that the king had irrevocably turned against the reformers, he responded that they had misjudged the king's wishes, and he warned them that if they persisted the king would turn against them too.[93] Cranmer was right.

On 20 July, at long last, the king's patience finally broke and he abandoned the hope that parliament would voluntarily approve his *via media*. On that day, Thomas Audley delivered a new bill on the king's behalf 'concerning Christ's religion'. By the close of business the following day, it had passed through both houses and was ready for the king's assent.[94] The bill announced that, seeing as 'nothing so much troubleth the commonwealth and hindereth quiet and concord as diversity in opinions and belief', the king had appointed his two committees on doctrines and ceremonies. However, since 'the true definition, determination and declaration thereof requireth ripe and mature deliberation and advice', the king had decided that the deliberations of those committees should not be limited to the present parliament but might continue until they concluded their work. This was, in other words, an elaborate retreat by the king, accepting that nothing would be accomplished for the moment – and indeed, the so-called 'King's Book' that grew from these deliberations would not be published until 1543.

But if this bill was a retreat by the king, it was an angry and defiant one, and he put into the bill a further provision which boldly staked out his own claim to be the sole arbiter of religion in his realm. The text is worth quoting extensively:

Be it therefore enacted . . . that all and every determinations, declarations, decrees, definitions, resolutions and ordinances, as according to God's word and Christ's gospel, by his majesty's advice and confirmation by his letters patent under his grace's great seal, [that] shall at any time hereafter be made . . . by the said archbishops, bishops and doctors now appointed, or other persons hereafter to be appointed by his royal majesty or else by the whole clergy of England, in and upon the matters of Christ's religion and Christian faith and the lawful

---

[92] Susan Brigden, *London and the Reformation* (Oxford, 1989), pp. 320–2.
[93] Foxe, *Acts and Monuments* (1583), p. 1866.
[94] Lehmberg, *Later Parliaments*, pp. 120–1.

rites, ceremonies and observations of the same, shall be in all and every point, limitation and circumstance thereof by all his grace's subjects . . . fully believed, obeyed, observed and performed to all purposes and intents, constructions and interpretations, upon the pains and penalties therein to be comprised.[95]

One key phrase here was 'or other persons hereafter to be appointed by his royal majesty'; the king was making it clear that if the present committees were not capable of following his instructions, he would appoint others who were. But other points are worth noting as well. The penalties for noncompliance were left open-ended – 'the pains and penalties therein to be comprised' – which gave the king potentially enormous coercive power. Most importantly, the bill stipulated that subjects were liable to penalties not only if they failed to *obey* the terms of any future religious articles, but also if they failed to *believe* them. This was, by any standard, a remarkable requirement for a civil statute. Here, following the broad definition of *adiaphora* proposed by Thomas Starkey, the government claimed the right to make formal requirements not only of outward behaviour but of inward belief in all matters that were not incompatible with 'God's word and Christ's gospel'. In failing to achieve his stated goal of a religious *via media* for the Church of England with statutory legitimacy, Henry VIII instead achieved something far greater: statutory authority for a remarkably broad interpretation of his own power.

All of this was not lost on the French ambassador, who reported that parliament had 'entirely transferred their authority and power to their king, whose sole opinion from now on will have the same efficacy as the acts which they were accustomed to make in parliament'. While everyone had always 'condescended' to the king's will, at least there was formerly 'some form and pretext of justice'; now that justice will exist 'only if it pleases the king'.[96] The ambassador believed that, as a result, no more parliaments would be called in England; in this he seriously erred, no doubt because he was better placed to report on events in England than to predict them. But he did note one concrete result of these recent events that he found both novel and distasteful:

I will not speak at length of the pamphlets and books which the bishops have printed daily in which, in order to be found good and faithful ministers, in treating

[95] *SR*, vol. III, pp. 783–4 (32 Hen.VIII. c.26).
[96] Kaulek (ed.), *Correspondance politique*, p. 211: 'Les estatz ont entièrement transféré leur auctorité et puissance à leur roy, duquel doresnavant la seulle opinion sera d'aussi grand efficace que les actes qu'ilz soulloient faire en parlement, qui est entierment se despouiller de la liberté qui restoit seulement au peuple à faire loix, et ce qui estoit de trois la remectre en ung seul. Et bien que auparavant tout le monde s'i condescendit à ce qu'on le veoit estre enclin, toutesfois les affaires bien ou mal s'expédi[oi]ent soubz quelque forme et prétexte de justice, où maintenant l'on recherchera seullement s'il plaist au roy.'

of true obedience, they give their king, in divine law, more power to interpret, augment, take away and make [doctrine] than the apostles or their vicars and successors ever dared to undertake. According to which, by their fine reasons, everything he says must be held as the law of God or the oracle of his prophets, and they not only want to attribute to him the proper obedience for a king to whom all honour, obedience and worldly service is due, but they also make him into a true statue for idolaters.[97]

This, then, was the context for the executions of three Catholics and three evangelicals on 30 July 1540, the greatest public statement of the Henrician *via media*. It was a statement written in blood because it had to be. The king would have preferred if subjects restrained their own religious passions, but what he got instead was a vivid statement of his own moderation: his authority to govern subjects who could not govern themselves. Henry VIII's moderation was thus simultaneously a plea for peace and an act of war. As the French ambassador put it, the king's middle way provided 'fresh fuel for greater butchery than ever'.[98]

## Conclusion

To assert a moderate middle way through the minefield of the Reformation might seem irenic in the cerebral world of formal theology, but in the more mundane world of politics it was an aggressive and antagonistic manoeuvre. By appealing to a notional centre, but locating that centre on ground that was barely inhabited, Henry VIII effectively denounced his subjects as extremists, raising rather than lowering the temperature of religious discourse. The executions of 30 July 1540 represent that process as it reached the boiling point; the violence of the act did not undermine the king's search for a middle way so much as it underlined the king's vision of moderation.

In large part, this connection between violence and moderation was a result of the regime's overarching preoccupation with the concept of *adiaphora*. Henry VIII conceived of a *via media* in which law and obedience trumped dogma and belief, subordinating theology to civil order. What he never quite understood, however, was that this attempt to domesticate

---

[97] *Ibid.*, p. 211: 'Je laisse à faire discours des cayers et livres que ces évesques font imperimer tous les jours, ès quelz, pour estre trouvez fidelles et bons ministres, en traictant de la vraye obéissance, itz permectent à leur roy, en loy divine, de povoir plus interpréter, augmenter, oster et faire que les appostres ny leurs vicaires et successeurs osairent oncques entreprendre; de sorte que, par leurs belles raisons, tout ce qu'il dict doibt es[t]re tenu comme loy de Dieu or oracle de ses prophètes, et luy veulent atribuer non pas seulement obéissance de roy auquel tout honneur, obéissance et service appartient en terre, mais en faire une vraye statue pour ydolâtres.'

[98] *Ibid.*, pp. 209–10: 'matière fresche pour une plus grand boucherye que jamays'.

theology was itself a theological position. The theory of *adiaphora* that underwrote the king's demands for obedience was in no sense neutral; it contradicted *both* the desire for Christian liberty at the heart of the Reformation *and* the desire for continuity at the heart of traditional Catholicism. It may have been a middle way, but in a world where ideas mattered and people were willing to die for their beliefs, that moderation could only ever be achieved from above through bloodshed.

# 3 Conformist moderation

## The *via media* and the moderation of the Church

In the half-century following the Elizabethan religious settlement of 1559, influential defenders of the Church of England came to imagine that settlement as a *via media* in the Reformation and argued that strict adherence to its ordinances was constitutive of religious moderation. This is not to say that they imagined an alternative 'Anglican' branch of Christianity between Catholics and Protestants; that vision would not emerge until the nineteenth century.[1] Rather, their *via media* lay in a straightforwardly Protestant Church between on one side Roman Catholics and on the other side puritans, whose unrestrained calls for further Reformation seemed to threaten the disorder of continental Anabaptism. These early opponents of puritanism, who systematically developed earlier, Henrician ideas of the Church of England as a *via media*, are known to historians as 'conformists', a scholarly term of art recognising their preference for obedience to the Church by-law-established as the basis for an orderly Christian society.

Historians have studied Elizabethan and early Stuart conformists, especially the most famous of them, Richard Hooker, from a variety of perspectives, and we now understand a great deal about their debts to the European Reformed tradition, their relationship to later 'Anglican' thought, their polemical engagement with puritanism and other important issues.[2] Yet no one has thought to ask just what the conformists

---

[1] See Peter Knockles, *The Oxford Movement in Context: Anglican High Churchmanship, 1760–1857* (Cambridge, 1994); Diarmaid MacCulloch, 'Richard Hooker's Reputation', *EHR* 117, no. 473 (2002), pp. 773–812.

[2] See, for instance, Lake, *Anglicans and Puritans?*; Ferrell, *Government by Polemic*; Patrick Collinson, *The Elizabethan Puritan Movement* (Oxford, 1989; first published 1967); Charles Prior, *Defining the Jacobean Church: The Politics of Religious Controversy, 1603–1625* (Cambridge, 2005); Anthony Milton, *Catholic and Reformed: The Roman and Protestant Churches in English Protestant Thought, 1600–1640* (Cambridge, 1995); Nicholas Tyacke, *Anti-Calvinists: The Rise of English Arminianism c.1590–1640* (Oxford, 1987); Eppley, *Defending Royal Supremacy*; W. J. Torrance Kirby, *Richard Hooker's Doctrine of the Royal*

meant by moderation. Since Catholicism and puritanism appear to be near opposite ends of a normative Christian spectrum – from dogmatism to individualism, from outward worship to inward spirituality, from centralisation to fragmentation – it has seemed self-evident that a middle space between them actually existed and that contemporaries would try to claim it. If, however, for early modern thinkers moderation implied not merely peace but governance, and the golden mean was not merely a point on a spectrum but a condition of authority, then conformist moderation may have meant something considerably different than historians have assumed. The purpose of this chapter is thus to demonstrate that the self-proclaimed moderation of the Church of England in its ethical, *internal* sense – a restrained and reasonable Church rather than an unbridled and fanatical one, a Church virtuously limited in its Reformation and thus a *via media* between Roman Catholicism and the Radical Reformation – was utterly dependent upon the Church of England's *external moderation* of its subjects through state power and coercive restraint.

It is not surprising to find that conformists favoured increased government power; the whole idea of 'conformity' implies it, and Peter Lake has argued that within conformist refutations of Presbyterian populism 'we can perhaps discern the English origins of Stuart absolutism'.[3] What is surprising and significant, however, is that for these thinkers moderation was not the opposite of strong authority but its essence. I want to suggest that a core issue in Tudor-Stuart religious debates was the relationship between internal and external moderation in the constitution of the Church. All English Protestants believed in the need for a moderate Church: one that was governed, whose passions were restrained, rendering it a *via media* between the universal monarchy allegedly sought by papists (usually described as tyranny) and the surrender of governance to the passions of the multitude allegedly sought by Anabaptists (usually described as anarchy). The question, however, was where did the power of ecclesiastical moderation lie and what were the limits of this authority over the Church? As this chapter will demonstrate, the conformist position was based upon the premise that the Church was incapable of self-restraint and thus had to be moderated externally by magistrates who settled disputes and set firm rules to regulate *adiaphora*. On this view, the institutional Church was inevitably prone to corruption and required the strong hand of civil authority to moderate its abuses; indeed the historical

*Supremacy* (Leiden, 1990); Nigel Atkinson, *Richard Hooker and the Authority of Scripture, Tradition and Reason* (Carlisle, 1997); Nigel Voak, *Richard Hooker and Reformed Theology: A Study of Reason, Will, and Grace* (Oxford, 2003).

[3] Lake, *Anglicans and Puritans?*, pp. 64–5.

rise of papal Antichrist was precisely the process whereby tyrannous clerics had thrown off the bridle of civil governance and claimed authority over kings, and the Reformation was in considerable part a process of restoring external moderation. Within this structure of civil governance, the maintenance of order was dependent upon moderation in the form of bishops – often described as 'moderators' – whose authority was necessary to restrain both the ideological fragmentation of the clergy and the seething turbulence of the laity. The bishops were of course clerics, but the lynchpin of the conformist system was that they were also civil officers, not merely spiritual doctors for troubled souls but worldly authorities whose coercive power was authorised by the monarch and the law.

In sum, the conformist position was based upon the impossibility that the visible Church could ever achieve genuine self-moderation. Because the Church inevitably included dangerous and ungodly elements within its worldly walls, the Bible had ordained obedience to civil government as the bulwark against the centrifugal forces that always threatened to tear apart God's house; right religion was inseparable from external order. As such, conformists built strong restraints to repress the passions of the Church's unruly members and to keep the Church as a whole on the middle path. The nature of these restraints varied considerably, and, as we shall see, the structures of Elizabethan conformity contained two potentially contradictory claims about the limits of ecclesiastical authority: an absolutist reliance on the monarch as supreme moderator, and a reliance on law that limited power over the Church at the same time that it limited the Church itself. But in all cases, moderation was virtually synonymous with strong and effective authority. The *via media* of the Church of England was an argument for governance.

### John Whitgift and the origins of the Elizabethan *via media*

The logical starting point for this discussion is the controversy sparked by the *Admonition to Parliament*, the puritan manifesto that in 1572 definitively rejected the half-measures of the Elizabethan settlement and demanded a full Presbyterian Reformation. The so-called Admonition Controversy was the first great debate between Protestants over the government of the Church of England, fought in a war of words between the puritan scholar Thomas Cartwright and the conformist Dean of Lincoln and future Archbishop of Canterbury John Whitgift.

While the idea of moderation and the middle way would become a major theme of later Elizabethan conformity, it was only a relatively minor theme in the writings of John Whitgift in the Admonition Controversy. This was undoubtedly because it still seemed somewhat strange for Whitgift to use such belligerent Reformation polemic, developed by Reformed Protestants against Anabaptists and by Henry VIII against Reformed Protestants, against his own supposed co-religionists. Indeed, in the previous thirty years the rhetoric of moderation had waned from its Henrician heights, and while it was far from absent – as Catherine Davies has shown, Edwardian Protestants practically invented indigenous English Anabaptists in order to present themselves as a middle way – it was used in more or less unified fashion by English Protestants rather than in intra-Protestant debate.[4] The battle for moderation between English Protestants, then, only began in earnest in the 1560s with the vestments controversy and the emergence of puritanism, and it was only in response to the appearance of a Presbyterian platform in the 1570s that John Whitgift first tentatively applied the concept to the English system of Church government.

In Whitgift's *The Defence of the Answer to the Admonition* (1574), then, while moderation reared its head at several key moments, and the twin dangers of ecclesiastical anarchy and tyranny were implicit throughout, nonetheless Whitgift declined numerous invitations to appeal to the logic of moderation. When his opponent claimed a middle way between 'contempt and excessive estimation' of the clergy, for instance, Whitgift's reply refused to engage the question of moderation.[5] Whereas later conformists described the need to balance democratic, aristocratic and monarchical estates as a form of moderation in the ecclesiastical polity, Whitgift flatly denied that government in England was or should be mixed.[6] Moreover, while in some places Whitgift placed his Presbyterian opponents at the opposite extreme from popery, more often he stressed that 'touching malice against the form and state of this our Church, I see no great difference betwixt them and the papists, and I think verily they both conspire together'.[7] Nonetheless, the Admonition Controversy provided the occasion for Whitgift to experiment with a variety of claims for moderation and the middle way that would become essential to the Church of England's self-image over subsequent decades. So it is in that spirit that

---

[4] Catherine Davies, *A Religion of the Word: The Defence of the Reformation in the Reign of Edward VI* (Manchester, 2002).

[5] *WJW*, vol. II, p. 396.     [6] *WJW*, vol. III, p. 197.

[7] *WJW*, III, p. 527. This would remain commonplace in more purely political texts accusing papists and puritans of shared sedition. See, e.g., Richard Bancroft, *Dangerous Positions and Proceedings* (London, 1593), with its claims that Geneva is the 'new Rome'; Oliver Ormerod, *The Picture of a Puritane* (London, 1605), especially 'Puritano-Papismus: Or, a Discovery of Puritan-Papisme'.

we begin with the Admonition Controversy: as an embryonic moment when we can see the outlines of the conformist *via media* in gestation.

At several points, Whitgift was pushed into adopting the language of the *via media* by the polemical need to rebut Thomas Cartwright's puritan appropriations of that space. For instance, Cartwright claimed to be 'as far from this tyranny and excessive power which now is in the Church' as he was from 'confusion and disorder wherein you travail so much to make us to seem guilty'. Against this claim for a Presbyterian *via media*, Whitgift hastily replied that 'this authority, which you call "tyranny and excessive", is moderate and lawful and according both to the laws of God and man'.[8] Whitgift's *via media* was here an afterthought and a reaction rather than a premeditated strategy. Another defensive moment was Whitgift's rebuttal of Cartwright's Aristotelian commonplace that 'contraries are cured by their contraries', hence in a Reformation context the best way to combat Antichrist was not merely to remove idolatrous ceremonies but to eradicate all popish ceremonies however indifferent they might be. Cartwright had argued that if you want to bring a drunken man to sobriety, you must not just give him moderate drink but no drink at all; if you want to straighten a crooked stick, you must not merely bend it straight but bend it towards the opposite side.[9] Whitgift's response was that such heathenish logic was ignorant of St Paul's precept that 'we must not do evil that good may come thereof'; both extremes are vices, and curing one vice with another is sinful regardless of what Aristotle may say about it. For Christians, then, the way to Reformation was not curing one extreme with another but strict adherence to moderation:

The ordinary means whereby a Christian man must come from vice to virtue, from an extreme to a mean, is the diligent reading and hearing of the word of God, joined with earnest and hearty prayers. The best way therefore to 'bring a drunken man to sobriety' is not to persuade him to a superstitious kind of abstinence or fasting, but to lay before him out of the word of God the horribleness of that sin and the punishment due unto the same. The similitude of a crooked stick is apt to set forth so crooked a precept, but not so apt to make manifest the way unto virtue.[10]

In part, then, Whitgift's *via media* was defensive and almost accidental. Yet throughout his work he assumed that the immoderate excesses of his Presbyterian opponents lay near the root of their dangerous assaults on the Church of England. Puritans, almost by definition, were ruled by passions and affections rather than religion and reason. At the beginning of his massive tome, Whitgift wrote that his opponents 'be not able to judge

---

[8] *WJW*, II, p. 280.    [9] *Ibid.*, pp. 441–3.    [10] *Ibid.*, p. 443.

of controversies according to learning and knowledge, and therefore are ruled by affection and carried headlong with blind zeal into diverse sinister judgments and erroneous opinions'.[11] He accused Cartwright of being 'full of passions' and repeatedly condemned his opponent's 'boiling stomach'.[12] He lamented that 'every line' of the *Admonition to Parliament* contained 'almost nothing else but... intemperate speeches'.[13] Complaining of puritan laymen who spat in the faces of conformist clergymen, Whitgift attacked such 'excessive raging' and asked, 'How did you move the people to this extremity?'[14] His conclusion was that 'if these men be not by discipline bridled, they will work more harm to this Church than ever the papist did'.[15]

This presumption of puritan immoderation – unbridled, boiling over, blinded by passions – was the lynchpin of Whitgift's *via media*. For if the puritans themselves were dangerously ungoverned, it followed that the Presbyterian programme for the Church was a form of *un*government, a release rather than a moderation of sinful affections. The Presbyterian platform was essentially a recipe for governance of the Church by the people rather than governance of the people by the Church. This appeared most explicitly in the Presbyterian reliance upon elections, especially the election of ministers by their congregations, which were *ipso facto* excessive because the people are 'commonly led by affection' in their votes.[16] Whitgift wrote, 'The people... through affection and want of judgment are easily brought by ambitious persons to give their consent to unworthy men'; they are so 'bent to novelties and factions', so prone to favour doctrines that 'inclineth to liberty', that they simply elect 'such as would feed their humours'.[17] While popular elections had been permitted in the primitive Church, the multitude had long since been 'secluded from such elections' because of their 'contentions' and 'sinister affections'; early in Church history 'the rage of the people' was sometimes 'so intemperate that they fell from voices to blows'.[18] Popular election was thus not a form of moderation but an excess that required moderation. In a particularly gleeful moment, Whitgift was able to appropriate the authority of the Presbyterian hero Theodore Beza

---

[11] *WJW*, I, p. 49.    [12] *WJW*, II, p. 105; I, pp. 124, 141; III, p. 277.
[13] *WJW*, I, p. 94.    [14] *WJW*, II, p. 2.
[15] *WJW*, I, p. 290. This would later become a conformist mantra. For instance, in a 1585 letter to Lord Burghley, Andrew Perne claimed that if the 'fantastical humours' of the puritans 'should take root in the university as they do in other places, both the Church and consequently the commonweal shall soon come to ruin thereby', hence he called upon colleges to 'study and labour to bridle and restrain the licentious affections of the youth of the university': BL Lansdowne MS 45, fo. 125v. See Lake, *Moderate Puritans*, pp. 62–3.
[16] *WJW*, I, pp. 372–3.    [17] *Ibid.*, pp. 466–7.    [18] *Ibid.*, p. 463.

for this view, translating a long passage: 'Because the multitude is for the most part ignorant and untractable, and oftentimes the greater part doth overcome the better, even in a popular state lawfully appointed all things are not committed to the unruly people but certain magistrates are appointed by consent of the people to govern the common sort and multitude. Now, if this wisdom be required in worldly affairs, much more is a moderation necessary in those things wherein men oftentimes see but little.'[19]

The other side of Whitgift's *via media* was opposition to the tyranny of the papacy. The Presbyterians argued that the Bible required parity of ministers and suggested that any hierarchy within the ministry, or any appropriation of civil power by ministers, was a form of tyranny. Whitgift, by contrast, argued that the Bible forbade not clerical government *per se* but 'the ambitious desire of the same and the tyrannical usage thereof'. As such, the scriptural passages Presbyterians used against English bishops were more appropriately used 'against the pride, tyranny and ambition of the bishop of Rome, which seeketh tyrannically to rule'.[20] Cartwright had provided a wonderful hostage to fortune when he wrote that there could be no 'moderate and well-ruled government' by clerics since they properly had only spiritual authority. Whitgift responded that the Bible prohibited not superiority but only 'pharisaical, ambitious and arrogant affection of superiority', and he countered with his own version of the *via media*: 'Surely, as Christ condemneth here the ambitious affection of such as ambitiously desire these names of superiority, so doth he in like manner condemn those who be so puffed up with pride and arrogancy that they condemn and disdain to call men in authority by the titles of their offices.'[21]

The middle way between tyranny and licentious liberty, then, was the restraint of popular affections, not through arbitrary rule but through law. In this sense, far from civil authority and jurisdiction making the English bishops tyrannical, it was precisely what prevented them from being tyrannical: power in the Church was authorised by its moderation. English bishops could not be tyrants because 'concerning jurisdiction they be bound to the laws themselves, and do but execute laws made, not of their own private authority, but by parliament and by the prince. Neither can they control the worst minister in their diocese if he observe the laws and rules prescribed.'[22] Episcopal power was moderate because it was limited by law, 'for the mind of man, even of the best, may be over-ruled by affection; but so cannot the law'.[23] Likewise, Royal Supremacy

---

[19] *Ibid.*, p. 415, repeated with a slightly different translation at p. 458.
[20] *Ibid.*, pp. 148, 150, 169.   [21] *Ibid.*, p. 168.   [22] *WJW*, II, p. 209.   [23] *Ibid.*, p. 240.

over the Church was moderate because it was generated and structured by law: 'Betwixt a king and a tyrant this is one difference, that a king ruleth according to the laws that are prescribed for him to rule by and according to equity and reason; a tyrant doth what him list, followeth his own affections.'[24] Whitgift told Cartwright: '"Liberty" and "tyranny" be too common in your mouth. It is no "tyranny" to restrain the people from that liberty that is hurtful to themselves and must of necessity engender contentions, tumults and confusion.'[25]

Beginning from a highly defensive position, then, John Whitgift established a positive *via media* for the Church of England in which moderation was constructed in and through exactly those structures which Presbyterians regarded as tyrannical: the law's investment of bishops and monarchs with strong and enforceable authority over the Church. This framework, here achieved almost accidentally and haphazardly, would later become the core of the conformist argument for moderation, and conformists would apply it to virtually every conceivable aspect of the English Church. In the 1570s, however, the ideological reach of this framework was still relatively limited, and Whitgift stressed in particular two areas where strong authority both was authorised by and constituted moderation: the controversy over Church ceremonies and the controversy over 'moderators' in Church debates.

On the issue of *adiaphora*, Whitgift cited Reformed authorities like Calvin, Bucer and Musculus to argue for a *via media* based upon order: the government's enforcement of uniformity for the sake of worldly order was a middle way between the disorder of free choice and the superstition of positing genuine spiritual necessity in outward ceremonies. Whereas puritans demanded that all indifferent ceremonies should be abandoned if they were not edifying, for Whitgift this demand was meaningless because by definition 'such laws and orders as keep godly peace and unity in the Church do edify'. Laws to enforce unity were necessary because of the 'crooked and rebellious nature of man', and therefore 'God had appointed magistrates and given them authority to make orders and laws to maintain the peace and unity of the Church, [so] that those which of conscience and good disposition will not, by such laws and orders may be constrained at the least to keep the external peace and unity of the Church'.[26] Or, as he put it late in the text, 'If any man shall say that this is to bring us again in bondage of the law and to deprive us of our liberty, I answer, no: for it is not a matter of justification but of order; and to be under a law is no taking away of Christian liberty.

---

[24] *Ibid.*, pp. 239 and 244.    [25] *WJW*, I, p. 408.    [26] *WJW*, II, pp. 61–2.

For the Christian liberty is not a licence to do what he list but to serve God.'[27]

The second area in which Whitgift stressed that genuine but restrained authority constituted moderation was in the appointment of 'moderators' to settle controversies. A key part of the Presbyterian platform was that, since there should be no superiority of one minister over another, Church assemblies required 'moderators': elected chairmen who maintained order but were merely *primes inter pares* with no authority over their brethren. Whitgift gleefully pointed out the logical contradictions in this attempt to institute order without superior authority: how could a moderator be chosen in an orderly way before there was a moderator to moderate the election of a moderator? Who would even have authority to call such an assembly?[28] More broadly, since moderation was government, real 'moderators' were not merely chairmen who directed discussion but authorities who 'might declare the state of the question', resolving issues in dispute; otherwise 'moderation' was not government but anarchy.[29] Quoting John Calvin, Whitgift stressed the need for a 'moderator' – that is, a ruler with authority over the rest – in every company: 'This thing doth nature allow, and the disposition of man require, that in every society, though all be equal in power, yet some should be as it were moderator of the rest, upon whom the other might depend. There is no court without counsel, no session of judges without a praetor or justice, no college without a governor, no society without a master.'[30] Unlike later conformist writers of the 1580s and 1590s, Whitgift did not turn this argument into a full-fledged justification for episcopal authority; he merely stressed the anarchy of the Presbyterian position and, latterly, the authority of Christian princes to appoint 'moderators' to govern the Church.[31]

In sum, then, John Whitgift's articulation of moderation and the *via media* in the 1570s was nowhere near as extensive, integrated or capacious as it would become in the writings of later conformists. The ideas he was exploring were new to him and to his readers. They were revisions of arguments invented by Henrician conformists like Thomas Starkey against Protestants, and arguments invented by continental reformers like John Calvin against Anabaptists, for novel use against members of Whitgift's own Church. As such, they were hesitant and often defensive, constructing from available materials – the need to refute charges of

---

[27] *WJW*, III, p. 488. Here Whitgift was following not only Thomas Starkey but also Matthew Parker and others who wrote against puritans in the vestments controversy of the 1560s: see e.g. Matthew Parker, *A Briefe Examination* (London, 1566), sig. ****3v.
[28] *WJW*, II, pp. 269–71.   [29] *Ibid.*, p. 276.
[30] *Ibid.*, p. 425.   [31] *WJW*, III, pp. 304–7.

tyranny, belief that puritans were led by passions rather than reason, fear of democratic energies in the Church – the outlines of a powerful new position. But if necessity was the mother of invention, Whitgift was a master inventor.

## The mediocrity of John Bridges

The full articulation of a conformist vision of the moderate *via media* thus had to wait thirteen more years for the publication of *A Defence of the Government Established in the Church of Englande* (1587) by the Dean of Salisbury, John Bridges. At 1,400 pages, it was one of the longest books that had ever been published in England, earning it eternal fame as the butt of Martin Marprelate's wit: 'a portable book, if your horse be not too weak, of an hundred, threescore and twelve sheets of good demy paper'.[32] For our purposes, it is interesting that Martin also repeatedly ridiculed Bridges's claims for a *via media*, telling him, 'You have to your mediocrity written against the papists' and mocking the alleged 'mediocrity' of the bishops whom Bridges has defended.[33] It took no subtle reading, then, to understand that near the heart of Bridges's project was a claim for moderation.

The contours of Bridges's argument for moderation can be found in the first section of *A Defence*, where he rebutted the claim in William Fulke's puritan manifesto *A Briefe and Plaine Declaration* (1584) that the Presbyterians desired merely for the Queen to 'appoint on both sides the best learned, most godly and moderate men to debate all differences of weight between them and us'. This call for a formal disputation, and the claim to moderation within it, Bridges immediately denounced as fraud on three grounds. First was the logic of *adiaphora*: if the Presbyterians were willing to admit that there were indeed 'moderate' men on both sides, this was as much as to admit that reasonable people could disagree, hence the points in dispute were not of such necessity that they were worth disturbing the peace of the Church. Second was the issue of Presbyterian passions: if there were really moderate men on the Presbyterian side, they should show 'better moderation' in their polemic and 'lay aside . . . indecent terms and violent demeanor'. Third was the question

---

[32] Joseph Black (ed.), *The Martin Marprelate Tracts: A Modernized and Annotated Edition* (Cambridge, 2008), p. 56.

[33] *Ibid.*, pp. 14, 16, 18. The OED cites this as the first pejorative usage of the word 'mediocrity'. See also p. 64, where Martin accuses Bridges of faulty logic by claiming that he ought to read 'Friar Titleman's rules *de inveniendis mediis*', a reference to a work of scholastic logic that in fact concerned the middle terms in syllogisms, but here was intended literally to mean 'inventing the mean'.

of who would 'moderate' the proposed disputation; this was the core of the matter, and it cut to the heart of Bridges's understanding of the *via media* of the Church of England. In Bridges's view, the Presbyterians wanted no moderator because they would accept no binding determination against them, and as Bridges put it in a telling simile, a disputation without a moderator to arbitrate it was no more than a 'prophecying'.[34] Here, then, in the first twenty pages of a 1,400-page book, we see the outline of Bridges's position: moderation was established through government authority over things indifferent, restraint of criticism in the Church and the binding authority of 'moderators'.

First, on the issue of ceremonies and conformity, Bridges linked moderation, obedience to the Church and Christian liberty. Glossing Calvin, he argued that Christ had 'left in our liberty external rites or ceremonies, lest we should think his worship to be included in them', providing only the general rule that 'comeliness should be kept and confusion should be avoided'. Thus, rather than binding our consciences 'as things of themselves necessary', ceremonies bind the conscience 'so far forth as they should serve to comeliness and peace'. That is, no *particular* form of ceremony was prescribed in Scripture, but *some* form of comely and orderly ceremony – in other words uniformity – was required. This was as much as to say that Christian liberty meant the liberty of Churches to alter their required ceremonies, not the liberty of individuals to disobey those requirements. Bridges described this necessity of obedience in the language of moderation: God had left indifferent ceremonies to our liberty, but 'he hath not in the mean season permitted unto us a varying and unbridled licence . . . He hath encompassed round about (that I may so term them) lattices (or cross bars) either else, hath he indeed so moderated the liberty which he gave, that at length we may by his word esteem what is right. This place therefore rightly weighed, will show the difference, between the tyrannical edicts of the Pope, which press the conscience with a cruel bondage; and the godly laws of the Church, in which discipline and order is contained.'[35] The point here was that the authority to determine indifferent ceremonies was by definition moderation – a restraint of licentiousness through public order – and that authority had to be binding and enforceable or else it was no moderation at all: 'What authority at all call ye that . . . when every man may do as

---

[34] John Bridges, *A Defence of the Gouernment Established in the Church of Englande* (London, 1587), pp. 14–18.

[35] *Ibid.*, p. 671. Conformists disagreed whether laws on *adiaphora* technically 'bind the conscience'; some argued that they bind merely the 'external action'. See, e.g., Robert Some, *A Godly Treatise, Wherein Are Examined and Confuted Many Execrable Fancies* (London, 1589), pp. 38–9.

he please and is not so much as bounden to hold them or to account of them as they be judged, determined and disposed, but may dispose of them at his own pleasure without any restraint?'[36]

Bridges's second framework for moderation was based upon the requirement for Christians to be peaceable, moderating their passions in order to conduct debates harmoniously and construe their opponents' positions charitably. Bridges was scrupulous to fulfil this requirement himself, working hard to maintain a civil tone. He stressed throughout the text that Presbyterians were erring brethren rather than heretics or enemies, and while he wrote that Presbyterian positions sometimes 'savoured' of Anabaptism, or that Presbyterians picked up the broken splinters of Anabaptism and used them to attack civil government, he never accused Presbyterians of *actually being* Anabaptists as many conformists later would.[37] Yet external moderation was embedded in this vision of Christian harmony, since Bridges's attacks on his erring brethren were tantamount to claims that they were incapable of moderating their own passions. So, for instance, in attacking the Presbyterian campaign against episcopacy Bridges wrote, 'So far hath this immoderate beat of their inconsiderate zeal inflamed their passions and patience against the lawful authority of the bishops.'[38] The Presbyterians displayed 'no link of love, no bond of peace, no bowels of mercy, no affection of compassion, but all of passion in this too, too black rhetoric'.[39] On no less than seven occasions, Bridges accused the puritans of 'overshooting' the mark in their zeal for the truth, for instance writing, 'If ever our brethren have overshot themselves, it is in their humour for this presbytery.'[40] The word 'humour' here is no accident: puritanism was an imbalance that needed moderation.

Perhaps the most subtle and interesting example was Bridges's analogy of the puritans, trading England's good Reformation for the vain hope of a better one, to Aesop's fable 'The Dog and the Shadow': 'The goodly show of a fairer bone persuaded Aesop's dog to leave the good bone that he had already in his mouth, and to leap into the water after the shadow of another. I pray God our brethren allure us not with the like bait of some fair shadow, to leave the good state we have of government established.'[41] This was an odd translation of the fable; ordinarily the

---

[36] Bridges, *A Defence*, p. 117.

[37] *Ibid.*, pp. 134, 143, 547. See Lake, *Anglicans and Puritans?*, pp. 108–9 and ch. 3 *passim*. For an unusually egregious example, see Richard Cosin's accusations of puritan sorcery, cannibalism, lechery, drunkenness and Anabaptism in *Conspiracie, for Pretended Reformation* (London, 1592), pp. 4–8.

[38] Bridges, *A Defence*, p. 1315.    [39] *Ibid.*, p. 1390.

[40] *Ibid.*, p. 1054. See also pp. 92, 656, 657, 964, 1194, 1212.    [41] *Ibid.*, p. 82.

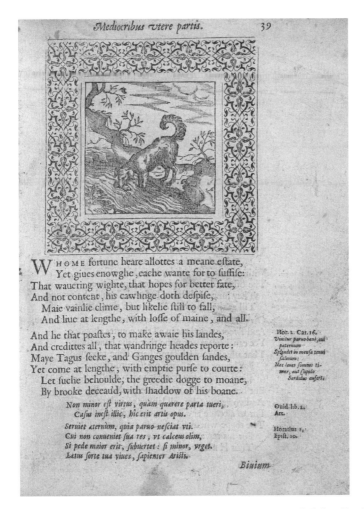

Figure 7. Geffrey Whitney, *A Choice of Emblemes, and Other Deuises* (Leiden, 1586), p. 39. The emblem 'Mediocribus utere partis', showing Aesop's fable known in the sixteenth century as 'The Dog and the Shadow'.

dog had in his mouth a 'piece of flesh' rather than a bone.[42] This makes it almost certain that Bridges's source for this reference was a sumptuous new emblem book published just the previous year, Geffrey Whitney's

---

[42] See, e.g., Aesop, *The Fables of Esope in Englishe* (London, 1570), fo. 36r–v; Aesop, *Here Begynneth the Book of the Subtyl Historyes and Fables of Esope*, trans. William Caxton (Westminster, 1484), fo. 33r.

*A Choice of Emblemes* (1586), which featured an emblem of the fable depicting a bone rather than a piece of flesh.[43] It is thus instructive that this emblem was an extended tutorial on moderation, with the heading *Mediocribus utere partis* – 'Use your portion with moderation' – and a series of warnings in English and Latin on the benefits of mediocrity over striving for perfection. In Bridges's interpretation, a puritan was no more than a greedy dog moaning for more.

Bridges's third and most significant framework for moderation was that the parity of ministers proposed by Presbyterians was fundamentally dangerous because without some 'moderator' with authority over the rest, presbyteries would inevitably descend into democratic chaos and confusion. Even Presbyterians accepted the need for the 'moderating of these governors, to bridle and repress all these inconveniences', but the way they sought to moderate them was not from above but from below, through popular election and the consent of the 'whole multitude'. This, in Bridges's view, was not moderation but the creation of 'a plain popular state'.[44] Instead, Bridges argued that the proper and essential role of the bishops was to be moderators of their presbyteries. It made no sense for a moderator merely to be first among equals rather than a genuine ruler, for 'how can he moderate his fellows except he have some authority over his fellows'? A true moderator 'in all deliberations determineth, that is, endeth and knitteth up the matter'. By definition, the moderator must have governance: 'To moderate the sentences of them all, his last voice strikes the stroke and hath the first and highest authority in the company . . . If he must moderate all their actions, how hath he not in this moderation an authority over them and an higher office?'[45] At one point, mocking the hypocrisy of Presbyterian demands for parity given the pre-eminence of Theodore Beza in Geneva, Bridges noted with rare humour his approval that such an excellent man should 'have a continuing and standing moderate office over all the residue of his fellow brethren there in the ministry to oversee and govern them'.[46] A moderate office was an office of governance.

Yet such governance was authorised by its limitation, and Bridges repeatedly described moderation by bishops as a middle way between the tyranny of papal supremacy and the anarchy of Presbyterian parity. Presbyterianism was 'as directly contrary to the right institution of bishops and archbishops as Antichrist's mystery of iniquity and his intolerable

---

[43] Geffrey Whitney, *A Choice of Emblemes, and Other Devises* (Leiden, 1586), p. 39.
[44] Bridges, *A Defence*, pp. 862–3 and the continuation of this discussion on pp. 954–5.
[45] *Ibid.*, p. 344.    [46] *Ibid.*, p. 461. See also pp. 1165 and 428.

pride and presumption is', with episcopal government '*in medio*' and the other two positions '*ab extremo in extremum*', like the 'mediocrity of justice between *minus* and *nimium*'.[47] The problem with the papacy was not superiority but 'excessive superiority', and as long as bishops maintained authority over their ministers without claiming universal authority over other bishops or princes, 'there was neither tyranny in this superiority but very good and necessary order'.[48] Indeed, the crucial point was that authority *was* moderation, the capacity to moderate schism and error, hence the Reformed Church 'confutes the immoderate pride of the pope, but denieth not a moderate superiority in the ministry'. 'Moderate superiority' here meant simultaneously a *limited* superiority and a *coercive* superiority, the authority to govern the ministry in their dioceses but not the 'unbridled tyranny' or unlimited authority claimed by the pope.[49] Hence Bridges quoted Calvin's letter to the King of Poland allowing for the existence of bishops to maintain order among the presbyters: 'Even as nature suggesteth this unto us, that out of all colleges one ought to be chosen upon whom the chiefest care should lie. But it is one thing to bear a moderate honour, to wit, so far as the faculty (or power) of man extendeth itself; another to comprehend the whole compass of the world in a government unmeasurable.'[50] The office of bishop, far from being a slippery slope towards 'Antichrist's pride and presumption', was instituted as 'the readiest way to restrain and repress it'.[51]

### Thomas Bilson and episcopal moderation

In Bridges, then, we see the outline of an argument for episcopacy as moderation, but this argument only reached full maturity with Thomas Bilson's *The Perpetual Government of Christes Church* (1593). Bilson's central thesis, far more overtly than for Bridges, was that churches required strong and effective government to restrain the concupiscence of both lay and clerical members. Using the familiar metaphor for moderation, he wrote on the first page that God had ordained government and discipline to 'bridle the unruliness of our affections', instituting the 'rod of correction, as well to guide the tractable as to repress the obstinate, lest disorder endured should breed confusion, the forerunner of all ruin'.[52] Moreover, Bilson's crucial polemical corollary to this thesis was that Presbyterian experiments in ministerial parity amounted not to government but to anarchy, the opposite extreme from the tyranny of Rome.

---

[47] *Ibid.*, p. 80.    [48] *Ibid.*, pp. 321, 324.    [49] *Ibid.*, pp. 346–8. See also p. 285.
[50] *Ibid.*, p. 416. See also p. 462.    [51] *Ibid.*, p. 79.
[52] Bilson, *Perpetual Government*, pp. 1–2.

The rationale behind Bilson's condemnation of Presbyterianism was that if governance were distributed too widely and too diffusely, it became merely the self-government of each member, which is to say it lost the restraining function for which government was ordained in the first place. 'For there can be no order but confusion in a commonwealth where every man ruleth, so would there be no peace, but a pestilent perturbation of all things in the Church of Christ, if every presbyter might impose hands and use the keys at his pleasure.'[53] Or, to put it slightly differently, government and parity were logically inconsistent concepts: 'The Church of God . . . hath been always governed by an inequality and superiority of pastors and teachers amongst themselves, and so much the very name and nature of government do enforce. For if amongst equals none may challenge to rule the rest, there must of necessity be superiors before there can be governors. It was therefore a ridiculous oversight in our new platformers [i.e. the Presbyterians] to settle an ecclesiastical government amongst the pastors and teachers of the Church and yet to banish all superiority from them.'[54]

For Bilson – who aspired to be a bishop and whose polemical writings won him preferment to the see of Worcester in 1596 and Winchester the following year – this superiority in the Church belonged to bishops, whom he considered biblically and apostolically ordained and vital. 'If order and discipline be necessary for all persons and ages in the Church . . . so much of the apostolic power as is requisite for the perpetual regiment of the Church must remain to those that from time to time supply the apostles' charge and succeed in the apostles' rooms.'[55] Episcopal power was by its very nature a moderate power, a middle way between anarchy and tyranny. He described the bishops' governance as 'fatherly moderation' and 'pastoral moderation' – literally the processes by which fathers restrain wayward children and shepherds restrain wayward sheep – in contrast to the 'tyrannical domination' of Rome.[56] He described a middle way between an absence of authority and the false claim of Roman authorities to civil lordship, for 'too much honour inflameth ambition, as too little engendereth contempt'.[57] At his most effusive, he described how, 'to avoid tumults and dissentions, God hath authorised one in each place and Church able to maintain a presbytery, who with pastoral and fatherly moderation should guide as well the presbyters and assist them, as the people that are subject to him according to the laws of God and man. The execution whereof is chiefly committed to his charge that is

---

[53] *Ibid.*, epistle to the reader, sig. ¶7v.    [54] *Ibid.*, epistle to the reader, sig. ¶2v.
[55] *Ibid.*, p. 207 (wrongly printed as p. 208).
[56] *Ibid.*, epistle to the reader, sig. ¶¶3v–¶¶5v.    [57] *Ibid.*, pp. 64–6.

the leader and overseer of all the rest, whom we call a bishop. His power I call a moderation and not a domination, because the wisdom of God hath likewise allowed and provided Christian means as well to bridle him from wrongs as to direct him in doubts.'[58]

As this last reference to the 'bridle' suggests, crucial to Bilson's understanding of the moderation inherent in episcopacy was that bishops themselves were also subject to moderation. This came most crucially from civil authorities, including the prince first and foremost, but also parliaments, convocations and other lawfully constituted organs of the national Church under the prince's watchful eye. For Bilson, then, 'there can be justly no suspicion nor occasion of tyrannical dealing so long as diocesans and metropolitans are limited by written laws in each case what they shall do, and every man that findeth himself grieved permitted to appeal from them to synods and princes'.[59] Or, as he put it elsewhere addressing the Presbyterians directly, 'If the execution of laws be dominion and *imperie* in your conceit, when as there is a present remedy by appeal to the prince's audience if any wrong or hard measure be offered, what will you call it to judge by discretion as your presbyteries do? Which is the greater kind of *imperie*, to determine all matters as you list, or to be limited in every point by the laws of the realm?' Here tyranny and anarchy, ordinarily opposite sides of the spectrum, doubled back upon one another as ten thousand petty tyrannies ('a pope in every parish') produced a more general anarchy in the realm: 'Would you have no laws at all but every case as it falleth out to be censured at the pleasure of the presbyters? That were a right tyranny indeed, not tolerable in any commonwealth that hath a Christian magistrate.'[60]

Bilson also admitted some limitation or moderation of the bishops from 'below', as it were: 'To temper the pastoral power of bishops that it might be fatherly... and not princely... the Church of Christ did in certain cases of importance not suffer the bishop to attempt anything without the consent of his presbyters.'[61] Likewise, Bilson admitted that the popular election of bishops 'was usual in the apostles' times' and that some manner of obtaining the 'consent of the people in the election of their bishops' had often been practised in Christian history.[62] Yet the weight of Bilson's analysis was to suggest that these more disorderly forms of moderation had been appropriate to the primitive Church before the advent of Christian magistrates, but now under a Christian prince

---

[58] *Ibid.*, pp. 304–5.    [59] *Ibid.*, epistle to the reader, sig. ¶¶5v.
[60] *Ibid.*, pp. 401–2. The danger of 'a pope in every parish' is described throughout ch. 14, with the exact phrase on p. 311.
[61] *Ibid.*, p. 313.    [62] *Ibid.*, pp. 339 and 344.

the need for such popular participation was radically attenuated. 'The people's right to elect their bishop never depended on God's express commandment but on the foundation and reason of human government', hence that right could and should lawfully devolve to the Christian prince who was 'the principal part and head of the people'.[63] Princes are 'by God's and man's law trusted with the direction and moderation of all external and public government as well in religion as in policy', hence they are to be 'trusted with elections if they please to undertake the charge'. In a 'popular state' like Geneva the election of bishops might still be appropriate, but in a kingdom like England the people had long ago 'submitted and transferred their right and interest to the prince's judgment and wisdom, which lawfully they might and wisely they did, rather than to endanger the whole commonwealth with such tumults and uproars as the primitive Church tasted of, and lay the gap open again to the factions and corruptions of the unsettled and unbridled multitude'.[64] Only in the most unusual and unnatural circumstances, in other words, did it make sense to give over the bridle of moderation to those who most needed bridling.

This brings us to the role of 'aristocracy' as a middle way between monarchy and democracy in the Church. In his epistle to the reader, Bilson mocked the way the Presbyterians misused this concept, imagining that every parish or congregation could be ruled by its own aristocracy, as if these were really the best men.[65] But Bilson nonetheless argued for the importance of aristocracy in the Church as a whole, as in ancient Israel, where God had ordained 'certain of the chiefest, who for their nobility and authority were preferred above the rest'.[66] He particularly invoked the moderation of an episcopal aristocracy in his discussion of the power of the keys, the ability to bind and loose sinners from the Church. Here the problem was that there were three seemingly competing injunctions by Christ that bore on the matter. In Matthew 16:19, the proof text of papalism, Christ seemed to give the power of the keys exclusively to Peter. In Matthew 18:17, the proof text of Presbyterianism, Christ seemed to give the power of the keys corporately to 'the Church'. Bilson, however, argued that both were compatible with an aristocratic reading, and that the two passages were in fact reconciled by a third, later passage, John 20:23, where the resurrected Christ gave the power of the keys jointly to his disciples, behind closed doors and without the rabble present.[67] On this reading, the power of the keys rested with the 'few', the aristocracy of the Church, which might in special circumstances include all ministers

---

[63] Ibid., pp. 348–9.    [64] Ibid., p. 356. See also pp. 310–11.
[65] Ibid., epistle to the reader, sig. ¶3r-v.    [66] Ibid., pp. 13–14.    [67] Ibid., pp. 213–214.

but ordinarily referred only to men with the 'highest calling amongst the clergy'. The apostles had thus ordained 'particular and preeminent moderation of the churches in each place by bishops'.[68]

The Presbyterians, Bilson wrote, fully understood the theoretical impossibility of trying to create a government for the Church alongside the parity of ministers. He bitterly mocked their attempts 'to reconcile their own contrarieties' through the creation of rotating or elected 'moderators' who guided the presbyteries but lacked authority over them. Either these 'moderators' lacked real authority, in which case the Presbyterians had no government for the Church at all, or else they had real authority, in which case they were essentially bishops by another name and Bilson could declare victory QED.[69] Elsewhere he ridiculed their contradictions: 'And so according to your manner you will have this power to be proper, and yet common; to be extraordinary, and yet usual; to cease with their persons, and yet to endure forever with your presbyteries. Fire will better agree with water than you with yourselves.'[70] In one extraordinary passage laying bare many of his assumptions, Bilson likened impotent Presbyterian 'moderators' with the civic republicanism practised in English towns: 'This is the right description of the mayor and aldermen of a city, or bailiffs and burgesses of a lesser town with us in England, but this is no description of a bishop in the Church of Christ.'[71]

Given their utter failure to reconcile Church government with ministerial parity, Presbyterians had tried to create government through the influx of the laity into positions of power in the Church: the establishment of lay elders. This Bilson regarded as irresistibly linked to democracy because the lay elders would outnumber, and hence out-vote, their pastors and teachers. He described the thousands of rural parishes that lacked learned laymen, ensuring that their elderships would be packed with 'silly governors . . . husbandmen and artisans', fit for rule in 'popular states and persecuted churches' but not in Christian kingdoms.[72] While the Presbyterians claimed to restrain the 'ambition of one that should be highest [i.e. the bishop]' they actually 'increase the pride of an hundred that should be lowest, for where we have one bishop in a diocese tied to the laws of God, the Church and the prince, you would have three hundred in a diocese . . . all of equal power and set at liberty to consult and determine of all matters at their pleasures'.[73]

The core of the problem was a failure of moderation. God had ordained two types of moderators, ministers and magistrates, and lay elders were

---

[68] *Ibid.*, pp. 109, 221–3.     [69] *Ibid.*, epistle to the reader, sig. ¶¶4r. See also pp. 216–18.
[70] *Ibid.*, p. 301.     [71] *Ibid.*, p. 239.     [72] *Ibid.*, pp. 150 and 156.     [73] *Ibid.*, p. 295.

apparently neither. If the lay elders were magistrates, then they must immediately 'relinquish all their authority' to the prince, or admit that they 'derive it from him', else *ipso facto* they 'establish another regiment against him'; there cannot be an alternative source of magistracy independent of the prince.[74] If, instead, the lay elders were ministers, this would be an intolerable intrusion of the flock upon the shepherds, the followers upon the leaders, the stones upon the builders – in others words, the essence of disorder rather than government.[75] As a result, the Presbyterians lit upon both extremes and missed the virtuous middle way between them: 'If laymen [i.e. elders] may intermeddle with ecclesiastical functions, why not the people? If the people may not, why should the elders, since both are lay? If they renounce the execution and challenge the supervision of ecclesiastical duties, they fly from one rock to fall on another; they clear themselves from the Word and entangle themselves with the sword.'[76]

## Stuart supremacy and absolute moderation

As the preceding argument has shown, Elizabethan conformist moderation was an argument for strong authority in and over the Church. Yet within that argument there were two alternative poles of authority available, and in the rest of this chapter I want to show how they led in substantially different political directions. I want first to discuss how, in the altered political circumstances of James I's reign, religious conformity produced a synthesis of moderation and absolutism. Second, I want to discuss how one creative alternative to this synthesis developed at the end of Queen Elizabeth's reign – the strikingly original model of Richard Hooker – offered a more subtle authoritarianism of law that would in the end prove more attractive to Englishmen searching for ways to justify state power paradoxically through its limitation.

The major development that came with the advent of the Stuart dynasty was the elaboration of the monarchical potential within the Elizabethan *via media*. Of the major Elizabethan conformists only one, the *sui generis* Flemish refugee Hadrian Saravia, had developed a genuinely absolutist interpretation of English Church government.[77] After all, most of the others were bishops or would-be bishops who shared a deep clericalism and lingering suspicion of their Supreme Governor; Elizabeth may have been their prince and font of moderation, but she was still a layperson and a woman. In the writings of Whitgift, Bridges and

---

[74] *Ibid.*, p. 148.    [75] *Ibid.*, p. 208.    [76] *Ibid.*, p. 209.
[77] See Lake, *Anglicans and Puritans?*, pp. 135–9.

Bilson, then, there was a studied ambiguity as to whether the monarch or the law was the proper agent of moderation in the Church. From the beginning of James I's reign, however, a new generation of writers tended to emphasise the most overtly monarchical tendencies within conformist thought to defend the position the king himself had staked out in his *Basilikon Doron*: that absolute monarchy was the principal defence against both popery and puritanism. It is useful to begin with Thomas Bell's *The Regiment of the Church* (1606), because Bell himself was a very different sort of conformist from the likes of Whitgift, Bridges and Bilson.[78] Bell was an ex-Catholic: he studied at the great English Catholic colleges at Douai and Rome, he was ordained a Roman Catholic priest in 1582, and he participated actively in the Catholic mission to England in the 1580s. By the early 1590s, however, he suggested that Catholics could conscientiously attend Protestant services, a position that earned him the hatred of many of his co-religionists. Thus by 1592 he was in communication with Archbishop John Whitgift, betraying his former allies. In 1593 he formally recanted his Catholicism and began a long career as a paid polemicist for the Church of England, living off a government stipend of £50 per annum. In *The Regiment of the Church*, then, we have a text in defence of the Church of England by a man significantly less committed to clericalism than his conformist predecessors and utterly dependent upon monarchical largesse for his livelihood. As such, its central argument was that 'the monarchical governance of our English Church is both the best and most laudable of all others'.[79]

*The Regiment of the Church*, in sharp contrast to most works of Elizabethan conformity, thus begins with a long discussion of Aristotle's three ideal types of government, devoted to proving that monarchy is best and that absolute monarchs like James I cannot be resisted for any reason, even atheism or apostasy.[80] This absolutist position was of course entirely compatible with a defence of episcopacy, and like his predecessors Bell contrasted the 'tyrannous' supremacy of the pope with the 'moderate and lawful' supremacy of the bishops, arguing that the bishops exercise jurisdiction granted to them by 'the whole Church assembled in parliament'.[81] Bell could sound, in other words, much like an Elizabethan. At several key points, however, Bell gave the civil magistrate

---

[78] Thomas Bell, *The Regiment of the Church as It Is Agreeable with Scriptures* (London, 1606). Other important examples include: John Buckeridge, *A Sermon Preached at Hampton Court before the Kings Maiestie* (London, 1606); David Owen, *Herod and Pilate Reconciled: Or, the Concord of Papist and Puritan* (Cambridge, 1610).

[79] Bell, *The Regiment of the Church*, sig. A3v.

[80] *Ibid.*, pp. 1–5.    [81] *Ibid.*, pp. 36, 110–11.

significantly greater and more direct control over the Church than most Elizabethans had been prepared to contemplate. In his discussion of the 'supreme government of the civil magistrate over all causes within his realms', for instance, Bell argued that Moses, wielding 'power like unto a king's, appointed order for all manner of religion in the people of God, and prescribed to Aaron himself and to the order of the Levites both what they should do and what they should avoid'. Later in Israelite history this royal power over the Church was delegated to people whom Bell identified with bishops, but he stressed that their power over the Church was always delegated royal authority rather than ecclesiastical authority *per se*. In his most pointed example he wrote, 'In the person of Samuel there did cohere both the magistracy and the priesthood; but he received the charge of moderating religion not as he was a priest but as he was a magistrate greater than whom there was none at that time in Israel.'[82] Moderation belonged to the chief magistrate.

Another example was Bell's discussion of lay elders in the Church. Like his predecessors, Bell argued that the form of Church government may be altered to suit different times and places, and that elements of democracy, while technically licit, were dangerous. As such, while councils of lay elders might be suitable for the Church in 'free cities and commonweals', they were generally unsuitable for 'Christian monarchies'. Bell took this argument one step further, however. When he admitted (as his predecessors had done) that, before the advent of Christian princes, lay elders had served a useful role in the Church, he further granted that a lay eldership might lawfully be retained under a Christian prince, 'so it be with his assent, good pleasure and moderation'.[83] Here Bell not only raised the spectre of the prince unilaterally dictating the form of Church government in his realm, he also imagined the prince, if he so chose, effectively sitting atop the presbytery and dictating its commands.

A third example was Bell's discussion of excommunication. Bell argued conventionally that the power of the keys had originally been given to the whole Church, but 'to avoid confusion, it is meet that some out of all be chosen, who may put the keys in use', since the 'vulgar sort want judgment and are often carried away with affections'. Most unconventionally, however, Bell also argued 'that the moderation and chief power of disposing and committing' the power of the keys 'resteth principally in the Christian magistrate, where the Church receiveth such a blessing'. This did not mean, Bell hastened to add, that the king could excommunicate people himself; 'none save only lawful ministers of God's word and sacraments can lawfully denounce the sentence of excommunication'. But it meant that the power of excommunication did not lie in the bishops by

---

[82] *Ibid.*, pp. 11–12.    [83] *Ibid.*, p. 143.

virtue of their episcopal office but only by direct royal grant, hence the
king could delegate that power to any ministers he chose. The choice
of the verb 'denounce' is also interesting, implying that clerics merely
promulgated the disciplinary decisions of the monarch.[84]

The idea that monarchs might enjoy direct authority over Church discipline was further developed in *De Adiaphoris*, published in Latin in
1606 and in an extremely literal English translation in 1607, by Gabriel
Powel, chaplain to the bishop of London. Powel's treatise, an answer to
William Bradshaw's puritan analysis of *adiaphora*, was probably the most
subtle and complex work ever written on the subject by an Englishman,
and it repeatedly delineated a now-familiar middle way between licentious liberty in things indifferent and the false belief that things indifferent
were a form of worship pleasing to God: moderation lay in conformity in
*adiaphora* for the sake of order. It was on the issue of royal authority, however, that Powel broke new ground. As we have seen, Elizabethan conformists were conflicted about whether to stress the monarchical aspect
of the English Church (ruled by a supreme head, reflecting the monarchical structure of the English State) or whether to stress the aristocratic
aspect of the English Church (ruled by bishops, a middle way between
tyranny and anarchy). Powel stepped into this conundrum with a new
argument. On one side, he wrote, it was tyranny for the laity to be simply
bound 'to assent and applaud all, without choice, whatsoever the bishops shall decree'. On the other side, the puritan position that 'every man
promiscuously should have licence to cry out, to move doubts, to propose doctrine, to ordain ceremonies' was dangerously democratic. The
middle way, then was that the Church

ought to be aristocratical, wherein the chief rulers and magistrates, the bishops
and princes, ought orderly to communicate their counsels. For the cognition both
of the doctrine and rites belongeth unto the Church, that is, to the bishops and
princes. Who also, when the matter shall be decided and agreed upon, ought
to be the keepers, maintainers and defenders of the external discipline, and the
putters in execution of the sentence and decree of the synod. So as they prohibit
and forbid idolatrous worship, blasphemies, perverse and wicked opinions, also
the contempt of mere indifferent and profitable rites, and punish the professors
thereof.[85]

This argument might be thought to limit the power of the monarch by
making him coequal with the bishops, but this would be to severely mis-
understand Powel's nuances. Previous conformists had seen the monarch
as possessing ultimate jurisdiction over the Church but in practice, as

---

[84] *Ibid.*, pp. 155–7.
[85] Gabriel Powel, *De Adiaphoris: Theological and Scholastical Positions, Concerning the Nature
and Use of Things Indifferent* (London, 1607), p. 14.

a layman, necessarily delegating that jurisdiction to the clergy: princes moderated bishops and bishops moderated the Church. Here, by contrast, the monarch was not only the source of episcopal authority but, to prevent the *bishops* from becoming tyrannical, princes partook of that power themselves, personally overseeing doctrine, ceremonies and discipline. As Powel noted a few pages later, bishops were necessary in the Church 'because both kings and princes, which do govern worldly empires, are very often times busied in other affairs, little regarding the ecclesiastical business'.[86] Hierarchy in the Church was absolutely necessary, but bishops only occupied the top rung because kings were too busy to do it themselves. Here, royal supremacy over the Church was *de facto* rather than simply *de jure* supremacy.

We can see the apotheosis of royal authority over Church discipline in *A Triple Antidote* (1609), written at the height of the Oath of Allegiance controversy by John Tichborne, a Cambridge scholar and client of Richard Bancroft. Tichborne began with a simple premise: there are two types of excommunication, separation from the invisible Church and separation from the visible Church. The first kind is a power that exists prior to any sort of settled Church government and adheres to the clergy by virtue of their ordination. But the second kind is dependent upon the constitutions of the visible Church to which it is attached and thus changes with circumstances. In particular, this second form of excommunication can be either ecclesiastical, civil or mixed: ecclesiastical excommunication is merely spiritual, the binding and loosing of sins, while civil excommunication is an expulsion from the outward government of the Church – in other words, *real* excommunication as it was normally understood. As such, while the clergy had government of souls, the civil State had government of the bodies of churchgoers: 'Albeit this censure [mere ecclesiastical excommunication] doth properly and evermore of right belong to the power of the Church and immediate government of souls, yet can no such power exercise any part of outward government or more public administration whatsoever within the territories and dominions of any civil magistracy, without the special good allowance or indulgence at the least of the chief magistrate there.'[87] The prince, in other words, had direct authority over membership in the visible Church, a power framed as a middle way between the opposite errors of clerical control over civil excommunication and lay control over spiritual excommunication. Ministers might have a limitless authority over spiritual absolution

---

[86] *Ibid.*, p. 19.

[87] John Tichborne, *A Triple Antidote, against Certain Very Common Scandals of this Time* (London, 1609), pp. 9–10.

and the kingdom of heaven, but that authority meant nothing in worldly kingdoms without the approbation of the king.

Tichborne continued his exploration of the relationship between the *via media* and royal power in part three of the tract, on the subject of indifferent ceremonies. Following earlier Jacobean writers like Gabriel Powel, Tichborne accused puritans of Manichaean dualism, unwilling to acknowledge a middle way between things commanded and things forbidden.[88] From this conventional starting point, however, he elaborated a remarkably capacious conception of *adiaphora*. For one thing, it was strikingly broad, even by conformist standards: if the Church's doctrine were sound, Tichborne argued, then all of its outward circumstances which were not evil in themselves were allowable, regardless of edification, order or comeliness.[89] It was also strikingly deep: *adiaphora*, once accepted as such, become so radically indifferent that 'no conscience . . . can arise from them'.[90] By this logic, no possible 'abuse, albeit in the highest degree of anything whatsoever', can 'discharge the subject from his due obedience to things of this nature once commanded by the magistrate'; even the most appalling superstition and idolatry would not release a subject from his duty.[91] Most importantly, unlike earlier writers (including Gabriel Powel) who had stressed the Church's authority to command obedience in things indifferent, Tichborne stressed the king's own authority:

Neither doth our freedom from that severity of the ceremonial law abridge any whit the authority of the magistrate in decent ceremonies agreeable to the gospel; but clean contrary (as we have above remembered) investeth rather that whole perfection, meaning and authority of the ceremonial law in those Christian magistrates to whom God committeth any part of his Church under the gospel. The ceremonial law indeed being nothing else but an order appointed by God himself for the outward polity and discipline of the Church being then under the pedagogy of the law, which now is left to the liberty of Christian princes as they shall see their times and occasions to require.[92]

In this remarkable passage, James I's *True Law of Free Monarchies* blended with Martin Luther's *Freedom of a Christian Man*, producing a Protestant absolutism based on moderation.

### Richard Hooker and the moderation of law

A very different trajectory out of Elizabethan conformity can be found in the moderation of Richard Hooker. Hooker's eight books *Of the Lawes*

---

[88] *Ibid.*, p. 85. See also pp. 104–5.    [89] *Ibid.*, p. 66.
[90] *Ibid.*, p. 86.    [91] *Ibid.*, p. 101.    [92] *Ibid.*, p. 106.

*of Ecclesiastical Politie* were written in the 1590s at the height of the conformist reaction against Presbyterianism, but they had a complex publication history. The first five books were published in Hooker's lifetime,
the first four in 1593 and the massive fifth in 1597. The later books,
however, remained in manuscript at various levels of completion and
with varying degrees of scribal circulation; the sixth and eighth were
not published until 1648, while the seventh was only printed after the
Restoration in 1662. Thus the corpus of Hooker's work did not exercise
a unitary historical influence, as neither the novel discussion of episcopacy in Book 7 nor the radical discussion of the limitation of royal power
in Book 8 were available to most readers. The books were conceived
together, however, hence we can find within their pages a more or less
coherent vision of ecclesiastical moderation and the *via media*.[93] For evidence that moderation was perceived by contemporary readers as lying
near the heart of Hooker's work, we need look no further than the title
page, created in 1611 and used in virtually all subsequent editions, where
the allegorical figure of the Church in the top left corner holds a Bible in
one hand and a bridle in the other.[94]

Richard Hooker was primarily a theorist of law, and, as we shall see,
law was at the heart of his vision of moderation. But law for Hooker was
always corollary to reason, and so it is with reason that we must begin.
Hooker wrote in his preface that there are two ways the Holy Spirit
leads human beings to truth: revelation, an extraordinary gift given only
to a few, and reason, given to 'all that are of God'.[95] We shall return
below to the very high capacity Hooker afforded 'reason' compared with
most Protestant theologians. But for the moment it is worth noticing
that in an Aristotelian framework 'reason' was also the principal restraint
upon the passions, affections or appetites that held them in moderation.
Hooker wrote that reason produces will, which it uses to control the affections, defined as the 'sundry fashions and forms of appetite': 'Appetite
is the will's solicitor, and the will is appetite's controller.'[96] In a religious
context, this became the basis for Hooker's contention that errors arise
'when men's affections do frame their opinions'.[97] For Hooker, heresy
was religious affection unbridled by reason, and heretics were those who

---

[93] On the production of the *Lawes*, see P. G. Stanwood, 'Works and Editions I' and W.
Speed Hill, 'Works and Editions II', both in Torrance Kirby (ed.), *A Companion to
Richard Hooker* (Leiden, 2008).

[94] Richard Hooker, *Of the Lawes of Ecclesiastical Politie* (London, 1611). I know of no other
images of the Church bearing a bridle, but a 1609 pageant for the new lord mayor of
London featured Religion with a book in one hand and 'a silver rod in the other' for the
'desertful chastisement of such as by over-heady zeal, or too cool remissness, shall dare
to disturb her laws and instructions': *Camp-Bell: or, the Ironmongers Faire Field* (London,
1609), sig. B1r.

[95] *WRH*, I, p. 17.    [96] *Ibid.*, pp. 77–8.    [97] *Ibid.*, p. 17.

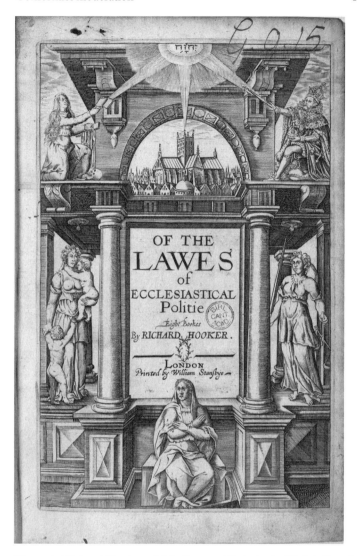

Figure 8. Richard Hooker, *Of the Lawes of Ecclesiastical Politie* (London, 1622), title page. The upper left corner shows an allegorical figure of the Church with a bible in one hand and a bridle in the other.

obstinately follow 'their own ambitious or otherwise corrupted affections instead of framing their wills to maintain that which reason taught'. Whereas true religion bends the will to reason, heretics '[bend] their wits to find how reason might seem to teach that which their wills were set to maintain'.[98] Here puritanism, like other sorts of religious error, was an uncontrolled appetite, a failure of reason to tame zeal and greed.

It is in this philosophical context of reason and the passions, then, that we must read Hooker's famous claim in Book 3 that human reason is a fundamental component of religion, coequal with scripture and tradition in achieving knowledge of God. The error he attributed to puritans – that scripture is the only source of secure religious knowledge, hence 'reason were an enemy unto religion, childish simplicity the mother of ghostly and divine wisdom' – was tantamount to accusing his opponents of *excess*, not properly moderating their passions with reason, and as such it was part of his argument that the Church of England was a *via media* between Rome and the radical Reformation.[99] On the Roman side was the erroneous opinion that 'only tradition' was the basis of the Bible's textual authority. On the other side, Presbyterians argued that revelation from the Holy Spirit was the sole basis of the Bible's textual authority. To both of these errors, Hooker posited reason as a moderating middle way, 'a necessary instrument without which we could not reap by the scripture's perfection that fruit and benefit which it yieldeth'.[100]

This was only the first of a long series of middle ways claimed by Hooker for the Church of England.[101] Another was the middle way between superstition and irreligion, between too much religion and too little. Superstition or 'superfluity in religion' was the product of two affections, zeal and fear.[102] On the other side, irreligion was the product of more sensual appetites like lust and greed. Since Hooker believed that

---

[98] *Ibid.*, pp. 224–5.    [99] *Ibid.*, p. 222.    [100] *Ibid.*, pp. 221–33.

[101] An older historiographical tradition claimed that Hooker's system was a genuine middle way between Roman Catholicism and Reformed Protestantism; for more recent historians making this claim see Philip Secor, *Richard Hooker and the Via Media* (Bloomington, Ind., 2006); Lee Gibbs, 'Richard Hooker: Prophet of Anglicanism or English Magisterial Reformer?' *Anglican Theological Review* 84, no. 4 (Fall 2002), pp. 952–4; William Harrison, 'The Church', in Kirby (ed.), *A Companion to Richard Hooker*. For an argument that associates Hooker with a mean in politics, see Charles Davis, '"For Conformities Sake": How Richard Hooker Used Fuzzy Logic and Legal Rhetoric against Political Extremes', in Arthur McGrade (ed.), *Richard Hooker and the Construction of Christian Community* (Tempe, Ariz., 1997). With more subtlety, H. C. Porter claimed that Hooker was 'especially successful as a sustained and thoughtful exponent of the balance of prerogative and consent in the Christian commonwealth of Tudor England': H. C. Porter, 'Hooker, the Tudor Constitution, and the *Via Media*', in W. Speed Hill (ed.), *Studies in Richard Hooker: Essays Preliminary to an Edition of His Works* (Cleveland, 1972), p. 77. For Hooker's moderation as a polemical tactic, see W. D. J. Cargill Thompson, 'The Philosopher of the "Politic Society": Richard Hooker as a Political Thinker', in W. Speed Hill (ed.), *Studies in Richard Hooker: Essays Preliminary to an Edition of His Works* (Cleveland, 1972); Patrick Collinson, 'Hooker and the Elizabethan Establishment', in McGrade (ed.), *Richard Hooker and the Construction of Christian Community*.

[102] *WRH*, II, pp. 27–9.

genuine atheists were few in number, he instead devoted his discussion to what he called 'affected atheism': intentional opposition to principles of religion to justify enjoyment of 'what sensual profit or pleasure soever the world yieldeth'. The word 'affected' here implied not only a contrivance but an 'affection' in the sense of a perturbation of the soul, and Hooker claimed that this 'irreligious humour' was so hard to suppress precisely because religion itself usually 'serveth as a bridle' for such concupiscence.[103]

The most important example, however, was Hooker's *via media* on the issue of indifferent ceremonies. Hooker's argument that ceremonialism constituted a middle way in the Reformation came at the conclusion of Book 4, where he discussed 'both kinds of Reformation: as well this moderate kind which the Church of England hath taken, as the other more extreme and rigorous which certain Churches elsewhere have better liked'. Other nations and Churches had tried to eliminate all Roman Catholic ceremonies, 'under colour of hatred towards things that are corrupt' throwing away even the most 'harmless ordinances'. God had saved England from such a dangerous fate, an action Hooker described as the very essence of moderation: 'The Almighty which giveth wisdom and inspireth with right understanding whomsoever it pleaseth him, he foreseeing... what tragedies the attempt of so extreme alteration would raise in some parts of the Christian world, did for the endless good of his Church (as we cannot choose but interpret it) use the bridle of his provident restraining hand, to stay those eager affections in some, and to settle their resolution upon a course more calm and moderate.'[104]

In his discussions of ceremonies, then, Hooker indulged in his most prolonged and sophisticated application of Aristotelian principles of moderation to the problem of Reformation. While Roman Catholics had 'over-superstitiously' abused religious ceremonies, puritans, by contrast, advised the Church to 'cure one contrary by another', a very dangerous practice since 'vices have not only virtues but other vices also in nature opposite unto them'. As such, Hooker wrote, we should not simply 'measure good by distance from evil, because one vice may in some respect be more opposite to another than either of them to that virtue which holdeth the mean between them both'. As he wrote elsewhere, the physician who will 'take away extreme heat by setting the body in extremity of cold' would undoubtedly cure the disease but would also kill the

---

[103] *Ibid.*, pp. 22–7.
[104] *WRH*, I, pp. 341–3. For later use of this analysis, see Francis Mason, *The Authoritie of the Church in Making Canons and Constitutions Concerning Things Indifferent* (London, 1607), p. 41.

patient.[105] Instead, to remedy the superstitious abuse of ceremonies the proper course is not to abolish them but rather 'to bring them back to a right perfect and religious usage, which albeit less contrary to the present sore is notwithstanding the better and by many degrees the sounder way of recovery'.[106]

Ceremonies also produced moderation because they limited Christians within regular and due bounds. Fast days, for example, serve three purposes: 'The first, a token of piety intended towards God; the second a pledge of moderation and sobriety in the carriage of our own persons; the last a testimony of our meaning to do good to all men . . . as contrariwise the very mass of general corruption throughout the world, what is it but only forgetfulness of God, carnal pleasure, immoderate desire after worldly things, profaneness, licentiousness, covetousness?'[107] Other ceremonies also exist in part to moderate the passions of Christians. Singing psalms in church, for instance, is requisite because music can carry us to 'ecstasies filling the mind with an heavenly joy', but it can also 'draweth to a marvelous grace and sober mediocrity' when the time for ecstasy is done. Hooker thus proposed a sort of artistic middle way in which affective worship through music is 'able both to move and to moderate all affections'.[108]

It is clear from this discussion that Hooker was more sanguine about human reason than most Protestants. But the core of the idea of reason in Hooker's view of the Church was not that *individual* reason was somehow unsullied by original sin so that reasonable people could moderate themselves, but rather that the *collective* reason of the Church should moderate its subjects. The existence of puritanism in fact proved that people could not be trusted to moderate themselves and needed some external reason to moderate them. And this brings us back, by a roundabout path, to Hooker's central contention that *law* constituted the moderation of the Church of England, for it was through law, the consensual and communal enactment of human reason, that order in the Church was enforced.

At even the most theoretical level, Hooker saw law as moderation: using Aristotelian teleology, Hooker posited that everything in the universe is shaped according to the ends for which it was made, and 'that which doth assign unto each thing the kind, that which doth moderate the force and power, that which doth appoint the form and measure of working, the same we term a law'.[109] This was true of the laws of nature, the laws

[105] *WRH*, II, pp. 319–20; *WRH*, I, p. 298.
[106] *WRH*, II, pp. 319–20.     [107] *WRH*, III, p. 60. See also *WHR*, II, p. 399.
[108] *Ibid.*, pp. 151–3.
[109] *WRH*, I, p. 58. On law as moderation, see W. J. Torrance Kirby, 'Reason and Law', in Torrance Kirby (ed.), *A Companion to Richard Hooker*. On teleology, see Barry

of scripture and the laws of human government: laws were simply forces that restrained objects to keep them on their proper path. Since human societies are made for the common good, then, the role of positive human law is to moderate the sinful excesses of individuals so that society as a whole may achieve that *telos*:

> Laws politic, ordained for external order and regiment amongst men, are never framed as they should be unless presuming the will of man to be inwardly obstinate, rebellious and averse from all obedience unto the sacred laws of his nature; in a word, unless presuming man to be in regard of his depraved mind little better than a wild beast, they do accordingly provide notwithstanding so to frame his outward actions that they be no hindrance unto the common good for which societies are instituted.[110]

This was the authoritarian side of Hooker: 'Authority is a constraining power, which power were needless if we were all such as we should be, willing to do the things we ought without constraint. But because generally we are otherwise, therefore we all reap singular benefit by that authority which permitteth no men, though they would, to slack in their duty.'[111] What rendered this authority moderate rather than excessive, however, was that laws were reasonable. Elaborating on a claim by Thomas Aquinas, Hooker argued that if laws are made by the consent of 'entire societies' through their representatives in 'parliaments, councils and the like assemblies' they embody the collective reason of the commonwealth and hence are by definition moderate rather than extreme.[112]

In the context of the controversy against the puritans, this meant that claims of private conscience against the laws governing religious worship

Rasmussen, 'The Priority of God's Gracious Action in Richard Hooker's Hermeneutic', in W. J. Torrance Kirby (ed.), *Richard Hooker and the English Reformation* (Dordrecht, 2003); Ranall Ingalls, 'Sin and Grace', in Kirby (ed.), *A Companion to Richard Hooker*.

[110] *WRH*, I, p. 96.

[111] *Ibid.*, p. 242; *WRH*, III, p. 256. It is largely literary critics rather than ecclesiastical historians who have noticed Hooker's strangely authoritarian constitutionalism. See, e.g. Brian Vickers, 'Authority and Coercion in Elizabethan Thought', *Queen's Quarterly* 87, no. 1 (Spring 1980), pp. 114–23; Debora Shuger, '"Societie Supernaturall": The Imagined Community of Hooker's *Lawes*', in McGrade (ed.), *Richard Hooker and the Construction of Christian Community*, p. 319: 'Although Hooker's Church is inclusive – or rather, precisely because it is inclusive – it is also fundamentally and essentially a coercive institution, employing "the rod of corporal punishment" to repress schism, dissidence, heresy, and all other such outbursts of individual dissent and ambition.' Rudolph Almasy, 'Language and Exclusion in the First Book of Hooker's *Politie*', in Kirby (ed.), *Richard Hooker and the English Reformation*, p. 241: 'True reconciliation, with the Church, with the state, and with Richard Hooker, is finally seen in terms of surrender. Law and order, peace and tranquillity . . . are possible only through submission.'

[112] *WRH*, I, pp. 82–3, 102–3. For Aquinas, see *ibid.*, pp. 236–7, quoting *Summa Theologica* I.2.q.91.art.3. Aquinas was expanding on ideas in Cicero's *De Legibus*.

fundamentally missed the point of those laws, which represented the external bridle of the commonwealth's collective reason upon the unruly passions of individuals. As Hooker put it in Book 5, 'Jurisdiction is a yoke which law hath imposed on the necks of men, in such sort that they must endure it for the good of others; how contrary soever it be to their own particular appetites and inclinations, jurisdiction bridleth men against their wills.'[113] As followers of private will rather than public law, puritans fulfilled Aristotle's dictum that 'the best men otherwise are not always the best in regard of society', and Hooker sarcastically suggested that the puritans would be among the best men in the world 'if they did not live amongst men but in some wilderness by themselves' – an argument more subtle than it appears, since the separation of the godly from the reprobate was indeed central to puritan ecclesiology. For Hooker, this separation was a violation of moderation because it removed constraint.[114]

Likewise, puritan claims for individual liberty in *adiaphora* were by definition dangerously excessive rather than moderate because they threw off the external moderation of law. Instead, the determination of *adipahora* by positive law was true moderation, a middle way between the 'over-extreme and violent' demand of Roman Catholics that all Churches must have the same outward forms, and the 'anarchy and mere confusion' of the puritans who claimed that each individual was free to do as he or she wanted. True Christian liberty was not liberty for individuals but for Churches to order their internal affairs through law: 'Those things which the law of God leaveth arbitrary and at liberty are subject unto positive laws of men, which laws for the common benefit abridge particular men's liberty in such things as far as the rules of equity will suffer. This we must maintain or else overturn the world and make every man his own commander.'[115]

This did not mean that there was absolutely no place for private conscience; like virtually all other sixteenth-century thinkers Hooker accepted that God should be obeyed before man and that to obey human law against one's own conscience was sinful. But he distinguished sharply between necessary or demonstrative claims of conscience and those that were 'mere probabilities only', arguing that the peace of the Church should trump mere probabilities. Most importantly, Hooker's criteria for certainty – an argument which 'being proposed unto any man and understood, the mind cannot choose but inwardly assent' – emptied the

---

[113] *WRH*, I, pp. 282–3.
[114] *WRH*, I, pp. 139–40. See Cosin, *Conspiracie, for Pretended Reformation*, preface sig. A4r–v.
[115] *WRH*, I, pp. 329–32; see also *WRH*, II, pp. 374–5.

concept of all content within an outwardly Christian polity. Within this framework, there was simply no issue of controversy on which conscience could trump law, because controversy itself was a priori proof that the claim of private conscience was merely probable rather than certain and hence should be abandoned before the public conscience of the law.[116] As he put it to the puritans, 'A law is the deed of the whole body politic, whereof if ye judge yourselves to be any part, then is the law even your deed also. And were it reason in things of this quality to give men audience pleading for the overthrow of that which their very own deed hath ratified?'[117]

The point, then, is that what made laws moderate for Hooker was the consent of the whole commonwealth through the legislative process, rather than anything kind or gentle about the laws themselves. Law was a sort of internal moderation of the commonwealth's passions through its collective reason, at the same time that it served as an external bridle upon the passions of individual members. As such, the rigorous enforcement of the law, or the use of law to strengthen authority, or the severe punishment of scofflaws like the puritans, was not excess but moderation. With this framework in mind, we are now in a position to understand Hooker's principal polemical claim against his puritan opponents, the moderation of the government of the Church of England. We must consider the issue in two parts: the authority of the bishops, and the authority of the prince.

The authority of bishops within the Church of England was moderate, according to Hooker, because it was limited or restrained by law.[118] This was not to deny their genuine authority; bishops existed to 'moderate all things' in their presbyteries, and while they ought to rule through consent, in the final analysis governance was theirs alone.[119] But while their authority had to be genuine in order to moderate the passions of those they governed, that authority was itself moderated by laws and was merely the judicial determination and executive enactment of laws positively determined by the whole commonwealth. As Hooker put it in Book 5, the disposition of ecclesiastical cases

resteth not now in the hands of popes, who live in no worldly awe or subjection, but is committed to them whom law may at all times bridle and superior power control. Yea to them also in such sort that law itself hath set down to what persons, in what causes, with what circumstances, almost every faculty or favour shall be granted, leaving in manner nothing unto them more than only to deliver what is already given by law.[120]

---

[116] *WRH*, vol. I, p. 33.     [117] *Ibid.*, pp. 27–8.
[118] The best discussion of Hooker and the bishops is A. S. McGrade, 'Episcopacy', in Kirby (ed.), *A Companion to Richard Hooker*.
[119] *WRH*, vol. III, pp. 175–84, 255–6.     [120] *WRH*, II, p. 45.

In answer to Theodore Beza's denunciation of episcopal power as tyrannical, then, Hooker answered, 'Is it possible that one so grave and judicious
should think it in earnest tyranny for a bishop to excommunicate, whom
law and order hath authorised to do so?'[121] Moreover, while English
positive law commanded government by bishops, all positive law was
alterable by new laws, hence bishops might be removed if they became
tyrannical and hence immoderate: 'Let this consideration be a bridle
unto them, let it teach them not to disdain the advice of their presbyters,
but to use their authority with so much the greater humility and moderation, as a sword which the Church hath power to take away from
them.'[122]

Likewise, the diocesan bishop in the English Church was by definition
restrained because his jurisdiction was limited by law to his diocese. In
Hooker's discussion of episcopacy, he divided bishops into two sorts:
bishops 'at large' and bishops 'with restraint'. The apostles were 'bishops
at large', with an unlimited commission to preach to all the nations of the
world, but over the course of time this regimen was replaced by 'bishops
with restraint' – a term which became, remarkably enough, Hooker's
ordinary idiom for diocesan bishops throughout Books 7 and 8. On the
one hand, it was precisely this 'restraint' that the pope violated by claiming universal jurisdiction, rendering popery hopelessly immoderate. Yet
on the other hand, Hooker told the Presbyterians, within their dioceses bishops were necessary to restrain anarchy.[123] Rule by 'bishops with
restraint' was a middle way.

But if bishops were moderate because they were restrained by law,
bishops were also agents of moderation in the ways they used the law
to restrain others. In particular, bishops were necessary as moderators
of the nobility; as clerical aristocrats themselves, bishops were perfectly
placed to act as a 'courteous bridle, a mean to keep them lovingly in awe
that are exorbitant, and to correct such excesses in them as whereunto
their courage, state and dignity maketh them over-prone'.[124] But more
generally, bishops were necessary to moderate the tumultuous populism
of the Presbyterians, which threatened to divide the Church into votes
and voices. In this sense, bishops *were* the moderation of the Church of
England, as Hooker put it in an extraordinary panegyric to episcopal
power: 'Prelacy, the temperature of excess in all estates, the glue and sol-
der of the public weal, the ligament which tieth and connecteth the limbs
of the body politic each to each other'.[125] Here Hooker perfectly captured the interrelation of internal and external moderation, the way the

---

[121] *WRH*, vol. III, pp. 229–30.    [122] *Ibid.*, p. 168.    [123] *Ibid.*, pp. 152–61.
[124] *Ibid.*, pp. 260–1.    [125] *Ibid.*, p. 263.

self-regulation of the body was achieved through a forcible 'tempering' of excessive members.

If we move finally to the authority of the prince as Supreme Head of the Church, we find in essence an extension of these arguments about bishops, the same reciprocal relationship between internal and external moderation, only now these arguments seem infinitely more radical because they involve the 'moderation' of royal authority.[126] In the first instance, as with the bishops, royal authority over the Church was moderate for Hooker insofar as it was limited or restrained by law, thus rendering the Church of England a *via media* between the tyranny of unbounded Roman primacy ('that one universal Nimrod') and the anarchy of the Anabaptists.[127] It was in this context that Hooker made his most extraordinary – and in his lifetime unpublishable – claims for the limitations of English monarchy by law. In general, Hooker wrote, 'the best established dominion is where the law most rule the king'. Hooker suggested that while kings who owe their thrones to conquest have only 'the law of God and nature for bounds', in monarchies created by consent, kings are bound by the positive laws of their kingdoms. This certainly was the case in England, where 'the axioms of our regal government are these: *lex facit regem* . . . Our kings therefore, when they take possession of the room they are called into, have it pointed out before their eyes, even by the very solemnities and rites of their inauguration, to what affairs by the said law their supreme authority and power reacheth'.[128] In ecclesiastical affairs in particular, English kings 'have dominion . . . but according to the laws of the Church'. Or, as he put it elsewhere, 'What power the king hath he hath by law, the bounds and limits of it are known. The entire community giveth general order by law how things publicly are to be done, and the king as the head thereof, the highest authority over all, causeth according to the same law every particular to be framed and ordered thereby.'[129]

Likewise, as with the bishops, royal authority was limited and hence moderate because of its spatial constraints: monarchs were only sovereign within their territories. While the queen's dominion over the Church of England was 'supreme' in the sense that 'that power be such as hath not any other to overrule it', it was only 'supreme so far as the bounds thereof do extend'. As territorially bounded power, it was a middle way between Roman Catholic claims to universal jurisdiction and puritan

---

[126] See Kirby, *Richard Hooker's Doctrine of the Royal Supremacy*; Eppley, *Defending Royal Supremacy*.
[127] See e.g. *WRH*, vol. III, p. 355 and Book 8 *passim*.
[128] *Ibid.*, pp. 336–42.    [129] *Ibid.*, pp. 434–5.

claims for the local authority of presbyteries over their congregations. This was why the Presbyterians were silly to object that the term 'Head of the Church' derogated Christ's own headship: Christ was universal head, but it seemed to him 'expedient to divide his kingdom into many portions and to place many heads over it, that the power which each of them hath in particular with restraint might illustrate the greatness of his unlimited authority'.[130]

But finally, if princely authority over the Church was moderate because it was restrained, princes were also the highest moderators, given awesome power by law to moderate the realm. Headship of the body politic – which for Hooker was precisely synonymous with headship of the Church – was both a directing and a restraining power, since within a body the head 'hath dominion over all the rest, it is the fountain of sense, of motion, the throne where the guide of the soul doth reign, the court from whence the direction of all things human proceedeth'.[131] In making ecclesiastical law, then, princes enjoyed extraordinary precedence: 'Peace and justice are maintained by preserving unto every order their rights and by keeping all estates as it were in an even balance. Which thing is no better done than if the king, their common parent whose care is presumed to extend most indifferently over all, do bear the chiefest sway in the making of laws which all must be ordered by.'[132] Here moderation was achieved not through a modern balance-of-powers theory but rather through a theory of the prince as balancer-in-chief.

Most importantly, kings enjoyed a plenitude of jurisdiction and executive authority over the Church, since 'only the king's royal power is of so large compass that no man commanded by him according to the order of law can plead himself to be without the bounds and limits of that authority'.[133] The king was the ultimate limitation, the final boundary of authority that constrained all. The very essence of royal power was that since individuals and parts of the body politic inevitably acted for their own private interests, 'there must of necessity in all public societies be also a general mover, directing unto the common good and framing every man's particular to it'.[134] This was not just the bridle but the carpenter's square, moulding or fashioning each part so that together they make a functional whole. So, for instance, if there was conflict and competition between civil and ecclesiastical jurisdictions, the solution was a third, pre-eminent jurisdiction 'whereby the king hath a transcendent authority . . . in all causes over both'.[135] Likewise, if individual ecclesiastical judges transgressed the authority of the law and 'do otherwise than

[130] *Ibid.*, pp. 370–2.    [131] *Ibid.*, p. 362.    [132] *Ibid.*, p. 394.
[133] *Ibid.*, p. 422.    [134] *Ibid.*, p. 349.    [135] *Ibid.*, p. 430.

they ought to do', the king provided a 'universal power, which reacheth over all, importing supreme authority of government'.[136]

In the end, then, Richard Hooker's unique vision of the moderation of the Church of England was built upon his new and radical solution to the problem of how authority can be restrained and yet nonetheless remain absolute and inviolable, the problem of finding a middle way between tyranny and anarchy. Hooker's solution was, in essence, to moot the problem by denying any meaningful difference between inside and outside, between authority and what it restrained, between moderation *of* the Church and moderation *by* the Church. Since positive law was defined tautologically as the product of the commonwealth's reason, every act produced through law was *ipso facto* moderate no matter how violent or aggressive, while every act of aggressive moderation upon those unwilling or unable to moderate themselves was always already a consensual enactment of the community's god-given reason. The middle way between popery and puritanism enforced absolute obedience upon its subjects, yet the obedience it enforced was obedience to their own reason; the Church had to moderate its unruly passions, but since those passions were also people, this necessitated high levels of repression and coercion. This was the logic, then, of Richard Hooker's strangely authoritarian constitutionalism, his gift of *public consent* to all members of the body politic so that their capacity for *private conscience* could be taken away. The Church of England was a *via media* because, rather than giving any power of moderation to popes or people, who themselves required moderation to restrain their excesses, it instead gave a plenitude of moderation to the corporate Church. In a context where the Church was also the state, the result was a new and distinctively English Leviathan.

## Conclusion

The moderation of Elizabethan religious conformity was always about authority and obedience; in this sense, the Church of England acquired its peculiar reputation as a moderate *via media* in the Reformation not because it was particularly calm, measured or reasonable, but because it was so very governmental. In this model, the Church's capacity to enforce uniformity upon its members, its willingness to punish dissent, was precisely what made it a middle way between the tyranny of Rome and the lawlessness of the puritans. Yet from this Elizabethan framework established most influentially by Whitgift, Bridges and Bilson, two alternatives emerged. The first, positing the need for an ultimate or

[136] *Ibid.*, p. 424.

supreme moderator to restrain excesses in the Church, led quickly to royal absolutism. This framework would remain a powerful magnet for conformists and High Churchmen throughout the seventeenth century, as their Church was repeatedly hijacked by puritans from within and assaulted by Catholics and sectaries from without. The second, positing a structure of legal moderation in which no power could be left unrestrained, had limited utility in the decades after it was conceived, but in the long run it would become far more influential. The peculiar genius of Richard Hooker was to be the first to encapsulate what would become a central contradiction of English government: the precocious development of the modern state combined with a liberal ideology that sought to limit state authority. In Hooker's iteration of the rule of moderation, uniquely among his contemporaries, the limitation of authority *by law* is what authorises that authority, so that the law itself takes on an almost magical capacity to render moderate what would otherwise be excessive. As the embodiment of restraint, it is always already restrained, hence legitimating an almost infinite expansion of legally constituted power for the state to discipline its subjects. It should be no surprise, then, that, while Hooker's vision of the ecclesiastical polity would be obsolete within a century after it was written, his larger vision of law and authority would prove constantly attractive in subsequent centuries when the most powerful and spectacularly intrusive state on earth acquired its reputation for moderation.

# 4    Puritan moderation

## Puritan self-government

In 1582, a bookbinder named Thomas Gibson painted disquieting graffiti in a church in Bury St Edmonds. Next to the royal arms, which Queen Elizabeth had erected in every parish church, Gibson wrote God's condemnation of the Laodiceans from Revelation 3:15–16: 'I know thy works, that thou are neither hot nor cold. I would thou were cold or hot. Therefore because thou art lukewarm, and neither cold nor hot, it will come to pass, I will spew thee out of my mouth.' These dangerous sentiments remained for 'a quarter of a year, in a most public place, without concealment' until Richard Bancroft, who was passing through the puritan stronghold of Bury to preach against the 'pretended Reformation there', notified local officials. According to the later reminiscence of Archbishop Whitgift, Bancroft was 'greatly maligned, by no mean persons, for doing his duty'. When Church authorities painted over Gibson's quintessentially *immoderate* text with less provocative verses, he countered by adding Revelation 2:20: 'Notwithstanding, I have a few things against thee: that thou sufferest the woman Jezebel, which maketh herself a prophetess, to teach and deceive my servants; to make them commit fornication, and to eat meat sacrificed to idols.' This remarkable incident was remembered the following year by the queen herself, who used it as an opportunity to remind her clergy that the Church of England was a moderate *via media* between puritans and papists who questioned her authority: 'I have heard that some of them of late have said that I was of no religion – neither hot nor cold, but such a one as one day would give God the vomit. I pray you, look unto such men . . . Both of these join together in one opinion against me, for neither of them would have me to be Queen of England.'[1]

---

[1] See BL Lansdowne MS 36, no. 65, fo. 164r; CUL MS Mm.I.47, pp. 333–5; Nash, *An Almond for a Parrat*, sig. C2r; Elizabeth I, *Elizabeth I: Collected Works*, ed. Leah Marcus, Janel Mueller and Mary Beth Rose (Chicago, 2000), p. 179; Diarmaid MacCulloch, *Suffolk and the Tudors: Politics and Religion in an English County* (Oxford, 1986),

This confrontation corresponds to our textbook understanding of puritanism: an almost Manichaean worldview in which the binary opposition of true religion and popery, the godly and the ungodly, left little room for moderation. Puritanism, in this view, was generated by the rejection of compromise – most famously the Elizabethan Settlement of 1559 – and was committed to replacing lukewarm conformity with hot, zealous faith. This propensity for continuous Reformation, interrogating every thought and action for signs of compromise with the world, encouraged puritans to generate increasingly radical factions, until in the 1640s the regulatory apparatus that had restrained their centrifugal energies was removed and puritanism itself flew apart into sectarian chaos.

There is certainly some truth to this picture, but, as historians have shown, it is at best half the story. This received wisdom has been most usefully complicated by Peter Lake, who stressed the ways so-called 'moderate puritans' – those who defended various sorts of accommodation with the demands of conformity in order to retain the capacity to reform and edify the Church of England from within – claimed a middle way between withdrawal from the reprobate world and submergence in it.[2] Patrick Collinson has explored puritan uses of the Aristotelian golden mean and argued that the immoderate zeal of puritan theology can be contrasted with the imperative of moderation in puritan biographical writings.[3] Many other historians have noticed the tendency of mainstream puritans to bolster their claims to legitimacy by contrasting themselves with separatist radicals, claiming a middle way between Rome and 'Brownism'.[4]

What has not been deduced more generally from these observations, however, is that, despite their habitual attacks on Laodicean lukewarmness, puritans – even the most 'extreme' of them – could be every bit

pp. 204–6; Anne McLaren, *Political Culture in the Reign of Elizabeth I: Queen and Commonwealth, 1558–1585* (Cambridge, 1999), pp. 21–2; John Craig, *Reformation, Politics and Polemics: The Growth of Protestantism in East Anglian Market Towns, 1500–1610* (Aldershot, 2001), pp. 104–5. Craig's reliance on the Lansdowne MS leads him incorrectly to deny that the verses regarding lukewarmness were really painted. Gibson, an associate of Robert Browne, was convicted of denying the queen's supremacy at the Bury assizes in June 1583 but submitted and was released, while his compatriots Elias Thacker and John Coppin were executed.

[2] Lake, *Moderate Puritans*.
[3] Patrick Collinson, '"A Magazine of Religion Patterns": An Erasmian Topic Transposed in English Protestantism', in Derek Baker (ed.), *Studies in Church History* 14 (Oxford, 1977), pp. 223–49.
[4] In addition to the works of Lake and Collinson, see Milton, *Catholic and Reformed*; Timothy McGinnis, *George Gifford and the Reformation of the Common Sort* (Kirksville, Miss., 2004), ch. 4; Stephen Foster, *The Long Argument: English Puritanism and the Shaping of New England Culture, 1570–1700* (Chapel Hill, N.C., 1991). For the period after 1642, this becomes a significant theme of the historiography.

as preoccupied with the middle way as their conformist opponents.[5] But crucially, the puritan vision of moderation was not largely concerned with compromise or consensus. As we have already seen, the middle way implied governance, hence puritan claims for moderation encompassed both self-control and control of others while parsing and negotiating the relationship between them. Puritan moderation did not merely limit or restrain the centrifugal impulses of puritanism itself; it also embodied claims for external authority and proposed forms of governance between tyranny and anarchy to moderate excesses in the Church.

This chapter thus argues that the core logic of puritan moderation, what made it fundamentally incompatible with the conformist position analysed in Chapter 3, was the belief that the Church could, and indeed must, moderate itself rather than yielding to the external moderation of the world. In puritan ecclesiology, every Church possessed the means of self-moderation through 'discipline': the divinely ordained process of admonition, correction and excommunication through which churches restrain their members and exclude the ungodly. This disciplinary apparatus was habitually described as a form of moderation, bridling sin and purging impenitent sinners, as well as a *via media* between tyranny and anarchy. Discipline thus both *was* moderation and provided the *precondition* for moderation: having moderated themselves through discipline, Churches were capable of self-government, and any external government over them without their own consent was not moderation but tyranny.

As such, the fundamental error of the conformists, the whole reason they thought the Church needed the moderation of an ecclesiastical hierarchy, was that the Church of England did not practise proper discipline. In essence, while the conformists argued that the Church could never moderate itself because of its disorderly members, puritans responded that the Church was required to moderate itself by reforming or purging those members. This self-moderation did not usually mean independence from civil authorities, but it meant that in ordinary circumstances the life of the Church did not depend upon them. In this sense, the puritan *via media* could appear remarkably liberal: its very essence was self-government, publicly achieved through collective governance and a plurality of voices. But the corollary of this liberalism was that moderation became a process of endless restraint and purgation as ungodly members were disciplined or excised from the Church to produce a rump capable of self-government.

---

[5] Rejection of lukewarmness was a common trope found in conformist writings as well. See, e.g., Lancelot Andrewes, *XCVI Sermons* (London, 1629), p. 977.

Puritan moderation was thus based upon the idea that the godly them-selves were in some sense capable of self-control. Yet this was an idea whose radical potential puritans usually did their best to deny, and ethical moderation for puritans was always imbricated in complex ways with formal mechanisms of collective discipline. It was precisely on this issue – how, when and in what sense self-government was moderate for the godly even though it was almost literally the definition of immoderation for others – that the great debates among puritans occurred.[6]

Within the core logic of puritan moderation, then, there was virtually endless room for conflict over how exactly self-moderation worked, who was capable of exercising it for the visible Church and what sort of balance should be struck between the anarchic tendencies of moderation-from-within and the tyrannical tendencies of moderation-from-without. Puritans of all stripes sought, as Stephen Brachlow has described it, 'an Aristotelian point of equilibrium between popular consent and executive rule in the distribution and use of power'.[7] Self-government was possible and indeed obligatory through the moderating power of the discipline, yet at the same time virtually all puritans accepted that self-government was precarious and could easily devolve into no government at all. This was, to put it mildly, a narrow path to walk, and it was balanced along this knife's edge that puritans fought their battles. For puritans, as much as for conformists, moderation meant governance; where that moderation came from was not so clear.

## Thomas Cartwright and the moderation of discipline

Any analysis of Puritan claims to moderation and the *via media* must begin with the Presbyterian activist and great hero of Elizabethan puri-tanism, Thomas Cartwright. As we have already seen briefly in Chapter 3, Cartwright deployed arguments for moderation extensively in his debates with John Whitgift in the Admonition Controversy of the 1570s, the first great debate between puritans and conformists over the government of the Church of England. Cartwright, just as much as his conformist oppo-nent, equated moderation in the Church with government of the Church,

---

[6] In New England, where puritans had freer rein, the possibilities multiplied. See Mark Peterson, *The Price of Redemption: The Spiritual Economy of Puritan New England* (Stanford, 1997), ch. 1; Michael Winship, 'Godly Republicanism and the Origins of the Massachusetts Polity', *WMQ* 63, no. 3 (July 2006), pp. 427–62; Foster, *The Long Argument*, chs. 4–5; James Cooper, *Tenacious of Their Liberties: The Congregationalists in Colonial Massachusetts* (Oxford, 1999), ch. 2.

[7] Stephen Brachlow, *The Communion of Saints: Radical Puritan and Separatist Ecclesiology, 1570–1625* (Oxford, 1988), p. 194.

hence like his opponent he sought a moderate *via media* between tyranny and anarchy.

The principal difference, however, was that Cartwright regarded any clerical hierarchy as a form of tyranny. There could be no such thing as 'moderate and well-ruled government' of one minister over another; God had forbidden not merely ambitious or irresponsible superiority but all superiority to the clergy.[8] As such, even rule that is 'moderate and lawful in a prince over his subjects' would be 'tyrannical' and 'violent in a pastor . . . over his flock'.[9] Rule by the bishops was thus by definition 'tyrannous lordship', an 'excess of authority' or 'immoderate power', and Cartwright used numerous metaphors of excess to describe episcopacy.[10] The bishops were 'superfluous branches' which 'spread their boughs and arms so broad that for the cold shade of them nothing can grow and thrive'; pruning was needed 'to take away the superfluous lop and spread of their immoderate offices'.[11] Likewise, the office of archbishop is a 'superfluous thing' that should be 'thrown out of the Church, as a knob or some lump of flesh, which being no member of the body doth burden it and disfigure it'.[12]

Since all higher ranks of ministry like bishops and archbishops were anti-Christian, God had ordained moderation of the Church from within and between the congregations rather than from above. For the conformist John Whitgift, as we have seen, this sort of internal or self-moderation of the Church was no moderation at all; authority and subordination existed precisely because people could not be trusted to rule themselves. Cartwright, however, had an ace up his sleeve, the core of the Presbyterian *via media*, which neutralised conformist arguments about anarchy: discipline. Cartwright argued that the Church was capable of self-moderation through proper discipline, and since proper discipline was not merely described but mandated by scripture, self-moderation was required of the Church.

Whitgift and the conformists had argued, in essence, that the Church was incapable of self-moderation because of its worldly corruptions and impurities. Apostolic forms of self-government like the election of ministers and excommunication by elected colleges of elders might have made sense for the small, persecuted congregations of the primitive Church, but they were patently inappropriate for large, obligatory, national Churches

---

[8] *WJW*, I, pp. 165–6.
[9] Thomas Cartwright, *The Second Replie of Thomas Cartwright* (Heidelberg, 1575), p. 431. See also *WJW*, II, p. 20.
[10] *WJW*, I, p. 140; Cartwright, *The Second Replie of Thomas Cartwright*, p. 551; *WJW*, II, p. 265.
[11] *WJW*, I, p. 39; *WJW*, II, p. 80.    [12] *WJW*, II, p. 99.

that included 'drunkards and whoremongers', the tares as well as the wheat. As such, as the Church had grown, God had given the Church the gift of Christian magistrates to rule over such tumultuous and disordered assemblies, and democracy in the Church had quickly yielded to forms more consonant with monarchical civil government, especially rule by bishops. For Cartwright, by contrast, this argument reeked of popish corruption, failing properly to distinguish 'between a confused multitude and the Church of God'.[13] The only reason there appeared to be 'drunkards and whoremongers' in the Church, the only reason the Church seemed to need external moderation, was that popery had robbed the Church of proper discipline. 'In the Churches of Christ', Cartwright wrote, 'there be no drunkards or whoremongers, at least which are known; for either upon admonition of the Church they repent and so are neither drunkards nor whoremongers, or else they are cut off by excommunication (if they continue stubborn in their sins) and so are none of the Church'. While the visible Church contained both tares and wheat, both sheep and goats, which could only finally be sorted out by God, that Church did not contain 'acorns' or 'swine', for the Church itself 'can discern between wheat and acorns, between swine and sheep' and cast out the offenders.[14] In other words, for Cartwright the whole reason the Church could moderate itself, and indeed the very essence of the Church's moderation, was its reform of penitent sinners and purgation of unrepentant ones through discipline. The Church, in this model, was not coterminous with civil society in the conformist mode, nor was it merely a voluntary Church in the Anabaptist mode, but rather it was an exclusive Church, limited in full, politically active membership to the reformed community capable of self-government.[15]

Cartwright repeatedly described this proper discipline through the familiar emblem of moderation, the bridle. 'The final end of this discipline', Cartwright wrote, 'is the reforming of the disordered, and to bring them to repentance, and to bridle such as would offend.'[16] This was social control rather than merely punishment: the bridle repressed sin and encouraged proper self-limitation. Through the discipline, everyone 'may be kept within the limits of his vocation, and a great number be

---

[13] Cartwright, *The Second Replie of Thomas Cartwright*, p. 291.

[14] *WJW*, I, pp. 382–3.

[15] See the Presbyterian John Udall's response to the objection that ecclesiastical elections are dangerous because drunkards and papists would elect drunkards and papists to rule: 'Such are not of the Church, but without, 1. Cor. 5.12, and therefore are not to meddle in any holy action. But if the people should choose an unmeet man, the eldership that governeth the action is to reform them.' John Udall, *A Demonstration of the Trueth of that Discipline* (1588), p. 31.

[16] *WJW*, III, p. 223, quoting *The Admonition to Parliament*. See also *WJW*, III, p. 416.

brought to live in godly conversation'.[17] Likewise, while there were certainly 'hypocrites' in the Church, tares who could not be distinguished from wheat and hence could not be expelled, it was precisely thanks to the 'bridle' of discipline that these tares kept their sins hidden and remained hypocrites rather than open sinners.[18] This bridling also explained why the conformists refused the yoke of biblically mandated discipline even after it was explained to them: because they 'will not suffer their untamed lusts to come under any yoke of correction nor their loose affections of riotous pleasures, proud ambition and unsatiable covetousness to be bound with any bands of wholesome discipline'.[19] This was to turn the tables on the conformists and posit Presbyterian discipline as *orderly*, a middle way between papal tyranny and conformist refusal of good government: it was incredible that 'the same which cry out of the tyranny of Antichrist should refuse the moderate and wholesome government of Christ'.[20]

Another crucial element in Cartwright's middle way between tyranny and anarchy concerned the procedures and protocols of discipline. Excommunication had to represent the consent of the whole Church rather than either the unbridled will of one man over the multitude, the very essence of tyranny, or 'the other extremity', the unbridled will of the multitude over their leaders.[21] Discipline thus belonged to the presbyteries, the aristocracy of the Church in the form of its elders and pastors; these men were elected, but because they were elected by a body already purged of its extremities they were nonetheless moderate. The classic puritan proof text for excommunication was Matthew 18:17, 'And if he shall neglect to hear them, tell it unto the church: but if he neglect to hear the church, let him be unto thee as an heathen man and a publican', which seemed to indicate some sort of corporate or consensual process but left ambiguous who exactly was meant by 'the Church' to whom the power of the keys was granted. Cartwright interpreted the crucial phrase 'tell the Church' not as meaning 'tell it to the pastor alone', as the conformists argued, nor 'tell it to the whole congregation', as the Anabaptists argued, but tell it to the 'pastor with the ancients or elders'.[22]

The point of this internal discipline was not only that it made the Church into a self-moderating body, capable of genuinely ethical

---

[17] *WJW*, III, p. 231.

[18] Cartwright, *The Second Replie of Thomas Cartwright*, p. 230.

[19] *Ibid.*, epistle, sig. XXX4v.

[20] *Ibid.*, epistle, sig. X3r. For similar arguments, see Laurence Chaderton, *A Fruitfull Sermon, vpon the 3.4.5.6.7.&8. Verses of the 12. Chapter of the Epistle of S. Paule to the Romanes* (London, 1584), pp. 72–4. See Lake, *Moderate Puritans*, pp. 34–5.

[21] *WJW*, III, p. 257.      [22] *WJW*, III, p. 168.

behaviour; moderation also became complicit in the brutal punishment *by the state* of those excluded from the Church: Catholics, adulterers and other excommunicates. For Cartwright, excommunication was not the end of the story; rather, after excommunication the civil magistrate should implement the judicial penalties of the Old Testament that mandated execution for blasphemy, adultery and idolatry, hence putting the 'bridle of fear' upon potential sinners.[23] The principal issue in contention was the countless thousands of papists who remained ostensibly members of the Church of England, whom Cartwright wanted to exclude from the Church through discipline but Whitgift wanted to include in the Church if they were willing to attend.[24] Cartwright argued that once such papists were purged they became solely the responsibility of the magistrate, who ought to force them to attend sermons so that they might be converted. They were to be regularly 'examined how they profit' by the magistrate, and 'if they profit not, to punish them. And, as their contempt groweth, so to increase the punishment, until such times as they declare manifest tokens of unrepententness; and then, as rotten members that do not only no good nor service in the body, but also corrupt and infect others, cut them off.'[25] Whitgift had shown false 'mildness and moderation' in refusing to condemn papists to death; this was not true moderation but anarchy, since it was not to govern but to leave papists to their affections.[26]

Just as discipline required some measure of popular consent to be moderate rather than tyrannous, so did the government of the Church. For Cartwright, this balance took the form of a Polybian mixed polity:

For the Church is governed with that kind of government which the philosophers that write of the best commonwealths affirm to be the best. For, in respect of Christ the head, it is a monarchy; and, in respect of the ancients and pastors that govern in common and with like authority amongst themselves, it is an aristocraty [sic], or the rule of the best men; and, in respect that the people are not secluded but have their interest in Church matters, it is a democraty [sic] or a popular estate.[27]

---

[23] Cartwright, *The Second Replie of Thomas Cartwright*, p. 99.

[24] *WJW*, III, pp. 102–3.

[25] *WJW*, I, p. 386. This tension between exclusivity and coercion was typical of Presbyterianism and was raised to sharp relief by separatists who argued for voluntary churches but nonetheless favoured coercion to force the ungodly to hear sermons: see Brachlow, *The Communion of the Saints*, pp. 253, 265; George Selement, 'The Covenant Theology of English Separatism and the Separation of Church and State', *Journal of the American Academy of Religion* 41, no.1 (March 1973), pp. 66–74.

[26] *WJW*, I, p. 115.

[27] *WJW*, I, p. 390. On Elizabethan Presbyterian arguments for a mixed polity, see Michael Mendle, *Dangerous Positions: Mixed Government, the Estates of the Realm, and the Making of the Answer to the xix Propositions* (University, Ala., 1985), ch. 4.

Cartwright repeatedly described this mixture as a moderation or *via media*: 'As there is in this government a defect, so there is an excess, and between both a mean which is to be holden'; judgements in the Church should be 'handled by a company' to prevent tyranny, but to refer every issue to a 'great multitude' would produce confusion.[28] Whereas Whitgift had quoted Theodore Beza to show that the common people had to be moderated and thus should not participate in elections, Cartwright argued that Beza had merely meant that popular elections should be organised and directed by suitable moderators; with that proviso the people might be 'called to some moderation' of the Church, in other words take their proper role in its governance.[29] Repeatedly in Church history, Cartwright wrote, 'the people bridled the rage of the Scribes and Pharisees against the truth', protecting Christianity against tyranny.[30]

Within the mixed estate of the Church, Cartwright made no secret of his preference for aristocracy and democracy over monarchy, for 'although it be granted that the government of one be the best in the commonwealth, yet it cannot be in the Church. For the prince may well be monarch immediately between God and the commonwealth, but no one can be monarch between God and his Church but Christ, which is the only head thereof.'[31] Glossing and reworking a claim from Book 3 of Aristotle's *Politics*, he argued, 'It is harder . . . that many should be carried away by their affections than one.'[32] Furthermore, tyranny in the Church was much more dangerous than tyranny in the state: 'There can be no tyranny in the commonwealth so extreme wherein there is not something

---

[28] Thomas Cartwright, *The Rest of the Second Replie* (Basel, 1577), pp. 66–7. See also *A Briefe and Plaine Declaration* (London, 1584), pp. 84–6: 'Therefore there ought to be in every Church a consistory or seniory of elders or governors, which ought to have the hearing, examination, and determining of all matters pertaining to discipline and government in that congregation. Which authority of theirs nevertheless ought to be moderated, that their judgment may be rightly accounted the judgment of the holy Church. Which thing consisteth in these two points: first, that the elders be elected and chosen by consent of the whole congregation . . . second . . . that when the consistory hath travailed in examining of causes pertaining to ecclesiastical discipline, and agreed what judgment ought to pass upon the matters, they propound it to the whole multitude that it may be confirmed by their consent.'

[29] Cartwright, *The Second Replie of Thomas Cartwright*, p. 284.

[30] *Ibid.*, p. 290. For a succinct Presbyterian statement that ecclesiastical elections can be moderated by superior powers but that the people's prerogative of election cannot be alienated, see William Stoughton, *An Assertion for True and Christian Church-Policie* (Middelburg, 1604), pp. 213–14.

[31] *WJW*, III, p. 198.

[32] *WJW*, II, p. 238, and see Cartwright, *The Second Replie of Thomas Cartwright*, pp. 229 and 134. See Aristotle, *The Politics and the Constitution of Athens*, trans. Stephen Evereson (Cambridge, 1996), p. 86, and the broader discussion on pp. 76–86 that 'if the people are not utterly degraded, although individually they may be worse judges than those who have special knowledge, as a body they are as good or better'.

tending to the preservation of it'; in other words, at least tyranny produces a kind of order. In the Church, however, 'uncontrolled authority' produces 'nothing but destruction and ruin'.[33]

One crucial kind of moderation within this balance of estates was the creation of 'moderators' for the presbyteries and synods. Moderators were to be elected by their assembly, they were to hold their position for the duration of that assembly only and their role was to guide the assembly rather than dominate them.[34] This 'moderate rule', as Cartwright called it, was moderate rather than tyrannical because it was elective and temporary, the very opposite of episcopacy.[35] This had been the form of government in the Church until the advent of popery; afterwards 'the further off they were from this moderation . . . the nearer they came to that tyranny and ambitious power which oppressed and overlaid the Church of God'.[36] Rather than being the absence of rule, as Whitgift had argued, it was the essence of rule: 'And withal you see that, as we are far from this tyranny and excessive power which now is in the Church, so we are by the grace of God as far from confusion and disorder.'[37]

In sum, Cartwright answered the conformist charge that self-government was no government by turning the tables on his opponents and arguing that it was really the bishops and the unreformed Church of England who were dangerously ungoverned. By contrast, puritan discipline and its balance of monarchical, aristocratic and democratic elements provided an architecture for moderate rule that satisfied the requirements of both scripture and classical political theory. While this was not yet a structure that empowered all members of the congregation to moderate each other, it was nonetheless what we might call an 'ascending theory of moderation' in which moderation emerged in some sense from the (godly) people. But as Michael Winship has noted, Cartwright and the Presbyterians 'had not completely solved the problem of creating a foolproof route between the Scylla and Charybdis of the tyranny of absolute rule and what was almost universally feared in this hierarchical age as the confusion of democratic excess'.[38] When confronted with the crucial problem of how conflicts between elders and people could be adjudicated without either overruling Christian liberty or generating schism, Cartwright could only throw up his hands and hope that, once the Church obtained proper discipline, God would show them the way.

---

[33] Cartwright, *The Second Replie of Thomas Cartwright*, p. 579.
[34] *WJW*, II, pp. 269–71.    [35] *WJW*, II, p. 275.    [36] *WJW*, II, pp. 277–8.
[37] *WJW*, II, p. 280.    [38] Winship, 'Godly Republicanism', p. 434.

## Puritan anti-separatism: government in an impure Church

The content of the Presbyterian platform changed little in the decades after the Admonition Controversy, as Peter Lake has noted.[39] Its polemical positioning, however, changed enormously as a result of two factors: a separatist movement that portrayed rejection of the Church of England as the logical conclusion of Presbyterianism, and an anti-puritan reaction that tarred all puritans with the brush of radical separatism. Thus in the years after 1588, Presbyterians were forced to do what they had largely resisted before: positing themselves as a middle way not between episcopacy and Anabaptism, but between episcopacy and their own erring brethren, the separatists.[40] The core of this position was an awkward and backhanded loyalism: given that obedience to the corrupt and popish government of the Church of England was a moral necessity until such time as it could be reformed in an orderly manner, such obedience had to be squared with right discipline and thus rendered a moderate middle way between the tyranny of the bishops and the disordered proceedings of the separatists. Or, to put it slightly differently, where Cartwright had stressed formal correction and excommunication, his successors stressed informal admonition, two different faces of disciplinary moderation.

Perhaps the first tract to make this argument at length was *The Rasing of the Foundations of Brownisme* (1588) by the puritan layman Stephen Bredwell. In the preface Bredwell explicitly identified himself with the *via media*, stating that his work had two parallel goals. First, he wrote in order to stop 'that violent stream of seducing, wherein daily such numbers of the younger and weaker sort of Christians are carried out of our assemblies' into the hands of separatists; second, he wrote in hopes that 'those impure mouths shall be dashed' that attempted to clothe honest reformers of the Church in 'one livery with these schismatical spirits, that so they might purchase unto them, both from magistrate and common people, equal hatred and avoidance'.[41] In other words, Bredwell positioned himself as a middle way between separatists on one side and conformists on the other. Later, Bredwell argued for a middle way between separation *from* the Church of England and full acceptance *of* the Church of England, arguing that the godly *via media* is to be *in but not of* the corrupt worldly Church. He asked rhetorically, 'Is there no mean betwixt

---

[39] Lake, *Anglicans and Puritans?*, p. 6.
[40] On earlier resistance among puritans to associate their wayward brethren with the radical extreme, see Lake, *Moderate Puritans*, ch. 5.
[41] Stephen Bredwell, *The Rasing of the Foundations of Brownisme* (London, 1588), epistle to the reader, sig. ¶4r–v.

these two extremities, but we must be either unnatural or careless?' and then answered his own question: 'We see flatly that as on the one side we are bound generally to shun private conversation with ungodly ones, so on the other side we must necessarily observe withal whatsoever special duties are to be required at our hands by anyone.' In other words, the godly must shun 'inward familiarity and delightful accompanying' with the ungodly, but nonetheless they must communicate with them in Church.[42] This was the very essence of the 'moderate puritan' position identified by Peter Lake: 'Puritan moderation was the product of a real battle between extremes and the only means by which the tension between compete submergence in the world and complete withdrawal from it could be controlled . . . Such a tension was, of course, typical of the ambiguities and contradictions inherent in the position of the godly, trapped in the world and inextricably mixed with the ungodly.'[43]

In an ecclesiological context, Bredwell argued, like Cartwright, that the Church of England should weed out the unworthy from communion. But unfortunately it lacked the proper discipline to do so, and he argued against the separatists that private Christians had no authority to perform such weeding themselves. For private men to excommunicate sinners would be to erect an unscriptural form of Church government, or indeed an anarchy, that was opposite to episcopal tyranny but every bit as unlawful. Thus, in the unfortunate current condition, when 'we cannot remove them' from the Church, presence at communion with the wicked was allowable, 'not securely or carelessly' but as a last resort that was preferable to the anarchy of open schism.[44] However, even though the godly had no binding disciplinary power when they found themselves in a corrupt Church, they did have one option open to them: publicly and repeatedly to admonish the wicked. This provided the godly with a positive obligation to pick fights with their reprobate neighbours, even while remaining in communion with them, all for the sake of moderation: private men had no power beyond 'admonition' to censure the wicked, but that admonition cleansed the consciences of the godly and allowed them to take communion with the ungodly.[45] If the proof text of Presbyterian discipline was Matthew 18:17, 'Tell the Church', then it was the godly Christian's duty 'at length to tell the Church' of every corruption of every member, 'but not withdraw himself, though the Church should not separate the same unworthy one'. The Christian fulfilled his

---

[42] Bredwell, *The Rasing of the Foundations of Brownisme*, pp. 39–40.
[43] Lake, *Moderate Puritans*, p. 149.
[44] Bredwell, *The Rasing of the Foundations of Brownisme*, p. 15.
[45] *Ibid.*, pp. 5–6, 18, 29–31, 37.

responsibility by performing his part of the disciplinary process and could not be blamed if others failed in theirs.[46]

In an important sense, then, Bredwell's tract was just such an admonition to the Church of England, a salve for the author's conscience that allowed him to remain in the English communion. He thus argued that the Church of England remained a true Church precisely because of godly members like himself who 'labour according to our places to recover that liberty the word giveth to every congregation for executing the discipline'.[47] Bredwell's own 'labour' was to denounce corruptions in the Church of England and to warn the people that without further Reformation the Lord's wrath would smite the proud English clergy.[48] Bredwell thus believed, like Cartwright, that the Church was ideally capable of self-moderation through discipline; given the failure of its governors to erect proper structures of governance, however, such general moderation remained in abeyance and godly individuals had to focus on their own moderation. The essence of this expedient Presbyterian position was that moderation remained obligatory for godly individuals, even if it was temporarily out of reach for the corporate Church.

Another text in this tradition was George Gifford's *A Short Treatise against the Donatists of England whome We Call Brownists*, published in 1590 after a long manuscript dispute between Gifford and Robert Browne. Gifford himself had been deprived of his benefice for refusing to subscribe to the Three Articles in 1584, but he had been quickly reinstated due to Lord Burghley's patronage, and he emerged unscathed from the later purges of puritans in 1588–91, largely because of his strong opposition to separatism. Richard Bancroft, however, remained convinced that Gifford was a dangerous puritan ringleader – which indeed in some sense he was. Given this context, Gifford's *Short Treatise* must be seen as a particularly violent instance of moderation: written at a moment when the separatist leaders Henry Barrow and John Greenwood rotted in prison, Gifford's text both authorised his patron Lord Burghley not to protect the separatists and also helped save Gifford from their grisly fate on the gallows in 1593.

In Gifford's preface, he gave a textbook account of the *via media*, describing how the devil used two opposite sorts of sinners to challenge the Church: 'His chief vassals, the tyrants and heretics, do wonderfully bestir them to effect his cursed desires. By the one sort he doth breathe out terror, and as it were spit fire. By the other he speweth up deadly poison and casteth his poisoned darts.' The tyrannous papists relied upon human tradition, falsely claiming that all who separated from them

---

[46] *Ibid.*, p. 18.     [47] *Ibid.*, p. 50. See also p. 96.     [48] *Ibid.*, p. 111.

had no true sacraments or ministry. 'Opposite to these . . . like a raging tempest from a contrary coast', were the Brownists, who claimed that 'our assemblies be Romish, idolatrous, antichristian synagogues'.[49]

The tract was in essence an assault on the Church of England's government and discipline conducted through the language of moderation, attacking the separatists for wrongly accusing the Church of England of being *altogether* anti-Christian whereas in fact it was merely corrupt, decrepit and sinful. Thus, Gifford's ostensible defences of the Church of England provided a framework in which all of its corruptions could be anatomised. As Gifford put it, the Church may be compared to a man who ceases to be a man and becomes instead a 'dead carcass' when 'the soul and life' departs his body; this is what the Brownists *wrongly* believed had happened to the Church of England. Yet while Gifford argued that the Church of England still clung to life, he highlighted just how tenuous its vital signs were: 'If he be sick and diseased, so that all parts are feeble, or if he be deformed with sores and maims, wanting hand, foot, eye, nose, or such like, yet is he still a man so long as the soul and life remain in him.'[50] As he put it later, 'The Church may be holden by force from executing God's commandment touching external government, and yet be the true Church of God.' For his example, Gifford alleged 'the Church that was held captive in Babylon'.[51] The Church of England did not benefit from such defences.

Gifford also employed the quintessential 'moderate puritan' technique of defending the Church of England as legitimate precisely because it contained the godly who reformed it from within. He argued that the Church remained alive because 'there were but a few true worshippers that frequented the temple among multitudes of profane and ungodly men'.[52] The Brownists were wrong to abandon a Church in which 'there be many particular persons which study earnestly to please God, mourning for their own sins', and where one whole party condemned corruptions within the prayer book and eagerly sought its reformation.[53] More broadly, Gifford argued that the disciplinary apparatus of the Church of England, while woefully corrupted, occasionally and accidentally got something right, and on those occasions only its actions were ratified by God. To suggest that the Church of England's excommunications were only just 'to the desert of them that be excommunicated', not in respect to 'those which excommunicate', was precisely to deny the disciplinary authority of the institutional Church.[54]

---

[49] George Gifford, *A Short Treatise against the Donatists of England, whome We Call Brownists* (London, 1590), sigs. A1r–A2v.
[50] *Ibid.*, sig. A1v.    [51] *Ibid.*, p. 44.    [52] *Ibid.*, p. 59.
[53] *Ibid.*, pp. 4, 16.    [54] *Ibid.*, pp. 56–8.

The most important thing about Gifford's *via media* was that it expressly located moderation in godly discipline, not in the Erastian power of the magistrate. In many places, of course, Gifford tried to yoke these things together and claim that godly discipline was a prop to magisterial power, for instance declaring that the Brownists 'be utter violators of ecclesiastical discipline, they abridge the power of the civil magistrate'.[55] Yet time and again, Gifford placed power in the hands of the Church. He argued that reform of the Church was not the prerogative of private men, hence the Brownists usurped lawful authority when they claimed the right to establish discipline themselves. But the authority they usurped was the Church's authority, over which the magistrate had no veto, because the erection of godly discipline is a perpetual obligation upon the Church. This argument can be seen, for instance, in a wonderfully subtle attack on Queen Elizabeth's authority over the ordination of ministers, presented ironically as an attack on unauthorised and disorderly religion:

If all the Brownists in the land should come together and choose a minister, and ordain him, should it make him any more a minister indeed before God than if all the apprentices in London, taking upon them to choose a Lord Mayor of the City, and to minister an oath unto him, should make him a Lord Mayor? The queen's majesty hath granted no such authority in the commonwealth to the apprentices; no more hath the Lord God in the Church unto the Brownists.[56]

For Gifford, therefore, like Thomas Cartwright, the discipline constituted a middle way. While on one hand the Church of England allowed wicked and profane men into the Church willy-nilly, and on the other hand the separatists allowed no one in the Church but their own quasi-perfect brethren, godly discipline erected a biblically sanctioned *via media* in which the visible Church contained both sheep and goats but nonetheless overt sinners could be rehabilitated or excluded. While on the one extreme the Church of England put discipline into the tyrannical hands of the bishops, and on the other extreme the separatists put discipline into the anarchic hands of the rabble, the godly *via media* made discipline the proper duty of the visible, corporate Church.[57] Like all conforming puritans, Gifford accepted the power of the magistrate to compel obedience in Church matters, but for Gifford this meant first and foremost that 'the civil power is an outward mean to drive men to hear the Gospel preached, and to obey the discipline'.[58] In the absence of proper discipline, godly Christians had to see to their own consciences: they were not permitted to join the wicked in idolatrous worship, but the wicked might be permitted to join them in true worship, if the magistrate insisted,

---

[55] *Ibid.*, sig. A2r.   [56] *Ibid.*, p. 103.   [57] *Ibid.*, pp. 47–50.   [58] *Ibid.*, p. 108.

without pollution of godly souls.[59] The Church of England sinned by not excluding wicked men from communion, but private persons sinned just as badly by excluding them without proper authority.[60] Perhaps most importantly, in the absence of formal mechanisms for parishes to choose or assent to their own ministers, the English godly should entreat patrons of livings for particular ministers and thus construct a version of consent within an otherwise corrupt system.[61] In sum, it was mere 'Anabaptistical freedom' to believe that Christianity freed the godly from the yoke of obedience to tyrants; Christian liberty freed only faith and conscience, not outward obedience.[62]

These anti-separatist Presbyterian texts were much less explicit than Thomas Cartwright in defining the moderate middle way as a form of government over the Church; after all, their purpose was not to describe a perfect ecclesiastical polity but to delineate the parameters of obedience to a decidedly imperfect one. Their conclusion was, in essence, a *via media* between usurping a public role and acquiescing to a private one. But I want to stress that they shared with Cartwright and other Presbyterians an intense belief in godly self-government as the essence of moderation. Public discipline was the path to a moderate Church, but if a moderate Church were temporarily out of reach, godly Christians could still moderate themselves.

### The Congregationalist *via media*

Separatists, however, responded with their own *via media*, stressing that biblically sanctioned discipline remained the path of moderation regardless of what Lord Bishops and High Commissioners might say to the contrary. And while all separatists made some version of this claim, justifying their freedom from episcopal authority while insisting that they erected a more legitimate power in its place, the most important version of the separatist *via media* was the one proposed by Congregationalists.[63] While the split between Presbyterian and Congregationalist models of Church

---

[59] *Ibid.*, pp. 60–3.    [60] *Ibid.*, p. 69.    [61] *Ibid.*, pp. 72–3.

[62] *Ibid.*, p. 86. For similar views see *A Most Grave, and Modest Confutation of the Errors of the Sect, Commonly Called Brownists, or: Separatists* (London, 1644), first published in the *Apologeticall Narration* controversy of 1644 but written and circulated in manuscript in the early 1590s.

[63] On the political theory of mixed government in Congregationalism, see Cooper, *Tenacious of their Liberties*; Foster, *The Long Argument*; Michael Winship, 'Freeborn (Puritan) Englishmen and Slavish Subjection: Popish Tyranny and Puritan Congregationalism, c.1570–1606', *EHR* 124, no. 510 (October 2009), pp. 1050–74. I am also indebted to the forthcoming work of both Michael Winship and Polly Ha, which they generously shared with me prior to publication.

government was more gradual and tentative than historians have some-times believed, and while some Congregationalists like William Bradshaw and William Ames tried hard to claim that they were not separatists at all, from the late 1580s onwards there was a growing tendency among puritans to see any obligatory national Church, rather than simply the unreformed Church of England, as tyrannous. After all, if churches pos-sessed their own apparatus for internal moderation through discipline, this raised the question: by what warrant did any superstructure claim authority over the congregations?

The Elizabethan Congregationalist version of moderation was most influentially advocated by the separatist firebrand Henry Barrow, whose most detailed framework appeared in his 1590 prison treatise *A Brief Discoverie of the False Church*. Barrow's middle way stressed the need for a more absolute scriptural purity in the Church:

God hath especially committed these holy oracles to the careful custody of the Church, there to be inviolably preserved . . . without corrupting, mixing, hiding, obscuring, perverting, wresting, there to be precisely observed with all reverence and fear, without any willing or known transgression, or swerving either to the right hand or to the left, of the whole Church or any member thereof.[64]

Later, using a common metaphor for the *via media*, he wrote that if people would take God's word 'as our lodestar, we shall no doubt by the light thereof (God's gracious spirit blowing upon the sails of our faith) safely sail through all these difficulties, even with a straight course to the free and sincere practice of the gospel; neither striking against the rocks of popery, nor falling upon the shelves and quicksands of Anabaptistry'.[65]

These claims for strict biblicism as a middle way found expression first and foremost in Barrow's construction of a true visible Church, his principal bone of contention with the Presbyterians. Barrow argued, like the Presbyterians, that godly discipline was necessary in the Church, with ministers and congregations excommunicating profane and ungodly persons and excluding them from the body of God. Yet he pushed his interpretation of this process much further, to the point that only the visibly godly should be included in the visible Church. As such, Barrow explicitly imagined an England where there would not be churches in every parish, because there might be no godly Christians there.[66] On the popish 'extreme', then, Barrow placed all churches which violated God's ordinance by admitting the ungodly to communion:

[64] Henry Barrow, *The Writings of Henry Barrow 1587–1590*, ed. Leland Carson (London, 1962), p. 270.
[65] *Ibid.*, p. 443.　　[66] *Ibid.*, p. 359.

He hath commanded [his faithful servants] to watch, and diligently to take heed, that no profane or wicked impenitent person be admitted unto, or kept in his Church; but diligently to watch both without and within, that the one sort be kept out, the other cast out of his Church. The legal pollutions, leprosies, ulcers, running issues, infections and unclean diseases for which then the people were separated from the temple and the congregation, are now in this Church all manner known sins obstinately held and maintained.[67]

Yet Barrow did not claim perfection on earth (as he caricatured the Anabaptist position) and he explicitly denied that any worldly congregation could be entirely without sin. It was *open* sin that mattered, because the Bible commanded the discipline of open sin by churches. Hidden sin was beyond the reach of the world: 'When I resort and walk together with the Church, and worship God to all outward seeming unreprovably, though I be inwardly never so great an hypocrite, until my sin apparently break out, the Church can no more censure me than the civil magistrate can punish me before I have broken the law.'[68] He admitted that, as scripture said, 'many glorious hypocrites shall there be which make a fair show in the flesh', and hence that the visible church would always be a mixture of the elect and the reprobate. But this by no means implied that the church could 'mingle and joineth such reprobate *known* chaffe, cockles, tares and darnel with the Lord's wheat *wittingly*'.[69] On the opposite 'extreme' from popery, then, Barrow placed Anabaptist perfectionism, the absurd claim to live without sin in this world.[70]

This *via media* was in some ways very similar to Cartwright's, and indeed both Barrow himself and conformists like Richard Bancroft portrayed it as the logical conclusion of the Presbyterian platform. Yet in this view, if the middle way was located in a visible Church consisting solely of the visibly godly, then the 'popish' extreme, which allowed the promiscuous civil multitude into the Church, included all the magisterial Churches of Europe, including Calvin's Geneva. Barrow repeatedly stressed the need for further reformation past where Calvin had stopped: 'I gladly acknowledge [Calvin] a painful and profitable instrument, in the things he saw and times he served in, yet not without his many errors and ignorances, especially touching the planting, government and ordering of the Church of Christ; and no marvel, for being so newly escaped out of the smoky furnace of popery, he could not so suddenly see or attain unto the perfect beauty of Sion.'[71] Barrow made it clear that Calvin's

---

[67] *Ibid.*, p. 327.     [68] *Ibid.*, p. 411.     [69] *Ibid.*, pp. 293–303. My emphasis.
[70] On the distinction in separatist ecclesiology between a Church of the visibly godly and a church of the elect, see John Coolidge, *The Pauline Renaissance in England* (Oxford, 1970).
[71] *The Writings of Henry Barrow*, p. 287.

overweening desire to refute the Anabaptists had driven him too far in
the opposite direction, into the hands of popery:

This and other like detestable stuff hath Mr. Calvin in his ignorance, partly to
suppress and confute that damnable sect of the Anabaptists, which fantastically
dream unto themselves a Church in this life without spot, and for every transgression that ariseth are ready to leave and forsake the fellowship of the Church,
without due and orderly reproofs, etc. Partly also is this stuff brought to defend
his own rash and disorderly proceedings at Geneva, whiles he at the first dash
made no scruple to receive all the whole state, even all the profane ignorant
people into the bosom of the Church.[72]

In *A Plaine Refutation of M. G. Giffardes Reprochful Booke* (1591), a
reply to Gifford's *Short Treatise against the Donatists of England*, Barrow
joined with his fellow prisoner John Greenwood to defend separatism
and Congregationalism against Presbyterian accusations of disorder. In a
blunt bid for political support, the tract was dedicated to Gifford's patron,
Lord Burghley, and attempted to convince him that Gifford was secretly
in league with the forces of counter-Reformation to brand the moderate
Congregationalist position as extremist Anabaptism or Donatism.[73] In
fact, Barrow and Greenwood argued, Gifford's hypocritical defence of
a Church he despised was tantamount to Familism, separating inward
belief from outward action in a way that undermined all conscience and
led to anarchy.[74]

One important component of Barrow's and Greenwood's claim to
moderation was that Congregationalists, unlike both Catholics and Presbyterians, had no designs to overthrow the Established Church or 'meddle with the reformation of the State otherwise than by our prayers'; the
'Babylonish deformities' of the Church of England were God's business
to sort out, not theirs.[75] Indeed, Barrow and Greenwood posited the
gathering of autonomous churches as a kind of obedience to the prince
in which they 'attempted nothing beyond our calling' but simply acted
as private men, unlike the very public and hence seditious calls for alteration of the Church by Presbyterians on one side and Catholics on the
other.[76] On this view, separation was not schism but a sort of inverted
discipline in which rather than sinners leaving the Church, the Church
leaves sinners: 'In separating from them we have not rent ourselves from
the Church or body of Christ, but rather separated the Church from them
and obeyed the commandment of God that calleth us out from amongst

---

[72] *Ibid.*, p. 316.
[73] Henry Barrow and John Greenwood, *A Plaine Refutation of M. G. Giffardes Reprochful Booke* (Dordrecht?, 1591), dedication.
[74] *Ibid.*, pp. 2, 12, 16.    [75] *Ibid.*, p. 4.    [76] *Ibid.*, pp. 197–8.

them.'[77] It was an odd kind of obedience, arguing in essence that they did not bother to condemn the Church of England because it had never been 'rightly gathered to Christ' in the first place.[78]

The core of Barrow's and Greenwood's *via media*, however, involved the restraint of membership in the Church. They had separated from England's 'parish assemblies' because of 'the profaneness, wickedness [and] confusion of the people which are here received, retained and nourished as members'. True churches were instead gathered congregations in which members made 'voluntary or particular confession of their own faith' as criteria of entry.[79] But on the other side, Barrow and Greenwood separated themselves from the Anabaptists by rejecting perfectionism or the limitation of the visible Church to God's elect: 'We judged not of God's secret election which he hath in all places amongst all sorts of men, but of the apparent odious sins of your congregations, from which whilst you will not be purged, we may have no spiritual fellowship or communion with you in this estate.'[80] This notion of purgation was absolutely central to Barrow's and Greenwood's ecclesiology: the properly purged Church was the Church of the middle way. Against charges of anarchy for allowing popular participation in Church governance, they responded that those charges 'fitlier agree to these tumultuous assemblies where all the profane are received as members, than unto the holy churches of Christ where none but the faithful are admitted or remain'.[81]

This was all brought to a head in an extraordinary section in which Barrow and Greenwood described the power of the keys, combining biblical and classical concepts to describe autonomous, self-governing discipline as a middle way between extremes. According to Matthew 18:17 and other scriptural passages, excommunication is given 'to the whole congregation', and 'every Christian is a king and a priest unto God to spy out, censure and cut down sin as it ariseth'. The phrase 'Tell the Church', however, had been variously misinterpreted. Some had misunderstood 'Church' to mean only some members of the Church who spoke for the rest, whether pope, bishops or presbyteries. On the other side, 'in a clean contrary extremity', were the radicals who 'would have the people without the elders to excommunicate, elect, etc., and that by plurality of voices'.[82] Since Barrow and Greenwood were specifically arguing against George Gifford, they narrowed the field of discussion to just two sorts,

---

[77] *Ibid.*, 'Wisdome to the reader', sig. B1v.     [78] *Ibid.*, p. 183.
[79] *Ibid.*, 'Wisdome to the reader', sig. A2r.
[80] *Ibid.*, p. 21. They also admitted the children of members: see pp. 55–6.
[81] *Ibid.*, p. 76.     [82] *Ibid.*, p. 74.

the Presbyterians and the radicals, 'the one whereof giveth this power of excommunication unto the consistory of elders without the people, the other unto the people by plurality of voices without the elders'.[83] The first of these was directly contrary to the 'liberty of the whole Church', since elders were created 'for preservation of the order of the Church and not for the subversion thereof; for the defence of the liberty of the least, and not to pluck away the liberty of all'.[84] 'On the other side', by contrast, lay 'monstrous confusion and high rebellion', for the choosing of officers by votes and divisions was a violent rending of Christ's body, a 'custom amongst the heathen in their popular governments but . . . insufferable in the Church of Christ'.[85] The middle way, then, lay in balance and distribution of authority, leading to the moderation of people and elders by one another:

God . . . hath made the body to consist of diverse members, hath distributed diverse gifts in diverse measure unto them . . . The people are commanded to obey their leaders, and to submit, to acknowledge, to honour them and to have them in super-abundant love. These are of God set over the flock, to watch, to instruct, admonish, exhort, rebuke &c., yet not to pluck away the power and liberty of the whole Church, or to translate and assume the public actions of the whole Church into their own hands alone. They are men and may err: they themselves even for all their doctrines and actions are subject to the censure of the Church, or of the least members of the Church, if in any thing they be found to err or transgress. Yea if they remain obstinate, that congregation whereof they remain ministers and members is to proceed against them and to excommunicate them as any other member.[86]

Here, Polybius and St Paul worked in tandem to defend constitutionalism in the congregations.

Developing directly from this Elizabethan tradition, the great advocate of a Congregationalist middle way at the beginning of the subsequent reign was Henry Jacob, often described as a 'non-separating' congregationalist because he remained in at least hypothetical communion with the godly in the Church of England.[87] Jacob, like William Bradshaw and William Ames, was something of a link between the Presbyterian movement and the later Congregationalist brethren in a period when they were not yet so ideologically and personally distinct as they would become: on the one hand Jacob believed in the reformation of the national Church and was instrumental in crafting the Millenary Petition and the puritan platform at Hampton Court in 1603–4, but on the other hand even

---

[83] *Ibid.*, p. 75.    [84] *Ibid.*, p. 76.    [85] *Ibid.*, p. 77.    [86] *Ibid.*, p. 77.
[87] For a cogent overview of the debate over non-separating or semi-separating Congregationalism, see Tom Webster, *Godly Clergy in Early Stuart England: The Caroline Puritan Movement, c.1620–1643* (Cambridge, 1997), esp. ch. 15.

then he clearly regarded individual congregations as wholly self-sufficient ecclesiastical polities.

In his 1604 appeal for biblically mandated discipline aimed at the newly crowned James I, the core of Jacob's argument was a radical limitation of the category of *adiaphora*: 'We believe (and the truth is) God's word never knew any indifferency in matters of the Church or of religion, wherein all things (whether great or small) have ever been either simply good or evil.'[88] This apparent denial of moderation, however, became the basis for Jacob's moderation: his insistence that obedience to scripture provided moderate government for the Church, while mere human government led to anarchy or tyranny. He ridiculed the conformist argument that scriptural 'examples are no precepts' and hence the Church might change with changing times: by that logic 'scarce anything in God's word shall suffice to constrain and bind us'.[89] Or, as he put it in his *The Divine Beginning and Institution of Christs True Visible or Ministeriall Church* (1610), by this argument 'a wide door is opened and an easy way made for libertines to walk in'.[90]

But if biblically mandated government, not human expediency, was the path to strong and effective rule of the Church, that necessarily meant government containing a strong democratic component. He wrote, 'The Christian Church's true and right government (in this regard that the whole company of people do give their free consent therein) is a certain democratie [sic].' But since that government was to be 'guided by the pastor chiefly, and also by the grave assistant elders', it was therefore 'not simply and plainly democratical, but partly aristocratical and partly monarchical. And so it is that mixed government which the learned judge to be the best'. This was in sharp contrast to the 'diocesan, provincial and Catholic' governments of the Church, which were 'monarchical, or at the best they are aristocratical' and hence 'differ formally and essentially' from biblically mandated government.[91]

This discussion of mixed government was written in 1610; in 1604, still hoping to convince a sceptical James I, Jacob had stressed that certain

---

[88] Henry Jacob, *Reasons Taken out of Gods Word and the Best Humane Testimonies Proving a Necessitie of Reforming our Churches in England* (Middelburg, 1604), sigs. A2v–A3r. See also William Bradshaw, *A Treatise of the Nature and Use of Things Indifferent* (London?, 1605), where Bradshaw adopts the full Aristotelian framework of moderation to subvert the idea that there could be anything truly indifferent in God's Church.

[89] Jacob, *Reasons Taken out of Gods Word*, p. 46

[90] Henry Jacob, *The Divine Beginning and Institution of Christs True Visible or Ministeriall Church* (Leiden, 1610), sig. *3r–v.

[91] Jacob, *The Divine Beginning*, sigs. A2v–A3v. Here we find a strong refutation of Michael Mendle's claim that 'mixed government disappeared in the early seventeenth century': Mendle, *Dangerous Positions*, p. 39.

sorts of episcopacy might be compatible with democracy in the Church. He delineated six types of 'bishops' in the world: from Type 1, the 'bishop' in a congregation whose title was synonymous with pastor or presbyter, to Type 6, the Universal Bishop at Rome. While he endorsed Type 1 and rejected Types 3–6, Jacob grudgingly accepted Type 2, the 'diocesan or titular bishop, who was bishop of a diocese in title and name only in ecclesiastical government having no more power than any other common pastor. He differed not in any essential part of the ordinary pastoral office, but was only president or moderator constantly (yet by his fellow pastors' free consent) over the pastors in a diocese.' Appealing to the new king, Jacob identified this second type of bishop with Scottish episcopacy.[92] Here the role of the moderator – a voice of government within rather than above the Church, always subject to the consent of his colleagues – was part of moderation, despite Jacob's Congregationalism.

In both 1604 and 1610, however, Jacob made the same argument that the requirement of democracy in the Church rendered Congregationalism the only moderate form of Church government, a middle way between tyranny and anarchy. The conformists had argued that elections of ministers and other forms of popular government in the Church 'cannot but bring with them commonly tumult and much trouble, if not confusion and peril'. Jacob replied that 'this were very true indeed . . . if we desired or sought for popular elections of diocesan bishops', because it would involve such a vast, promiscuous multitude in the democratic process, but fortunately 'such running together of a whole city or diocese, such voice-giving of such multitudes of people, we desire not, neither do we any ways allow it'. Instead, Jacob advocated democratic participation only at the local level by 'the Christian people of one parish' – an exclusivist vision of the congregation – where the minister and elders 'first prepare and determine the whole matter, namely in such sort that the people may not need to do ought afterward but only consent with them and freely signify their consent in it'.[93] For Jacob, then, the conformists had played right into the Congregationalists' hands. Conformists thought popular Church government would lead to disorder and threaten the State because they wrongly imagined Church government to function at a diocesan or national level, where it would indeed yield chaos.

---

[92] Jacob, *Reasons Taken out of Gods Word*, pp. 7–9.

[93] *Ibid.*, pp. 26–7. In this earlier part of his career Jacob's ideal version of a popular election looked like the 'parliamentary selection' process described by Mark Kishlansky, with a single candidate presented by elders to the congregation for approbation; he would later focus much more on the necessity of positive choice: see Mark Kishlansky, *Parliamentary Selection: Social and Political Choice in Early Modern England* (Cambridge, 1986). I owe thanks to Polly Ha for discussing this issue with me.

But this was proof that real Church government was merely congregational, because at the congregational level popular government could never threaten the State.

This distinction allowed Jacob to redefine the royal supremacy and the role of civil authorities. While magistrates should have no authority *within* the Church, their role *over* the Church was activated if the Church overflowed its bounds. He wrote that popular government in the Church, 'being limited within the bounds of one particular congregation, neither is nor ever hath been nor can be in the least sort dangerous to any civil State whatsoever, but may easily, yea with violence be resisted and punished by any the meanest next dwelling officer of justice, if any person or persons in the Church become seditious and refractory'.[94] This was Jacob's answer to the riddle of how, as he put it, 'every true visible and ministerial Church' is a 'body politic' rather than 'anarchy' despite the absence of either episcopal rule or civil jurisdiction.[95] Popular governance of congregations was possible precisely because they were utterly without worldly power, charged with regulating and moderating their own spiritual affairs but so impotent in civil affairs that they might be overpowered by the village constable.

A further, influential version of Congregationalist moderation was produced by Francis Johnson, known to conformists as the 'Bishop of Brownism',[96] pastor of the 'ancient' separatist Church in Amsterdam during James I's reign. Johnson indulged in a series of schisms from his Amsterdam brethren from nearly the moment he arrived in the Netherlands, hence his writing condemned erstwhile allies as often as the Church of England. Beginning in 1607, Johnson split definitively from two other groups of separatists in his congregation whom we shall examine below: John Smyth and his followers, who revived the practice of adult believers' baptism, and Henry Ainsworth and his followers, who held that power in independent Churches lay in the whole body of the congregation rather than in their eldership. Johnson considered both of these doctrines dangerously populist, hence his writings began self-consciously to stress the need for a moderate middle way between communion with the Church of England and anarchy in Church government.

In his most important work, *A Short Treatise Concerning the Exposition of Those Words of Christ, Tell the Church, &c. Mat. 18.17* (1611), Johnson argued for a middle way between 'the apostasy of Antichrist on the one hand, and the erroneous confused courses of the Anabaptists on

---

[94] Jacob, *The Divine Beginning*, sig. A3r.     [95] *Ibid.*, sig. B1v.
[96] Henoch Clapham, *A Chronological Discourse* (London, 1609), sig. I2v.

the other hand, that we may by the mercy of God stand free and safe from both'.[97] The content of this middle way was a congregation fully separated from the anti-Christian Church of England, where authority over discipline had been falsely stolen by the bishops from the congregations, but one in which that authority did not therefore fall promiscuously upon the whole body of the Church but rather upon 'Church officers, so ordained by the Lord, and chosen by the Church itself'.[98] The fact that those officers were chosen by the whole congregation ensured that their authority over excommunication did not abridge the Christian liberty of members.[99] That authority, however, extended only to the 'public' duty of excommunication, a duty which Christ had ordained to be carried out with utmost order by responsible (male) magistrates, not by the whole congregation (including its female members) as Ainsworth and the 'Anabaptists' allegedly believed. However, individual members of the congregation retained their own duty of 'private' admonition and censure, hence they were still part of the congregational disciplinary process, unlike in the corrupt Church of England.[100]

Perhaps most importantly, Johnson stressed that his middle way required a distinction between separation and excommunication. Individual Christians had a private authority not only to admonish one another but also to separate from error where they found it; this defined Johnson's difference from the Presbyterians. But they did not have authority to excommunicate one another, because that power lay solely in the public authority of the eldership; this defined Johnson's difference from his enemies in Amsterdam. As he put it, 'Separation . . . implieth the power we have over ourselves, whereas excommunication implieth power and authority over others.'[101] In this view, a separatist congregation was really separatist only at the moment of its foundation; thereafter it became a moderate government that exercised lawful discipline to restrain the sinful impulses of its members.

### Towards a populist *via media*

Francis Johnson was such an important figure in puritan circles that his tract on Matthew 18:17 drew fire from both 'sides'. On the more conservative side, it became the vehicle for the leading non-separating Congregationalist, William Bradshaw, to restate the boundaries of his

---

[97] Francis Johnson, *A Short Treatise Concerning the Exposition of Those Words of Christ*, Tell the Church, &c. Mat. 18.17 (Amsterdam?, 1611), To the Reader, sig. A2v.
[98] Johnson, *A Short Treatise*, sig. B4v.
[99] *Ibid.*, sig. C3v.  [100] *Ibid.*, esp. sigs. C3r–C4v.  [101] *Ibid.*, sig. D1r.

commitment to the national Church. Bradshaw's *The Unreasonablenesse of the Separation* (1614) was so committed to the ideology of the *via media* that its preface, probably written by William Ames, ended with the words, 'Read therefore with understanding, and learn a mean betwixt all and nothing.'[102] The whole text of *The Unreasonablenesse of the Separation* was in some sense an extended commentary on the middle way between popery and separatism, since the tract took the form of a debate with Francis Johnson, whose name was abbreviated throughout as 'Fr. Iohn'. Here the pun – Francis Johnson is really Friar John – put readers continuously on notice that the two extremes of 'all' and 'nothing' represented the same anti-Christian enemy.[103] But more importantly for our purposes, Bradshaw's break with the Presbyterian middle way came in the final section of the text, where he addressed the question of whether 'every true visible Church of Christ be not a company of people called and separated out from the world'. Bradshaw admitted that in some sense every true Church must be separated from the world and its 'false worship and ways'; here and elsewhere, he pointed clearly towards the independence of individual churches. Yet this did not preclude true Christians from remaining in communion with the world due to 'their infirmity and ignorance'. This was the essence of Bradshaw's middle way: Congregationalism might be preferable, but this did not warrant separation from an institutional Church that had not yet realised the truth about Church government. Thus, Bradshaw argued:

They may in time become the true visible Church of Christ, which at the first were not in the said manner and form called, separated and joined together, but forced and constrained against their will by the sword of the magistrate . . . Many of those churches in our kingdom from which you [Francis Johnson] separate, as they now stand, are such a company of people.[104]

Here Bradshaw hoped that English congregations might someday achieve true gospel independence, thus he endorsed Congregationalism as a form of moderation, as long as it was *not enacted today* while it remained illegal, but at the appropriate historical moment.

But if Bradshaw attacked Johnson from the right, much more innovative and significant arguments came from his left. The populist, democratic *via media* was artfully constructed against Johnson by his former

---

[102] William Bradshaw, *The Unreasonablenesse of the Separation* (Dort?, 1614), sig. A3v.

[103] This was an almost irresistible tactic among Johnson's many enemies; *The Prophane Schisme of the Brownists or Separatists* likewise mocked Johnson's followers as 'Franciscans': Christopher Lawne, John Fowler, Clement Sanders and Robert Bulward, *The Prophane Schisme of the Brownists or Separatists* (London, 1612), pp. 11–13.

[104] Bradshaw, *The Unreasonablenesse of the Separation*, sig. P1v.

colleague Henry Ainsworth, a renowned Hebrew scholar who found in the Old Testament ample proof for the power of the people in the Church. Ainsworth's faction in Amsterdam seceded from Francis Johnson's 'ancient' separatist Church in December 1610 over what they saw as Johnson's backsliding towards authoritarianism. Ainsworth's version of moderation, however, was presented most forcefully three years later in his *An Animadversion to Mr Richard Clyftons Advertisement* (1613), where he argued that Johnson and his ally Clyfton had adopted the arguments of papists, conformists and Presbyterians: the false distinction between the public judgement of elders or clerics and the merely private judgement of laypeople in the congregation.[105] This, for Ainsworth, was the source of what he called 'popish succession', the notion that the Church was constituted through a chain of rulers endowing one another with authority, rather than through the voluntary association of its members; this was the very essence of papal tyranny, now reproduced not only among the Presbyterians but among the separatists.[106] As Ainsworth summarised his opponents' willingness to retain elements of Roman hierarchy: 'Their fear lest they should fall into Anabaptism is before defrayed; but as some mariners to avoid Charybdis have fallen into Scylla, so these to shun the shelves of Anabaptistry have run their ship upon the rocks of popery.'[107]

Yet Ainsworth also detested and feared anarchy in the Church, especially the anarchy of John Smyth, another apostate from the 'ancient' separatist Church who in January 1609 had rebaptised himself and his followers without any external authority. In a 1609 tract against Smyth, Ainsworth had called for a middle way between Presbyterian tyranny and Anabaptist 'mere confusion and abuse of the holy ordinances of the gospel, if everyone in the Church should administer and perform the works of Christ's ministers'.[108] Now in 1613, Ainsworth called for a middle way between Anabaptism and the tyranny of 'succession': 'We hold it necessary that all Church actions be orderly carried, either by the officers if there be any, or by the magistrates as in Israel, or by the fathers of families, or the most excellent in gifts requested thereunto by the congregation. This we firmly maintain, against all popular confusion and disorder whatsoever.' This was essentially to argue that the powers of discipline exist in a gathered Church prior to the election of officers – how else could the first officers lawfully be elected? – hence a gathered

---

[105] Henry Ainsworth, *An Animadversion to Mr Richard Clyftons Advertisement* (Amsterdam, 1613), preface, sig. \*\*\*3r–v.
[106] *Ibid.*, pp. 5–6, 11.     [107] *Ibid.*, p. 85.
[108] Henry Ainsworth, *A Defence of the Holy Scriptures* (Amsterdam, 1609), p. 131.

Church is capable of moderation rather than anarchy without the obedience of the many to the few.[109]

The core of this claim was Ainsworth's distinction between power and government in the Church, 'acknowledging government to be in the officers, but power in the whole body of the Church'. The proper balance of these two attributes was the essence of the Church's *via media*: 'Between these two is the matter so conveyed, as while we plead for the Church's right and power, we are said to oppugn government, and when we yield the elders to govern, they thereby would enclose the whole power in their hands.'[110] This *via media* depended centrally upon the franchise or power of election, which was not an office of government in itself but 'a power and right that the saints out of office have'. This distinction made perfect sense, from a political theory viewpoint, when the 'election' in question was the choice of officers: the people chose their government and delegated power to them but were not the government themselves. But Ainsworth, rather remarkably, also applied this distinction to congregational discipline through votes of excommunication: 'We infer also that to give voices in deciding of controversies and judging of sinners is not a part of government, but a power and a right that the saints out of office have.'[111] To claim that the power of excommunication was not *part* of government but rather was the proper *basis* of government was novel, but it reinforced the same argument we have seen from all our puritan writers: the moderation of the Church's government was produced by purging the Church of undesirable elements, rendering the Church a self-moderating body.

Ainsworth left no doubt that this moderation was largely the job of 'the brethren', the common members of the congregation. 'Brethren' was a carefully chosen word; he repeatedly denied that women could participate in discipline or give their voices in elections.[112] But within the limits of early modern England's gender and age hierarchy, Ainsworth made extraordinary claims for the role of the multitude in moderating the excesses of elites. The real threat of disorder, Ainsworth wrote, were those modern Pharisees, the lay elders of the Presbyterian churches, whose three of four votes were enough to 'carry matters, though it be against

[109] Ainsworth, *An Animadversion to Mr Richard Clyftons Advertisement*, pp. 58, 5.
[110] *Ibid.*, p. 10.
[111] *Ibid.*, p. 11. See also pp. 118–19. Henry Jacob made a seemingly similar distinction between the possession and use of power in the Church. Brachlow has argued that Jacob did not take it to the same populist ends (*The Communion of Saints*, pp. 186–93) but Jacob's *The Divine Beginning* emphasises that the congregation not only holds the power of church censure but also ultimately enforces it. I owe this point to Polly Ha.
[112] Ainsworth, *An Animadversion to Mr Richard Clyftons Advertisement*, pp. 33–4.

pastor, teacher and 500 brethren'. Francis Johnson had suggested that in such a case the pastor, teacher and people retained the right of separation, but this Ainsworth 'abhorred' as 'unruly': proper discipline prevented such tyranny rather than running from it.[113] The correct answer was thus to give the 500 their due votes, 'for if the people have some understanding and insight into matters as well as the elders, why should they not be used also in consulting and determining public things which concern all?'[114] The radicalism of this question was surpassed only by the radicalism of another on the subsequent page, at the end of a long argument that within the Pauline simile of the Church as a body, there was no reason why ordinary Christians could not be eyes or hands as well as feet: 'A woman in Abel when it was in danger to be spoiled persuaded all the people with her wisdom to cut off Sheba's head, and so preserved the city. Was she in this action a part of the foot, or of the heart and head in that body, may we think?'[115]

### Radical moderation?

This brings us finally to the English Baptist progenitors John Smyth and Thomas Helwys, the epitome of extremist radicalism for almost all subsequent discussions of the *via media*, but also claimants to the *via media* themselves. For they, too, desired an orderly, governed, moderate Church rather than an excessive one, and they, too, tried to balance the rights of Christians with the prerogatives of officers to find a middle way in which power was authorised by its moderation. Their difference from other puritans, in the end, was one of degree rather than kind, since they began from the same premise that a properly constituted Church was a machine of self-moderation through discipline.

It is useful to begin with John Smyth's *The Differences of the Churches of the Separation* (1608), written to justify his schism from the 'ancient' Amsterdam congregation but finished just before that schism resulted in his remarkable self-baptism. The core of Smyth's ecclesiology was that the three-fold order of presbytery followed by his opponents – an officer corps in every congregation consisting of pastor, teacher and lay elders – was a new Antichrist, an ungodly division of labour between clergy and laity that re-erected the stubborn clericalism of both popery and prelacy. Rather, Smyth argued (in a claim that ironically tracked with conformist arguments for the worldly authority of bishops) that there was only one proper eldership in the Church, since the different gifts described in scripture could all be held by the same people. Hence the

---

[113] *Ibid.*, p. 39.    [114] *Ibid.*, p. 40    [115] *Ibid.*, pp. 41–2.

various names often given to Church officers – bishops, pastors, teachers, governors, leaders – were in fact 'several names for one and the same office'. That office, called the presbytery, Smyth defined as 'the company of the elders which are for the Church in the public actions of the Church, either of the kingdom or priesthood', hence all presbyters were simultaneously preachers, dispensers of sacraments, governors and leaders of the Church 'in public affairs'.[116] The immediate import of this argument was to elide any distinction between clergy and laity: an elder elected because he 'excelleth in government' might 'properly . . . be called a ruler or governor', yet by virtue of his office he had the right to preach and administer the sacraments; contrariwise, an elder elected because of his gifts as an expositor of doctrine might most properly be called a teacher or doctor, yet he retained by virtue of his office the right to govern the Church. An immediate corollary of this conclusion was that every congregation was to have many pastors rather than one.[117]

We can see already, then, Smyth's desire to overcome the tyranny of puritan clerisy by distributing power among a broader coterie of officers. But on the other hand, this creation of a unified officer corps, despite its radicalism, was still at heart the constitution of a government whose role was to 'moderate' the Church. Smyth split this role into two halves – 'the works of the presbytery in the priesthood of the Church' and 'the works of the presbytery in the kingdom of the Church' – but he stressed the moderating function of both. Within the works of the priesthood the job of presbyters was 'to lead and moderate the Church in . . . spiritual sacrifices' while within the works of the kingdom the job of presbyters was 'to lead and moderate the Church actions and speeches in these matters and causes of the kingdom and government'.[118]

Like other puritans, Smyth argued that what made these moderators 'moderate' rather than tyrannous was that they were subject to their congregations. He simply pushed this relationship further, and framed it somewhat differently, than his erstwhile brethren. On the worship side, Smyth was in fact deeply conflicted and largely failed to resolve his contradictions. In addition to the presbyters being elected by their brethren, Smyth wrote, 'although the presbytery lead and moderate these spiritual sacrifices, yet the brethren [are] interested in using their gifts for the performance of all these parts of spiritual worship'. Here we see an apparent

[116] John Smyth, *The Differences of the Churches of the Separation* (Middelburg, 1608), pp. 22–4.
[117] *Ibid.*, p. 26.    [118] *Ibid.*, pp. 27–8.

admission that all members of the congregation have equal authority as priests in Christ. Yet he concluded that sentence by reminding readers that 'things must be done in order', and he mentioned one large 'exception' to the parity of brethren and presbyters: 'The administration of the seals of the covenant seemeth to appertain only to the elders or presbytery, as sacrificing did only to the priests.' The word 'seemeth' speaks volumes here of Smyth's ambivalence.[119]

On the discipline side, however, Smyth was less conflicted and pushed his populism past where Ainsworth had stopped: 'The brethren are all interested in all the parts of administration though the elders lead and moderate them.' Here, rather than distinguishing between power and government in the Church, the common people retained the governmental authority that they enjoyed 'immediately from Christ'. This had several implications. It meant, first of all, that even 'when the Church wanteth an eldership' it retained the power 'to preach, pray, sing psalms, and so by consequent to administer the seals of the covenant; also to admonish, convince, excommunicate, absolve and all other actions either of the kingdom or of the priesthood, by necessary consequent'. Here, beginning from the position he shared with Ainsworth that a Church without elders could still be moderate, we have the basis for Smyth's extraordinary belief in the moderation of his own imminent self-baptism, and in fact that extraordinary act of ecclesiological bootstrapping – simultaneously an act of literal self-government and the creation of a public polity in Smyth's own person – is a neat example of the simultaneity of internal and external moderation. Second, it meant not only that the whole Church retained the power to remove the presbytery for just cause, which Ainsworth and other separatists admitted, but that the congregation might exercise *independent* authority over election and excommunication 'to use when occasion seweth [sic]' without the support or guidance of the eldership.[120]

If we move to Smyth's writings after his self-baptism, we see the end point of these arguments. If any two or three Christians possess the full disciplinary and governmental apparatus of the Church, then that includes control of entry into the Church through baptism:

Now, for baptising a man's self, there is as good warrant as for a man churching himself. For two men singly are no Church, jointly they are a Church and they both of them put a Church upon themselves, so may two men put baptism upon themselves. For as both those persons unchurched yet have the power to assume the Church each of them for himself with others in communion, so each

---

[119] *Ibid.*, p. 28.     [120] *Ibid.*

of them unbaptised hath power to assume baptism for himself with others in communion.[121]

The key word here was 'unbaptised'. True Church government described in scripture, what Smyth called 'the true apostolic constitution', was radically limited to adult believers capable of exercising their governmental role, 'baptised disciples that confessed their faith and their sins'.[122] By this logic, the baptism of unbelievers was the font and wellspring of *tyranny*, because in Smyth's model Church members were also Church governors.[123] Infant baptism thus gave the Church of England its 'false constitution', and only by separating from this constitution could a new government be established in its place.[124] It was in this sense that Smyth claimed to be a supporter of Church government rather than its enemy.

About a year after Smyth's self-baptism, having made contact with Dutch Mennonites in Amsterdam, he partially relented. He concluded that while self-baptism by independent congregations was perhaps licit *in extremis*, in contexts where other Churches practised adult baptism it was more orderly for Christians to join those Churches rather than beginning their own, so he urged his followers to become Mennonites. The result was a schism in which a faction led by Thomas Helwys accused Smyth of backsliding and excommunicated Smyth and thirty-one of his supporters. In Helwys's 1611 tract *An Advertisement or Admonition unto the Congregations*, then, we see the culmination of Smyth's earlier *via media*. Part II of the tract was organised around the problem of 'succession', the anti-Christian notion that once a Church is established all other Christians in the vicinity must 'be one with you and receive power and all the holy things from you' rather than beginning their own churches. This was tyranny, the removal of divinely appointed governmental authority from 'all that are called of God'.[125] In this sense the Dutch Anabaptists were no better than the 'Antichrist of Rome', claiming to be mother of all churches.[126] If only the baptised can baptise, then all churches and ministry must derive from previous churches and ministry, reproducing a carnal succession of the Church as the papists did rather than accepting the spiritual succession of true believers. For Helwys, then, the right of self-baptism was an essential deterrent to tyranny, exactly equivalent to denying the authority of bishops or synods over individual congregations,

---

[121] John Smyth, *The Character of the Beast, or the False Constitution of the Church* (Middelburg, 1609), p. 58.
[122] *Ibid.*, p. 48.     [123] *Ibid.*, p. 53.     [124] *Ibid.*, epistle, sigs. A2v–A3r.
[125] Thomas Helwys, *An Advertisement or Admonition unto the Congregations* (Amsterdam?, 1611), p. 20.
[126] *Ibid.*, p. 24.

for if gathered communities of Christians could not baptise themselves then they were always beholden to external authorities.[127]

Other parts of the tract, however, were organised around the need to combat the radical excesses of the Anabaptists (a label that Helwys, like Smyth, never accepted), especially the quintessential Anabaptist errors of pacifism and denial that the godly could be magistrates. For Helwys, God wanted absolute parity among Christians so that none wielded spiritual authority over another; any spiritual authority was tyranny. But, as Thomas Cartwright had argued forty years earlier, to deny civil authority its 'sword of justice' would be anarchic, undermining the conditions in which true churches could flourish. For, as Helwys put it, 'Who would obey their orders and decrees if they had no power to constrain? Would evildoers be persuaded by words to do well?'[128] Moderation of the wicked was always necessary.

This, then, was how Helwys's explicitly self-baptising, radically decentralised and self-actualising *via media* could still, within its own logic, be an argument for governance rather than anarchy, a mode of restraint rather than liberation:

For whilst some church or congregation settled in the dregs of error, and overtaken with a secure, cold, frozen profession of the gospel; and some other church or congregation carried away with a headstrong blind zeal into many errors . . . what hope is there of the growth of pure religion? We therefore earnestly beseech all people by the mercies of God (in whom there is any faithful love of God's truth) not to respect any men.[129]

In this remarkable fashion, radical nonconformity became the essence of moderation, because only by limiting Church membership to its asymptotic limit of a handful of regenerated saints, utterly alienated from other churches but protected from sin by civil magistrates, could the Church truly be moderated: 'Hold not errors for company's sake, nor walk in by-paths by affections; it is better to hold the truth alone, and to walk in the ways thereof contrary to all the affections of the heart, which is deceitful.' Only under conditions of maximum liberty, predicated upon almost unlimited exclusion of those incapable of such liberty, were the godly free to moderate their own affections.[130]

### Conclusion

This chapter has explored the development of puritan moderation from the 1570s to the 1610s. It has suggested that puritans shared (against the

---

[127] *Ibid.*, pp. 29, 35, 51.    [128] *Ibid.*, p. 70.    [129] *Ibid.*, p. 54.    [130] *Ibid.*, p. 83.

conformists) a belief in the Church's capacity for self-government, using divinely ordained discipline that was simultaneously the external and coercive moderation of a reprobate world and the internal and consensual self-moderation of the saints themselves. Yet despite these similarities, puritans differed from one another enormously over the mechanics of self-moderation: from an elitist reliance upon aristocratic moderation; to a balance of aristocratic and popular elements in the Church moderating one another; to a conception of popular government in which the Church had to be radically limited because every member of the Church was entrusted with its moderation. We have seen, then, a process or progression in which the core logic of puritan moderation produced ever-expanding definitions of tyranny, and the middle way between tyranny and anarchy was located in ever greater congregational autonomy and populism; yet the more such arguments stressed freedom and self-government, the more they relied upon discipline and exclusion as instruments of moderation. At each stage these new arguments were deposited atop previous ones like so many layers of sediment, producing an ever-larger and more heterogeneous composite of puritan ecclesiology, with each position claiming to be the *telos* that finally achieved full Reformation.

One consequence of this analysis is that we must rethink our assumptions about the relationship between puritanism and moderation. However fond puritans were of biblical verses condemning Laodicean lukewarmness, it is absolutely not the case that puritans lived within a binary or dualist mentality in which they were, as Stuart Clark has argued, 'incapable of any subtlety in categorising their foes'.[131] Puritans were every bit as preoccupied as their conformist opponents with moderation and the search for a middle way between extremes, a phenomenon not limited to the people we have learned to call 'moderate puritans'. But crucially, this does not mean that moderation was so relativised as to evacuate the concept of all meaning, or that it provided an infinitely fungible framework that anyone could apply to any position. Rather, a second consequence of this discussion is that moderation did not simply refer to a religious position being limited, compromised or reasonable, but rather moderation did a particular sort of ideological work authorising governance, control and restraint; early modern puritans used the framework of moderation and the *via media* to claim competency to govern or to describe the mechanisms whereby they would govern well. For puritans as much

---

[131] Stuart Clark, *Thinking with Demons: The Idea of Witchcraft in Early Modern Europe* (Oxford, 1997), p. 63. See Ethan Shagan, 'Beyond Good and Evil: Thinking with Moderates in Early Modern England', *JBS* 49, no. 3 (July 2010), pp. 488–513.

as conformists, the Reformation in England was moderate insofar as it governed, and for puritans that government always and necessarily combined informal structures of self-regulation with formal structures of rule. We must acknowledge, then, the *forcible* side of moderation itself in the seventeenth century as it underwrote the creation of new institutions of authority.

A final consequence of this analysis is that the English Reformation, in its most vigorous and experimental expressions, both anticipated some of the most important political theorising of the subsequent century and imbued that later tradition with some of its characteristic ambivalences. We shall see below that debates over liberty in the seventeenth century stressed that proper liberty was a middle way between tyranny and anarchy, hence calls for liberty were always predicated upon its restraint. This chapter has suggested that this 'rule of moderation' had a long English pedigree: it was central to puritan attempts to solve the problem of how self-government can be government indeed rather than anarchy by a different name. While, as we saw in Chapter 3, Richard Hooker's conformist solution invoked the rule of law as moderation, the puritan solution was to yoke freedom with discipline. Both versions would play important roles in the development of England's paradoxically repressive constitutionalism.

## Part III

# Moderate rule

We have seen in Part II the rule of moderation in broadly constitutional debates concerning authority in and over the Church. The essential problem was a catch-22 familiar since antiquity: government consists in the restraint of excess, but the power to restrain excess itself requires restraint. Yet, however timeless this agonism, Englishmen building their Church confronted it within unique institutional and ideological contexts. First, the English Reformation established the primacy of civil over ecclesiastical government, erecting a superstructure that all participants had to accept or else step beyond the pale of political legitimacy; for all the theological subtleties used to define religious moderation, it was hard to trump obedience to lawfully constituted authority. Second, humanism and Protestantism converged to emphasise the regenerative powers of virtue or godliness in the world; given the centuries that England had wallowed in anti-Christian corruption, the goal of government was not merely stability but improvement. Third, while both Christian liberty and strong government were essential, belief in the depravity of man and the fallen nature of all human institutions severely attenuated what both liberty and authority might be taken to mean. Time and again, then, the solution offered by English Protestants for navigating these conflicting imperatives was the rule of moderation: government was in some significant sense authorised by its limitation, but the government such limitation authorised was intrinsically interventionist, committed to the goals of discipline and regeneration through the active restraint of its subjects. Since external moderation needed to take over where internal moderation failed, the rule of moderation was committed to peace and harmony through restraint and exclusion, with routinely coercive and sometimes violent results.

Part III takes this religious framework as a foundation and opens outwards onto much broader social, cultural and political issues. Its chapters are not so tightly wound and technical but rather seek to understand how the politics of restraint that had first developed in an ecclesiastical setting came to permeate and structure English public life. In particular, we will see how this configuration shaped four key developments: the establishment of an English empire in the New World; the growing recognition and significance of a 'middle sort' of people; demands for political liberty in the English Revolution; and the rise of religious toleration. As we shall see, in sometimes surprising ways all of these were, like the emergence of the Church of England, broadly *constitutional* developments, creating middle paths between deficient and excessive government, between incivility and oppression. They were also bound within broadly similar constraints as those that shaped the emergence of the Church of England: strong central authority, the requirement of liberty, and a profound pessimism about the human condition that attenuated both. The result was the much more general development of English public life along the same lines as, and in some cases directly emerging from, the developments described in Part II: the rule of moderation. Government was authorised by its limitation, but the government such limitation authorised was the most robust the world had ever seen, dedicated not merely to stability but to discipline and regeneration through the active restraint of its subjects.

In each of these areas, then, we will see how the ubiquitous quest for moderation in English public life authorised particular sorts of restraint. In sum, Part III will argue that claims for empire, the 'middle sort', liberty and toleration, insofar as they were identified with moderation, were all claims for authority. Not coincidentally, these areas are also four of the central constituent elements of modern English history. The conclusion that follows will therefore suggest that the rule of moderation may be near the heart of a central paradox of English modernity: the contradiction between a developing liberal ideology that insisted upon the limitation of government and the expansion of that government's authority upon its own subjects and the world.

# 5 English expansion and the empire of moderation

## Introduction: 'between the old world and the new'

In 1578, the Elizabethan courtier and magus John Dee introduced his queen to the concept of a 'British Empire', in the process outlining the most expansive vision of Tudor authority ever written. In a self-conscious repudiation of Hapsburg claims to lordship over all the world, Dee argued historically and legally that Queen Elizabeth's empire included not only the whole of Britain and Ireland but also Denmark, Norway, Sweden, France, great chunks of Germany, the New World north of the forty-fifth parallel and even, via a fourteenth-century marriage treaty, Spain and Portugal and hence the New World in its entirety. Yet the title of Dee's remarkable work – *Brytanici Imperii Limites* – paradoxically stressed the moderation of his claims: these were the boundaries of Tudor authority, beyond which the law-abiding English would not extend themselves. Throughout the manuscript Dee affirmed the moderation of English aspirations and contrasted them with the excesses of foreign, especially Spanish, imperial projects. In proving English *imperium* over Scandinavia, for instance, Dee admitted that 'the common guise hath anciently been with all nations excessively to extol some one of their notable princes', passing off their 'registered fantasies' as history; in other words, most nations invented ancient conquests to make excessive claims to authority. The English, by contrast, relied upon the unimpeachable deeds of 'our incomparable Arthur', whose ancient conquests had been affirmed by a counsel of noblemen, scholars and lawyers who swore that 'so far as they were able, following the path of righteousness and straying neither to right nor to left, they would expound the venerable institutions of their laws and customs, omitting nothing, adding nothing and disguising nothing by prevarications'.[1] The British Empire, then, was moderate

---

[1] *John Dee: The Limits of the British Empire*, ed. Ken MacMillan with Jennifer Abeles (Westport, Conn., 2004), pp. 53–7. On Dee's text see Ken MacMillan, *Sovereignty and Possession in the English New World: The Legal Foundations of Empire, 1576–1640* (Cambridge, 2006); Charlotte Artese, 'King Arthur in America: Making Space in History for

regardless of its geographic expanse because it was legitimate, whereas other European empires were immoderate because they usurped lawful English authority.

Dee's claims underline a central tension within the English imperial imagination and represent a particularly significant iteration of the rule of moderation as it spread outward from the ecclesiastical sphere into English society. For of all the subjects discussed in these pages, few would seem more incongruous sites of moderation than imperialism, which was by definition about expansion rather than restraint. America's lure of limitless gold and global dominion brought to mind legends of Midas and Icarus, cautionary tales against overreaching natural limits; by any rational standard the moderate course of action would have been to stay home. Yet the representation of empire as the virtuous pursuit of moderation was fundamental to the creation and endurance of England's New World colonies; such language was ubiquitous, filling the interstices of other rationales that scholars have seen as founding ideologies of English imperialism.[2] As Andrew Fitzmaurice has recently shown, the pursuit of empire was imagined in England as a moral exercise as much as a commercial venture; it was an extension westward of the culture and values that the English believed made them a great people.[3] At the centre of those values was the *via media*, with England moderating excesses both at home and abroad, 'seated between the Old World and the New' in the words of Francis Bacon.[4]

Yet precisely because moderation was external as well as internal, the line between moral exercise and colonial conquest was never a sharp one; it was always understood that moderation required the containment or repression of dangerous extremes. This chapter will thus analyse claims for the moderation of English imperial ventures during the formative period from Queen Elizabeth's reign up until the uneven moment (different for different colonies, perhaps the mid 1620s for Virginia and the late 1630s for Massachusetts) when England's New World empire passed from imperial imagination to settled authority. In those years, I want to argue, the ideology of moderation paradoxically freed English

---

The Faerie Queene and John Dee's *Brytanici Imperii Limites*', *Journal of Medieval and Early Modern Studies* 33, no.1 (Winter 2003), pp. 125–41.

[2] The best work on this subject is Jeffrey Knapp, *An Empire Nowhere: England, America, and Literature from Utopia to The Tempest* (Berkeley, 1992).

[3] Andrew Fitzmaurice, *Humanism and America* (Cambridge, 2003).

[4] *The Letters and the Life of France Bacon*, ed. James Spedding (London, 7 vols., 1861–74), I, p. 388: 'Seated between the Old World and the New / A land there is no other land may touch, / Where reigns a Queen in peace and honour true; / Stories or fables do describe no such.'

government from its traditional, insular limits and authorised its global metastasis. Advocates of empire argued that English government was a restraining power, controlled and reasonable, a moderator of dangerous extremes, and as such they at least partially overcame the conventional association between expansion and excess that had permeated the classical tradition and linked empire with luxury, corruption and tyranny.[5] An empire of moderation, in this vision, was quite literally an empire that moderated: the *via media* of English government underwrote its limitless expansion as a form of restraint. This expansion did not primarily involve governance of North American natives – the English in this era were notoriously uninterested in ruling subject peoples – but rather governance of English subjects in new commonwealths under the English crown, imagined as bridles both to Old World excess and to New World deficiency. In this sense, claims for the moderation of English imperialism were nearly tautological – governance was moderation – and rival English interests could compete for the crown of moderation in and through the process of colonial development.[6]

Now, the primary literature of early colonial North America is vast, and its historiography is complex, erudite and in many ways beyond the scope of this book; I can do no more here than isolate one strand of thought from a rich tapestry, and I am well aware that specialists will have much to add. The goal of this chapter, then, is not to argue with those specialists but to distil from their work and their sources an argument with relevance to metropolitan English history. That is, not only did England's imperial aspirations germinate in the sixteenth and early seventeenth centuries, but so too did arguments authorising such expansion on the grounds of its limitation. In this sense, English imperialism required little ideological invention or intellectual borrowing; it required only the reorientation of materials well in hand. The rule of moderation at the core of early modern English society already embodied all of the contradictions between harmony and belligerence, between republican virtue and colonial domination – what Paul Stevens has called the paradox of exclusive universalism[7] – at the heart of the imperial project.

---

[5] See David Armitage, *The Ideological Origins of the British Empire* (Cambridge, 2000).

[6] Here I am indebted to Andrew Fitzmaurice's argument that imperialism was widely imagined as part of the humanist *vita activa*, a contribution to the life of the commonwealth, and hence incorporated the moral philosophy of civic humanist politics: Fitzmaurice, *Humanism and America*, ch. 3.

[7] Paul Stevens, '"Leviticus Thinking" and the Rhetoric of Early Modern Colonialism', *Criticism* 35, no. 3 (Summer 1993), pp. 441–61.

## Climate moderation and English governance

'The wise creator of the universal globe hath placed a golden mean betwixt two extremes: I mean the temperate zones, betwixt the hot and cold.'[8] So began Thomas Morton's *New English Canaan*, a long description of New England first published in 1632. This notion of a geographical middle way was an ancient conceit first proposed in the fifth century BC, but like so many other versions of the golden mean it was popularised by Aristotle, who argued that the earth contained two habitable sections, one in the northern hemisphere and one in the south. In the northern hemisphere, the region too far north was uninhabitable because of the cold, and he hypothesised that there must be a corresponding subtropical zone that was also uninhabitable because of the heat. Thus the habitable or temperate zone was the moderate middle way between the two. The notion of an uninhabitable 'torrid zone' near the equator was disputed by, among others, the influential first-century AD geographer Strabo, who pointed out that the equatorial region was in fact inhabited. But Strabo – in whose works John Dee scribbled over 2,000 marginal notes[9] – still followed Aristotle in imagining a 'temperate' zone between the 'torrid' and 'frigid' zones, and this became the basis for his speculation that there might be other inhabited continents unknown to the Greeks and Romans, since the length of the known world was not more than one-third of the total circumference of the globe in the temperate zone.[10]

The classical tradition also bequeathed to the Renaissance a notion of environmental determinism in which geography influenced human nature, so that more temperate climates produced more temperate people. Bluntly speaking, cold made men strong but stupid, while heat made men smart but lazy, so in temperate climates men might achieve a golden mean that partook of both. This was a commonplace in Tudor England, for instance in Robert Barret's *Theorike and Practike of Moderne Warres* (1598), where he wrote that the soldier of the 'north climate, by reason of his wide distance from the sun, doth abound in hot blood, and is of good courage and great strength, entering into battle without fear, but rash and inconsiderate in the same, void of consideration and counsel in most of his actions'. On the contrary extreme, 'the meridonal man, by reason of the nearness of the sun, the which they have almost for their zenith, are fearful and fainthearted and very loath to enter into

---

[8] Thomas Morton, *New English Canaan* (London, 1632), p. 11.
[9] MacMillan, *Sovereignty and Possession*, p. 53.
[10] E. H. Warmington (ed.), *Greek Geography* (London, 1934), pp. 231–2; E. H. Bunbury, *A History of Ancient Geography*, 2nd edn (New York, 2 vols., 1959), I, pp. 395–403 and II, pp. 223–8.

battle except constrained and urged thereunto, but withal very subtle, wary and sharp-witted'. Thus men of the 'middle climate, participating of both extremes' are the best.[11] Englishmen, not surprisingly, often asserted that their own climate provided this golden moderation. As Michael Drayton put it in the opening lines of his *Poly-Olbion* (1612):

> Of Albion's glorious isle the wonders whilst I write,
> The sundry varying soils, the pleasures infinite
> (Where heat kills not the cold, nor cold expels the heat,
> The calms too mildly small, nor winds too roughly great,
> Nor night doth hinder day, nor day the night doth wrong,
> The Summer not too short, the Winter not too long).[12]

This, then, was the background to Thomas Morton's claim that God had made the temperate zone a climatic golden mean. Within this framework, promoters of England's imperial ventures sought to convince potential investors and government officials that their projects partook of climatic moderation. According to Morton, for instance, New England was the most virtuously mediocre of all locations, 'situated about the middle of those two extremes':

> You may prove it thus: counting the space between the [equatorial] line and either of the poles in true proportion, you shall find it to be 90 degrees. Then must we find the mean to be near unto the centre of 90, and that is about 45 degrees, and then incline unto the southern side of the centre, properly for the best benefit of heat, remembering that *sol et homo generat hominem*. And then keep us on that same side, and see what land is to be found there, and we shall easily discern that New England is on the south side of that centre. For that country doth begin her bounds at 40 degrees of northern latitude, and ends at 45 degrees of the same latitude, and doth participate of heat and cold indifferently but is oppressed with neither.[13]

Similar rhetoric was often used for the plantation in Virginia. As early as 1610, the London minister William Crashaw wrote that in order to travel to other parts of the New World from England the 'passage is subject either to the intemperate heat of the sun on the one side, or the danger of the ice on the other side'. By contrast, 'only this passage into Virginia, being in the west-southwest or thereabouts, is in that true temper so fair,

---

[11] Robert Barret, *The Theorike and Practise of Moderne Warres Discoursed in Dialogue Wise* (London, 1598), p. 8. 'Intemperate climates' were also believed to generate disease: see Karen Kupperman, 'Fear of Hot Climates in the Anglo-American Colonial Experience', *WMQ* 41, no. 2 (April 1984), pp. 213–40. More broadly, Kupperman notes English fears of 'superabundance' in hot climates.

[12] Michael Drayton, *Poly-Olbion* (London, 1612), p. 1. For many more examples and an extended discussion of these issues, see Scodel, *Excess and the Mean*, ch. 3.

[13] Morton, *New English Canaan*, pp. 15–16.

so safe, so secure, so easy, as though God himself had built a bridge for men to pass from England to Virginia'.[14] According to Crashaw, even though Virginia was 'between the 34 and 45 degrees of northerly latitude' and hence might seem to lie 'not far enough from the *torrida zona*', nonetheless for reasons not yet fully discerned it turned out that the climate was 'temperate and indifferent'. Interestingly, the clinching evidence for this geographical moderation was the surprisingly light skin of the natives.[15] A dozen years later, when Englishmen had far more experience in Virginia, they could still write that because it was located 'near the middest of the world, between the extremities of heat and cold, [it] seems to partake of the benefits of both, and thereby becometh capable of the richest commodities of most parts of the earth'.[16]

Colonies farther to the north were also drawn into this rhetoric. Richard Eburne claimed in 1624 that Newfoundland was most 'healthy and temperate, very agreeable to the constitution of our English bodies', suggesting that it was 'very near in the same temperature for heat and cold that England is, rather warmer than colder, as which lieth above four degrees nearer the south than England'.[17] As we might suspect from this description, Eburne had never actually been to Newfoundland, but claims for the territory's geographical moderation had long been a staple of Newfoundland promotional texts, even among writers who should have known better. When Humphrey Gilbert first viewed Newfoundland (in August) with his men, 'they found the same very temperate, but somewhat warmer than England at that season of the year'.[18] Later in the 1580s, in a manuscript intended 'to induce some noble [persons] to conquer and possess the new found land', Edward Hayes protested, perhaps too much, against 'the common opinion that is had of the intemperature and extreme cold that should be in this country'. Hayes insisted that this was a myth and that most of the colony was temperate: 'I do grant that not alone in the Newfoundland but in Germany, Italy and Africa the mountains are extreme cold... [but] the valleys and lower grounds in the Newfoundland must likewise be hot and temperate as the clime doth seem. Wherefore all doubts may be removed, that by reason of the

[14] William Crashaw, *A Sermon Preached in London before the Right Honourable the Lord Lawarre, Lord Governour and Captaine Generall of Virginea* (London, 1610), sig. E1v.

[15] *Ibid.*, sig. E2r. This obsession with skin colour was common in tracts supporting colonisation, and authors generally seem to have believed that moderate or temperate climates produced whiter people. See Alden Vaughan, 'From White Man to Red Skin: Changing Anglo-American Perceptions of the American Indian', *AHR* 87 (1982), pp. 917–53.

[16] Edward Waterhouse, *A Declaration of the State of the Colony and Affaires in Virginia* (London, 1622), p. 3.

[17] Richard Eburne, *A Plaine Path-Way to Plantations* (London, 1624), p. 105.

[18] *NAW*, III, p. 39.

intemperature, the Newfoundland should be unhabitable throughout or in any part that lieth under so temperate climes.'[19]

Historians of colonial North America, most importantly Karen Kupperman, have described in detail this obsession with climatic moderation: both the desire to claim temperance for colonies despite mounting evidence to the contrary, and the intellectual problem of how to account for climate not behaving as early modern natural philosophy said it should.[20] But while these historians have paid ample attention to the way early modern imperialists associated moderate bodies with moderate climates, they have not much noticed the ethical implications of such assertions. The claim to possess bodies carefully tempered by God and England's climate was not only a physical claim but a moral one. This is nowhere more explicit than in Richard Barckley's great Neostoic compendium *A Discourse of the Felicitie of Man* (1598), where climatic temperance was closely associated with the moral superiority of the middle estate between riches and poverty, which we shall explore further in Chapter 6 below. For Barckley, 'the estates or kinds of life may be compared to the zones by which the cosmographers divide the world'. In this schema, 'high dignities and honourable estates may be likened to the burning zone . . . because they that live under that part of the heaven are continually parched and unquieted with the extreme heat of the sun', and this disquiet and lack of inner peace leads to their 'ambitious desire to enlarge their dominion or possessions . . . and therefore one calleth *imperium, honestissimam sepulturam*'. On the other extremity, 'they that live in poverty and lack' are likewise 'unquieted with continual care and fear of want' and hence 'may be likened to them that dwell under the cold zone, called *zona frigida*, who by want of the sun's heat . . . lead a painful life'. The golden mean of course lay in the *zona temperata* between excessive heat and cold: 'They that live in a mean estate are free from the troubles, cares and dangers to which high dignities are subject by their excess and superfluities, which allure to vice; and likewise from the fear of penury and want which tormenteth the poor estate. He therefore that

---

[19] *Ibid.*, p. 126. A more sceptical account of the classical tradition of climate moderation is in Samuel Purchas, *Purchas His Pilgrimage. Or Relations of the World and the Religions Observed in All Ages* (London, 1613), pp. 602–8. Yet Purchas still imagines America as enjoying a virtuously moderate climate.

[20] Karen Kupperman, 'Climate and Mastery of the Wilderness in Seventeenth-Century New England', in David Hall and David Allen (eds.), *Seventeenth-Century New England: A Conference* (Boston, 1984); Karen Kupperman, 'The Puzzle of the American Climate in the Early Colonial Period', *AHR* 87, no. 5 (December 1982), pp. 1262–89; Karen Kupperman, *The Jamestown Project* (Cambridge, Mass., 2007), ch. 5; Catherine Armstrong, *Writing North America in the Seventeenth Century: English Representations in Print and Manuscript* (Aldershot, 2007), ch. 2; Chaplin, *Subject Matter*, ch. 4.

is in a mean estate, or not over near extreme poverty, hath a sufficiency of riches to the help of felicity.'[21]

If temperate climate was therefore an ethical claim, linked to the restraint of avarice and ambition, it was also, *mutatis mutandis*, a political claim. Most importantly, in Book VII of the *Politics* Aristotle had famously described the Greeks as ideal citizens and governors because of their temperate climate. As the 1598 English translation put it:

> We will speak of what nature the citizens ought to be: which thing is easily known, if we consider the most famous cities of Greece, and all the habitable parts of the earth, considering how many sorts of people there are. For those nations which inhabit cold places, and in Europe, are full of courage, but have no sharpness of wit, nor cunning; for which cause they do the longer continue in liberty; but they are without any good form of government and cannot bear rule over their neighbours. They of Asia are witty, and more apt to the learning and practicing of arts, but they are not so courageous, and are therefore subject, and doe serve continually. The Greek nation as it is in the midst between these two places, so doth it participate of both, being courageous and ingenious, for which cause it doth continue and keep her liberty, and is well governed, and might command the whole world, if it had but one manner of government.[22]

For promoters of English empire this meant, first of all, that Englishmen were in some sense the natural or appropriate rulers of their prospective colonies; there was, in Joyce Chaplin's felicitous phrase, 'cosmic synchrony between the invaders and their new place of abode'.[23] Thomas Morton explained that because New England occupied a climatic golden mean, it was 'therefore most fit for the generation and habitation of our English nation of all other'.[24] *An Historicall Discoverie and Relation of the English Plantations in New England* (1627) told its readers that New England was 'so temperate as it seemeth to hold the golden mean, and indeed it is most agreeable to the nature of our own'.[25] In George Peckham's 1583 account of Humphrey Gilbert's voyage to Newfoundland, Peckham stressed not only climatic moderation – 'they found the same very temperate' and 'a temperate climate at all times of the year' – but also the naturalness for Englishmen of Newfoundland's moderation, 'whose country doth (as it were with arm advanced) above the climates both of Spain and France, stretch out itself towards England only'. Most importantly, by stressing the felicity of moderate climates for English habitation,

---

[21]  Richard Barckley, *A Discourse of the Felicitie of Man* (London, 1598), pp. 488–9.

[22]  *Aristotles Politiques*, p. 359.

[23]  Chaplin, *Subject Matter*, p. 157.     [24]  Morton, *New English Canaan*, pp. 15–16.

[25]  *An Historicall Discoverie and Relation of the English Plantations in New England* (London, 1627), sigs. D1v–D2v. This tract reproduced much material from the 1622 *Brief Relation of the Discovery and Plantation of New England*.

Peckham delineated a moral duty of empire: 'The climate mild and temperate, neither too hot nor too cold, so that under the cope of heaven there is not anywhere to be found a more convenient place to plant and inhabit in . . . Is it not therefore (I say) to be lamented that these poor pagans, so long living in ignorance and idolatry, and in sort, thirsting after Christianity (as may appear by the relation of such as have travailed in those parts) that our hearts are so hardened, that few or none can be found which will put to their helping hands, and apply themselves to the relieving of the miserable and wretched estate of these silly souls?'[26]

The payoff of this potent mixture of ethical, political and environmental writing was the extraordinary claim, repeated increasingly often as it was discovered that North America was not really so temperate as the colonisers had hoped, that the English empire literally moderated or tempered the climate of its colonies. The English constructed an empire of moderation in the active and external sense of the term: its industry and civility reduced its colonies to a golden mean.[27] In 1620, for instance, Richard Whitbourne argued that Newfoundland's 'unnecessary bushes' and 'unserviceable woods' should be burned to the ground, so that 'the hot beams of the sun might pierce into the earth and stones there, so speedily as it doth in some other countries, that lie under the same elevation of the pole, it would then there make such a reflection of heat, that it would much lessen these fogs, and also make the country much the hotter winter and summer, and thereby the earth will bud forth her blossoms and fruits more timely in the year then now it doth, and so bring the land more familiar to us, and fitter for tillage and for beasts'.[28] In John Mason's *A Briefe Discourse of the New-Found-Land* (1620), he posited the absence of English civility as the explanation for the fact that Newfoundland was colder than its moderate latitude suggested: 'The lands not manured and therefore more naturally cold, the country slenderly peopled, void of towns and cities, whereof Europe is full; the smoke whereof and heat of fires much qualifieth the coldness of the air.'[29] Many similar suggestions were made for New England. A 1634 tract claimed that God had made the climate of New England *more* temperate since the English arrived: 'They [the Indians] say he is a good God that sends them so many good things, so much good corn, so many cattle, temperate rains, fair seasons, which they likewise are better for since the arrival of the English; the times and seasons being much altered in seven or eight

---

[26] *NAW*, III, pp. 41–2.
[27] Here I am indebted to Kupperman, 'Climate and Mastery of the Wilderness'.
[28] Richard Whitbourne, *A Discourse and Discovery of New-Found-Land* (London, 1620), p. 57.
[29] John Mason, *A Briefe Discourse of the New-Found-Land* (London, 1620), sig. B2v.

years, freer from lightning and thunder, long droughts, sudden and tempestuous dashes of rain, and lamentable cold winters.'[30] Philip Vincent described the moderation of New England as being contingent on the successful planting of the English there: 'New England ... is in the same height with the North of Spain, and South part of France, and the temper not much unlike, as pleasant, as temperate and as fertile as either, if managed by industrious hands.'[31] In *Wonder-Working Providence* (1654), Edward Johnson of New England described a debate that had occurred in 1632 regarding how exactly the arrival of the English had moderated the climate: 'Here, reader, thou must be minded of another admirable act of Christ for this year, in changing the very nature of the seasons, moderating the winter's cold of late very much, which some impute to the cutting down the woods and breaking up the land; but Christ have the praise of all his glorious acts.'[32]

The 'moderation' of England's early imperial ventures, then, was paradigmatic of the reciprocal and indissoluble association between internal and external moderation. To the extent that the English associated their own moral superiority with moderate climate, their colonies were literally an empire of moderation where temperate climate was both a justification for, and a result of, English governance. And if the English literally moderated the climate of their colonies, then their expansion could always be defended as moderation rather than excess.

### Governing populations

If governing climate provided one rationale for the moderation of empire, another rationale was governing populations. This did not mean for the English, as it did for the Spanish, governing native populations in a political sense, but rather governing the size of populations, regulating both expansion and decline to produce a golden mean.

Historians have long stressed that Englishmen justified their invasion on the grounds that North America was *vacuum domicilium*, empty or unpopulated. Lying behind this claim were complex arguments about what constituted true habitation. God had commanded the children of Adam and of Noah to 'fill the earth and subdue it', not only to spread over all the land but to command all inferior animals, plants and even the rocks themselves. Moreover, in punishment for Adam's sins, men were

---

[30] William Wood, *New Englands Prospect* (London, 1634), p. 84.
[31] Philip Vincent, *A True Relation of the Late Battell Fought in New England* (London, 1637), sig. A4r.
[32] Edward Johnson, *Wonder-Working Providence of Sion's Saviour*, ed. William Frederick Poole (Andover, Mass., 1867), p. 55. An equally blunt example from 1641 is on pp. 170–1.

required to work the land with the sweat of their brows. Agriculture, then, provided the conventional Christian definition for habitation of land, and any piece of land that had not been somehow 'improved' was considered *res nullius* and fit for colonisation.[33] The failure of people to use and improve the land, moreover, constituted a violation of God's will: John White argued that 'it were a great wrong to God to conceive that he doth ought in vain, or tenders a gift that he never meant should be enjoyed; how men should make benefit of the earth, but by habitation and culture, cannot be imagined'.[34] Englishmen thus did not disguise their glee when Indians began dying in extraordinary numbers from a series of plagues to which they were miraculously immune. It seemed to them that God was punishing the Indians for not using the land; for instance, in a 1634 letter to Sir Simonds D'Ewes, John Winthrop described an Indian smallpox epidemic by which 'God hath hereby cleared our title to this place'.[35] When God made a country so nearly vacant, John Cotton wrote, 'there is liberty for the sons of Adam or Noah to come and inhabit, though they neither buy it nor ask their leaves'.[36]

Yet just as there were too few people in America, so likewise there were too many people in England. It was thus through plantation that *both* populations could be brought to a virtuous mean, and all the dangers of both under-use and over-use of the land could be avoided. This providential connection between England and America allowed proponents of empire once again to imagine an empire of moderation in a literal sense: empire moderated extremes. In this case, however, such moderation not only justified the expropriation of Indian lands but also justified the forced or coerced transportation of the London poor. The creation of an English empire was a remedy for social extremes, and negative representations of Indians went hand in hand with the need to moderate the excesses of England's labouring classes.[37]

Once again we must begin with Aristotle's *Politics*. In his discussion of population in Book 7, Aristotle began by refuting the commonplace that a large population was requisite for a successful commonwealth. 'Power' rather than 'multitude' was the true measure of greatness, in the sense that a city is great if it can perform its function; Hippocrates was

[33] See Anthony Pagden, *Lords of All the World: Ideologies of Empire in Spain, Britain, and France c.1500–c.1800* (New Haven, 1995), ch. 3; James Tully, *An Approach to Political Philosophy*, ch. 5.

[34] John White, *The Planters Plea* (London, 1630), p. 3.

[35] Cited in Armstrong, *Writing North America in the Seventeenth Century*, p. 67.

[36] John Cotton, *God's Promise to His Plantation* (London, 1630), pp. 4–5.

[37] For a cogent discussion of these issues, see Chaplin, *Subject Matter*, ch. 4. Chaplin suggests that English writers took a generally positive line on English fecundity and its benefits for empire, whereas I interpret these texts as depicting overpopulation as dangerously excessive and in need of remedy.

a great physician because of his skill not his size, and a fatter physician would be no greater. Likewise, even to the extent that population is indicative of greatness, one must be very careful to distinguish quality within the quantity: a populace city that consisted of slaves, foreigners and artificers but few soldiers would not be great. Most importantly, Aristotle stressed the need for population to remain moderate, because excessive populations were ungovernable:

It is known by experience to be very difficult, or rather impossible that a city which is too much peopled, can be well governed. Certes, of all the cities whose government is accounted good, we see not any which is too populous. And hereof reason itself doth assure us, for the law is a certain order, and the good instituting of laws, is of necessity good order: but the excessive number of inhabitants is not capable of order... There is also a certain measure of greatness in cities, as in all other things, in living creatures, plants and instruments, for each of them being too small, or of excessive greatness, cannot retain his power, but shall thereby wholly lose his nature, or remain unprofitable: as a ship of an hand breadth is not in very deed a ship, nor that also which is of two furlongs, but being come to some greatness, either through being too little, or through excessive highness, it will sail ill.[38]

Advocacy for population moderation can be found as early as the first generation of English humanists. In Thomas More's *Utopia*, for instance, the laws of Utopia stipulated that if 'the multitude throughout the whole island pass and exceed the due number, then they choose out of every city certain citizens, and build up a town under their own laws in the next land where the inhabitants have much waste and unoccupied ground'.[39] Thomas Starkey's *Dialogue Between Pole and Lupset* argued that 'if there be of people either too few or too many' the result would be 'miserable penury and wretched poverty', while a virtuous mean would produce a true commonwealth.[40] By the 1590s, given both the demographic reality of population expansion in England and the beginnings of English expansion into the New World, it is not surprising that the idea of population moderation linked the supposedly excessive population of England with

[38] *Aristotles Politiques*, pp. 356–7. For concern that London was not 'so great as populace', see John Stow, *A Survay of London* (London, 1598), p. 477. For important continental discussions translated into English, see Giovanni Botero, *A Treatise, Concerning the Causes of the Magnificencie and Greatnes of Cities*, trans. Robert Peterson (London, 1606), *passim* but esp. pp. 93–7; Jean Bodin, *The Six Bookes of a Common-Weale*, trans. Richard Knolles (London, 1606), pp. 640–1.

[39] St Thomas More, *A Fruteful, and Pleasaunt Worke of the Beste State of a Publyque Weale, and of the Newe Yle called Vtopia*, trans. Ralph Robinson (London, 1551), sig. I5v.

[40] Thomas Starkey, *A Dialogue between Pole and Lupset*, ed. Thomas Mayer (London, 1989), pp. 31–2. For related claims, see Armitage, *The Ideological Origins of the British Empire*, p. 50.

the supposedly deficient population of America. Perhaps the most overt early example comes from Edward Hayes and Christopher Carleill, who argued that in the so-called 'Northwest regions' of America

commodities are apparently known to be there, so as people only are wanting. And we in England are overburdened, and as it were pestered with people. If therefore many, yea 20 thousand of our spare people . . . were sent and employed into those countries there to inhabit . . . it should both ease the realm of our superfluous people and bring much wealth and happiness and honour unto the state.[41]

More surprising than the presence of this rhetoric is its obsession with issues of order and government. Let us look, for example, at Robert Gray's 1609 *Good Speed to Virginia*, where population pressure provided the crucial rationale for why so moderate a people as the English needed to leave their homes and colonise foreign lands. Gray wrote that a century earlier 'this kingdom was not so populous as it is now' and 'there was room enough in the land for every man, so that no man needed to encroach or enclose from another'. In that former state of sufficiency, empire would have been an excessive policy: 'Religion and piety taught us . . . rather to be content with our own than either politiquely or ambitiously to undertake uncouth enterprises unto which necessity did no way urge us.' Now, however, God had so increased the population in England that 'it behooves us to be both prudent and politic, and not to deride and reject good proffers of profitable and gainful expectation'. Indeed, the scriptural text for this sermon was Joshua 17:14, one of the most aggressive and expansionist Old Testament passages, where the Israelites told Joshua that they had not enough land because they had become 'a great people', and Joshua responded by ordering them to 'cast out the Canaanites'.[42]

Within Grey's rhetoric, moreover, were specific claims about overpopulation as excess in need of moderation in its governmental sense. As Aristotle had said, with increased population inevitably came civil disorder: 'There is nothing more dangerous to the estate of commonwealths than when the people do increase to a greater multitude and number than may justly parallel with the largeness of the place and country. For hereupon comes oppression and diverse kind of wrongs, mutinies, sedition, commotion and rebellion, scarcity, dearth, poverty and sundry sorts of calamities.' The multitudes of England, 'like too much blood in the body, do infect our country'. Overpopulation was a message from

[41] *NAW*, III, p. 164. See also pp. 31, 125 for other examples.
[42] Robert Gray, *A Good Speed to Virginia* (London, 1609), sigs. B1r, B2r–v.

God that England, like Israel, needed to expand for the 'disburdening and discharging of such unnecessary multitudes as pester a commonwealth'. This, in other words, was an extension into an imperial context of commonplace English arguments about the dangerous immoderation of the unbridled masses.[43]

The effect of this rhetoric was to link the two processes of civilising the Indians and governing the English poor. Grey complained bitterly of the idleness that led so many Englishmen to live like 'drones' and 'feed upon the fruits of other men's labours'. It was this idleness that prevented more of the English poor from emigrating to the colonies. Yet on the other side of the equation this was the same charge of idleness that Grey and other apologists for empire habitually made against the Indians, who lived off the vast American landscape without attempting to cultivate or improve it. Thus, when Grey linked the duty to colonise with the duty to civilise, his proposed cure for Indian incivility was the same moderation he applied to the 'intemperancy, incontinency and other luxurious and riotous courses' of the colonisers themselves:

It is not the nature of men, but the education of men, which make them barbarous and uncivil, and therefore change the education of men and you shall see that their nature will be greatly rectified and corrected. Seeing therefore men by nature so easily yield to discipline and government upon any reasonable show of bettering their fortunes, it is every man's duty to travel both by sea and land, and to venture either with his person or with his purse, to bring barbarous and savage people to a civil and Christian kind of government.[44]

Other supporters of the American plantations used similar arguments. The 1622 printed sermon *Virginia's God Be Thanked* congratulated the aldermen of London, 'who, seeing this city to be mightily increased, and fearing lest this overflowing multitude of inhabitants should like too much blood in the body infect the whole city with plague and poverty, have therefore devised in their great wisdoms a remedy for this malady, to wit, the transporting of their overflowing multitude into Virginia'.[45]

---

[43] *Ibid.*, sigs. B3v–C1r. One English imperialist even wrote in his commonplace book that the high levels of mortality from disease in the West Indies and the Chesapeake were helpful 'drains' for the overpopulation of England that would otherwise lead to rebellion: Nicholas Canny, 'The Origins of Empire: An Introduction', in Nicholas Canny (ed.), *The Origins of Empire* (Oxford, 1998), pp. 19–20.

[44] Gray, *A Good Speed to Virginia*, sigs. C1r, B1r and C2r. On the ubiquitous charge that Indian men were lazy and idle, see James Axtell, *Native and Newcomers: The Cultural Origins of North America* (Oxford, 2001), ch. 6. On the need to overcome the idleness of the English in order to create colonies, see Karen Kupperman, 'The Beehive as a Model for Colonial Design', in Karen Kupperman (ed.), *America in European Consciousness 1493–1750* (Chapel Hill, 1995).

[45] Patrick Copland, *Virginia's God Be Thanked* (London, 1622), p. 31.

Earlier in the plantation process, the reason for the colony's near-failure had been that these overflowing multitudes had not received proper discipline and hence became like Indians: 'Most of them at first, being the very scum of the land . . . neglected God's worship, lived in idleness, plotted conspiracies, resisted the government of superiors, and carried themselves dissolutely amongst the heathens.' Now, however, with the creation of proper discipline in the colony, the superfluous poor who had been a burden in England were 'through the good government there, and God's blessing upon the works [of] their hands, become men able to live of themselves in good sort and fashion'.[46] Once again, the dangers of deficient population and excess population were both answered by English government in America.

Of all the early Stuart texts encouraging empire, however, the most extensive and multifaceted call for population moderation was Richard Eburne's *Plaine Path-Way to Plantations* (1624), a long dialogue ostensibly (although surely not truly) addressed directly to the 'poorer and common sort' to convince them to migrate. From the first paragraph, Eburne lamented the misery of England 'by reason of the excessive multitude of people which therein at this present do swarm and superabound', and he suggested that 'God in his gracious providence' had provided colonisation as 'an infallible remedy'. The preface included some remarkably impolite language to convince readers to pack their bags and leave: 'Be not too much in love with that country wherein you were born . . . She accounts you a burden to her and encumbrance of her. You keep her down, you hurt her and make her poor and bare.'[47] England's population had been rising since Queen Elizabeth's reign, Eburne wrote, and 'unless it may again be reduced to that mediocrity at least, and there stand, it can be in no tolerable estate'.[48] On the opposite side of the equation, colonising the New World would also alleviate its deficiency in population:

For it was God's express commandment to Adam, Gen.1:28, that he should fill the earth and subdue it. By virtue of which charter, he and his have ever since had the privilege to spread themselves from place to place, and to have, hold, occupy and enjoy any region or country whatsoever which they should find . . . not pre-occupied by some other.

The goal of the English, Eburne wrote, was precisely to make 'No Land' into 'England'.[49]

---

[46] *Ibid.*, pp. 24 and 32.
[47] Eburne, *A Plaine Path-Way to Plantations*, sigs. A2r–v, B2v.       [48] *Ibid.*, p. 72.
[49] *Ibid.*, pp. 16–19. For the English representation of America as a 'nowhere' from *Utopia* onwards, see Knapp, *An Empire Nowhere*.

Within this rhetoric of population moderation, Eburne had complex arguments for how plantation would cure English social ills. For instance, one effect of rising population in England was 'the excessive high prices of all things to live by'; the remedy for inflation was thus 'the diminution of the people'.[50] The moderation of the population would also eliminate the great evil of idleness in England, since 'if the superfluous multitude of our land were removed' those left behind would 'need fall to work and leave idleness, because that multitude removed they should have none to do their work for them'.[51] Indeed, so convinced was Eburne of colonisation as a social remedy that he suggested money given for poor relief should instead go to plantations, and he was also one of the most vociferous early supporters of involuntary transportation for criminals and vagrants.[52]

Moreover, Eburne made a series of connections between the Indians and the English settlers. Like so many other early supporters of North American colonies, Eburne repeatedly described the Indians as 'tractable', willing to submit to English government, but similar submission was needed from the settlers themselves.[53] In England, 'unspeakable idleness' had 'corrupted and in manner effeminated our people generally'. Whereas in the classical tradition effeminacy had usually been seen as a product of empire, here colonies were the solution, providing government to turn vagrants into well-ordered subjects. In England, the government had made 'many good statutes and provisions for the beating down of drunkenness, for setting the poor and idle people to work', but these had failed because they 'strike at the boughs, but not at the roots'.[54] Colonies were the solution that struck at the root, and it was thus essential that in the colonies the poor had leaders of 'better breeding and experience' to rule over them: 'Nature herself teaching the Amazonian bees not to swarm without their Lady, and the cranes not to fly without their leader; [this] may easily teach us that we shall transgress the very order of nature if we shall make such a removal without the conduct of such men, as for their place and power, birth and breed, may be fit to order and rule, to support and settle the rest.'[55]

---

[50] Eburne, *A Plaine Path-Way to Plantations*, pp. 9–10.
[51] *Ibid.*, p. 13.    [52] *Ibid.*, pp. 48 and 59.
[53] *Ibid.*, pp. 28 and 32. See Karen Kupperman, *Settling with the Indians: The Meeting of English and Indian Cultures in America, 1580–1640* (Totowa, N.J., 1980), ch. 7.
[54] Eburne, *A Plaine Path-Way to Plantations*, pp. 13–14.
[55] *Ibid.*, pp. 68, 115. For a slightly unusual example of the same trope, see Thomas Scott, *Vox Populi, or Newes from Spayne* (London, 1620), sig. B4r–v, where the evil Spanish ambassador laments that Virginia and the Bermudas 'serve for drains to unload their [England's] populous state, which else would overflow its own banks by continuance of peace, and turn head upon itself or make a body fit for any rebellion'.

All of this suggests that virtuous moderation at home was closely linked, through the rhetoric of population, to the creation of an empire of moderation abroad. In 1978, Nicholas Canny argued in a classic essay that draconian discipline was instituted in the Virginia and Ulster plantations because 'most of those who ventured overseas came from the poorest elements of society, and were considered by their superiors to be incapable of self-discipline, to be barely civilised, and certainly not suitable instruments for transmitting civilisation to others'.[56] This is undoubtedly true, but the evidence here suggests that this discipline may have been more deeply inscribed in the colonial project: colonies were imagined as ideal sites for moderation of the English as well as the Indians, and strong government was thus an integral part of English imperialism rather than its unexpected outcome. It was as early as 1610, after all, that William Crashaw described how 'many of the vulgar and viler sort' who went to Virginia 'only for ease and idleness, for profit and pleasure', found instead a land where, in good Christian fashion, 'they must labour or else not eat, and be tied within the bounds of sharp laws and severe discipline'.[57] Likewise, the *True Declaration of the Estate of the Colonie in Virginia* (1610) suggested that the sloth of Englishmen in Virginia was alleviated by 'Sir Thomas Gates his experiment: he professeth that in a fortnight's space he recovered the health of most of them by moderate labour, whose sickness was bred in them by intemperate idleness'.[58] A dozen years later, John Donne put it best, as was his wont: 'If the whole country were but such a Bridewell, to force idle persons to work, it had a good use.'[59]

## Bridling Spain

Another important sense in which English expansion might paradoxically constitute moderation was built into the logic of imperial competition: the English empire was an empire of moderation because, as Richard Hakluyt wrote in 1584, it was 'a great bridle to the Indies of the king of

---

[56] Nicholas Canny, 'The Permissive Frontier: The Problem of Social Control in English Settlements in Ireland and Virginia 1550–1650', in K. R. Andrews, N. P. Canny and P. E. H. Hair (eds.), *The Westward Enterprise: English Activities in Ireland, the Atlantic, and America 1480–1650* (Liverpool, 1978), p. 19.

[57] Crashaw, *A Sermon Preached*, sig. F2r.

[58] *A True Declaration of the Estate of the Colonie in Virginia* (London, 1610), p. 33. This text is discussed in John Gillies, 'Shakespeare's Virginian Masque', *English Literary History* 53, no. 4 (Winter 1986), pp. 673–707, at pp. 679–80.

[59] John Donne, *A Sermon upon the Eighth Verse of the First Chapter of the Acts of the Apostles* (London, 1624), pp. 21–2.

Spain'.[60] This version of moderation was concerned to restrain Spanish and Catholic tyranny and instead offer good government to the New World. But it was also, at a very deep level, about economics: Spanish tyranny was the result of greed, epitomised by the gold and silver mines of the Spanish Empire, while English moderation was about trade, replacing extraction with balanced exchange.

The need to bridle Spain was deeply rooted in the anti-Spanish prejudices of late Elizabethan and early Stuart England. Works by that most famous critic of Spanish imperialism, Bartolomé de las Casas, were first translated into English in 1583 and thereafter excerpted in countless English texts.[61] But more broadly, attacks on the Spanish Empire, sometimes subtle and sometimes brimming with bile, permeated almost every discussion of English colonisation. Samuel Purchas, for instance, wrote that the first people whom Spaniards met in the Caribbean assumed that the Spanish invaders were cannibals, and 'such have they since proved, in effect'. North America, in contrast to the Caribbean, was 'virgin soil not yet polluted with Spaniards' lust'.[62] Robert Gray wrote, 'Far be it from the nature of the English to exercise any bloody cruelty among these people [the Indians]. Far be it from the hearts of the English to give them occasion that the holy name of God should be dishonoured among the infidels.'[63] Robert Johnson wrote that English 'dominions shall be enlarged . . . not by storms of raging cruelties (as West India was conquered) with rapier's point and musket shot murdering so many millions of naked Indians, as their stories do relate, but by fair and loving means, suiting to our English natures'.[64]

Some of the clearest descriptions of the excesses of Spanish imperialism come from letters concerning the treatment of English prisoners captured in 1607 by Spanish ships in the Caribbean. Henry Challons, for instance, described the 'extremities they use with us, as I conceive,

---

[60] Richard Hakluyt, *A Discourse Concerning Western Planting*, ed. Charles Deane (Cambridge, Mass., 1877), p. 45.

[61] William Maltby, *The Black Legend in England: The Development of Anti-Spanish Sentiment, 1558–1660* (Durham, N.C., 1971), ch. 2. The importance of Las Casas in England has been disputed in Alfred Cave, 'Canaanites in a Promised Land: The American Indians and the Providential Theory of Empire', *American Indian Quarterly* 12, no. 4 (Fall 1988), pp. 277–97.

[62] Purchas, *Purchas His Pilgrimage*, pp. 613 and 631. Anti-Spanish sentiment in English imperial texts differed depending upon the theological complexion of the writer and shifted significantly through the Jacobean period as the king's attempted rapprochement with Spain ebbed and flowed. On Purchas's rhetoric in this regard, see Armitage, *The Ideological Origins of the British Empire*, pp. 87–9.

[63] Gray, *A Good Speed to Virginia*, sig. C2v.

[64] Robert Johnson, *Nova Britannia: Offering Most Excellent Fruites by Planting in Virginia* (London, 1609), sig. C2v.

to enforce our men to their religion', including allegedly having English-men's 'noses, ears and privy members cut off'. Less pornographic but more revealing was a letter from Sir Charles Cornwallis to the Earl of Salisbury recounting his conversation with the president of the Spanish Council of the Indies. The Spaniard claimed that, despite his desire to comply with English demands that prisoners be released unharmed, control of the Indies was so important that 'in coercions and punishment, to restrain access to those countries, he had an inclination rather to cruelty than clemency'. Cornwallis, in response, 'much marveled that so wise a nation' would refuse to pursue 'some mean way, agreeable with their safety and honour, to have their pursuit of the absolute dominion and possession of the Islands united, whereby they seem to add so inestimable a power to their already overgrown greatness'.[65]

This Spanish unwillingness to accept a 'mean way' in empire was also reflected metaphorically in their love of intemperate heat, in contrast to the English, who, as we have seen, were naturally suited to environmental moderation. Edward Hayes and Christopher Carleill, for example, drew an axis of Roman Catholic excess through southern Europe: 'The heat of summer in Italy and all places else of Europe under 40 degrees (being not hindered by accidental causes) is unto our bodies very offensive, which cannot prosper in dry and scalding heats, more natural to the Spaniard than us.'[66] Such assumptions about the relationship between intemperate climates and intemperate subjects also underwrote William Crashaw's offhanded sleight in 1610 that Virginia was 'not so hot as Spain'.[67]

A more common framework for thinking about Spanish excess was their excessive government of the Native Americans. Accusations of Spanish 'tyranny' over the Indians always had notions of excess embedded in them, but sometimes this was made explicit, as in Hayes's and Carleill's claim that the 'silly people' of the New World had never attacked any European settlement except 'amongst the Spaniards, whose tyranny hath exceeded towards them'.[68] In a backhanded attack on the Spanish, Richard Whitbourne argued that the natives of Newfoundland were 'ingenuous, and apt by discrete and moderate governments to be brought to obedience'.[69] It was this framework of Spanish excess contrasted with English moderation that led Carleill to argue in 1583 that the natives would inevitably welcome English imperialism, since America was

---

[65] *NAW*, III, p. 414 for Challons's letter and pp. 415–16 for Cornwallis's letter.
[66] *Ibid.*, pp. 158–9 and p. 163.
[67] Crashaw, *A Sermon Preached*, sig. E1v.    [68] *NAW*, III, p. 167.
[69] Whitbourne, *A Discourse and Discovery of New-Found-Land*, sig. B1v.

'inhabited with savage people of a middle and tractable disposition'.[70] Perhaps the most explicit claim that moderation would succeed with the Indians where Spanish excess had failed comes from the pen of Samuel Purchas, describing the good-cop/bad-cop routine of the Virginia settlers John Smith and Christopher Newport:

[Smith and Newport] may by their examples teach the just course to be taken with such: the one breeding awe and dread, without Spanish or panic terror, the other disgraced in seeking to grace with offices of humanity those which are graceless. Neither doth it become us to use savages with savageness, nor yet with too humane usage, but in a middle path (*medio tutissimus ibis*) to go and do so that they may admire and fear us, as those whom God, religion, civility and art have made so far superior.[71]

But the most significant contrast between English moderation and Spanish excess was economic: Spain's excessive greed for silver and gold contrasted with the moderate sufficiency of English plantation. This was, at one level, a naked instance of sour grapes, since the English hoped and expected to find precious metals; Martin Frobisher's 1578 expedition, for instance, brought 148 skilled miners to the American arctic.[72] Moreover, since the promotional literature of English colonialism was largely aimed at investors, claiming that the English empire was not about riches but moderation sometimes required tortured casuistical contortions, a process that John Gillies has identified as the problem of balancing 'temperance' and 'fruitfulness'.[73] In an August 1585 letter to Francis Walsingham, for instance, Ralph Lane wrote that Virginia would yield more riches than 'all the kingdoms and states of Christendom their commodities joined in one together', but then in the very same letter he employed the language of economic moderation to explain why, despite these riches, his men were nearly starving: 'And for mine own part [I] do find myself better contented to live with fish for my daily food, and water for my daily drink, in the prosecution of such one action, than out of the same to live in the greatest plenty that the court could give me.'[74] Paradigmatic of this shiftiness was the tortured rhetoric of Sir Walter Raleigh, justifying his failed get-rich-quick scheme in Guiana as an effort to 'recover but the moderation of excess, and the least taste of the greatest plenty formerly possessed'.[75]

---

[70] *NAW*, III, p. 33. Here 'middle' may be *sic* for 'mild', as it appears elsewhere in closely related texts.
[71] Cited in Knapp, *An Empire Nowhere*, p. 2.     [72] Chaplin, *Subject Matter*, pp. 47–8.
[73] Gillies, 'Shakespeare's Virginian Masque'.     [74] *NAW*, III, p. 289.
[75] Walter Raleigh, *The Discouerie of the Large, Rich, and Bevvtiful Empire of Guiana* (London, 1596), sigs. A2v–A3r. Jeffrey Knapp has described this attitude as 'English otherworldliness', an allegedly disinterested interest, the early modern equivalent of what J. R.

The paradox here was that America was *potentially* rich, but unlike the Spanish, who extracted riches from the land without restraint, the English had to patiently manure, plant and cultivate the land to access its riches. John Smith described how the Spaniards in America had lived idly off the labour of conquered peoples, while by contrast the industrious English created a colony from scratch.[76] This was explained at length by William Wood in his 1634 *New Englands Prospect*, where he clarified that even though no Englishmen had got very rich in America, likewise none were very poor: 'They are well contented, and look not so much at abundance as a competency.'[77] This discourse has been described succinctly by John Gillies: 'Fruitfulness is linked to temperance by the necessity of labour.'[78] This issue was also at the heart of Richard Barckley's analogy, quoted above, between temperate climate and economic moderation. For Barckley, the extreme heat of the burning zone led kings and peoples to 'ambitious desire to enlarge their dominion or possessions . . . and therefore one calleth *imperium, honestissimam sepulturam*' – a neat description of Spanish excess and the graveyard of the Spanish Empire. The temperate zone, by contrast, was associated with a 'sufficiency of riches'.[79]

This trope played upon commonplace associations of New World gold with Old World greed. John Lyly's *Midas* (1592), written soon after the failure of the Spanish Armada, depicted Phillip II as a Midas obsessed with gold, belatedly repenting his immoderation in both greed and government: 'If I be rid of this intolerable disease of gold, I will next shake off that untemperate desire of government, and measure my territories, not by the greatness of my mind, but the right of my succession.'[80] The 1597 edition of William Warner's *Albions England* associated immoderate Spanish greed with misguided conquest: 'But godhood none in Indian gold, and pope-bulled hopes shall miss / Nor Macedonian Phillip's son Castillian Phillip is / But one who, whilst he wars for ours, hath lost even part of his'.[81] Richard Barnfield's *The Encomion of Lady Pecunia: or the Praise of Money* (1598), a satire modelled on Erasmus's *Praise*

---

Seeley would later call conquering half the world 'in a fit of absence of mind': Knapp, *An Empire Nowhere*, p. 193 and *passim*.

[76] John Smith, *The Generall Historie of Virginia, New-England, and the Summer Isles* (London, 1624), p. 82.

[77] Wood, *New Englands Prospect*, p. 48. On this issue see Daniel Vickers, 'Competency and Competition: Economic Culture in Early America', *WMQ* 3rd series, 47, no. 1 (January 1990), pp. 3–29. Vickers's understanding of 'competency' in early modern England incorrectly assumes that it required landed independence.

[78] Gillies, 'Shakespeare's Virginian Masque', p. 681.

[79] Barckley, *A Discourse of the Felicitie of Man*, pp. 488–9.

[80] John Lyly, *Midas* (London, 1592), sig. C2v.

[81] William Warner, *Albions England a Continued Historie of the Same Kingdome* (London, 1597), p. 226.

*of Folly*, called his text a song of 'fair Pecunia / The famous queen of rich America', and stressed that in money, as in all things, 'the mean is best':

> The juice of grapes, which is a sovereign thing
> To cheer the heart, and to revive the spirits;
> Being used immoderately (in surfeiting)
> Rather dispraise, than commendation merits:
> Even so Pecunia, as she is used;
> Good of her self, but bad if once abused.[82]

The golden mean, in these texts, was not made of gold at all.[83]

Edward Hayes and Christopher Carleill skillfully wove together strands of geographic, anti-Spanish and economic moderation in their 1590s 'Discourse concerning a voyage intended for the planting of Christian religion and people in the Northwest regions of America'. They argued against those who believed that 'no remote land newly to be planted is worthy regard or estimation unless the same be rich in gold and silver mines'. Hayes and Carleill responded:

> We have hope also of silver mines, and of other metals, assurance. Nevertheless gold and silver mines are found most plentiful in hot and untemperate regions. But seeing that other gross (yet needful) commodities, which our intended countries of new habitation do yield abundantly, and whereof those countries stand in need which possess the fountains of treasure: shall purchase unto us gold and silver, dwelling under temperate and wholesome climates. Then how much better shall it be for us there to possess gold and silver in health of body and delight, than for greedy desire to possess the mines, to deprive ourselves of all health and delight by dwelling in countries within the burning zones, where the heat or air shall be unto our complexions intemperate and contagious. Nature hath framed the Spanish apt to such places, who prosper in dry and burning habitations. But in us she abhorreth such.[84]

If Spanish greed and economic excess were associated with tyranny and cruel treatment of the Indians, so too was English economic moderation associated with beneficent treatment of the Indians and good government. This was accomplished through the economic language of balanced exchange: while the Spanish stole from the Indians, the English

---

[82] Richard Barnfield, *The Encomion of Lady Pecunia: or the Praise of Money* (London, 1598), sigs. A4r–v, C3v.

[83] On the deep scepticism of excessive profit among humanist-influenced imperialists, see Fitzmaurice, *Humanism and America*, ch. 2. He also notes in ch. 3 that English critics of imperialism specifically worried about the effeminising effects of American luxury.

[84] NAW, III, p. 163. Joyce Chaplin cites an anonymous manuscript advice on empire: 'The Spaniards may serve us for an example not to seek for mines of gold and silver' because 'the climate for that country where the gold is excessive is an enemy both to man and good husbandry'. Chaplin, *Subject Matter*, p. 152.

paid a just price.[85] So, for instance, in Walter Raleigh's account of his exploration in Guiana, he 'suffered not any man to take from any of the nations so much as a *pina* or a potato root without giving them content-ment . . . which course, so contrary to the Spaniards (who tyrannise over them in all things) drew them to admire her Majesty, whose commandment I told them it was, and also wonderfully to honour our nation'.[86] It was the essence of early modern economic theory – established by Aristotle, mediated by Thomas Aquinas and other scholastic theologians – that what made an exchange 'just' was that the two parties each benefited by removing a superfluity and filling a scarcity. If one party had too much wool but not enough wine, and the other party had too much wine but not enough wool, then an exchange between them was just; money was simply a medium that allowed for seemingly incommensurate objects of exchange to be valued relative to one another.[87] Most often in the case of the Indians and the English, however, the proposed rationale of economic balance was a specific one: the Indians had excess land but lacked faith and civility, while the English had faith and civility to spare but not enough land. Thus, out of an intellectual framework constructed to bridle the excess and tyranny of the King of Spain, there emerged a complex rationale for English expropriation of Indian land.

As early as 1583, the poet John Chester wrote in a preface to an account of Sir Humphrey Gilbert's voyages:

> The journey known, the passage quickly run
> The land full rich, the people easily won.
> Whose gains shall be the knowledge of our faith
> And ours such riches as the country hath.[88]

Within the account itself, George Peckham (who, incidentally, was a Roman Catholic) defended the justice of this exchange: 'The savages shall hereby have just cause to bless the hour when this enterprise was undertaken. First and chiefly, in respect of the most happy and gladsome tidings of the most gracious gospel of our savior Jesus Christ . . . And in respect

---

[85] This notion of payment was utterly inconsistent with the idea of *vacuum domicilium*. For a discussion of this ideological contradiction and the English practice of purchasing lands with cash, see Francis Jennings, *The Invasion of America: Indians, Colonialism, and the Cant of Conquest* (Chapel Hill, 1975), ch. 8; Fitzmaurice, *Humanism and America*, ch. 5.

[86] Raleigh, *The Discouerie of the Large, Rich, and Bevvtiful Empire of Guiana*, p. 52.

[87] See Kaye, *Economy and Nature*; Diana Wood, *Medieval Economic Thought* (Cambridge, 2002); Norman Jones, *God and the Moneylenders: Usury and the Law in Early Modern England* (Oxford, 1989); Andrea Finkelstein, *Harmony and the Balance: An Intellectual History of Seventeenth-Century English Economic Thought* (Ann Arbor, 2000).

[88] *NAW*, III, p. 37. See the discussion of this and similar sources in Knapp, *An Empire Nowhere*, pp. 75–7.

of all the commodities that they can yield us (were they many more) that they should but receive this only benefit of Christianity, they were more than fully recompensed.'[89] By the early seventeenth century these arguments had become commonplace. For example, the court preacher Daniel Price described a balanced exchange in 1609: 'You will obtain their best commodities, they will obtain the saving of their souls.'[90] An official publication of the Council of Virginia, called *A True and Sincere Declaration of the Purpose and Ends of the Plantation Begun in Virginia* (1610), claimed that '[we] do buy of them the pearls of the earth, and sell to them the pearls of heaven'.[91] In John Cotton's farewell sermon before leaving for New England, he reminded English colonists to 'offend not the poor natives, but as you partake in their land, so make them partakers of your precious faith. As you reap the temporals, so feed them with your spirituals.'[92]

A particularly blunt example of this rhetoric was William Crashaw's 1609 sermon in London for the new governor of Virginia. He insisted that, as a moral imperative, 'we will take nothing from the savages by power nor pillage, by craft nor violence, neither goods, lands, nor liberty, much less life (as some of other Christian nations have done, to the dishonour of religion)'. Crashaw's conclusion, however, was not that the English should not colonise America, but rather that 'we will take from them only that they may spare us: first, their superfluous land, secondly their superfluous commodities'. In other words,

We will exchange with them for that which they may spare and we do need; and they shall have that which we may spare and they do much more need. But what may they spare? First, land and room for us to plant in, their country being not replenished in many degrees . . . But what will we give them? First, we will give them such things as they greatly desire and do hold sufficient recompense for any of the foresaid commodities we take of them. But we hold it not so, and therefore out of our humanity and conscience we will give them more, namely such things as they want and need, and are infinitely more excellent than all we take from them, and that is 1. Civility for their bodies, 2. Christianity for their souls. The first to make them men, the second, happy men.[93]

This construction was made equally explicit in the 1609 tract *Nova Britannia*, which described the 'mutual interchange and commerce' between the English and the Indians:

---

[89] *NAW*, III, pp. 53–4.
[90] Richard Price, *Sauls Prohibition Staide* (London, 1609), sig. F3r.
[91] Cited in Knapp, *An Empire Nowhere*, p. 76. As Knapp notes, p. 281, this discourse of exchange was so ubiquitous that it was condemned and satirised by anti-materialists who saw English imperialism as becoming dangerously greedy and debased.
[92] Cotton, *God's Promise to His Plantation*, p. 19.
[93] Crashaw, *A Sermon Preached*, sigs. D3v–D4r.

To our great expense and charge, we make adventures to impart our divine riches to their inestimable gain, and to cover their naked misery with civil use of food and clothing, and to train them by gentle means to those manual arts and skills, which they so much affect and do admire to see in us. So in lieu of this we require nothing at their hands but a quiet residence to us and ours, that by our own labour and toil we may work this good into them and recompense our own adventures, costs and travels.[94]

Yet, while *Nova Britannia* was unremarkable in describing the exchange of wealth for religion and civility, it was unusually explicit in admitting and even celebrating the coercive aspect of that exchange; the commodities traded might be of comparable value, but the choice whether to trade was not left to the ignorant Indians. 'As for supplanting the savages', the author wrote, 'we have no such intent. Our intrusion into their possessions shall tend to their great good, and no way to their hurt, unless as unbridled beasts they procure it themselves.' The bridle, of course, was the emblem of moderation, which the Indians would receive either voluntarily by submitting to English law or involuntarily by submitting to English armies: 'God hath reserved in this last age of the world an infinite number of those lost and scattered sheep to be won and recovered by our means. Of whom so many as obstinately refuse to unite themselves unto us, or shall malign or disturb our plantation, our chattel, or whatsoever belonging to us, they shall be held and reputed recusant, withstanding their own good, and shall be dealt with as enemies of the commonwealth of their country.'[95]

## Religion, civility and moderation

This reference to Indian 'recusants' as 'enemies of the commonwealth of their country' brings us to the final sense in which English imperialists sought an empire of moderation: the English empire as government in a formal sense, reducing subjects to obedience and the rule of law. The English were notoriously uninterested in actually governing native populations: theirs was an empire over land not people, almost always establishing miniature commonwealths of English people abroad, displacing natives rather than absorbing or administering their polities.[96] I want to suggest, then, that the argument for civility was significant not only or primarily as an argument for moderating Indian lawlessness but also as an argument for bridling other sorts of 'recusants': religious extremists. As we saw in Part II, debates over the moderation of English religion

[94] Johnson, *Nova Britannia*, sigs. C1v–C2r.    [95] *Ibid.*, sigs. C1r and C2r.
[96] For the most recent and nuanced treatment of this issue, see J. H. Elliott, *Empires of the Atlantic World: Britain and Spain in America, 1492–1830* (New Haven, 2006).

were largely debates over governance. As those debates were transferred to an imperial setting, they were framed around the capacity of England's new colonies abroad to enforce religious moderation upon their populations, with the figure of the Indian now standing in as a cipher or foil against which religious extremism and rejection of government could be measured.

The need to 'civilise' the Indians was, of course, central to English understandings of empire, but 'civilise' had a very specific early modern meaning: to subject to civil authority. Thus one minister wrote in 1609, 'It is every man's duty . . . to bring the barbarous and savage people to a civil and Christian kind of government.'[97] Another writer suggested that the Indians were uncivilised precisely because their 'kings . . . have no laws to command by, nor have they any annual revenues'.[98] Yet another wrote that the Indians 'range and wander up and down the country without any law or government, being led only by their own lusts and sensuality'.[99] This was the derivation of the word 'civil' – pertaining to citizens – and many authors noted how thankful they still were to the Roman Empire and Julius Caesar's legions for having brought 'civility' to England.[100] This perception that Indians lacked settled government was, of course, a wilful suppression of the evidence, and Francis Jennings has noted succinctly, 'Europeans' pronouncements that Indians had no government were contradicted by their practice of dealing with Indian chiefs through the protocol of diplomacy with sovereign states.'[101]

Quite apart from England's notoriously patchy campaign to civilise the Indians, however, from the 1580s onwards it was a significant theme of imperial writings that the English empire would create a civil space for the government of religion, with puritans and papists mapped onto Indian incivility. For example, in 1610 William Crashaw described how to 'make the name of Christ honourable, not hateful' to the Indians:

Suffer no papists. Let them not nestle there, nay let the name of the pope for [sic] popery never be heard of in Virginia. Take heed of Atheists, the devil's champions, and if thou discover any, make them exemplary. And if I may be so bold as to advise, make Atheism and other blasphemy capital, and let that be the first law made in Virginia. Suffer no Brownists, nor factious separatists; let them

[97] Gray, *A Good Speed to Virginia*, sig. C2r.     [98] Wood, *New Englands Prospect*, p. 79.
[99] Gray, *A Good Speed to Virginia*, sigs. C2v–C4r.
[100] Johnson, *Nova Britannia*, sig. C2r; Crashaw, *A Sermon Preached*, sig. C4v. On the common conceit that ancient Britons were similar to modern Indians, see David Armitage, 'The New World and British Historical Thought', in Karen Kupperman (ed.), *America in European Consciousness 1493–1750* (Chapel Hill, 1995).
[101] Jennings, *The Invasion of America*, p. 111. See also Kupperman, *Settling with the Indians*, ch. 3.

keep their conventicles elsewhere. Let them go and convert some other heathen, and let us see if they can constitute such churches really, the ideas whereof they have fancied in their brains.[102]

The reason for this emphasis on Church of England loyalists as colonists was that civility was a prerequisite for true religion. As David Armitage has noted in his discussion of Richard Hakluyt's classicism, 'Civilization, defined in Ciceronian terms as the life of the citizen, was . . . prior to, and indispensable for, Christian salvation.'[103] Thus the conversion of the Indians to Christianity could only be attempted 'after they first be made civil men'. Or, as Crashaw put it elsewhere, the natives were inclinable 'first to civility, and so to religion'.[104]

Many writers particularly based their thinking about imperial moderation on the conformist rhetoric of anti-puritanism. As early as 1584, Richard Hakluyt had embedded this framework in his 'A Discourse Concerning Western Planting', arguing that, if Queen Elizabeth pursued an overseas empire,

> many inconveniences and strifes amongst ourselves at home in matters of ceremonies shall be ended. For those of the clergy which by reason of idleness here at home are now always coining of new opinions, having by this voyage to set themselves on work in reducing the savages to the chief principles of our faith, will become less contentious and be contented with the truth in religion already established by authority.[105]

There was no shortage of imperial apologists who insisted that, as much as America needed godly colonists, it also needed bishops and ecclesiastical judges 'lest faction and confusion, like tares among the wheat, grow faster there than religion, order and peace of the Church'.[106] One good example is a sermon entitled *Sauls Prohibition Staide*, preached at Paul's Cross by a chaplain to Prince Henry in May 1609 and printed soon thereafter. The text of the sermon was Acts 9:4, 'Saul, Saul, why persecutest thou me?' and the preacher, Daniel Price, used the occasion to suggest how to do God's work without becoming a Pharisee like Saul. The answer, Price suggested, was to imitate God in the gentleness of his rebuke: 'Speak thou unto thine enemy mildly without choler, moderately without fervor, as thy master here did, "Saul, Saul, why persecutest thou me?"' The goal of such moderation was the conversion of sinners, while zeal leads only to persecution. Of course, some zeal was necessary, but too much was deeply dangerous:

---

[102] Crashaw, *A Sermon Preached*, sig. L1r.
[103] Armitage, *The Ideological Origins of the British Empire*, p. 76.
[104] Crashaw, *A Sermon Preached*, sigs. K1v and C3v.
[105] Hakluyt, *A Discourse*, p. 12.     [106] Eburne, *A Plaine Path-Way to Plantations*, p. 69.

Zeal must stir up discretion, discretion must direct zeal. As the hope of a Christian, so the zeal of a Christian is as Susanna between two adulterers, as virtue between two extremes, as innocency between two tyrants, Hercules between two serpents, the grain between two millstones. Blind ignorance on the one side, proud insolence on the other side, a blind zeal, a proud zeal, the one superstitious, the other supercilious... The doctrine hence, is that every Christian let moderation govern the stern of his violent opinion, or else his zeal is abominable before God.[107]

Price equated the ignorance and superstition with Catholicism, while insolence and superciliousness he equated with puritanism. Most interestingly, in a stark inversion of puritan claims to oppose excessive religious persecution, puritans were here accused of being persecutors like Saul because 'you have been so zealous that you could have eaten up bishoprics and ecclesiastical endowments, and in zeal have persecuted our reverend fathers'.[108] But of particular interest is how this anti-puritanism was deftly converted, in the final six pages of the text, into a piece of imperial propaganda. Price located persecution particularly in those who 'have injuriously vilified and traduced a great part of the glory of God... I mean in the plantation of Virginia'. These persecutors of the Virginia project, especially the insolent puritans, set themselves up against the laws of the Church and state, most notably the Virginia project 'countenanced by our gracious king, consulted on by the oracles of the Council, adventured in by our wisest and greatest nobles'.[109]

Once puritans found themselves actually governing vast chunks of New England, however, they commonly appropriated this rationale of civilised moderation for themselves.[110] The clearest example comes from the so-called Antinomian Controversy of 1636–8, the first great intra-puritan controversy in New England and the first conflict to disturb the newly chartered government of Massachusetts Bay. The opening sentence of Governor John Winthrop's defence of his government's proceedings, *A Short Story of the Rise, Reign and Ruin of the Antinomians, Familists & Libertines, that Infected the Churches of New-England* (1644), stressed that

---

[107] Price, *Sauls Prohibition Staide*, sigs. C2v and D2v–D3r. Similar arguments are made on sigs. D3v–D4r.

[108] *Ibid.*, sigs. D4v and F2r.    [109] *Ibid.*, sigs. F2v–F3r.

[110] This was not altogether original to New England, which was a late and relatively insignificant province on the American scene. On the broader history of puritan appropriations of colonial ideals of governance and order, see Karen Kupperman, 'Errand to the Indies: Puritan Colonization from Providence Island through the Western Design', *WMQ* 45, no. 1 (January 1988), pp. 70–99. See also Stephen Foster, *Their Solitary Way: The Puritan Social Ethic in the First Century of Settlement in New England* (New Haven, 1971); T. H. Breen, *The Character of the Good Ruler: A Study of Puritan Political Ideas in New England, 1630–1730* (New Haven, 1970).

this controversy was singular because it represented a challenge not just to puritan theology but to puritan government:

> After we had escaped the cruel hands of the persecuting prelates, and the dangers at sea, and had prettily well outgrown our wilderness troubles in our first plantings in New England, and when our commonwealth began to be founded and our churches sweetly settled in peace... our wise God... sent a new storm after us, which proved the sorest trial that ever befell us since we left our native soil.[111]

At a doctrinal level, the controversy was principally over the issue of free grace: the question of whether God might save people purely of his own free will, without any human participation, and hence whether the whole puritan emphasis on the cycle of law, sin, despair, faith and regeneration was simply a new version of Jewish legalism or Catholic works theology.[112] At a political level, however, the controversy was about considerably more: the question of whether a commonwealth founded on the puritan ideals of self-government described in Chapter 4 was genuinely capable of moderating its excesses and bridling sin, or whether it was really no more than anarchy as its critics had claimed. As such, much of the public response to the antinomians by Winthrop and his allies was framed around the idea that New England government was government indeed, bridling the (literally) lawless antinomians. The result was a series of texts that rhetorically identified Anne Hutchinson, John Wheelwright and their followers as uncivil, part of the wilderness and partaking of Indian lawlessness, reduced to moderation by the strong hand of puritan government.

Because the leaders of puritan New England were so concerned not to be seen as persecuting the antinomians for their religion, they stressed that the civil trials of Anne Hutchinson and her colleagues were not for conscience but for sedition. The awkward difficulty with this strategy, however, was that the antinomians had done nothing overtly seditious. As such, prosecutors went to considerable (and, coming from at least semi-separatist puritans, ironic) lengths to show that their doctrinal errors led to contempt of authority, which inevitably led to the collapse

---

[111] David Hall (ed.), *The Antinomian Controversy, 1636–1638: A Documentary History*, 2nd edn (Durham, N.C., 1990), p. 201.

[112] Michael Winship, *Making Heretics: Militant Protestantism and Free Grace in Massachusetts, 1636–1641* (Princeton, 2002). For similar issues at the same time in England, see David Como, *Blown by the Spirit: Puritanism and the Emergence of an Antinomian Underground in Pre-Civil-War England* (Stanford, 2004). The term 'antinomian' means 'against the law', and while Winship argues persuasively that the theological issue of freedom from the moral law was not the essence of the controversy, nonetheless 'lawlessness' proved a potent weapon for puritan authorities to link the doctrinal and governmental aspects of the dispute.

of government.[113] So, for instance, in a rich passage of his *A Short Story* Withrop described how antinomianism literally undermined law, substituting populist anarchy for moderation:

The court declare Mr. Wheelwright guilty, they proclaim him innocent; the court judged his speech to be false and seditious, they affirmed it to be the truth of Christ . . . Further, in pretending their moderation, they put arguments in the people's minds to invite them to violence, by bringing the example of Peter drawing his sword, wherein they blamed not his fact but his rashness, and that of the people rescuing Jonathan, which to make the more effectual they say that it was not seditious.[114]

The leadership of a woman also provided an obvious target for accusations of immoderation. According to John Wilson, 'The misgovernment of this woman's tongue hath been a great cause of this disorder.'[115] According to Hugh Peters, Hutchinson 'was a woman not only difficult in her opinions, but also of an intemperate spirit'.[116] According to John Cotton, Hutchinson's opinions 'set an open door to all epicurism and libertinism'.[117]

It was in this sense that the antinomians were represented as part of the New England wilderness, brethren of the uncivil Indians rather than the civil English. A central exhibit in Winthrop's case that antinomians undermined civil government, for instance, was that after antinomianism infected the Church of Boston, they failed to send any members 'in the late expedition against the Pequots'.[118] John Cotton, combining traditional slanders against Anabaptists with more recent stereotypes of Native Americans, told Anne Hutchinson that her views of the mortality of the soul and the resurrection of the dead could not help but lead to 'that filthy sin of the community of women, and promiscuous and filthy coming together of men and women without distinction or relation of marriage'.[119] Perhaps the most striking piece of evidence is Winthrop's famous denunciation of Anne Hutchinson at the denouement of his *A Short Story*: 'This American Jesabel kept her strength and reputation, even among the people of God, till the hand of civil justice laid hold on her, and then she began evidently to decline.'[120] Here the essence of uncontrolled feminine disorder was quintessentially 'American' – a term English settlers of Winthrop's generation did not use to refer to themselves – until the law reduced her to civility.

The result was a series of blunt arguments by Winthrop and his allies that puritan self-government was not the same as licentious liberty, and

---

[113] Hall (ed.), *The Antinomian Controversy*, pp. 293–5, 299.    [114] *Ibid.*, p. 260.
[115] *Ibid.*, p. 384.    [116] *Ibid.*, p. 320.    [117] *Ibid.*, p. 372.
[118] *Ibid.*, pp. 253–4.    [119] *Ibid.*, pp. 371–2.    [120] *Ibid.*, p. 310.

that the government could and would intervene to civilise Anne Hutchinson and the antinomians. For instance, if ever there were concern that puritan demands for liberty of conscience implied broad religious toleration, Winthrop put a stop to it with a blunt exchange at the beginning of Hutchinson's civil trial: when Hutchinson claimed that her actions were 'matter of conscience', Winthrop responded, 'Your conscience you must keep or it must be kept for you.'[121] Likewise, when John Wheelwright attempted to appeal his conviction back to England, his appeal was denied on the grounds that the New England court had full jurisdiction by royal grant, and if such appeals were possible 'there would be no use of government amongst us'.[122] When William Aspin defended his role in drafting an antinomian petition, 'the court answered that this was no petition but a seditious libel; the misnaming of a thing doth not alter the nature of it'.[123] Perhaps most notably, in reply to John Cogshall's defence that he had merely spoken his mind as an enfranchised member of the court according to his rights as a citizen, the court responded, 'It is licentiousness, and not liberty, when a man may speak what he list.'[124]

Puritans, then, were every bit as capable as their conformist opponents of defending an empire of moderation. The creation of good government in the wilderness lay near the ideological core of early modern English imperialism. This good government was a middle way between the tyranny of the Spanish and the lawlessness of the Indians, but it also mapped neatly onto an alternative middle way between the tyranny of the papists and the anarchy of the radical Reformation. This was a game that puritans could play as well as anyone, and when faced with challenges to the first great experiment in puritan government, they justified (not without considerable irony) breathtaking acts of state-sponsored repression as virtuous moderation.

## Conclusion

The particular confluence of ideas described in this chapter – moderation of climate, population, Spanish tyranny and religious extremism – was of course temporary. The revolutions of the 1640s forever changed how puritanism and popery were perceived; the rhetoric of social crisis would change with the levelling-off of English population and the growth of commercial capitalism in the later seventeenth century; and the English perception of empire was inevitably transformed by its very success. By the 1660s, with several colonies now flourishing commonwealths, the

---

[121] *Ibid.*, p. 312.  [122] *Ibid.*, pp. 256–7.  [123] *Ibid.*, p. 260.  [124] *Ibid.*, p. 258.

slave trade established and a booming market in England for imperial commodities, the metropole would necessarily develop new languages for understanding its colonial possessions.

Yet despite these changes, it does not take much imagination to see that the early modern empire of moderation cast long shadows over the future of the British Empire. The names and faces would change, but the British long imagined themselves as the moderate alternative to the excesses of their imperial competitors: Dutch republicans in the later seventeenth century, French absolutists in the eighteenth century, German militarists in the nineteenth and twentieth centuries. Apologists for the British Empire often described with pride how much better subject peoples were treated by the British than by their competitors. Those apologists imagined empire as an agent of moderation for England's own excessive populace – Botany Bay springs instantly to mind – and they often described Britain as a moderating influence on the peoples they conquered, for instance bringing the virtues of law and order to decadent and effeminate South Asia. The ghosts of this rhetoric are still with us.

The point is not only that this rhetoric was always divisive and self-serving despite its irenic and universalist tone, but also that the rule of moderation was built into the imperial project from the very beginning, so that moderation became a wellspring of imperial violence. Scholars in recent years who have analysed the ideological origins of the British Empire have focused on its classical republican and Renaissance human-ist roots, supplanting a previous generation who had focused on its reli-gious and commercial aspects. These arguments are profoundly impor-tant, and it is not my purpose to dispute them. Yet at moments they seem to imply that the English had somehow to overcome the moder-ation of their own Renaissance culture in order to conquer the world. One such work attempts to understand how the English overcame the contradiction between a self-perception of neo-classical liberty at home and the creation of an empire abroad.[125] Another attempts to understand how the English overcame the contradiction between a self-perception of virtuous service to the commonwealth and the self-interested pursuit of wealth and glory in America.[126] Yet another examines how English legal theorists used the continental Civil Law to overcome the inherent inabil-ity of the English Common Law to function in an imperial setting.[127] These are valuable projects, but they are so committed to unravelling the

---

[125] Armitage, *The Ideological Origins of the British Empire.*
[126] Fitzmaurice, *Humanism and America.*    [127] MacMillan, *Sovereignty and Possession.*

tangled strands of ideologies that they may not pay sufficient attention to the ideological work done by the tangles themselves.[128]

The rule of moderation, with its promiscuous mixing of internal and external restraint, was just such a tangle. Its apparent paradox, the capacity of moderation to hold coercion and harmony in suspension, was what made it so useful to the muddled and contradictory process of empire-building. Moderation combined exclusivity and coercion with universalism and peace, resulting in a middle way that sharply divided the world into a single, normative centre and an infinitely varied but profoundly dangerous periphery. There could hardly be a more perfect synecdoche for the imperial project as a whole. Thus when the English began their quest for overseas colonies, it may be that they did not need or want to untangle the strands of their ideals, however real their sense of disquiet and occasional self-loathing. Those knots were woven into the cultural fabric of early modern England, and England rode them all the way to empire.

[128] See David Read, 'Colonialism and Coherence: The Case of Captain John Smith's General Historie of Virginia', *Modern Philology* 91, no. 4 (May 1994), pp. 428–48.

# 6　Social moderation and the governance of the middle sort

## Introduction: the politics of social moderation

Historians who do not feel comfortable talking about a 'middle class' in England before the nineteenth century instead often use the term 'middle sort'.[1] Whatever sleight of hand may sometimes be inherent in this manoeuvre – for the occupants of the two categories often seem eerily similar – early modern historians console themselves that 'middle sort' (or sometimes 'middling sort') was at least a *bona fide* early modern term. Using this term, and trying to understand its contemporary nuances, captures subjective understandings of early modern social relations in ways that more recent and ideologically freighted terms like 'middle class' simply do not. Thus a number of historians, most notably Keith Wrightson, have tracked the emergence of the idea of a 'middle sort', arguing that the 'middle sort of people' were only occasionally identified as such in the sixteenth and early seventeenth centuries, but that use of the term increased from the 1620s onwards, accelerating rapidly in the Civil Wars and Revolution, indicating the growing significance and cultural coherence of people whose wealth and status depended upon trade.[2] This

---

[1] For the most recent discussion of how to define the middle sort, see H. R. French, *The Middle Sort of People in Provincial England 1600–1750* (Oxford, 2007), 'Introduction: Definitions'. Craig Muldrew has defined the middle sort as 'yeomen, artisans and professionals such as lawyers who profited by selling goods or services on the market': Craig Muldrew, *The Economy of Obligation: The Culture of Credit and Social Relations in Early Modern England* (New York, 1998), p. 16. Peter Earle has described middling people as those 'who worked but ideally did not get their hands dirty. The majority were commercial or industrial capitalists who had a stock of money, acquired by paternal gift, inheritance or loan, which they continually turned over to make more money': Peter Earle, *The Making of the English Middle Class: Business, Society, and Family Life in London, 1660–1730* (Berkeley, 1989), p. 3.

[2] Keith Wrightson, '"Sorts of People" in Tudor and Stuart England', in Jonathan Barry and Christopher Brooks (eds.), *The Middling Sort of People: Culture, Society and Politics in England, 1550–1800* (New York, 1994); Keith Wrightson, 'Estates, Degrees and Sorts: Changing Perceptions of Society in Tudor and Stuart England', in Penelope Corfield (ed.), *Language, History and Class* (Oxford, 1991); Keith Wrightson, 'The Social Order in Early Modern England: Three Approaches', in Lloyd Bonfield, Richard Smith and

view has been nuanced by Henry French, who showed that even after the idea of a 'middle sort' came into vogue, the middle sort rarely deployed it themselves. It remained in the seventeenth century a term of theoretical analysis rather than self-identification, and in local contexts the middle sort usually referred to themselves as 'chief inhabitants', stressing their ascendancy rather than their mediocrity.[3]

As a result of these valuable investigations we now understand a great deal about the complex social and cultural position of the 'middle sort' in early modern England. On the upper end, the middle sort might mimic the qualities of their betters, purchase manors and over generations become gentrified; yet increasingly through our period they also might reject such aspirations and defend the life of useful trade over decadent gentility. On the lower end, the middle sort might claim entry into the oligarchies of their communities through the rhetoric of gentility; yet since a decreasing percentage of tradesmen actually owned their means of production, they might easily fall into dependency and become indistinguishable from wage earners. The seventeenth-century 'middle sort' thus appear in the historiography as ancestors of both the bourgeoisie and their skilled employees, and understanding the process of differentiation between these groups has become a significant scholarly enterprise. In sum, by paying attention to the terms by which contemporaries described themselves and others, historians have re-authorised the centrality (for the seventeenth century if not for the sixteenth) of tradesmen, shopkeepers, merchants and capitalist farmers within a cultural rather than a social or Marxist historiography.[4]

Yet this chapter will suggest that the agenda of this historiography – understanding how early moderns divided society into sorts, and later classes, of people – has unwittingly restricted the emerging concept of a 'middle sort' within a very narrow cultural space. To put it bluntly, in analysing the idea of a 'middle sort' historians have focused overwhelmingly on the second part of the term – 'sort' – while virtually ignoring

---

Keith Wrightson (eds.), *The World We Have Gained: Histories of Population and Social Structure* (New York, 1986).

[3] French, *The Middle Sort of People*, *passim*; H. R. French, 'Social Status, Localism and the "Middle Sort of People" in England 1620–1750', *P&P* 166, no. 1 (2000), pp. 66–99.

[4] In addition to the work of Wrightson, French, Earle and Muldrew already cited, some important examples include: Penelope Corfield (ed.), *Language, History and Class* (Oxford, 1991); Penelope Corfield, 'Class by Name and Number in Eighteenth-Century England', *History* 72, no. 234 (February 1987), pp. 38–61; Jonathan Barry and Christopher Brooks (eds.), *The Middling Sort of People: Culture, Society and Politics in England, 1550–1800* (New York, 1994); Margaret Hunt, *The Middling Sort: Commerce, Gender, and the Family in England 1680–1780* (Berkeley, 1996); John Smail, *The Origins of Middle-Class Culture: Halifax, Yorkshire, 1660–1780* (Ithaca, 1994).

the first part of the term – 'middle' – assuming that 'middle-ness' was self-evident, a sociological marker tied to an emerging group of people whose professions made them something less than gentle but whose wealth made them something more than common.[5] This focus has prevented historians from seeing the broader framework from which the idea of a 'middle sort' emerged and hence the full ideological significance of its emergence.

This broader framework was what I call 'social moderation', the widespread application of the Aristotelian ideal of virtuous mediocrity to questions of status. Social moderation as a philosophical category existed long before the idea of the 'middle sort', in uneasy tension with the hierarchical assumptions of the Great Chain of Being, drawing upon both classical and biblical sources that stressed the ethical superiority of a moderate estate between riches and poverty.[6] But crucially, as Mark Kishlansky has emphasised, 'In the early modern world there was no separation between the social and the political',[7] hence social moderation was in significant measure a *political* marker, referring to citizens neither corrupted by wealth nor debased by poverty and hence capable of participation in the polity. Moderation was government, and social moderation referred not only to the self-government or voluntary submission by which people restrained their social ambitions, but also to the capacity for public government attendant upon their social virtues. For this reason, social moderation was routinely appropriated for the landed elite; gentlemen and noblemen were described as belonging to the moderate estate, neither rich nor poor, in large part because of their public authority. But by extension, when writers from the late sixteenth century onwards applied the concept of social moderation to tradesmen, yeomen and other commercial subjects through the language of the 'middle sort', these were in large part novel *political* claims about participation in the English commonwealth.[8]

The argument of this chapter thus has three parts. First, in the century before 1640, the category of social moderation was often deployed not

---

[5] For a later period, this assumption has been forcibly questioned by Dror Wahrman, *Imagining the Middle Class: The Political Representation of Class in Britain, c.1780–1840* (Cambridge, 1995). For a comparative context, see Sarah Maza, *The Myth of the French Bourgeoisie: An Essay on the Social Imaginary, 1750–1850* (Cambridge, Mass., 2003).

[6] The most sophisticated discussions of these antecedents are Todd, *Christian Humanism*; Scodel, *Excess and the Mean*.

[7] Kishlansky, *Parliamentary Selection*, p. 15.

[8] On the governance of the middle sort in early modern England, see Hindle, *The State and Social Change*; Steve Hindle, *On the Parish? The Micro-Politics of Poor Relief in Rural England c.1550–1750* (Oxford, 2004); Phil Withington, *The Politics of Commonwealth: Citizens and Freemen in Early Modern England* (Cambridge, 2005).

merely to describe a sociological position between riches and poverty but to associate that position with governance; the 'mean estate' incorporated ideals of citizenship.[9] Second, when the idea of the 'middle sort' of people evolved in the later sixteenth and seventeenth centuries, it embodied and transmitted broader debates and anxieties over what 'sort' of people were in fact citizens with public rights and responsibilities and the extent to which the English commonwealth was governed from within rather than from above. Third, this emphasis on the rule of moderation explains why the term 'middle sort' exploded into view in the middle decades of the seventeenth century: it was part and parcel of the larger conflict over political participation and public governance that we associate with the Civil War and Revolution.

### Social moderation and the ideal of governance

Long before the emergence of a stable category called the 'middle sort', English people sometimes wrote as if they knew what it was. The medieval chronicler Thomas Walsingham reported that in the plague of 1379 the *'mediocribus'* evacuated their houses in large numbers.[10] In the forest laws of King Canute, the levy of *warscot*, a tax to pay for armour, differentiated between *primarii*, *mediocres* and *minuti*.[11] The life of St Dunstan of Canterbury divided the urban population into, *'ipsi divites, ipsi mediocres, ipsi pauperes'*.[12] In the early fourteenth century, people calling themselves *'les menes gentz de la cominaute de la ville de Norwich'* complained about tallage levied on them by *'les bailiffs et les riches'*.[13] In the mid fourteenth century the *'mediocris populi'* of London complained to the king that the mayor and sheriffs had interfered with their ancient right of selling small wares at the Cheap.[14] Moreover, as Andy Wood has shown, the

---

[9] Confusingly, the word 'mean' in a social context can signify either 'middle' or 'low', hence I have tried to be extremely careful in this chapter to incorporate only those examples where the term clearly refers to moderation rather than baseness.

[10] Samuel Cohn, *The Black Death Transformed* (London, 2003), p. 128. For similar examples outside England, see pp. 126–8.

[11] Thomas Blount, *Nomo-Lexikon, a Law-Dictionary* (London, 1670), sig. YYYr; Holinshed, *The First and Second Volumes of Chronicles*, p. 207.

[12] Henry Wharton, *Anglia Sacra* (London, 1691), part 2, p. 217.

[13] William Hudson and John Cottingham Tingley (eds.), *The Records of the City of Norwich* (Norwich, 2 vols., 1906–10), I, pp. 61–2.

[14] A. H. Thomas (ed.), *Calendar of Plea and Memoranda Rolls Preserved among the Archives of the Corporation of the City of London at the Guild-Hall* (Cambridge, 6 vols., 1926–61), I, p. 1. Sylvia Thrupp has suggested that the *mediocres* in these sources were men too poor to rent shops in better districts who were 'struggling to retain their independence against the wealthier shopkeepers and the great merchants': Sylvia Thrupp, *The Merchant Class of Medieval London* (Ann Arbor, 1962), p. 32.

English term 'middle sort' was occasionally used as early as Henry VIII's reign.[15] Henry Brinkelow, for instance, recommended in his *Complaint of Roderyck Mors* (1542) that monastic lands should be used to lower the tax burden on the commons so 'that the poor and middle sort of the people may be eased thereby'.[16]

These indigenous usages tended to refer to graduated taxation or other forms of legal differentiation. But since England recognised no formal social ranks with specific privileges below the nobility, there was no legally defined 'middle' rank equivalent, for example, to the *arti minori* of medieval Florence who sat between the *arti maggiori* and the *popolo minuto*, or to the German *gemeine Mann* who was legally differentiated from *das Volk*. In the social discourse of medieval England, then, the delineation of a middle rank occurred only on an occasional, *ad hoc* basis at moments when the binary division of society into gentle and ungentle was insufficient. While the notion of a social middle was available in a descriptive or relational sense, the theoretical development of this layer of society was impoverished by European standards.

The English Renaissance, however, imported a sophisticated tradition, most commonly found in translations of classical and continental works, that the 'moderate estate' between riches and poverty was the most virtuous condition. The *locus classicus* for this idea of social moderation was Book 4 of the *Politics*, where Aristotle argued (as the 1598 English translation put it), 'There are in all cities three sorts of inhabitants: the one very rich, the other very poor, the third in a mean between both. Since then it is granted that the mean is the best, it follows that mean wealth is likewise the best of all, as that which easily obeyeth reason.' Those with too great a fortune are over-mighty and unwilling to submit to authority; those with too little fortune are too degraded to participate rationally in government. 'The one cannot bear rule but servilely obey; the others cannot obey but in lordly manner bear rule.' Each leads to an unbalanced constitution: 'Whenever the one or the other succeed, viz. the rich men or the people, and transgress the mean, they draw the commonwealth unto them, whereon follows a democracy or an oligarchy.' Between the two, those neither rich nor poor tend to promote a balanced constitution:

A city therefore must be principally of men whose estates are equal and alike, as are they whose substance is mean . . . those citizens enjoy more safety than any other, for they desire not other men's goods, as the poor do, neither are their

---

[15] Andy Wood, *The 1549 Rebellions and the Making of Early Modern England* (Cambridge, 2007), p. 17. I owe thanks to Andy Wood for discussing these issues and providing several important references.

[16] Henry Brinkelow, *The Complaint of Roderyck Mors* (Strasbourg, 1542), sig. F3v.

goods desired by others, as the poor do covet the rich men's wealth...Thus we see that of all civil societies, that is the best which consisteth of men whose estate is mean; and that those cities are well governed, wherein there are many such inhabitants, which may have more power then the other two parts.[17]

This was first and foremost a discussion of how reasonable citizens contributed to the commonwealth; social moderation was defined not just by material conditions but also by attentiveness to reason and virtuous civic participation.[18] The result was that Renaissance texts routinely interpreted social moderation in terms of proper government: the reciprocal responsibilities of citizenship, ruling and being ruled. So, for instance, the 1586 English translation of Pierre de la Primaudaye's *The French Academie* described the virtue of social moderation in terms of political forms:

The third kind of a good and right commonwealth is of a Greek word called Timocratie, which we may call the power of mean or indifferent wealth. This kind of government was after a peculiar sort called of the ancients by the name of 'commonwealth' because this policy tended most of all to public profit, and was guided by laws, and compounded of an Oligarchy and a Democraty, which are two extremes, and of themselves vicious and corrupt. For of their mediocrities this form of commonwealth was instituted...Aristotle speaketh of this kind of commonwealth when he saith that civil society consisting of mean persons is very good, and that those cities are well governed wherein there are many of the middle sort.[19]

Likewise, the 1594 English translation of Justus Lipsius's *Six Bookes of Politickes* combined Aristotle's categories with Tacitean cynicism to describe why the Emperor Tiberius chose middling people as his advisors:

---

[17] *Aristotles Politiques*, pp. 219–21. Two contemporary Latin commentaries on the *Politics* were not specific about the English meanings of the *medii* but followed Aristotle's political interpretation of the category: John Case, *Sphaera Civitatis* (Oxford, 1588), pp. 374–80; John Lawrence, *Politica Decorum Commentationes* (London, 1590), sig. 2v–3r. These were based upon the late thirteenth-century continuation by Peter of Auvergne of Thomas Aquinas's unfinished commentary on the *Politics*. Auvergne devoted several long sections to the question of why the *medii* were *optimi cives*, concluding not only that they often exceeded the rich in nobility and virtue and were thus the most useful to the state, *dicitur pars civitatis*, but also that because of their love of king and country they were *bene consulunt bono reipublicae*: see *Sententia Libri Politicorum, Continuatio a Petro de Alvernia*, 4.10 *passim*, online at www.corpusthomisticum.org/iopera.html, last consulted 24 August 2010. I owe thanks to Geoffrey Koziol for help with a particularly obscure Latin passage.

[18] Another prominent *locus classicus* for the connection between social moderation and government is Plato's *Republic*, where the Guardians must guard against both wealth and poverty in their city, for both foment 'revolution': Plato, *Republic*, pp. 97 and 263 (422a and 591d–e).

[19] Pierre de la Primaudaye, *The French Academie wherein is Discoursed the Institution of Manners*, trans. Thomas Bowes (London, 1586), pp. 527–8.

'Fearing lest those that did so surpass might be a stumbling block in his own way; and those of the worser sort a shame and dishonour to the commonwealth'. Lipsius then inserted the moral: 'Those, then, of the middle sort are the best, to whose fidelity, both in times past and at this day, princes may with most safety commit their secret affairs.'[20]

It is worth noticing that Aristotle nowhere said who exactly possessed social moderation, hence its civic import was left open to interpretation and appropriation. For instance, while the criteria of mediocrity might refer to urban elites – Aristotle's *polis* was still translated as 'city' – they could also refer to the rural yeomanry. Thomas Smith's *De Republica Anglorum* (1583), for instance, gave barely ten lines to 'Citizens and Burgesses' but devoted more than three pages to 'Yeomen' as a middle degree: 'This sort of people confess themselves to be no gentlemen, but give the honour to all which be or take upon themselves to be gentlemen, and yet they have a certain preeminence and more estimation than labourers and artificers, and commonly live wealthily and keep good houses.' Smith described this yeomanry not only as a sociological category but as a political one, '*optimos cives in republica*, and such as whom the writers of commonwealths praise to have many in it'. Citing Book 4 of Aristotle's *Politics*, he praised yeomen for not meddling in public matters except when they are called, but he stressed that when they are called they become the most public-spirited citizens and the best soldiers.[21]

Above the level of the yeomanry, the Roman tradition offered ample resources for the 'moderate estate' to refer to wealthier, landed men in their capacity as governors. According to a 1600 translation of Livy's *History of Rome*, for instance, it was from the ranks of the *patres* whom Romulus chose as his personal bodyguards that there emerged 'the order of the knights or gentlemen of Rome, a mean degree between the two estates of nobles and commons, as it were the seminary, to replenish the Senate when the places were void, and to augment the number of them'.[22] Here the middle estate showed their virtue through service to the prince, and their moderate position authorised their government in the commonwealth. It should be remembered, in this context, that Aristotle's criteria of social moderation – neither too rich nor too poor, both

---

[20] Lipsius, *Sixe Bookes of Politickes*, p. 55.

[21] Thomas Smith, *De Republica Anglorum* (London, 1583), pp. 29–33. Francis Bacon would later adopt the military perspective on these 'middle people' but largely abandon the governmental one: see Francis Bacon, *The Historie of the Reigne of King Henry the Seuenth* (London, 1629), p. 74; Francis Bacon, *The Essayes or Counsels* (London, 1625), pp. 173–4.

[22] Livy, *The Romane Historie Written by T. Livius of Padua*, trans. Philemon Holland (London, 1600), sig. E5r.

obedient subjects and virtuous governors, having equal estates between them – were also the self-defining features of the Elizabethan gentry, whose sense of citizenship flowed from obedience to the crown combined with the ability to counsel with reason, and whose common gentility made them equals in an important sense despite their incessant squabbles for precedence.

Social moderation could also reach to the very top of the social ladder. In a 1563 translation of Seneca's *Oedipus*, for instance, Creon asked:

> Alas would I my sister of
> her lawful kingdom spoil?
> Think you such Treason may have place
> in brother's breast to boil?
> If that mine oath could me not keep
> content with my degree:
> But that condemning mean estate,
> I would climb aloft to be.[23]

Here the 'mean estate' was claimed by the noble Creon, brother of the Queen, for whom it meant remaining content with his position as counsellor to the Queen rather than claiming the crown of Thebes for himself.[24] Finally, social moderation with this civic connotation could even apply to kings. The puritan John Dod described in 1611 the biblical case of King Uzziah, 'who being in a moderate estate, did exceeding much good for the Church and commonwealth; but when he was grown mighty and strong, his heart was lifted up, and then he could not content himself with his kingly dignity but he would needs take upon him the office of the high priest also'.[25]

The result of this tradition was that humanists could deploy the notion of a 'middle estate' to describe the idealised attributes of landed elites who moderated their ambition and avarice to hold the golden mean. Even Erasmus, so often taken as a supporter of meritocracy and social mobility, often used the idea of *mediocritas* as advice to the rich to moderate their ambition rather than support for a rising coterie of new men. For example, his colloquy *Philodoxus* appealed repeatedly to the need for moderation in the social world – *In omni re memento, ne quid nimis: sed*

---

[23] Seneca, *The Lamentable Tragedie of Oedipus*, trans. Alexander Neville (London, 1563), sig. C8r. 'Mean estate' here is an interpolation by the translator for the Latin *fortuna*; there is nothing in the original to suggest either a middle degree or a 'mean' degree in the sense of baseness or inferiority.

[24] Very similar understandings of 'the man of mean estate' can be found in Seneca, *The Eyght Tragedie of Seneca. Entituled Agamemnon*, trans. John Studley (London, 1566), sig. B5v.

[25] John Dod, *Foure Godlie and Fruitful Sermons* (London, 1611), p. 20.

*tamen mediocriter omnia esto* – but the point of the colloquy was to convince men to be satisfied with virtuous office-holding rather than fame and glory.[26] In the 1542 English translation of the *Apophthegmes*, Erasmus advised men 'not to extend beyond the compass of sufficiency, but to consist within the bounds of mediocrity', but in context the import of this advice was that 'purchase of lands ought to be moderate', a warning to great men not to burden their heirs with excessive troubles.[27] This may have been an elaboration of Cicero's dictum in Book 1 of his *De Officiis*, which in the 1556 English translation warned gentlemen that in the building of 'manorplaces . . . there must doubtless be used a measure, that to a meankeeping must be reduced'.[28] Nicholas Bacon's poem 'In Commendation of the Mean Estate', written between 1553 and 1565, likewise imagined social moderation as restraint by great men. The poem advised the landed elite to moderate the size of their estates, the size of their serving staff and the number of women they brought to bed. Overlarge estates created cares upon a gentleman's head which 'the wise man of mean degree / For his estate need not foresee'. Gentlemen with forty servants usually 'use well scant ten'; the rest are superfluous. Wealthy men ordinarily enjoyed 'Venus at will, beds of delight'; moderate men know that 'Venus rights the man may have' but 'to exceed nature's desire / Is to seek heat where needs no fire'.[29]

The Ciceronian ideal of the *vita activa* was close to the heart of these visions of the 'mean estate': striving for self-control, epitomised in the restraint of worldly appetites, authorised participation in the commonwealth. It was in this spirit that Erasmus wrote in his *Institutio Christiani Principis* that citizens should be neither too rich nor too poor, 'for the pauper is of no use and the rich man will not use his ability for public service'.[30] For the Elizabethan Catholic humanist William Blandie, the virtue of moderation – 'the measure of things ordered, according to reason's prescription' – authorised governance, and he offered the example

---

[26] 'Philodoxus', from Desiderius Erasmus, *Familiarum Colloquiorum Opus* (London, 1571), p. 626. This was apparently the first edition published in England, but educated Englishmen read Erasmus's colloquies in continental editions from 1518 onwards. See also the colloquy *Gerontologia sive Ochma* for repeated uses of *mediocritas* to describe the control of ambition or greed among social elites.

[27] Erasmus, *Apophthegmes*, fo. 38v.

[28] Cicero, *Marcus Tullius Ciceroes Thre Bokes of Duties*, trans. Nicholas Grimald (London, 1556), fo. 55r–v. 'Quarum quidem certe est adhibendus modus ad mediocritatemque revocandus. Eademque mediocritas ad omnem usum cultumque vitae transferenda est': online at www.thelatinlibrary.com/cicero/off.shtml, last consulted 27 September 2010.

[29] Printed in Nicholas Bacon, *The Recreations of His Age* (Oxford, 1919), pp. 5–8. See Patrick Collinson, 'Sir Nicholas Bacon and the Elizabethan *Via Media*', in his *Godly People: Essays on English Protestantism and Puritanism* (London, 1983).

[30] Cited in Todd, *Christian Humanism*, p. 133.

of 'Numa Pompilius, a Roman of mean estate, who by upright dealing, and supporting of justice, was thought and proclaimed by the whole consent of the Romans worthy to succeed Romulus in the state of royal majesty'.[31] Edwin Sandys likewise praised those 'who in a middle degree of condition possess also a moderate temper of affections; which is ordinarily the greatest part in all well-ordered commonwealths; and withal the far surest and firmest to the state'.[32] A more elaborate example comes from Richard Barckley's Neostoic masterwork, *A Discourse of the Felicitie of Man* (1598). Within Barckley's long discussion of the dictum that 'they that be in a mean estate be best', he argued, 'He is accounted a great estate that hath dominion and power over others, but he is a great estate indeed that hath himself in his own power. And therefore if thou desire to be great, and to make all things subject to thee, make thyself subject to reason: thou shalt rule much if reason rule thee.'[33] Self-government was here the essence of felicity, and Barckley stressed that glory, rule, honour and reputation are unnecessary to human contentment. Yet he also stressed that wealth and rule are compatible with social moderation so long as one's worldly place retains 'respect to nature and to civility, measured by the sound judgment of a mind void of all perturbations'. Here, in keeping with Seneca's complicated and seemingly contradictory espousal of public duty for men who understood the irrelevance of the world, 'civility' was the prerogative of those who disdained wealth and power rather than seeking it.[34]

In these and other texts before the widespread elaboration of the 'middle sort', classicising English Renaissance writers and translators imagined a deep connection between the quality of social moderation – being neither rich nor poor, hence demonstrating appropriate control of worldly appetites – and public life.

### Labour, moderation and governance

The same was often true by the end of the sixteenth century in discussions of the key biblical text describing social moderation, Proverbs 30:8–9, part of what is known as 'Agur's Prayer'.[35] Here Agur son of

---

[31] William Blandie, *The Castle, or Picture of Pollicy Shewing Forth Most Liuely, the Face, Body and Partes of a Commonwealth* (London, 1581), p. 10.

[32] Edwin Sandys, *A Relation of the State of Religion* (London, 1605), sig. R4v.

[33] Barckley, *A Discourse of the Felicitie of Man* (London, 1598), pp. 495–6.

[34] *Ibid.*, pp. 486–90.

[35] Agur's middle state between riches and poverty was also routinely employed in Christian social ethics as a warning against greed, in ways that had nothing to do with political participation but rather stressed the virtuous life of the spirit. My point in this section is

Jakeh, sometimes identified with Solomon but usually not, prays (in the 1611 Authorised Version), 'Remove me far from vanity and lies; give me neither poverty nor riches, feed me with food convenient for me. Lest I be full and deny thee and say who is the Lord? Or lest I be poor and steal and take the name of God in vain.'[36] The medieval tradition had almost entirely allegorised this passage. In the first influential discussion of Agur's Prayer, St Jerome insisted that 'food convenient for me' was the spiritual food described in Isaiah 55:2, far removed from worldly power, strong wine, beautiful wives and other desires.[37] St Bernard used Agur's Prayer in a Lenten sermon on the depravity of man to describe how all worldly conditions are dangerous: 'Things that soothe and things that trouble, I fear: both hunger and refreshment, both sleep and wakefulness, both work and rest wage war against me. Give me neither riches nor poverty, says the wise man (Proverbs 30:8): undoubtedly because on both sides lies a trap, on both sides danger. And therefore temperance restrains concupiscence.'[38] The influential thirteenth-century exegete Hugo of St Cher glossed 'food convenient for me' with the discussion in Ecclesiasticus 39:26 of things 'basic to the needs of man's life', but these he explained allegorically: water cools the passions, fire inflames belief, oil is piety, clothes (*vestimentum*) are good works and so forth.[39] Moreover, Agur's association of poverty with theft and impiety was an enormous hostage to fortune after the onset of Protestant attacks on

---

to stress that a commonwealth reading of Agur's Prayer became available, not to suggest that this was the only reading.

[36] In the fourteenth century, following the Vulgate, Wyclif had rendered the text, 'Give thou not to me beggary or riches; give thou only necessaries to my livelihood.' The Coverdale Bible (NSTC 2065) abandoned 'beggary' but followed Wyclif on the second half of the passage: 'Give me neither poverty nor riches, only grant me a necessary living.' These earlier versions may suggest a somewhat different and more egalitarian interpretation of the middle condition than the later 'convenient for me', with its implication that different people had different sorts of 'convenience'. This translation was first introduced in the 1560 Geneva Bible.

[37] St Jerome, *S. Eusebii Hieronymi Stridonensis Presbyteri Commentariorum in Isaiam Prophetam Libri Duodeviginti*, Book 15, column 0530C-0531B, from the online *Patrologia Latina*, last consulted at http://pld.chadwyck.com on 24 August 2010. See also Venerable Bede, *In Proverbia Solomonis*, printed in *Corpus Christianorum*, Series Latina (177 + vols, Turnholti, 1953–), CXIX B, p. 142.

[38] St Bernard of Clairvaux, *Sermo VI in Quadragesima. De Oratione Dominica*, column 0182C, from the online *Patrologia Latina* last consulted at http://pld.chadwyck.com on 24 August 2010. My translation. 'Et quae mulcent, et quae molestant, timeo: et esuries et refectio, et somnus et vigiliae, et labor et requies militant contra me. Divitias et paupertatem ne dederis mihi, orat sapiens (Prov. XXX, 8): nimirum quia utrobique laqueus, utrobique periculum. Quod si reprimit temperantia concupiscentiam.'

[39] Hugo de Sancto Charo, *Opera Omnia in Universum Vetus & Novum Testamentum* (Coloniae Agrippinae, 8 vols., 1621), III, fol. 64v.

voluntary poverty, especially because the Vulgate rendered 'poverty' as *mendicitatem* (beggary), with obvious connotations of the mendicant orders for sixteenth-century readers. Hence Catholic writers after 1520 developed elaborate new allegorical interpretations of the text. For François Vatable, Professor of Hebrew at the Collège de France, Agur's poverty was not material but rather a poverty of religious understanding. Taking as his source Romans 12:3, where St Paul advised Christians to use 'the measure of faith' given by God, Vatable argued that riches and poverty referred to an 'excess and defect of understanding' (*sapientiae excessum et defectum*). Too much understanding led to pride, too little understanding led to idolatry, so the wise man prayed for a middle way.[40]

Later Tudor Protestant exegetes, by contrast, were much more literal and associated Agur's Prayer closely with the idea of labour in a calling, which restrained wealth and rendered it moderate.[41] In one of the earliest examples, a sermon posthumously printed in 1562, Hugh Latimer advised his auditors:

Let not this affection take place in your hearts to be rich; labour for thy living, and pray to God, then he will send thee things necessary. Though he send not great riches, yet thou must be content withal, for it is better to have a sufficient living than to have great riches. Therefore Solomon, that wise king, desired of God that he would send him neither too much nor too little.[42]

In the first great English commentary on the Book of Proverbs in 1580, Michael Cope's interpretation of Agur's Prayer stressed that poverty was

---

[40] Printed in John Pearson, *Critici Sacri* (London, 1660), columns 4392–3. For other sixteenth-century Catholic texts using allegorical interpretation to deny that Agur's Prayer contradicted clerical poverty, see Cornelius Jansen, *Paraphrasis in Psalmos Omnes Dauidicos... Eiusdem in Prouerbia Salomonis & Ecclesiasticum Accuratissima Commentaria* (Lugduni, 1592), pp. 228–30; Joannes Arboreus, *Commentarii Ioannis Arborei Laudunensis, Docoris Theologi, in Proverbia Salomonis* (Paris, 1549), fol. 101v.

[41] See Naomi Tadmor, *The Social Universe of the English Bible: Scripture, Society and Culture in Early Modern England* (Cambridge, 2010). This book appeared too late to incorporate its arguments here.

[42] Hugh Latimer, *Certayn Godly Sermons* (London, 1562), fo. 58v. While not using Agur's Prayer, Latimer also discussed social moderation in his *A Most Faithfull Sermon Preached before the Kinges Most Excellente Maiestye* (London, 1550), sigs. G2r–G3v: 'Here by this ye may perceive that it is not the abundance of riches that maketh a man to live quietly and blissfully, but the quiet life is in a mediocrity. *Mediocres optime vivunt* (sayth he) they that are in a mean do live best. And there is a proverb which I read many years ago, *Dimidium plus toto*, the half sometimes more than the whole. The mean life is the best life and the most quiet life of all. If a man should fill himself up to the throat he should not find ease in it but displeasure.'

a scourge of God and that labour was the divinely sanctioned remedy: 'It is lawful to avoid the same by the means that God teacheth us by his word, the which are labour and prayer.' Hence Agur's Prayer against poverty was in fact a prayer 'that God would grant him grace that he might be able to labour, and that he would bless his travail'.[43] Thomas Cartwright similarly argued that Agur's Prayer required Christians to acquire such wealth as was suitable to their rank 'through honest labour and devotion' (*labore studioque honesto*).[44]

In the hands of one of the most influential Elizabethan religious commentators, William Perkins, this interpretation of moderation through labour was strongly linked to the 'calling' as a civic office. For Perkins, labour in a calling represented moderation in the sense that it restrained the labourer: men 'must keep within the compass, limits, or precincts thereof'.[45] The point of the calling was that every man must 'restrain his affection from the world' and must 'turn and dispose' that affection to better things, for 'our affection is like a sea, which being suffered to pass his banks, overflows the whole country'. Hence for the 'better restraining of our affections' we must seek 'no more but things that be necessary and sufficient for us and ours, for to seek for abundance is not lawful'; in this context Perkins quoted Agur's Prayer.[46] Yet if labour was moderation because it restrained the labourer, it also gave the labourer a public office of restraint. Perkins defined every calling as 'some particular office arising of that distinction which God makes between man and man in every society'. The office of the magistrate is 'government over his subjects'; the office of master is 'government over his servants'.[47] While these callings were the essence of civility, other callings were likewise offices for the 'good, happy and quiet estate of a society'. A merchant, a carpenter, a soldier – all these were callings that 'serveth to uphold and maintain . . . the estate of the commonwealth'.[48]

The point is that labour became a crucial link between internal and external moderation: labour not only rendered one's social condition moderate and hence virtuous but was also a public office that restrained

[43] Michael Cope, *Godly and Learned Expositions upon the Proverbs of Solomon* (London, 1580), pp. 608–12.

[44] Thomas Cartwright, *Commentarii Succincti & Dilucidi in Proverbia Salomonis* (Leiden, 1617), columns 1438–46: 'Quia tamen modum in divitiis acquirendis non tenuit, non dubium est, quin misera ejus defectio ab hac radice primario pullulaverit. Quamobrem unusquisque conditionem vitae suae, & stationem, in qua Deus illum constituit, debite, & attente expendat, ut illas divitias a Deo petat, & labore studioque honesto comparet, quibus se, & ordinem suum tueatur.' See also William Perkins, *The Whole Treatise of the Cases of Conscience* (Cambridge, 1608), Book III, pp. 52–69.

[45] *Ibid.*, I, p. 751.    [46] *Ibid.*, I, p. 769. See also *Workes*, II, p. 126.

[47] Perkins, *Workes*, I, p. 755.    [48] *Ibid.*, p. 758.

the concupiscence of the commonwealth.[49] We can thus find any number of early Stuart texts that closely associated social moderation, virtuous labour and governance. Perhaps the central example comes from the Wiltshire minister George Webbe, who would later be promoted by Charles I to become Bishop of Limerick. In 1621, Webbe published *Agurs Prayer, or, the Christians Choyce, for the Outward Estate and Condition of this Present Life*, the first full printed work devoted solely to the idea of social moderation.[50] Webbe stressed that riches, while often abused, were nonetheless good in themselves rather than indifferent.[51] The key to their benefits was to use them well, which most people were unable to do because of their sinfulness; riches were like an untamed horse who threw off unskilled riders. Thus, God has commanded us 'to labour and to take pains in our lawful callings, that we may have sufficient, not only to relieve our own wants, but also to relieve the necessities of others'.[52] This meant not only relief of the poor and alms for the Church, as in medieval exegesis, but also the use of wealth 'for the good of the commonwealth, when as we shall have wherewithal to pay tribute, scot and lot, and to perform such public services as shall be required at our hands. In this respect we may pray for riches.' Webbe's choice of terms speaks volumes: 'scot and lot' was the medieval term for the reciprocal relationship between paying taxes and civic responsibility for freemen of corporations, while 'public service' obviously referred to the active participation of citizens in governance.

The converse was also true: if it was socially moderate to increase one's wealth through labour for the sake of the commonwealth, it was gross public irresponsibility to become impoverished. For Webbe, even though God sometimes chose to use poverty for the benefit of the godly, poverty in a pejorative sense was associated with sin. He claimed that 'it is a rare

---

[49] Andrew McRae has shown that in seventeenth-century Georgic literature, labour was increasingly associated with public service to the commonwealth: Andrew McRae, *God Speed the Plough: The Representation of Agrarian England, 1500–1660* (Cambridge, 1996). See also the discussion of Richard Deloney's 1597 *Jack of Newberry* in Laura Stevenson, *Praise and Paradox: Merchants and Craftsmen in Elizabethan Popular Literature* (Cambridge, 1984), p. 120, where a beehive represents a 'flourishing commonwealth, where virtuous subjects labour with delight' and where the prudence and fortitude of clothiers support the commonwealth and drive out the allegorical figure of Treason.

[50] George Webbe, *Agurs Prayer: Or, the Christians Choyce* (London, 1621).

[51] *Ibid.*, pp. 190–203. This was a technical splitting of hairs: riches are good *in themselves* because they are called 'gifts of God' and 'blessings of God' in scripture, but they are indifferent *to us* because they are subject to abuse or alteration by their owner. This distinction fit well with broader Protestant understandings that good works depended upon God's blessings of those works rather than the works themselves, and it authorised Webbe's fundamental argument that accumulation of wealth was divinely sanctioned for the devout. See pp. 281–2 for a nearly identical argument about 'prosperity'.

[52] *Ibid.*, p. 121.

thing' to see a righteous man in poverty, and that 'the original cause' of poverty was sin: 'Before sin, there was no poverty, no want, no indigency; but when man by transgression fell from God, then he lost all his former wealth and poverty was laid upon him as a curse.' Webbe thus attacked those who fell into poverty through neglect of their worldly callings: 'As we have seen the truth of it already against the vow of poverty in popery, so we are to observe it against the poverty of many among ourselves, occasioned willfully and woefully through their own negligence. It is a sin for any, through their own negligence or want of providence, to bring poverty upon themselves.'[53] This claim allowed Webbe to embark on theologically sophisticated attacks on the excesses of the poor, 'those droves of drones, the shame of our land, the swarms of vagrant beggars'. Because of their 'love of idleness and contempt of pains in a lawful calling', the poor are generally 'given up to most horrible sins of injustice and uncleanliness'.[54] While he advocated charity for the poor whom God had made, for the 'thriftless poor' Webbe had only contempt, arguing that the only 'alms' they should receive are admonition, reformation and correction, notably 'corporal punishments . . . according to the good and warrantable orders of the state'.[55]

In the same period, other interesting examples can be found in the works of Robert Aylett, an ecclesiastical lawyer, high commissioner and prolific poet.[56] Aylett's *Thrifts Equipage* (1622), a collection of poetic meditations organised around socio-economic issues, was preoccupied with the issue of social moderation. For Aylett, thrift was 'That virtue, or that golden mean / Twixt avarice and prodigality / The constant moderation between / Base niggardise, and wasting luxury'. Allegorically, Thrift was the eldest daughter of Temperance, hence she 'moderateth all delights and pleasure . . . / For she not only is a moderation / In meats, and what to clothing doth pertain / But she eke and moderates our recreation / Lest for it we do lose a greater gain'.[57] According to Aylett this virtue was conspicuously lacking in both rich and poor, but he admitted its presence among a wide variety of other persons, defined by their labour for the public good: 'Artificer, good husband, merchant, knight / And magistrate, this virtue doth defend'.[58] Aylett stressed that all the saints of both the Old and New Testaments were farmers or tradesmen,

---

[53] *Ibid.*, p. 140.    [54] *Ibid.*, pp. 141–3.    [55] *Ibid.*, pp. 170–8.

[56] Aylett, like George Webbe, was a Laudian. There was clearly no sense in which the connection between labour in a calling, public authority and social moderation can be linked to puritanism.

[57] Robert Aylett, *Thrifts Equipage viz. Fiue Diuine and Morall Meditations* (London, 1622), pp. 2–3.

[58] *Ibid.*, p. 23.

working in their lawful callings before God called them to the ministry. Most notably, 'The apostles all were fisherman, and gained / Their living by enduring wet and cold / Divines think, Joseph blessed Jesus trained / In his own trade, till he thrice ten years old'.[59] Here, then, social moderation was constituted in and through labour. Yet *Thrifts Equipage* made a series of connections between the moderation of industrious labour and the moderation of political rule. Men not 'made in husbandry to sweat' might instead 'sweat in arts or laws political / 'Tis fit all earn their bread, before they eat'. Diligence is particularly to be found 'In highest rulers which the public sway / Who are set over us for our own gain / If them as God's vicegerents we obey'.[60] In the Bible, 'Of Moses, Joshua, Kings and Judges good / Have they not all for labour stoutly stood?'[61]

If *Thrifts Equipage* stressed that governance was a form of moderation through labour, Aylett's sequel, *Ioseph, or, Pharoah's Favourite* (1623), stressed that labour in a moderate estate authorised governance. The text was an atrocious epic poem on the political capacities of Joseph as 'Lord Keeper' of Pharoah's Great Seal, centred on his moderate husbanding of Egypt's resources through seven years of plenty and seven years of famine. Here the avatar of social moderation was Joseph's father Jacob, the self-sufficient yeomen who wanted nothing more than a mean estate:

> Some pass through sickness, poverty, some wealth,
> Honour, preferment, pleasure, strength and health,
> Some equally of both participate,
> This is the mean, yet safe and happiest fate,
> The highest I did ever aspire:
> And in this state I still to live desire.

Yet, as Jacob noted a few lines later, the essence of happy government was when the proud were cast down and moderate men were raised up to positions of authority in the state.[62] During Joseph's rule over Egypt, his brilliance, befitting his socially moderate background, was to 'take care for the public good' by preventing all 'excess' during the fat years, storing grain for the lean years.[63] Later, when Pharoah welcomed Jacob and his other sons into Egypt, he made them 'rulers of my fold', giving them public authority even as they maintained their social moderation through labour as shepherds.[64]

Thus, in the discourse based upon biblical sources, much as in the discourse based upon Graeco-Roman sources, social moderation could function as a civic ideal as much as an economic one. The middle

[59] *Ibid.*, pp. 8–9.    [60] *Ibid.*, pp. 11, 23 and 29.    [61] *Ibid.*, pp. 43–5.
[62] Robert Aylett, *Ioseph, or, Pharoah's Fauorite* (London, 1623), p. 81.
[63] *Ibid.*, p. 61.    [64] *Ibid.*, p. 82.

station between riches and poverty was a position of citizenship, insofar as the occupant of that social position was in some inadequate but meaningful sense self-governing – disciplined, independent, in control of the appetites – and used that self-government in service to the commonwealth.

### The 'middle sort' as governors

Having uncovered the political signification of social moderation, we are now in a position to analyse what it meant for a particular 'sort' of people to be invested with that ideal. The development of the idea of the 'middle sort' was part and parcel of a wider debate over whether tradesmen, yeomen and others who worked for their wealth were mere ungentle mechanics, manual labourers born to obey rather than to rule, or whether they might be sufficient governors of their own passions to participate in the public life of the commonwealth.

It is worth noting that the political significance of the middle sort in seventeenth-century England has been an important theme in recent historiography. As Mark Goldie has shown, seventeenth-century householders really did participate in government in enormous numbers as petty officeholders in what he called 'the unacknowledged republic'.[65] More recently, Phil Withington has described how urban citizens not only participated in the governance of their towns and cities, but also imagined themselves in explicitly republican terms as active citizens of the *polis*. To be a freeman practising a trade was also to be an enfranchised citizen and in many cases an officeholder, and according to Withington urban freeman, burgesses and citizens in the seventeenth century came to 'personify qualities of civility and governance'.[66] The current argument suggests, then, that as those same urban citizens became the 'middle sort', their newfound moderation was recognition not merely of their social condition but of their political participation. Before turning in

---

[65] Mark Goldie, 'The Unacknowledged Republic: Officeholding in Early Modern England', in Tim Harris (ed.), *The Politics of the Excluded, c.1500–1850* (New York, 2001). See also Hindle, *The State and Social Change*; Patrick Collinson, 'The Monarchical Republic of Queen Elizabeth I', in his *Elizabethan Essays* (London, 1994); John McDiarmid (ed.), *The Monarchical Republic of Early Modern England: Essays in Response to Patrick Collinson* (Aldershot, 2007).

[66] Withington, *The Politics of Commonwealth*, p. 12. See also Phil Withington, 'Public Discourse, Corporate Citizenship, and State Formation in Early Modern England', *AHR* 112, no. 4 (October 2007), pp. 1016–38; Jonathan Barry, 'Civility and Civic Culture in Early Modern England: The Meanings of Urban Freedom', in Peter Burke, Brian Harrison and Paul Slack (eds.), *Civil Histories: Essays Presented to Sir Keith Thomas* (Oxford, 2000); French, *The Middle Sort of People*, pp. 253–4.

the next section to specific debates over this issue in the context of the English Revolution, in this section I want briefly to survey arguments about the 'middle sort' – those who made their living through trade, identified as a mean between gentle and plebian  that foregrounded the political in ways that have not been fully appreciated by social historians.

Early appropriations of social moderation for tradesmen, merchants and shopkeepers, as well as early usages of the 'middle sort' as a term-of-art, were often conspicuous in their emphasis on service to the commonwealth; historians have not noticed this theme simply because they were not looking for it. So, for instance, one of the earliest significant considerations of the 'middle sort' occurred in Richard Mulcaster's *Positions... Necessarie for the Training Vp of Children* (1581). In his discussion of the need for moderate provision for young scholars – since too large a stipend 'breedeth a loose and dissolute brain' while too small a stipend produces 'a base and servile conceit' – Mulcaster argued that:

The middle sort of parents, which neither welter in too much wealth nor wrestle with too much want, seemeth fittest of all, if the children's capacity be answerable to their parents' state and quality; which must be the level for the fattest to fall down to, and the leanest to leap up to, to bring forth that student which must serve his country best.[67]

There is a clear sense here that the child of those neither wealthy nor poor, when properly prepared by education and religion, becomes fittest for active citizenship to 'serve his country best'. Later in the text, Mulcaster made clear both whom he meant by the 'middle sort' and why they were so fit for government. In a fierce attack on the idleness of the rich, Mulcaster lamented the great multitude of gentlemen in England, 'which groweth on daily too far and too fast, and lessen the middle commoner too much: whose bigness is the best mean, if Aristotle say true, as his reason seems great, for peace and quietness in public estate, to desire the rich gentlemen which have most, and the poor meany which have least, to hold their hands and put up their weapons when they would be seditious, as the two extremities in a public body'.[68] Here, following Aristotle, the moderation of the 'public estate' comes from the increase and aggrandisement of the 'middle commoner'. But importantly, the word 'commoner' in the sixteenth century typically referred not simply to those below gentle rank but to rights-bearing citizens of corporations and more generally urban elites like burgesses.[69] The appropriation of

---

[67] Richard Mulcaster, *Positions Wherin Those Primitiue Circumstances Be Examined, which Are Necessarie for the Training Vp of Children* (London, 1581), pp. 139–40.
[68] *Ibid.*, p. 209.      [69] *OED*, cap. 1a.

social moderation for these urban citizens was part and parcel of a claim for their citizenship.

At roughly the same time, *A Description of the City of London* (published in Stow's 1598 *Survay of London*, but written some twenty years earlier) stressed that, even though London had grown to an enormous population, because 'the greatest part of them be neither too rich nor too poor, but do live in the mediocrity, I conclude with Aristotle that the prince needeth not to fear sedition by them'.[70] Far more than a mere exculpation of the urban middle sort from charges of disloyalty, this was an argument for their political superiority. The anonymous author wrote that there had been two great causes of rebellions in English history: ambition, which 'reigneth in the minds of high and noble personages', and covetousness, which 'possesseth the miserable and needy sort'. In London, however, there was no political ambition: high office was an 'onus' men accepted only reluctantly, and there was no faction or dangerous popularity because government revolved in a regular pattern regardless of who held office. Likewise, covetousness could not bear 'great sway' in London because 'the multitude and most part there is of a competent wealth and earnestly bent to honest labour'. The result was civil peace through the rule of moderation.[71]

Another example was Thomas Gainsford's magnum opus of nationalist propaganda *The Glory of England* (1618), a work popular enough to go through four editions within four years. The work was in large part a tribute to England's 'sufficiency' – a commonplace synonym for social moderation in the exegesis of Agur's Prayer and in other Christian social ethics – which Gainsford contrasted with 'Venetian riches, the many millions coming out of India into Spain, so many crowns of the sun coined in France'.[72] Gainsford's point was not that England was poorer than these other countries but that its wealth was moderate and sufficient rather than excessive because it belonged to urban tradesmen and yeomen farmers.[73] So, for instance, while Venice and Paris were dominated by nobles and priests, Gainsford praised the city of London, where 'tradesmen and

---

[70] Stow, *A Survay*, p. 480. For an earlier account that included 'handicraftsmen' and merchants within Aristotle's 'mean sort of men', see Francesco Patrizi, *A Moral Methode of Ciuile Policie* (London, 1576), sig. 5r. This work, significantly, was translated by 'Richard Robinson, citizen of London'.

[71] Stow, *A Survay*, p. 477.

[72] Thomas Gainsford, *The Glory of England, or, a True Description of Many Excellent Prerogatives and Remarkeable Blessings, whereby She Triumpheth over All the Nations of the World* (London, 1618), preface sig. ¶6r.

[73] Gainsford's emphasis on sufficiency is ironic, given that he fell from a successful goldsmith's family into a life of debt, forcing him to sell his inheritance and work as a mercenary soldier and hack writer: *ODNB sub nomine*.

shopkeepers' were unmatchable in their 'order, government, liberty of meeting, diet, purchasing of land, delicate furniture and all the particulars whereby a city is made famous, worthy and wealthy'. On the other side, while Europe's peasants were mired in serfdom, 'you shall find our yeoman of England a title of estimation in regard of his wealth, antiquity and maintenance of his family', and from the ranks of yeomen now came England's 'lawyers, citizens and merchants'.[74] In sum, while nobles and peasants dominated most countries, England was dominated, as Aristotle had recommended, by its middle sort. Most significantly, while other countries grew excessively rich through military conquest by monarchs, the true glory of kingdoms comes from 'the enriching of private men' who then contribute to the public. To this end, the great hero of England is the 'merchant-adventurer, as he is one way the supporter of political states by commerce, conversation and bringing in of wealth, so is he another way the Atlas of honour and majesty by his customs, filling the store-houses of the court, supplying the wants of a palace, pleasing the desires of novelty, cooling the heats of pride, and satiating the vanity of wishes'.[75]

Many of these themes were combined in a wonderful little pamphlet entitled *A Dialogue Between Riches, Poverty, Godliness, Gravity, Labour and Content* (1659).[76] The pamphlet began by setting the stage: 'There dwelt once, as hath been said, two inhabitants in one town, one called Riches, the other Poverty.' These two men were notoriously bad neighbours, constantly bickering: 'Riches would be insulting over poverty, either wronging or oppressing him', while Poverty 'was as much to blame too, for he was as stout as Riches . . . and very foul mouthed, and could never afford Riches a good word'. Riches drank from a cup called 'excess, a great foul cup it was', while Poverty was descended from Cain and had a 'nasty slut' for his wife. Into the midst of this, then, 'there happened to come into those parts' a man named Godliness, 'a stranger nobly born, and of a far better descent than either of the former two'. Godliness was a refugee from the Civil Wars in search of an honest living, but he was quickly driven out by both Riches and Poverty, neither of whom would have anything to do with him. The local magistrate named Gravity thus intervened and advised Godliness instead to go live with another neighbour: 'He bids him return to the town again, and about the middle of it, turn aside a little out of the road; there dwelt just midway, as he could guess, between Riches and Poverty, old Labour, a good honest neighbour,

[74] Gainsford, *The Glory of England*, pp. 269 and 307–8.    [75] *Ibid.*, p. 317
[76] *A Dialogue Between Riches, Poverty, Godliness, Gravity, Labour and Content* (London, 1659).

and the best house keeper in all the parish. He had a convenient house to let, and would be glad of a good tenant.' Labour represented all the best qualities of the middle sort. He was married to Prudence, and together they raised children who wore 'no lace or trimming that was costly', but rather clothes that were 'whole and handsome'. Labour travelled the world and built great cities, while in England he 'improved lands, levelled mountains, drained fens, invented all arts and sciences'. Indeed, the 'commonwealth was upheld by Labour' and he 'set many poor people a work, and paid them daily . . . yea, Labour provided stocks and pensions for the widows and children of such, who had been honest and careful in their business'. Just as importantly, Labour was also a political citizen, for he had 'stablished the wholesomest laws and rules of government', he had 'conquered most nations, gained the greatest dominions'. In the end, then, after Godliness and Labour worked together to rebuild the parish church, there arrived in the community a man named Content, whom the author identified with the biblical figure of Melchisedech, the priest-king and antetype of Christ. When Content arrived he first 'called in at Poverty's shed, enquiring if there was any room for such guests; they said no'. Next he tried the home of Riches, where he was informed that 'none neither knew him or any of his company'. Thus the home of Labour became 'Contentment's lodgings'. The moral of the tale, then, was to equate 'Godliness with Content' at the house of Labour, who upheld the commonwealth.

As a result of these new associations, in the later seventeenth century, when the term 'middle sort' became commonplace, so too did usages which presumed or implied the political participation of this 'sort'. Henry Neville's *Plato Redivivus* (1681) noted that 'there is scarce any amongst the middle sort of people, much less within the walls of the House of Commons, who do not perfectly know, that we can have no alliance with any nation in the world that will signify any thing to them, or to our selves, till our government be redressed and new modeled'.[77] James Tyrrell's *Bibliotheca Politica* (1694) described how the 'middle sort of men' in Saxon times included both rural and urban freemen who 'should have their representatives in parliament'.[78] In the same year, William Atkins described his role as a doctor for the middle sort as epitomising moderate public service:

A great part of the inhabitants in and about London are a middle sort of trading people; my business hath been much among them, and I am content with a middle station. If I had studied to serve my own interest more than to serve the

---

[77] Henry Neville, *Plato Redivivus* (London, 1681), pp. 208 and 247.

[78] James Tyrrell's *Bibliotheca Politica: or an Enquiry into the Ancient Constitution of the English Government* (London, 1694), p. 387.

public, I might have set up a coach and six horses, but I am content to ride in a hired coach . . . God hath given me enough to my full content, and now I am ready to be serviceable to any according to my ability.[79]

The point of these brief, impressionistic examples is not to suggest that approbation of the 'middle sort' as a political signifier was unanimous or unidirectional. In fact, as we shall see below in the context of the Revolution, many writers rejected any association between social moderation, the 'middle sort' and public responsibility. As early as 1557, many of the poems in the great anthology of English poetry known as 'Tottel's Miscellany' associated the 'moderate estate' with the rejection of politics. For instance, a poem entitled 'Of the Mean and Sure Estate' identified withdrawal from politics as social moderation: 'Unknown in court that hath the wanton toys / In hidden place my time shall slowly pass'.[80] A poem entitled 'They of the Mean Estate are Happiest' attacked riches insofar they were a symbol of immoderate love of power: 'For riches hates to be content / Rule is enemy to quietness. / Power is most part impatient / And seldom likes to live in peace'.[81] Another poem argued that:

> Who waiteth on the golden mean . . .
> Hides not his head in sluttish coats,
> Ne shrouds himself in filthiness.
> Ne sits aloft in high estate,
> Where hateful hearts envy his chance:
> But wisely walks betwixt them twain,
> Ne proudly doth himself advance.[82]

This was to anticipate a broad swathe of Elizabethan pastoral literature in which social moderation was associated with rural leisure rather than labour, and in which withdrawal from the cares of public life was the beginning of wisdom.[83] Later, when social moderation was increasingly associated with tradesmen and yeomen, Joseph Hall's *Quo Vadis?* (1617)

---

[79] William Atkins, *A Discourse Shewing the Nature of the Gout* (London, 1694), p. 112. For more examples see *The Practical Works of the Rev. Richard Baxter*, ed. William Orme (London, 23 vols., 1830), VI, p. 51; Henry Care, *An Answer to a Paper* (London, 1688), p. 18; Antoine de Brunel, *A Journey into Spain* (London, 1670), p. 146; George Morley, *The Bishop of Winchester's Vindication* (London, 1683), pp. 452–3; Robert Atkyns, *The Power, Jurisdiction and Privilege of Parliament* (London, 1689), p. 30; Robert Atkyns, *A Treatise of the True and Ancient Jurisdiction of the House of Peers* (London, 1699), p. 14; John Tutchin, *A New Martyrology* (London, 1693), p. 29.

[80] Henry Howard, *Songes and Sonettes, Written by the Right Honourable Lorde Henry Haward Late Earle of Surrey, and Other* (London, 1557), fo. 44r.

[81] *Ibid.*, fo. 51r–v.     [82] *Ibid.*, fo. 64v.

[83] See Scodel, *Excess and the Mean*. The *locus classicus* for these claims were the Odes and Epistles of Horace, translated into English as: *Certain Selected Odes of Horace, Englished*, trans. John Ashmore (London, 1621), esp. sig. C2r–v and sig. C3v; *Horace His Arte of Poetrie, Pistles and Satyrs Englished*, trans. Thomas Durant (London, 1567), esp. sig. C5r and sig. E1r.

seems to have been thoroughly derogatory when it described men of the 'middle rank' as 'either followers of the great, or commanders of the meaner sort', and hence responsible for the 'lukewarm indifferency' of both.[84] In a 1688 tract on Protestant unity, Gilbert Burnet claimed that while 'persons of the middle rank and condition' contributed to the strength and prosperity of the commonwealth, 'yet they make not that figure in the government, nor stand in that capacity of having influence in public affairs' necessary to protect true religion from its enemies.[85] More broadly, even if few sources flatly denied that the middle sort possessed some public competence, there were very real disagreements about what sort of competence they possessed and its significance for public life

My point, then, is not to suggest consensus but to show that discussions of social moderation came to embody debates and anxieties over the political participation of the 'middle sort'. While some writers nuanced or even rejected the claims to political competency elaborated through the rhetoric of social moderation, even these writers, through their explicit use of political categories, signalled that the idea of the 'middle sort' bore a political significance that historians have not heretofore noticed. This was not – except in the unique circumstances of the Civil War – a debate with clear sides or coherent positions that lined up according to ecclesiastical or political ideology. I do not mean to argue, for instance, that Gilbert Burnet opposed the political authority of the middle sort in some fundamental sense while George Webbe supported it (although undoubtedly the *term* 'middle sort' was almost always a mark of approval). Rather, I want to suggest that nearly all seventeenth-century commentators acknowledged the political implications of talking about a particular 'sort' of people through the language of social moderation; by listening to that language with an ear open to the relationship between moderation and government, we can hear them trying to make sense of, and appropriate for their own diverse purposes, a novel, confusing and sometimes disquieting political phenomenon.

### The revolution of the middle sort

This brings us to the conflagration of the mid seventeenth century. It was in the context of the Civil War and its messy aftermath that the concept of a 'middle sort of people' exploded into common parlance. Not

---

[84] Joseph Hall, *Quo Vadis? A Iust Censure of Travell as It Is Commonly Vndertaken by the Gentlemen of Our Nation* (London, 1617), p. 52.

[85] Gilbert Burnet, *The Ill Effects of Animosities among Protestants in England* (London, 1688), p. 19.

coincidentally, this was also the one context where we can see positive and negative assessments of the political competency of the 'middle sort' lining up along clear partisan lines. While the rapid emergence of the term 'middle sort' was undoubtedly tied to real social change, its timing can be closely associated with the fact that governance itself, and particularly the role of the 'middle sort' in the governance of the commonwealth, was among the central issues at stake in the conflict.[86] I want to suggest that in debates over the participation of the 'middle sort' in the English Revolution we can see most clearly the early modern linkage between social moderation and public government.

The association between parliamentarians and the 'middle sort' has been ensconced in modern scholarship since R. H. Tawney inserted it there nearly a century ago. More recently, Christopher Hill and Brian Manning made more sustained arguments that the parliamentarian cause had the support of the middle sort,[87] while with far more subtlety Keith Wrightson suggested that contemporary observers evolved and developed the socio-linguistic concept of a middle sort precisely to make sense of Civil War parliamentarianism.[88] Certainly the relationship between Roundheads and the middle sort was recognised both during the Civil War and afterwards, giving credence to modern claims for links between employment and ideology. The most famous version is Richard Baxter's:

It is of very great moment here to understand the quality of persons which adhered to the king and to the parliament, and their reasons. A great part of the Lords forsook the parliament, and so did many of the House of Commons, and came to the king... A very great part of the knights and gentlemen of England in the several counties (who were not parliament men) adhered to the king... And most of the tenants of these gentlemen, and also most of the poorest of the people, whom the other called the rabble, did follow the gentry and were for

---

[86] Here my interpretation fits closely with that of Wahrman, *Imagining the Middle Class*, concerning the politicisation of the language of class in the 1790s, and in fact in one paragraph on p. 68 Wahrman seems to have intuited much of my argument about the seventeenth century.

[87] R. H. Tawney, *Religion and the Rise of Capitalism: A Historical Study* (London, 1926); Brian Manning, *The English People and the English Revolution, 1640–1649* (London, 1976). Much of the enormous corpus of Christopher Hill's work is devoted to the idea of the Civil War as a bourgeois revolution, see, e.g., Christopher Hill, *The World Turned Upside Down: Radical Ideas in the English Revolution* (London, 1975); Christopher Hill, *Puritanism and Revolution: Studies in Interpretation of the English Revolution of the Seventeenth Century* (London, 1958). For critical assessments, see Roger Howell, 'The Structure of Urban Politics in the English Civil War', *Albion* 11, no. 2 (Summer 1979), pp. 111–27; John Morrill, 'Provincial Squires and "Middling Sorts" in the Great Rebellion', *HJ* 20, no. 1 (March 1977), pp. 229–36.

[88] Wrightson, '"Sorts of People" in Tudor and Stuart England'.

the king. On the parliament's side were (besides themselves) the smaller part (as some thought) of the gentry in most of the counties, and the greatest part of the tradesmen, and freeholders, and the middle sort of men, especially in those corporations and counties which depend on clothing and such manufactures. If you ask the reasons of this difference, ask also why in France it is not commonly the nobility nor the beggars but the merchants and middle sort of men that were Protestants.[89]

An equally sophisticated but less famous account comes from Peter Pett, a political maverick whose strong belief in religious toleration later led him to support alternately the radical Whigs and James II's dispensing power. In his 1661 *Discourse Concerning Liberty of Conscience*, he gave an elaborate sociological explanation for both the Civil War and religious debate more generally. Pett suggested that 'such as live on trade', whose livelihood depended upon 'the honesty of their servants', were naturally drawn to puritan preachers who 'are most passionate and loud against vice and the appearance of it'. Likewise, those people 'engaged in trade and traffic' also 'hate ceremonies in general, that is, forms and set behaviours that are necessary, as being not at leisure for them, and as they are expenseful, and as contrary to their education'. This amounted to an explanation for the whole Reformation: in southern Europe, where 'things grow of their own accord, that is, without industry', people remained Catholics, while in northern Europe, where people are 'more addicted to trade', they became Protestant. In particular, in the disputes over ceremonies that led to the Civil War in England,

If we reflect on those that did love ceremonies heretofore in our nation, we shall find them to have been persons of the greatest rank and quality among us, who did affect ceremonies in civil things; or of the poorest sort, who did get their daily bread by the charity of the other. The middling sort of men, and especially the substantial tradesmen of corporations, did generally disgust them.[90]

There are many other, less elaborate examples, as Keith Wrightson, Brian Manning and others have noted. At Bristol, for instance, 'the King's cause and party were favoured by two extremes in that city; the one wealthy and powerful men, the other of the basest and lowest sort, but disgusted by the middle rank, the true and best citizens'. According to Lucy Hutchinson, in Nottingham 'most of the gentry' were for the King, while 'most of the middle sort, the able and substantial freeholders and the other commons, who had not their dependence upon the malignant nobility

---

[89]  Richard Baxter, *Reliquiae Baxterianae* (London, 1696), p. 30.
[90]  Peter Pett, *A Discourse Concerning Liberty of Conscience* (London, 1661), pp. 29, 33, 35–8.

and gentry, adhered to the parliament'.[91] It is clear from these quotations that claiming 'middle sort' status for the parliamentary cause was a moral as much as a sociological exercise, identifying parliament with the normative virtue of social moderation. Thus, as a rule, the identification of parliament with the middle sort was undertaken by writers who favoured both. This is not to deny that there were real sociological differences between supporters of the two sides; tradesmen and merchants may well have been more likely to favour parliament. But given the previous discussion of the ways in which the idea of a 'middle sort' carried political claims, it also suggests that the normative association of parliament with the middle sort might have been related to claims about 'middle sort' participation in government.

If we want a representative of this position, we need look no further than the principal propagandist for the English Free State, John Milton. In Milton's 1650 Latin treatise *Pro Populo Anglicano Defensio*, he sought to defend republican governance against claims of anarchy and disorder. He wrote (as the 1692 English translation put it):

You inveigh against the common people, as being blind and brutish, ignorant of the art of governing, you say there's nothing more empty, more vain, more inconstant, more uncertain than they. All which is very true of yourself, and it's true likewise of the rabble, but not of the middle sort (*plebe... media*), amongst whom the most prudent men, and most skilful in affairs are generally found; others are most commonly diverted either by luxury and plenty, or by want and poverty, from virtue, and the study of laws and government.[92]

Here, then, the advent of the English Commonwealth was precisely the entry of a new category of men into government, the *prudentissimi*, distinguished both from the lowest of common people and from gentlemen. This middle sort were by their very nature the most suitable for virtuous participation in authority.

The 1640s and 1650s also saw a swell of allusions to the passages of Aristotle's *Politics* concerning the moderate estate, now typically using a phrase that had been absent from the 1598 translation: the 'middle sort'. An August 1642 declaration by parliament – later quoted by William

---

[91] Wrightson, '"Sorts of People" in Tudor and Stuart England', p. 46; Manning, *The English People*, pp. 170–80, 254–65.

[92] John Milton, *A Defence of the People of England* (Amsterdam?, 1692), p. 170. The 1650 Latin original is: 'Inveheris deinde in plebem, caecam eam et brutam, regendi artem non habere, nil plebe ventosius, vanius, levius, mobilius. Conveniunt in te optime haec omnia; et de infima quidem plebe sunt etiam vera, de media non item; quo ex numero prudentissimi: caeteros hinc luxus et opulentia, inde egestas et inopia a virtute, et civilis prudentiae studio plerunque avertit': John Milton, *Ioannis Miltoni Angli Pro Populo Anglicano Defensio* (London, 1650), p. 167.

Prynne in 1655 to hoist the government on their own petard – claimed, 'The most mischievous principles of tyranny are practised that ever were invented, thereby to disarm the middle sort of people, who are the body of the kingdom.'[93] John Milton wrote in 1643 that Europe's Catholic powers intended to set up in England 'a government by discretion', against which the greatest defence was 'the middle sort of people of England . . . who here live like men, and are wont to fight or die like men in honour or defence of their country'.[94] A radical tract by Edward Harrison in 1649 argued that democracy was virtuous government by the middle sort: 'The third of right is democracy, the power of the people, when mean and indifferent men are by them chosen; neither of the richest, to avoid tyranny, nor of the poorest, to avoid confusion. Of which Aristotle saith that those societies which consist of mean persons in power, is very good, and those cities and commonwealths are well governed, wherein there are many of the middle sort, who have more power then both the other parties.'[95] A 1654 text purporting to be a translation of Hugo Grotius, published under the title *Politick Maxims*, claimed, 'Tis expedient that betwixt the peers and the plebeians there should be a middle sort and degree of persons, as a seminary of nobility, such as were the knights and gentlemen of Rome: for this degree is a kind of tie, or ligament of both the other.'[96]

The new category of the 'middle sort', then, had both appropriated the traditional virtue of social moderation and embodied its more overtly political connotations, at least according to those favourably disposed to parliament's struggle against the king. But this raises the question: if claims to political rights, rather than merely sociological reportage, were at stake in contemporary accounts of the 'middle sort', how did parliament's opponents interpret the social context of the Civil War?

First of all, it is important to note that there was a populist, radical framework that located social moderation in the common people and advocated the redistribution of wealth to restore their moderation, hence rejecting parliament's own claim to represent the middle sort. Perhaps the most famous such claim in the Revolution came from the pen of

---

[93] *Journal of the House of Lords*, vol. V, 20 August 1642, online at www.british-history.ac. uk/report.aspx?compid=34880, last consulted 24 August 2010. For Prynne, see William Prynne, *A New Discovery of Free-State Tyranny* (London, 1655), p. 32.

[94] John Milton, *A Soveraigne Salve to Cure the Blind* (London, 1643), p. 26.

[95] Edward Harrison, *Plain Dealing: or, the Countreymans Doleful Complaint and Faithful Watchword, to the Statesmen of the Times* (London, 1649), p. 7. I am grateful to Elliot Vernon for this reference.

[96] Hugo Grotius[?], *Politick Maxims and Observations* (London, 1654), pp. 128–9. Many other texts of the 1640s and 1650s also made explicit use of Aristotle's idea of a moderate estate, famously James Harrington's *Oceana*, for which see Chapter 7 below.

George Foster, who described a vision in which God's angel, with sword drawn, rode through the countryside 'cutting down all men and women that he met with that were higher than the middle sort, and raised up those that were lower than the middle sort, and made them all equal, and cried out, "Equality! Equality, in that I have now made all men alike!"' Historians have quoted this passage as a colourful anecdote, but they have not considered just what Foster's 'middle sort' signified. For Foster, the 'middle sort' were decidedly not the urban tradesmen or rural capitalists who had supported parliament; these were Whores of Babylon. Instead, the 'middle sort' were small farmers, 'enjoying the fruits of the earth and so no longer to work for others, or others to have the benefit of their labours, but every man shall now enjoy the fruits of his own labour'. Excess, for Foster, consisted in 'self-interest', 'striving for riches' and 'ambition', and eventually God will 'make these that have riches give them to them that have none'. The point was to create a permanent society of self-sufficient labour.[97]

Another version was *A Declaration of the Wel-Affected in the Country of Buckinghamshire* (1649), which purported on the title page to represent 'the middle sort of men within the three Chiltern hundreds of Disbrough, Burnum and Stoke, and part of Alisbury hundred'. The 'middle sort' here were contrasted on one side with 'chief commanders' in the army and parliament, who 'are grown to an extreme height of avarice, pride, hypocrisy and apostasy, mere arbitrary politicians preferring their filthy lucres and diabolical interests, gain and ugly honour, more than the common freedom'. On the opposite side were the poor, whose 'rights, dues, etc' had been unjustly stolen from them. The solution, proposed in a series of numbered grievances, was to raise the poor up to the middle sort by allowing them to dig the commons – a vision that included 'common freedom' as an explicitly political claim.[98] While these two tracts were unusual in using the term 'middle sort', the idea that social moderation was an attribute of the commons can be found much more broadly in the radical pamphlet literature of the period, describing both the

---

[97] George Foster, *The Sounding of the Last Trumpet* (London, 1650), pp. 17–18, 42, 46–7. A remarkable precedent for this framework, although one that Foster is unlikely to have known, can be found in Hans Hergot's 1525 German tract *On the New Transformation of the Christian Life*: 'There have been three tables in the world. The first was superfluous and had too much on it. The second had a moderate amount and enough to satisfy the needs [of those who sat at it]. The third was completely wanting. Then those from the superfluous table came and wanted to take away the bread from the table that had least. The conflict arose from this, and God will overturn the superfluous table and the table with the least, and he will uphold the middle table.' Translated in Michael Baylor (ed.), *The Radical Reformation* (Cambridge, 1991), p. 225.

[98] *A Declaration of the Wel-Affected in the Country of Buckinghamshire* (London, 1649).

political and economic rights from which they had been unjustly excluded. This was, in essence, to deny the commonplace association of the middle sort with parliamentarianism, not by challenging its sociological claims but by challenging its political meanings: parliament had betrayed the commons and thus could have no affinity with social moderation.

It is within the literature of royalism, however, that we find a full-fledged alternative to the claim that the 'middle sort' supported parliament. Royalists refused to surrender the valuable currency of social moderation and made elaborate arguments that parliamentarian Londoners were not the middle sort at all but a coalition of the greedy rich and the ignorant poor. We might usefully begin with an insignificant but representative tract by Peter Heylyn entitled *Lord Have Mercie Upon Us* (1643) which identified the source of the civil wars as 'the factious and disloyal carriage of that wealthy city' and argued that London was the enemy of the independent landowner: 'We spent our wealth amongst them to make them rich, and they employ that wealth to no other purpose than to make us miserable.' The tract described how the city's greed and wealth, based upon trade and accumulation, had corrupted the nation:

By venting their commodities into all parts of the kingdom ... they draw into their hands all the wealth thereof, which they pour out again to foment war; and by the wretchedness of their example make the whole nation guilty of their own undoing. So as we may affirm of that factious city, as an ancient author did of Rome in the state of heathenism, that there is little hope of rest to the Church of God till that city be once humbled.

In addition to the rich, moreover, the poor of London also fomented war, 'those tumultuous assemblies of unruly people, gathered from all parts of that potent but unquiet city to awe the parliament and terrify those discrete and moderate members of both houses who had no other thoughts than the peace and honour of their country'. Between these social extremes, then, were 'moderate' members of parliament and a minority of 'moderate' Londoners who put peace and law ahead of profit, 'fellow citizens, many of which were very cordially affected to his sacred majesty, right honest patriots and zealously inclined to such moderate counsels as did conduce to the advancement of the public peace'.[99]

Another early example was Thomas Fuller's *Jacobs Vow* (1644), based upon a sermon preached before Charles I at Oxford in May 1644. This was in essence a reminder to royalists, many of whose lands had been sequestered, that Jacob's biblical request for 'necessaries for the present'

[99] Peter Heylyn, *Lord Have Mercie Upon Us* (Oxford, 1643), pp. 3, 42, 5–6, 44 and 34.

had been 'very moderate and reasonable', providing a lesson for royalists 'to teach us how moderate we should be in the desire of earthly things'.[100] Agur prayed 'expressly against riches . . . as well as poverty', and likewise Jacob prayed 'neither for riches, nor honour, nor any other outward thing, but only for bread to eat and clothes to put on', so it should be no surprise to virtuous royalists that this was now their condition. Although Fuller avoided preaching *ad hominem*, it did not take much imagination to see parliamentarians and Londoners in the 'horse leaches' and 'worldlings' for whom riches, honours and earthly pleasures were the holy trinity.[101] This did not mean that Fuller opposed the association of the middle sort with social moderation more generally – two years earlier he had written, 'It is no breach of contentment for men by lawful means to seek the removal of their misery and bettering of their estate. Thus men ought by industry to endeavor the getting of more wealth, ever submitting themselves to God's will' – but rather that he refused to associate this moderation with parliamentarians.[102]

In the years around the regicide, the narrative solidified that London's excessive riches had produced a collapse of morality, leading to the sins of rebellion and irreligion. Charles Dallison, for instance, argued in 1648 that the puppeteers controlling parliament's war effort were 'a faction in the city of London, who were the moneyed men and so interested in buying the Church lands'.[103] The following year, *Eikon Basilike* (1649) included a prayer from the king: 'Divert, I pray thee, O Lord, thy heavy wrath justly hanging over these populous cities, whose plenty is prone to add fuel to their luxury, their wealth to make them wanton, their multitudes tempting them to security, and their security exposing them to unexpected miseries.'[104] The royalist Samuel Butler's 1652 poem 'The Reformation' argued that the parliamentarians 'lay their consciences aside / And turn with every wind and tide / Puff'd on by ignorance and pride / And all to look like gentry / . . . See the tradesman, how he thrives / With perpetual trouble / How he cheats and how he strives / His estate t'enlarge and double / Extort, oppress, grind and encroach / To be a 'squire and keep a coach'.[105]

---

[100] Thomas Fuller, *Jacobs Vow: A Sermon Preached before His Majesty* (London, 1644), pp. 4–6.
[101] *Ibid.*, pp. 7–8.
[102] Thomas Fuller, *The Holy State* (Cambridge, 1642), p. 196.
[103] Charles Dallison, *The Royalist's Defence* (London, 1648), sig. A4v.
[104] Charles I [?], *Eikon Basilike: The Porvtraictvre of his Sacred Maiestie in His Solitudes and Svfferings* (London, 1649), p. 210.
[105] Samuel Butler, *The Second Volume of the Posthumous Works of Mr. Samuel Butler* (London, 1715), pp. 248–55.

As the Cromwellian regime ground to a halt, William Sanderson's *Compleat History of the Life and Raigne of King Charles from His Cradle to His Grave* (1658) began the process of converting this narrative from propaganda to history. Sanderson admitted that, while the gentry generally inclined to the king so as 'better to rule over the commons their vassals', the common people 'consisting chiefly of Yeomen, Farmers, petty Freeholders and others, men of manufacture, bred up sparingly, but living in plenty' generally supported parliament. The important phrase here was 'bred up sparingly but living in plenty'; these were the *nouveau rich* who exceeded their appropriate moderation, just like the Londoners who were 'luxuriant in wealth' and 'pampered with ease' and hence experimented with Presbyterianism. The one time Sanderson referred to the 'middle sort', he was quoting the August 1642 declaration by parliament falsely claiming that the king intended to 'disarm the middle sort of people, who are the body of the kingdom'. But while parliament's declaration had identified the 'middle sort' very imprecisely with 'gentlemen, yeomen and townsmen', for Sanderson this piece of misinformation was aimed squarely at 'the gentry of the northern countries'.[106] Parliamentarians, by definition, could not represent social moderation because they were self-evidently disobedient and rebellious subjects.

It was in the great royalist histories produced after the Restoration that this framework fully matured, challenging the connections between parliament, the middle sort and virtuous citizenship. Thomas Hobbes's history of the Civil War, *Behemoth: Or, the Long Parliament*, completed in 1668, gave a retrospective account of Civil War allegiance. Noting London's support for parliament, Hobbes wrote that throughout history 'those great capital cities, when rebellion is upon pretext of grievances, must needs be of the rebel party, because the grievances are but taxes, to which citizens, that is, merchants, whose profession is their private gain, are naturally mortal enemies; their only glory being to grow excessively rich by the wisdom of buying and selling'. Later the same point is made about 'rich subjects, that have made themselves so by craft and trade' who 'never look upon anything but their present profit'. When the interlocutor in the dialogue answers that merchants are 'said to be of all callings the most beneficial to the commonwealth, by setting the poorer sort of people to work', Hobbes's mouthpiece replies that they merely make 'poor people to sell their labour to them at their own prices; so

---

[106] William Sanderson, *A Compleat History of the Life and Raigne of King Charles from His Cradle to His Grave* (London, 1658), pp. 543, 187, 561. See also Thomas Cartwright, *The Danger of Riches, Discovered in a Sermon* (London, 1662), pp. 2, 6–7, 16. This Cartwright was the grandson of the famous puritan.

that poor people, for the most part, might get a better living by working at Bridewell'. Indeed, it was the utter dependence of the urban poor on the rich citizens, and their subsequent exploitability, that made them so active against the king: 'And as most commonly they are the first encouragers of rebellion, presuming their own strength; so also are they, for the most part, the first to repent, deceived by them that command their strength.'[107] Here, then, Hobbes agreed with Baxter that parliament's support came from urban merchants, tradesmen and their workers, but he utterly disagreed about the 'middle' or 'moderate' nature of that support.

Another example is Edward Chamberlayne's *Angliae Notitia: Or, the Present State of England* (1669), in which he considered at length why the disease of rebellion 'infected some of the worse natured and worse nurtured gentry, divers of the inferior clergy, most of the tradesmen and very many of the peasantry'. The answer was that England was too abundant in natural resources, so that 'the wealth, insolence and pride of these . . . have rendered them so distasteful, not only to the few strangers who frequent England but even to their own gentry, that they could sometimes wish that either the country were less plentiful or that the impositions were heavier'. It was because the supposed middle sort had lost their moderation and grown rich that they abandoned their senses and became politicians, and it was necessary to make them less rich again, perhaps by increasing taxes, to return the nation to good order. Indeed, Chamberlayne wrote that 'in England it is no paradox to affirm that, as too much indigency in the inferior sort of people doth depress the spirits and dull the minds of them, so too plentiful and wanton a fortune causeth in them a laziness and less industry; that state commonly enjoying most peace and order and happiness, where either the moderate barrenness of the country, or want of ground, or multitude of imposts (as in Holland) do necessitate the common people to be industrious in their callings'.[108]

One final example comes from David Llyod, whose 1668 panegyric for royalist martyrs described one 'Thomas Berkley of Worcester, gentlemen' as 'one of those happy men that are only found in England, living in the temperate zone between greatness and want (France and Italy . . . hath no point between sink and ace, nobility and peasantry)'. Here the notion

---

[107] Thomas Hobbes, *Behemoth: Or, the Long Parliament*, ed. Ferdinand Tönnies (Chicago, 1990), pp. 126 and 142. A slightly different manoeuvre can be seen in Edward Hyde, *The History of the Rebellion and Civil Wars in England* (Oxford, 3 vols., 1707), I, pp. 372–5.

[108] Edward Chamberlayne, *Angliae Notitia: Or, the Present State of England* (London, 1669), pp. 59–61.

of social moderation was clearly employed but referred to a gentleman of considerable means, since his great sacrifice for the king's cause was that

> he was forced, besides several irregular sums extorted from him, to lay down for his loyalty in the corban of the conspiracy, Goldsmith's Hall, four hundred twenty-six pounds fifteen shillings and six pence: a sum that deserves a mention, for we are resolved none shall be denied admittance to the temple of honour, who hath been at so great a charge to go through the temple of virtue.[109]

From both parliamentarian and royalist perspectives, then, sociological claims about the Civil War had significant political implications. For parliamentarians, 'middle sort' support for parliament was an act of political engagement both authorised and explained by their social moderation. For royalists, by contrast, the support of urban tradesmen and capitalist farmers for parliament was a product of avarice and ignorance, demonstrating their self-interest and incapacity for political participation; unable to restrain their social appetites, it was no wonder they had rebelled.

## Conclusion

In conclusion, the new concept of a 'middle sort' invested a particular 'sort' of people with a pre-existing ideal of social moderation that encompassed not only or even principally economic status but also a constellation of attributes related to reason, citizenship and service to the commonwealth. Moderation meant government, and the 'governance of the middle sort' captures with some precision the complex interrelationship between ethical self-restraint, reasonable subjection to government and reasonable participation in government. The emergence of the 'middle sort' was thus imbricated with broader early modern debates over the proper role of that 'sort' of people in public authority, debates which only in the crucible of the Revolution crystallised into coherent positions or sides, but which nonetheless permeated and percolated through much of the social and political commentary of Tudor-Stuart England. This explains why the term rose to prominence in the middle of the seventeenth century, when the Civil War and its aftermath raised into sharp relief the question of how far England was to be a participatory commonwealth. It explains why parliamentarians were so concerned to associate the middle sort with their cause, while both royalists and radicals

---

[109] David Lloyd, *Memoires of the Lives, Actions, Sufferings & Deaths . . . for the Protestant Religion and the Great Principle Thereof, Allegiance to Their Soveraigne, in Our Late Intestine Wars* (London, 1668), p. 123. For a later example, see the discussion of 'the moderate sort of men' in John Dryden, *Absalom and Achitophel* (London, 1681), p. 3.

questioned that claim on ideological rather than sociological grounds. It explains why, as Henry French has noted, the term 'middle sort' appears most often in printed texts but not as a self-referent or locus of social identity-formation. And it foregrounds the emergent authority of tens of thousands of citizens who were increasingly acknowledged, at least by certain observers in certain polemical contexts, as appropriate moderators of England's passions.

In the decades around 1700, much of this cultural framework dissolved, even as the social reality underpinning it hardened. The concepts of moderation and the middle way lost their political connotations; both Aristotle's *Politics* and Agur's Prayer lost their cultural authority; the social and the political were gradually differentiated. I have tried to suggest, then, that the emergence of the idea of a 'middle sort' of people in Tudor-Stuart England can be precisely located to a particular historical moment when social moderation implied political authority, and as such the 'middle sort' signified different things than historians interested in objective social conditions, or historians looking forward to the Industrial Revolution, have been conditioned to hear. While there is no doubt that urban tradesman and rural yeomen increased in numbers and social significance in this period, their 'moderation' was by no means obvious; to claim it for them, or to contest that claim, was a way of commenting on the parameters of English government.

Given that the term 'middle sort' bore significant political connotations, historians might perhaps rethink their fondness for the term as a supposedly neutral sociological signifier. We are often told that 'middle class' is a problematic term in pre-industrial contexts, but it has been presumed that 'middle sort' is a merely descriptive term that more or less transcends time, space and culture. Hence Anglophone historians of medieval China, ancient Rome and virtually every other pre-industrial setting routinely use the early modern term 'middle sort' as if it can be unproblematically and unambiguously grafted onto any society. But if, as this chapter had suggested, the emergence of the term 'middle sort' was part of a debate over new forms of political authority, then using the term 'middle sort' as a category of historical analysis may do more damage to our understanding of pre-industrial society than importing the wholly alien, and hence perhaps safely heuristic, category of class.

## Introduction: 'the mean of liberty'

In modern political thought, we like to imagine 'liberty' as a simple antonym of 'tyranny', yet a moment's reflection reveals that this dualism is illusory. When we use the word 'liberty' in a political context, we implicitly assume a series of appropriate limitations; even the strictest libertarians admit that some forms of coercion and some limits to self-determination are not incompatible with liberty but essential to it. Political liberty, then, is ordinarily presumed to exist on a continuum, and its limitations are as significant as its core in defining what liberty means in particular political contexts.[1] In the seventeenth century, when political ideals were routinely imagined as middle ways between extremes, this idea of limited liberty as true liberty was inevitably expressed in terms of moderation.

The interconnection between liberty and moderation can be found anywhere in early modern England that the idea of liberty came into vogue. But there is no better laboratory for studying this association, and no place where its ideological implications were more significant, than in the great, extended controversy over the nature of liberty we call the English Revolution. So, for instance, as Quentin Skinner has recently noted, Thomas Hobbes described himself in the dedicatory epistle to his *Leviathan* as responding to 'those that contend, on one side for too great liberty, and on the other side for too much authority'.[2] Far from being a novel claim for moderation in 1651, this was a commonplace. The parliamentarian theorist Henry Parker, for instance, wrote in 1642, 'Long it was ere the world could extricate itself out of all these

---

[1] John Locke put this idea succinctly in 1693: 'No government allows absolute liberty; the idea of government being the establishment of society upon certain rules or laws which require conformity to them; and the idea of absolute liberty being for anyone to do whatever he pleases. I am as capable of being certain of the truth of this proposition as of any of the mathematics': John Locke, *An Essay Concerning Human Understanding* (Amherst, New York, 1995), p. 448.

[2] Quentin Skinner, *Hobbes and Republican Liberty* (Cambridge, 2008), pp. 208–10.

extremities . . . to avoid the danger of unbounded prerogative on this hand, and too excessive liberty on the other.'[3] In a tract significantly entitled *The Arraignment of Licentious Liberty and Oppressing Tyranny* (1647), the erstwhile parliamentarian and future royalist Nathaniel Hardy hoped that 'neither royal majesty may invade the subjects' liberty, nor the subjects' liberty entrench too far on royal majesty'.[4] In 1649, John Lilburne and his fellow Levellers admitted, 'Though tyranny is so excessively bad, yet of the two extremes, confusion is the worst.'[5] The republican Marchamont Nedham in 1650 described the English Commonwealth as 'the only bank which preserves us from the inundation of tyranny on the one side, and confusion on the other'.[6] In 1656, the lawyer Michael Hawke argued that as a conjunction of 'liberty and principality' the Cromwellian protectorate was a 'mean between an abrupt service under the dominion of a tyrant, and dissolute licentiousness . . . To the best princes the mean of liberty is most pleasing, and so to rule their subjects by reason and law, that they do live civilly without injury and enjoy quietly their properties and liberty.'[7] The examples are nearly limitless.

Proper liberty, then, was habitually understood as a middle way. The word 'liberty' itself sometimes referred simply to this golden mean, implicitly denying that excessive liberty was really liberty at all; but even when authors instead described liberty as potentially either excessive or deficient, they concurred that the appropriate, beneficent liberty of a commonwealth must always be moderate. Recognising this seventeenth-century classification of true liberty as a middle way between extremes, necessarily moderate in order to be actualised, forces us to rethink our approach to political theory in the English Revolution. As Siep Stuurman has noted, the historiography of political thought remains largely trapped within a teleology that privileges rather than deconstructs the history of 'liberty'.[8] Once we have noticed that liberty acquired meaning through its moderation, however, every defence of liberty can be resituated as an attempt to restrain or bridle liberty in its own particular context. The goal of this chapter is thus to use the rule of moderation to provide a new context for reading political thought, and especially

[3] Henry Parker, *Observations upon Some of His Majesties Late Answers and Expresses* (London, 1642), p. 14.

[4] Nathaniel Hardy, The *Arraignment of Licentious Liberty and Oppressing Tyranny* (London, 1647), p. 15.

[5] Andrew Sharp (ed.), *The English Levellers* (Cambridge, 1998), p. 162.

[6] Nedham, *The Case of the Common-Wealth of England Stated*, pp. 87–8.

[7] Michael Hawke, *The Right of Dominion, and Property of Liberty* (London, 1656), pp. 104–5.

[8] Siep Stuurman, 'The Canon and the History of Political Thought: Its Critique and a Proposed Alternative', *History and Theory* 39, no. 2 (May 2000), pp. 147–66.

republican thought, in the English Revolution.[9] Studying how early modern writers sought to moderate liberty allows us to read texts calling for freedom, whether republican, royalist, or 'radical', as competing acts of exclusion and limitation. Thus, by tracing the creative topologies through which different writers redefined the spectrum from tyranny to anarchy, this chapter offers new insights into the aggression of English political thought, particularly the paradoxically repressive liberty advocated by the most influential revolutionary republican text, James Harrington's *The Commonwealth of Oceana* (1656).[10]

### The neo-Roman theory of moderate liberty

Let us begin in 1649, after the execution of Charles Stuart, with the outpouring of self-consciously 'republican' texts intended to shape the new, ostensibly republican regime of the English Free State. These texts have a clear historical importance as the first systematic expositions of non-monarchical government in England. Just as importantly, they have a remarkable historiographical prominence: since the 1970s they have been at the heart of the 'history of ideas' as a discipline. John Pocock placed these texts at the centre of a centuries-long tradition of 'civic republicanism' – a political theory based on classical *virtu* and active citizenship – which eventually migrated to America as an alternative to the individualist ethos of Lockean liberalism.[11] Jonathan Scott placed these texts at the centre of a tradition of 'Christian humanist moral philosophy' that rejected private interest in favour of the public good, requiring a 'radical reformation of manners'.[12] Perhaps most importantly, Quentin

---

[9] I use the term 'republican' here as convenient but somewhat imprecise shorthand for writers who sought to structure the English commonwealth in accordance with classical republican principles rather than England's ancient constitution. The historiographical debate over who the classical republicans were in the seventeenth century I regard as distracting.

[10] The repressive nature of Harrington's scheme for the republic has been discussed in, for instance, Paul Rahe, *Republics Ancient and Modern: Classical Republicanism and the American Revolution* (Chapel Hill, 1992); Jonathan Scott, '"The Rapture of Motion": James Harrington's Republicanism', in Nicholas Phillipson and Quentin Skinner (eds.), *Political Discourse in Early Modern Europe* (Cambridge, 1993); Gary Remer, 'James Harrington's New Deliberative Rhetoric: Reflection of an Anticlassical Republicanism', *History of Political Thought* 16, no. 4 (Winter 1995), pp. 532–57; Johann Sommerville, 'English and Roman Liberty in the Monarchical Republic of Early Stuart England', in John McDiarmid (ed.), *The Monarchical Republic of Early Modern England: Essays in Response to Patrick Collinson* (Aldershot, 2007), pp. 215–16.

[11] J. G. A. Pocock, *The Machiavellian Moment: Florentine Political Thought and the Atlantic Republican Tradition* (Princeton, 1975).

[12] Scott, *Commonwealth Principles*; Jonathan Scott, 'What Were Commonwealth Principles?' *HJ* 47, no. 3 (2004), pp. 591–613.

Skinner found in these texts a 'neo-Roman theory of free states' based on the Roman law distinction between slavery and freedom, in which civil liberty depends upon neither the state nor its citizens being within any power external to their wills.[13] In these and many other works, the revolutionary moment of the regicide and its obvious discontinuity with England's 'ancient constitution' is seen as creating a unique intellectual space for a republican synthesis.

And so it did. But republican visions of 'liberty' were not so single-mindedly concerned with the dangers of 'tyranny', whether represented by kings, private interests, or conditions of dependence, as this scholarship would imply. Rather, their constant harping on 'liberty' was something of a shell-game, or at best a neat shorthand, for a much more complex vision of good government as equally free both from external domination and from the unbridled will or unrestrained appetites of its people. Or, to put it in a slightly different idiom, they described liberty as freedom from the passions as well as the interests. At the most basic level, they described true liberty not as the antithesis of tyranny/slavery, but as the moderate middle way between tyranny/slavery and 'populacy'.[14] I want to call this position – the first of several theories of restraint to be described in this chapter – the neo-Roman theory of moderate liberty.[15]

We can usefully begin with the ideas of Eutactus Philodemius – perhaps a pseudonym for Antony Ascham, a propagandist and ambassador for the Commonwealth – in *The Original & End of Civil Power* (1649).[16] Philodemius wrote, in unimpeachably republican terms, that the people's 'free choice' is the 'source and fountain from whence all forms of power and government flow', and that 'the people' in this sense are 'every single or particular person within any nation or kingdom, high and low, noble and ignoble, rich and poor, bond and free, without any limitation or restraint to any individual person whatsoever'.[17] The expression of this popular will and the absence of restraint, then, is the essence of political

---

[13] Quentin Skinner, *Liberty Before Liberalism* (Cambridge, 1998).
[14] Depending upon the perspective of the speaker, a deficiency of liberty might go under the heading of either tyranny or slavery: deficient liberty for the individual was slavery, while deficient liberty for the polity was a condition of tyranny. I have generally used the term 'tyranny' rather than 'slavery' in this chapter because I generally approach the question from the perspective of the state.
[15] I am indebted here to Graham Maddox, 'The Limits of Neo-Roman Liberty', *History of Political Thought* 23, no. 3 (Autumn 2002), pp. 418–31.
[16] Eutactus Philodemius, *The Original & End of Civil Power* (London, 1649). Richard Tuck has challenged the identity of Ascham with Philodemius on the grounds that *The Original & End of Civil Power* is far more republican than the rest of Ascham's corpus: Tuck, *Philosophy and Government*, pp. 257–8.
[17] Philodemius, *The Original & End of Civil Power*, pp. 3–4.

liberty. When free people delegate their power to magistrates, they do not thereby relinquish 'their proper rights and interests', but only the power to preserve those rights, and they thus retain their authority to judge tyranny.[18]

Yet Philodemius positioned himself and his Republic not as defenders of liberty against its tyrannical opposite that produced slavery, but rather as defenders of a moderate middle way between tyranny and 'populacy'. The whole question of the origins and goals of civil power, he wrote, could only be properly treated from a perspective of 'equidistant station between these two great and sharply controverted interests of populacy and magistracy'. Before the civil wars, the 'extreme of the magistrate's part' had been 'vigorously contested for and pursued, until at length it clashed with God's interest', and hence magistracy was destroyed in the Revolution. Now, however, 'the other extreme is hotly contested for, by men unacquainted with just and allowed policy . . . as if the bulk of the people, in their moliminous and confused body, were the supreme and sovereign power'.[19] The first extreme had put too much stock in the unlimited will of a 'degenerate magistrate', but the second extreme 'pulls down the great ordinance of magistracy under the unhallowed feet of an easily discontented vulgar'.[20] Philodemius's goal, then, was to describe how the people's liberty was precisely a *via media* between these extremes.

So where did Philodemius draw the line between liberty and anarchy, and how could he square his restraint of the 'vulgar' with his claim that lawful authority flows directly from the absence of such restraint? He argued that the people's natural power, in its raw state, was a 'vast and thronged bulk of underived majesty', useless and unprofitable, formless and void like the earth 'before God with his *fiat* did gather it together into one place'.[21] This 'underived' power was dangerous precisely because of its immoderation: 'The people's power and vigor, whilst it remains thus untransferred, is dangerous to themselves: they will soon range beyond the line and pale of private rights and properties; their appetites are their purveyors, and their wants are measured by their wills.' Nature, however, had provided a remedy for this 'shoreless excess': 'nature hath taught men to give up and concredit that power and vigor before mentioned,

---

[18] *Ibid.*, pp. 4–6.

[19] Philodemius's use of the word 'moliminous' in this context was likely taken from Henry Parker's 1642 *Observations*, p. 14: 'Till some way was invented to regulate the motions of the people's moliminous body, I think arbitrary rule was most safe for the world.' It is possible that Philodemius was really Parker.

[20] Philodemius, *The Original & End of Civil Power*, dedication sig. A2r–v.

[21] *Ibid.*, p. 7. On p. 10, in an equally arresting simile, Philodemius describes the people's undelegated power as like the letters of the alphabet, 'promiscuously thrown together in a heap', before they are formed into words.

which they have in themselves', into other men's hands.[22] Here, then, *representation* was the essence of Philodemius's vision of moderate liberty as an alternative to anarchy. As he put it, 'All sovereignties and royalties are *virtually* in the people, though it be *formally* in him or them whom the people set up over themselves.'[23] Representation is necessary here not merely because direct democracy or participation are impracticable but because they are dangerous, not properly bridling the unruly appetites of the people. The pseudonym Eutactus Philodemius, it is worth noting, did not just mean populist, but *disciplined* populist, or perhaps lover of well-disciplined people.[24]

What of the other side of the balance, and Philodemius's vision of liberty as an antidote to tyranny? Here again we find an apparent contradiction, because alongside Philodemius's blistering attacks on the tyranny of Charles I, he defended a level of *de facto* power for the Commonwealth government beyond what many of his contemporaries found tyrannical. Much of this was no doubt a polemical necessity for a (presumably) paid propagandist; for instance, despite his love for representative government, Philodemius defended the violently purged Rump Parliament as 'a parliament entire in its essence, though not a full parliament'.[25] But this was more than mere political posturing. In a general sense, Philodemius authorised and embraced state-sponsored violence for the common good. To make this argument, he reinterpreted the natural-law commonplace that self-destruction is unnatural, hence the people cannot delegate any power to hurt themselves. He argued that, while people did not have a natural right to commit suicide or enslave themselves, they certainly did have a right, and even a duty, to sacrifice their lives and property for the common good. Hence they delegated that right to their representatives, giving the Commonwealth government the power to take both their property and their lives. As Philodemius put it:

God doth not entrust any man to have power to destroy his own image, i.e. to take away man's life, but him or them whom he makes gods, i.e. magistrates, and to whom he deputes his own place. Yet this great, yea the greatest ingredient of supremacy, viz. power of life and death, that is thus affixed to the person of a ruler, or supreme, is derived to him from that authority or government from whence he is so denominated a supreme, and it is from his authority only that his diadem is environed with such glorious rays of majesty.[26]

Needless to say, this has all the hallmarks of the most vigorous absolutist theories, although it posits an absolute government derived from the

---

[22] *Ibid.*, pp. 7–9.     [23] *Ibid.*, p. 4. Emphasis in the original.
[24] I owe thanks to Sarah Ross for translating this Greek for me.
[25] Philodemius, *The Original & End of Civil Power*, p. 29.     [26] *Ibid.*, pp. 17–18.

people.[27] It in effect authorises magistrates to break the law and use any means necessary to promote the common good – in context, Philodemius is legitimising both extraordinary taxation and the creation of extralegal tribunals like the one that condemned Charles Stuart. So what distinguished this awesome state power from tyranny? The answer, once again, was representation. It is not the magistrates' actions but their authorisation that distinguishes tyranny from liberty, and proper authorisation renders the use of seemingly extreme force moderate. On these grounds, Philodemius was even willing to allow for monarchy as legitimate government as long as the monarch was elected. But hereditary government was *ipso facto* tyrannous, because it made the people into a mere 'footstool' by which kings 'ascend to their pompous majesty'.[28] The government of the English Commonwealth was free rather than tyrannical, then, precisely because it had finally conquered the hereditary principle of prerogative government.

Another good example of the neo-Roman theory of moderate liberty is Marchamont Nedham's *The Case of the Common-Wealth of England Stated* (1650).[29] Nedham, like Philodemius before him, straightforwardly defined liberty as a moderate middle way between extremes: his goal was to explain why the 'present government' of the English Commonwealth was 'the only bank which preserves us from the inundation of tyranny on the one side, and confusion on the other'. The dangerous extreme of 'tyranny' Nedham represented as not only monarchical but Presbyterian. The opposite extreme of 'confusion' he represented in 'those zealous pretenders to liberty and freedom', the Levellers.[30]

---

[27] See Tuck, *Philosophy and Government*, ch. 6. Tuck would see Henry Parker as a principal source of these ideas.

[28] Philodemius, *The Original & End of Civil Power*, p. 32.

[29] Nedham was a notorious turncoat, hired pen and 'jack of all sides', and we cannot trust that he actually believed anything he wrote. Nonetheless, an elaborate historiography has established that he was also an independent-minded troublemaker, unafraid to challenge his employers, and his republican tracts represent significant moments of intellectual synthesis. See Paul Rahe, *Against Throne and Altar: Machiavelli and Political Theory under the English Republic* (Cambridge, 2008); Blair Worden, 'Wit in a Roundhead: The Dilemma of Marchamont Nedham', in Susan Amussen and Mark Kishlansky (eds.), *Political Culture and Cultural Politics in Early Modern Europe: Essays Presented to David Underdown* (Manchester, 1995); Vickie Sullivan, *Machiavelli, Hobbes and the Formation of a Liberal Republicanism in England* (Cambridge, 2004), ch. 3.

[30] Nedham, *The Case of the Common-Wealth of England Stated*, pp. 87–8. Nedham had associations with John Lilburne and other Levellers in the mid 1640s, and, as always with Nedham, it is difficult to know whether he had changed his mind, was being disingenuous or was picking individual aspects of the Leveller platform to support or condemn. See Blair Worden, 'Marchamont Nedham and the Beginnings of English Republicanism', in David Wootton (ed.), *Republicanism, Liberty, and Commercial Society, 1649–1777* (Stanford, 1994); Scott, *Commonwealth Principles*, ch. 11. Samuel Glover has

Nedham's discussion of 'Presbyterian or monarchical tyranny' is a textbook argument for 'liberty before liberalism' as outlined by Quentin Skinner. Liberty for the state, the crucial antecedent to the liberty of the individual, is defined by non-domination or the absence of coercive pressure. One form of coercive pressure, external pressure from other nations, had appeared in the 1640s in the form of the Scots and their attempt to bind Englishmen with the Solemn League and Covenant.[31] But equally dangerous was internal coercion by Presbyterian ministers who threatened parliament's autonomy. Presbyterians used the 'popish trick' of 'drawing all secular affairs within the compass of their spiritual jurisdiction'; hence Presbyterianism will inevitably 'bring all people into the condition of mere galley-slaves'.[32] Liberty, in this model, was distinguished from tyranny by its freedom from domination by crown, Church, or foreign power. In his other major publication of the early 1650s, the newspaper *Mercurius Politicus*, Nedham explicitly added the hereditary nobility to this list of tyrants. He wrote, for instance, that the existence of a 'hereditary, distinct order of men from the people' was the 'bane of all in a commonweal', and that in classical Rome the continuance of power in the hands of the senators and their families, even after the declaration of a free state, was the cause of the people's liberties being 'trodden under foot'.[33]

Nedham was not only concerned with the absence of freedom, however, but with its excess. He thus viciously attacked the Levellers, who demanded 'chimeras of liberty as might fit their own ends and fantasies . . . not liberty but licentiousness'.[34] The root of Levellerism, according to Nedham, was excessive concern for personal or individual liberty, at the expense of the common liberty of the people. This was especially clear when the Levellers presumed to question the will of parliament, the people's representative institution, 'taking upon them, dictator-like, to define what is liberty . . . as if themselves alone were infallible and the only champions of universal freedom, and the parliament such as either regarded it not or sought its destruction'. It was precisely this self-interest, under the guise of concern for liberty, that undermined

---

usefully suggested that *The Case of the Commonwealth* was aimed as much against 'a more representative and popular republicanism that had been advocated by the Levellers' as it was against the royalists and Presbyterians: Samuel Glover, 'The Putney Debates: Popular versus Elitist Republicanism', *P&P* 164 (1999), pp. 47–80, at pp. 79–80.

[31] Nedham, *The Case of the Common-Wealth of England Stated*, pp. 58 and 67.

[32] *Ibid.*, pp. 74–5. This striking claim may be an ironic allusion to the fact that the great Presbyterian progenitor John Knox had actually been a galley slave.

[33] *Mercurius Politicus* 95 (1 April 1652), p. 1490; *Mercurius Politicus* 102 (20 May 1652), p. 1595.

[34] Nedham, *The Case of the Common-Wealth of England Stated*, p. 77.

the public good, and Nedham insinuated that the Levellers were only interested in politics as a vehicle to enrich themselves, to 'satisfy their natural appetites of covetousness and revenge upon the honourable and the wealthy'. According to Nedham, every 'plea for equality of right in government' was at base a demand for 'equality of estates, and the making of such laws as the agrarian laws enacted . . . in Rome, whereby it was made criminal for any man to grow richer than ordinary'.[35]

Nedham even went so far as to say that 'a democratic or popular form' of government is 'the greatest enemy of liberty', precisely because moderation is not within the competence of the common people:

> For the multitude is so brutish that . . . they are ever in the extremes of kindness or cruelty; being void of reason, and hurried on with an unbridled violence in all their actions, trampling down all respects of things sacred and civil, to make way for their liberty, which Clapmarius calls a most dissolute licentiousness, or a licence to do even what they list.[36]

Citing the great Florentine republican Francesco Guicciardini, Nedham wrote that 'many times, when a people have got loose from the yoke of a tyranny or kingly government, out of a desire of liberty they proceed from one extreme to another . . . and except they be restrained run headlong into licentiousness, which also might be rightly called a tyranny'.[37] The spectrum from anarchy to tyranny is here bent back upon itself so that the two extremes are almost contiguous, a topographical manoeuvre common in republican thought: tyranny can be imagined as the unbridled licence of the magistrate, while anarchy can be imagined as the empowering of a million petty despots.

Such was the 'neo-Roman theory of moderate liberty' as expressed by Philodemius, Nedham and many others: freedom as a middle way between tyrannical domination of the popular will and the unbridled expression of that will. Nedham would later put it succinctly in his *The Excellencie of a Free-State* (1656): 'Freedom . . . is above all other forms of government, if it be kept within due bounds and order.' This sort of striking juxtaposition tripped easily off republican tongues; over the course of two pages, Nedham managed to praise 'discipline and freedom', 'liberty and sobriety' and even 'pure principles of severity and liberty'.[38] Most fundamentally, the need for a real-but-moderated expression of the popular will meant for republicans that the right to vote had to be limited to those most capable of moderating their passions with reason, who might use their vote for the common good rather than their own self-interest. The author of *Salus Populi Solus Rex* (1648) wrote, 'It is

---

[35] *Ibid.*, pp. 78–86     [36] *Ibid.*, pp. 78–9.     [37] *Ibid.*, p. 80.
[38] Nedham, *The Excellencie of a Free-State*, pp. 24, 52–3.

not the major vote of the people that must bear sway but the rational vote, not *vox populi* but *salus populi*.'[39] Nedham likewise warned that 'when we mention the people, observe all along that we do not mean the confused promiscuous body of the people'. He thus argued that the franchise should extend only 'to the people (without distinction) in as great a latitude, as may stand with right reason and convenience'.[40]

This neo-Roman theory of moderate liberty, with its self-conscious moderation of popular sovereignty, sounds conservative to modern ears – and later in this chapter it will become clear that many contemporaries also regarded it as inadequate. But it is worth remembering that any theory of popular sovereignty was remarkable and revolutionary. To see this, we need to look briefly at how royalists understood the moderation of liberty. The most influential statement of constitutional royalism, *His Majesties Answer to the XIX Propositions of Both Houses of Parliament* (1642), argued in explicitly Polybian fashion that good government consists in a balance of the three ideal forms of monarchy, aristocracy and democracy.[41] Democracy, or government by the many, was the part of the mixed polity that brought to this balance 'liberty and the courage and industry which liberty begets'. Yet the role of the people in the constitution of the state, through their House of Commons, was the essentially negative power to deter tyranny, making sure that 'the prince may not make use of [his] high and perpetual power to the hurt of those for whose good he hath it'. On the opposite side, the danger of democracy lay in its positive expression, which tended inevitably towards anarchy, so it was the role of monarchy to elicit such 'fear and reverence from the people, as may hinder tumults, violence and licentiousness'.[42] Thus, despite the

---

[39] *Salus Populi Solus Rex. The Peoples Safety Is the Sole Sovereignty, or the Royalist Out-Reasoned* (London, 1648), unfoliated table of contents. See also p. 19: 'If the common vote of the giddy multitude must rule the whole, how quickly would their own interest, peace and safety be dashed and broken? It is not *vox* but *salus populi* that is the supreme law: if the common people do vote against common principles, they that vote not with them must not be included in them.'

[40] Nedham, *The Excellencie of a Free-State*, pp. 71 and 94. John Milton came close to both Nedham and *Salus Populi Solus Rex* when he answered the question of whether the Rump Parliament really spoke for the people: 'Populus inquam; quod enim Senatus pars potior, id est sanior, fecit; in qup vera populi potestas residebat, quid ni id populum fecisse dicam?' Milton, *Ioannis Miltoni Angli Pro Populo Defensio*, p. 151. On this idea of rule not by a majority of the people but by their 'sanior, valentior pars' see Paul Rahe, 'The Classical Republicanism of John Milton', *History of Political Thought* 25, no. 2 (Summer 2004), pp. 243–75, at pp. 252–60.

[41] On the connections between *His Majesties Answer* and claims to 'moderation', see Michael Mendle, *Dangerous Positions*, ch. 8; Arihiro Fukuda, *Sovereignty and the Sword: Harrington, Hobbes and Mixed Government in the English Civil Wars* (Oxford, 1997).

[42] Charles I?, *His Majesties Answer to the XIX Propositions of Both Houses of Parliament* (Oxford, 1642), pp. 22–4. The indispensable guide to these issues is Smith, *Constitutional Royalism*. While I have focused on *His Majesties Answer* here for the sake of brevity,

firm commitment of constitutional royalism to the liberty of the people, the people's role in the constitution consisted in a veto power over royal taxation, not in any active will or positive contribution for the House of Commons in the formation of policy. Not only the people but their representatives needed to be bridled.

What constituted anarchy in this system was thus any autonomous or independent voice of the people. The House of Commons was 'an excellent conservator of liberty' insofar as it represented the consent of the governed, but it was 'never intended for any share of government'.[43] In the constitutional royalist view, the House of Commons must never 'extend their debates and resolutions beyond what is proper to them', which was solely to advise the king when requested and consent to his laws.[44] Whenever the people found their own voice, or thought themselves fit to debate the king's policies, anarchy was the result; their discussions were to be strictly limited to the issues brought to them from above. And if ever the House of Commons were to 'discover the *arcanum imperii*' – as the authors of *His Majesties Answer* believed was occurring in 1642 – the common people would 'grow weary of journey-work' and under pretence of liberty 'destroy all rights and proprieties, all distinctions of family and merit; and by this means this splendid and excellently distinguished form of government end in a dark equal chaos of confusion'.[45]

## The Levellers

While the neo-Roman theory of moderate liberty was not at all 'conservative' in the manner of constitutional royalism, nonetheless many contemporaries offered different and potentially more subversive interpretations of the moderation of liberty. First among these were the Levellers, that loose group of activists who rose to prominence in the aftermath of the New Model Army's victory in the first Civil War, contributed to Cromwell's rise to power in 1648, and were betrayed and scattered by the new Commonwealth government in 1649. The Levellers embraced the

Smith's analysis suggests similar arguments in texts by Thomas Wriothesley, Henry Hyde, John Culpepper, Lucius Carey, John Bramall and others. On these issues, see also Mendle, *Dangerous Positions*; Fukuda, *Sovereignty and the Sword*.

[43] Charles I?, *His Majesties Answer*, p. 24.    [44] *Ibid.*, p. 14.

[45] *Ibid.*, pp. 27–8. On the more absolutist side of royalist theory, Robert Filmer identified liberty as the blessing of royal gifts rather than as a natural condition, so that anarchy became more or less simply the absence of royal constraint, while tyranny was so attenuated that at one point (p. 207) Filmer stressed that its true and original meaning was not misuse of government but only the 'the ill-obtaining of the government'. See Robert Filmer, *Patriarcha and Other Writings*, ed. Johann Sommerville (Cambridge, 1991), pp. 4, 44, 147, 237, 261–9.

emerging republican definition of liberty in the abstract, but they offered a strikingly different vision of its appropriate moderation.

When republican theorists spoke of 'slavery', whether for individuals or nations, they meant conditions of dependence that rendered someone no longer their own master – 'subject to the jurisdiction of someone else' in the terms of the Justinian *Digest* – and hence unable lawfully to dispose of themselves or their property.[46] This dependence was often conceived as a constraint on the will, identified in the political sphere with extra-legal force or even the mere presence of a 'negative voice' or veto power in government. To quote Quentin Skinner,

The thesis on which the neo-Roman writers chiefly insist...is that it is never necessary to suffer...overt coercion in order to forfeit your civil liberty. You will also be rendered unfree if you merely fall into a condition of political subjection or dependence, thereby leaving yourself open to the danger of being forcibly or coercively deprived by your government of your life, liberty, or estates.[47]

The Leveller understanding of these issues was virtually indistinguishable from republican theory, as has been suggested by Samuel Glover, Jonathan Scott and others.[48] The essential similarity between republican and Leveller views can be seen, for instance, in the 1646 *Remonstrance of Many Thousand Citizens*, which called on parliament to free the people from the 'negative voices' of the king and House of Lords, or else 'tell us that it is reasonable we should be slaves...For in this way of voting in all affairs of the commonwealth, being not chosen thereunto by the people, they are therein masters and lords of the people – which necessarily implies the people to be their servants and vassals.'[49] William Walwyn's *Gold Tried in the Fire* (1647) denounced 'the pretended negative voice (most destructive to freedom)' and condemned the Presbyterian plan to dismantle the New Model Army as 'something equally evil to a negative voice'.[50] A petition to General Fairfax from Northumberland Levellers claimed that the king had 'subdued the law-giving power of the free

---

[46] Skinner, *Liberty before Liberalism*, p. 41.

[47] *Ibid.*, pp. 69–70. Thomas Corns has summarised John Milton's republicanism in terms of opposition to a negative voice: 'A commonwealth without a king is a commonwealth in which citizens enjoy rights without permission, and what is permissive is not really a right': Thomas Corns, 'Milton and the Characteristics of a Free Commonwealth', in David Armitage, Armand Himy and Quentin Skinner (eds.), *Milton and Republicanism* (Cambridge, 1995), p. 38.

[48] Most broadly, Scott has argued that Levellers, Diggers, Quakers and republicans all had 'a substantially shared definition of liberty': Scott, 'What Were Commonwealth Principles?' p. 595. See also Glover, 'The Putney Debates'; Nigel Smith, 'Popular Republicanism in the 1650s: John Streater's "Heroick Mechanicks"', in David Armitage, Armand Himy and Quentin Skinner (eds.), *Milton and Republicanism* (Cambridge, 1995).

[49] Sharp (ed.), *The English Levellers*, p. 38.    [50] *Ibid.*, pp. 77 and 81.

people of England in their parliament, to the negative voice of himself and posterity . . . as if ourselves were naturally their born slaves'.[51]

None of this, however, means that republicans and Levellers *agreed* in any significant sense, because their mutual definition of liberty served almost no function in isolation from their views of how that liberty should be moderated. And on this crucial issue, the Levellers and the republicans were miles apart. Of course, the Levellers were notoriously heterogeneous – one scholar has called them 'a broad, fluctuating movement whose fringes merged into mainstream Independency on the one hand and egalitarian communism on the other'[52] – and it would be foolish to try to squeeze their views into too neat a package. But in general, the Levellers' fundamental response to the emerging republican vision of liberty was to point out that by the republicans' own definition the vast majority of English people remained slaves, living in conditions of perpetual dependence on both landlords and politicians in whose election they had no voice. Republicans, of course, saw this particular limitation on liberty as true, moderate liberty, restraining or bridling the irrational impulses of the people, while the Levellers saw it as tyranny; conversely, the Levellers saw an end to this domination as true, moderate liberty, constructing a government which would restrain the appetites of landlords and politicians, while the republicans saw this as anarchy. Rarely have two ideologies been so divided by a common language.

The neo-Romans did not generally think of tyranny in terms of coercive pressures in civil society, the law, the labour market or the family; they preferred a more straightforwardly governmental framework.[53] The Levellers, however, stressed that domination could come in many forms. Most importantly for our purposes, they extended the idea of tyranny to include various forms of economic domination; this was what made the Levellers so frightening to their contemporaries, and it is what made some people believe that they intended radical social levelling or even communism. One version of this radicalism was the theory of the 'Norman yoke': the Norman Conquest of 1066 had reduced the

---

[51] *To His Excellency Thomas Lord Fairfax . . . The Humble Representation of the Desires of the Officers and Souldiers in the Regiment of Horse, for the County of Northumberland* (London, 1648), pp. 2–4.

[52] Norah Carlin, 'The Levellers and the Conquest of Ireland in 1649', *HJ* 30, no. 2 (1987), pp. 269–88, at p. 272.

[53] Skinner, *Liberty before Liberalism*, p. 17. John Milton was certainly a partial exception to this rule, imagining liberty very much in the sense of a public sphere of thought and communication.

formerly free people of England to a state of unfreedom under the domination of a foreigner and his descendants.[54] Less radical versions of this theory simply called for the protection of ancient liberties that had managed to survive under Norman tyranny, but according to more radical versions the distribution of property in England, and the laws that protected that property, were products of Norman tyranny that rendered English people unfree.

Arguments of this sort, for instance attacks on so-called 'base tenures' and other feudal property arrangements as forms of domination, can be found throughout the Leveller *corpus*, but they became especially prominent in later Leveller writings as neo-Roman thought was coming to prominence. In 1648, a Leveller petition to General Fairfax began by claiming

that the people of this nation, both by nature and as they are Englishmen, are a freeborn generation, but by conquest and captivity under William, the duke of Normandy's bastard, they were made slaves, the property of their lands removed from the British natives to the Norman invaders; the lands which were vouchsafed to their occupation, translated from their own fee-simples into strange tenures, by knight, homage, villain and other services (to the conqueror and his Norman earls, lords and knights, which of his commanders he made in every county).[55]

In 1649, *A Declaration or Representation* by the inhabitants of Hertfordshire lamented that the Commonwealth government intended to keep

those that have adhered to the first declared parliamentary principles, in slavery to themselves and the greatest cavaliers of the land, by base tenures, fines, hariots, fealty, homage, &c... For it is notoriously known... that the most part of those that did adhere to the parliament were not great men but such as were oppressed by great men, either in copyholds or tithes, or by the subtlety of the lawyers.

Later, in its call for new elections, the tract argued that

---

[54] See J. G. A. Pocock, *The Ancient Constitution and the Feudal Law: A Study of English Historical Thought in the Seventeenth Century* (Cambridge, 1957); Christopher Hill, 'The Norman Yoke', in his *Puritanism and Revolution*; R. B. Seaberg, 'The Norman Conquest and the Common Law: The Levellers and the Argument from Continuity', *HJ* 24, no. 4 (1981), pp. 791–806. Martin Dzelzainis has challenged the significance of the 'Norman yoke' in Leveller thought, arguing that there was only a brief anti-Norman moment in Leveller writing. However, Dzelzainis is really concerned with the extent to which Levellers attacked Magna Carta and regards this position as synonymous with anti-Normanism. My own understanding of the 'Norman yoke' is far less narrowly defined, and there is no doubt that even later Leveller texts that accepted the legitimacy of common law and Magna Carta nonetheless denounced the 'Norman yoke' as undermining English liberties: Martin Dzelzainis, 'History and Ideology: Milton, the Levellers, and the Council of State in 1649', *Huntington Library Quarterly* 68, no. 1 (2005), pp. 269–87.

[55] *To His Excellency Thomas Lord Fairfax*, p. 1.

if we ever recover our right of a new election of a new Representative, for which we engaged against the chief tyrant of the Norman race, we also resolve against all his creatures, and never intend to choose one of them more for a parliament man while we live; we mean lords of manors, impropriators and lawyers, whose interest is in our oppression, and at this day keep us in bondage like Egyptian task-masters.[56]

The idea that economic domination was a critical obstruction to English liberty can perhaps best be explored in the major newspaper that most reflected Leveller ideas, significantly called *The Moderate*, published in sixty-three weekly issues from June 1648 to September 1649.[57] In February 1649, for instance, the newspaper praised a petition from Buckinghamshire demanding 'that the people of the nation be made free by having their lands wholly cleared and discharged from all manner of fealty and homage claimed by any Lord, or others, as Lords of Manors, that being a badge and brute of the Norman slavery'.[58] In September 1648, it claimed that 'all the people of this nation will shake off their burden, and will be a free people, whereas they have been hitherto in no other capacity than slaves; all kings having assumed the crown lineally from the Conqueror, as appears by quit rents, and the tenure of villainage yet in force'.[59] In April 1649, it complained that the people's 'badges and marks of slavery, by fealty, homage, and base tenures' had been continued and confirmed by parliament after the regicide.[60]

The point of these attacks on England's land laws was that the legal distinction between 'holding' lands and having real property in those lands was a fundamentally tyrannous distinction, introduced by the feudalism of the Normans. This was the subtext of the long editorial, published just after Pride's Purge in December 1648, which denounced the 'absurd and pernicious' idea that 'all goods, chattels, possessions and whatsoever else a man hath, are properly the king's, and that the people have only the use thereof, without any propriety at all . . . If the people have only the use

---

[56] *A Declaration or Representation of the Actions, Intentions and Resolutions of Divers of the Inhabitants of the County of Hartford* (London, 1649?), pp. 4 and 7. George Thomason scrawled the words 'a Leveller' across the title page of his copy.

[57] The exact relationship between *The Moderate* and the Leveller movement has been the subject of some debate; the newspaper was usually independent of the Leveller leadership and could sometimes include critiques of Lilburne and his associates, but nonetheless it was a platform for ideas and debates within the Leveller community. See particularly Jürgen Diethe, 'The Moderate: Politics and Allegiances of a Revolutionary Newspaper', *History of Political Thought* 4, no. 2 (Summer 1983), pp. 247–79; Roger Howell and David Brewster, 'Reconsidering the Levellers: The Evidence of the Moderate', *P&P* 46 (February 1970), pp. 68–86.

[58] *The Moderate* 32 (20 February 1649), p. 313.

[59] *The Moderate* 10 (19 September 1648), p. 76.

[60] *The Moderate* 39 (10 April 1649), p. 397.

and no interest in their estates what other condition can the people be in but slavery?'[61] At issue here was not the absolutist claim that all land in England was the property of the king – a claim rare at any time, and utterly irrelevant by December 1648 – but the much more urgent idea, based in natural rights theory, that use rights constituted a form of real property, known as the *dominium utile*. If all tenants owned this form of property, then they were free men, and their relationship to their land-lords should be one of free exchange between equals rather than servile tenantry; if all tenants did not own this form of property, then they were no more than slaves, and their tenantry should immediately be ended. As the editorial continued, 'Aristotle saith that free men and slaves differ only in this, that slaves have only the use of things without property, or interest, and cannot acquire or get to themselves any dominion or true right in any thing.'

As this reference to free exchange suggests, economic liberty in *The Moderate* could take proto-liberal forms as easily as more redistributive ones. What mattered was that the poor be emancipated from their state of dependence, which might be accomplished *either* by redistributing property to the poor *or* by giving the poor a greater autonomy over their property. On the more genuinely 'levelling' side, for instance, we find in *The Moderate* a complaint that land was 'each man's birth-right' and that its expropriation by tyrants rendered it instead the 'greatest cause of most sins'.[62] Here a form of property redistribution was seen as the only cure for tyranny. Elsewhere in *The Moderate* there was a petition from Buckinghamshire that demanded 'raising a stock' of cash for the unemployed so that 'so many thousands be not suffered to beg'.[63] But we also find in *The Moderate* many bluntly capitalist demands and proposals. In November 1648, for instance, *The Moderate* printed a letter from Tavistock, Cornwall, supporting the Cornish tin miners' claim 'that prices have been imposed illegally upon them without their consent, by colour of preemption and the prerogative of first buying alleged to be in the king'. The miners demanded instead 'the common interest and privilege with other subjects, of selling their own goods, digged and obtained with the hazard of their lives, for their best advantage . . . and that they may not be left at last under perpetual bondage . . . they believing themselves a part of the free born people of England'.[64]

---

[61] *The Moderate* 23 (19 December 1648), p. 201.
[62] *The Moderate* 61 (11 September 1649), p. 701; see also *The Moderate* 56 (7 August 1649), p. 651.
[63] *The Moderate* 32 (20 February 1649), p. 313.
[64] *The Moderate* 18 (14 November 1648), pp. 151–2.

In sum, then, Levellers might either shade into economic levelling or embrace possessive individualism insofar as both offered equally reasonable solutions to the same problem: that only a condition of non-domination could make a person genuinely free.[65] There was little agreement in these texts about exactly what sort of economic coercion constituted tyranny. They lacked sophisticated discussions of whether wage labour made people more or less dependent. They lacked virtually any discussion of whether investment might be coequal with land as a mode of economic independence.[66] What they contained, however, was a palpable sense that, without some mode of economic independence, true liberty is impossible. This was a view of liberty which the republicans (and their allies in government like Henry Ireton) of course shared, but in mirror-reverse: the republicans denied citizenship to the poor because they lacked independence. But whereas the republicans did not seem to mind a commonwealth in which many or even most English people existed in this state of unfreedom, the Levellers insisted that such a state was by definition tyrannous.

If we turn to the other side of the *via media*, the dangerous absence of restraint, the Levellers – driven by the polemical need to defend themselves against charges of opposition to all government – agreed with the republicans that true liberty was a middle way between tyranny and anarchy. In their 1649 *A Manifestation*, for instance, and in numerous other places, the Leveller leaders claimed to be 'for government and against popular confusion'. The depravity and corruption of man made government necessary, hence, 'though tyranny is so excessively bad, yet of the two extremes, confusion is the worst'.[67] Yet while the Levellers agreed with their opponents that 'confusion' was the worst possible outcome in a polity, what needed moderation to prevent this confusion was not political participation by the common people but rather the licentiousness of

[65] See Quentin Skinner, 'Rethinking Political Liberty', *History Workshop Journal* 61 (Spring 2006), pp. 156–70. For older contributions see e.g. C. B Macpherson, *The Political Theory of Possessive Individualism* (Oxford, 1962); J. C. Davis, 'Levellers and Democracy', *P&P* 40 (1968), pp. 174–80; Keith Thomas, 'The Levellers and the Franchise', in Gerald Aylmer (ed.), *The Interregnum: The Quest for Settlement 1646–1660* (London, 1972); Alan Houston, '"A Way of Settlement": The Levellers, Monopolies, and the Public Interest', *History of Political Thought* 14, no. 3 (Autumn 1993), pp. 381–420, at 399.

[66] Steve Pincus has usefully highlighted these issues as points of disagreement among supporters of the Commonwealth in the 1650s: see Steve Pincus, 'Neither Machiavellian Moment nor Possessive Individualism: Commercial Society and the Defenders of the English Commonwealth', *AHR* 103, no. 3 (June 1998), pp. 705–36. Whether Levellers disagreed on these issues or merely chose not to parse them too finely is unclear. See also Houston, 'A Way of Settlement'.

[67] Sharp (ed.), *The English Levellers*, p. 162.

magistrates. In the vast majority of cases where Levellers discussed the need to moderate liberty, they referred not to popular liberty but to the liberty of the powerful. Anarchy for the Levellers was nothing more or less than the collapse of government, and as such it was not something the people did themselves, but rather something their governors did when they abandoned reason and pursued their own appetites, dissolving the bonds of government and driving the people to natural law with all its dangers. What distinguished this magisterial lawlessness from tyranny was that anarchy was the excess of magistrates against law, while tyranny was arbitrary rule over law itself.

So, for instance, in an untitled broadsheet published in August 1645, John Lilburne denied that election to parliament gave members 'a lawless unlimited power', and he mocked the claim that parliamentary privilege immunised members against 'known law'. As such, he delineated a middle way between anarchy and tyranny that specified parliamentary privilege as a form of anarchy: 'Unknown privileges are as dangerous as unlimited prerogatives – being both of them secret snares, especially for the best-affected people.'[68] Two years later, *An Agreement of the People* (1647) stressed the necessity that 'every person may be bound alike' by law, regardless of 'tenure, estate, charter, degree, birth or place', associating excessive freedom with the special liberties that freed landlords, peers and MPs from moderation; laws should 'bind all alike, without privilege of exemption'.[69] It was in this spirit, then, that Lilburne rather remarkably turned the tables on his critics and accused parliament of undermining private property. Because MPs were so dangerously free to follow their appetites without restraint, he called on them to 'bound yourselves and all future parliaments from abolishing propriety, levelling men's estates and making all things common'.[70]

It was in this sense, too, that Lilburne could make the seemingly oxymoronic claim that parliament intended the 'overthrow of magistracy', and Richard Overton could argue that the House of Lords was 'antimagisterial'.[71] The lawlessness of governors threatened the whole edifice of the state. Hence in August 1649 Lilburne argued on the one hand that 'it is no tumult to deliver petitions [to parliament] by

---

[68] *Ibid.*, pp. 5–7.

[69] *Ibid.*, pp. 95–6. John Warr, *The Priviledges of the People* (London, 1649), pp. 4–5, argued that 'the way to advance privilege is to keep it within its due bounds', hence 'liberty should not ascend to privilege, but privilege should stoop down to liberty as its centre and rest'. Warr cogently argued that law ought not to restrain the people's liberty but enlarge it by restraining the liberty of 'the mighty'. On the levelling of special privileges and liberties, see Rachel Foxley, 'John Lilburne and the Citizenship of "Free-Born Englishmen"', *HJ* 47, no. 4 (2004), pp. 849–74.

[70] Sharp (ed.), *The English Levellers*, p. 137.     [71] *Ibid.*, pp. 187 and 61.

popular multitudes', but on the other hand he attacked the 'boundless wills and humours' of members of parliament to whom he and his supporters petitioned.[72] This elite immoderation was understood as anarchy rather than tyranny insofar as it produced the dissolution of government in a strict sense: it reduced the people to a state of nature. In other words, if the Levellers themselves seemed anarchic, or if the people ceased to obey their rulers, it was generally the government's fault. Lilburne, for instance, accused the Rump Parliament of overthrowing magistracy, causing the people to 'fly to the prime laws of nature . . . that original state or chaos of confusion wherein lust is become law'.[73] In his *Legall Fundamentall Liberties* (1649) Lilburne claimed that members of parliament 'break all your oaths, protestations and covenants that you have taken to maintain the laws and liberties of the kingdom', and as such 'dissolve the whole frame and constitution of the civil policy and government of this kingdom [sic!] into the original law of nature'.[74] In sum, while popular confusion was as bad or worse than tyranny, it was the governors who produced it; hence it was they, more than the people, who in the first instance required moderation.

### The Diggers

More radical than most Levellers were the self-proclaimed 'True Levellers', known to posterity as the Diggers. Once again, analysis of Digger texts suggests a basic concordance with the neo-Roman definition of liberty, with the difference coming in the shape of the space between tyranny and anarchy and the ways liberty ought to be moderated. The Diggers adopted the Leveller idea that freedom from domination must include socio-economic domination but they argued that the whole system of monetary exchange, the whole regime of buying and selling, deprived people of their natural liberty in the earth and was therefore *ipso facto* tyrannous. If a person did not possess the earth and its fruits freely, he entered into the domination of those who did, because he depended upon them for his survival. True freedom from domination was only possible when a person could take what he needed without having to obtain permission.

The most comprehensive such reinterpretation of liberty was Gerrard Winstanley's final work, *The Law of Freedom in a Platform* (1652).[75] The

---

[72] *Ibid.*, p. 185.     [73] *Ibid.*, p. 192, and pp. 179–201 *passim*.

[74] John Lilburne, *The Legall Fundamentall Liberties of the People of England Revived, Asserted and Vindicated* (London, 1649), p. 7.

[75] A sophisticated historiography has addressed the question of whether this text was a culmination or betrayal of the Digger movement of 1649–50, and whether it should be

text began with such a lucid vision of liberty – both its allegedly moderate centre and the extremes of tyranny and licentiousness that required moderation – that it deserves to be quoted at length:

The great searching of heart in these days, is to find out where true freedom lies, that the Commonwealth of England might be established in peace. Some say it lies in the free use of trading, and to have all patents, licences and restraints removed: but this is a freedom under the will of a conqueror. Others say it is true freedom to have ministers to preach, and for people to hear whom they will, without being restrained or compelled from or to any form of worship: but this is an unsettled freedom. Others say it is true freedom to have community with all women, and to have liberty to satisfy their lusts and greedy appetites: but this is the freedom of wanton unreasonable beasts and tends to destruction. Others say it is true freedom that the elder brother shall be landlord of the earth and the younger brother a servant: and this is but a half freedom, and begets murmurings, wars and quarrels. All these, and such like, are freedoms, but they lead to bondage and not to the true foundation-freedom which settles a commonwealth in peace. *True commonwealths freedom lies in the free enjoyment of the earth.*[76]

Winstanley is here wrestling with precisely the issue of moderation, the question of how people's 'lusts and greedy appetites' can be restrained by reason without that restraint constituting tyranny. Historians have debated whether Winstanley regarded external restraint as temporary or permanent within his spiritual vision of human renewal, but restraint it was, not only on sexual licentiousness but on economic and religious behaviour. Unsettled freedom, freedom without restraint, was in an important sense not true freedom at all.[77]

To understand Winstanley's understanding of tyranny and its relationship to liberty, we must begin with his views of property. In many parts of the tract, Winstanley sounds like just another Leveller in his claims

seen as a pessimistic text constructed in defeat or an optimistic text demonstrating a broad utopian vision. This scholarship has unfortunately remained mired in attacks or defences of Winstanley's communism. See George Shulman, *Radicalism and Reverence: The Political Thought of Gerard Winstanley* (Berkeley, 1989); J. C. Davis, 'Gerard Winstanley and the Restoration of True Magistracy', *P&P* 70 (1976), pp. 76–93; Christopher Hill, *The Religion of Gerard Winstanley* (Oxford, 1978); Timothy Kenyon, *Utopian Communism and Political Thought in Early Modern England* (London, 1989); Michael Rogers, 'Gerard Winstanley on Crime and Punishment', *SCJ* 27, no.3 (1996), pp. 735–47; Darren Webb, 'The Bitter Product of Defeat? Reflections on Winstanley's Law of Freedom', *Political Studies* 52 (2004), pp. 199–215. For our purposes, these debates are not so important as the fact that in this most elaborate of all revolutionary utopias, truly aggressive moderation was necessary to prevent liberty from becoming licentiousness.

[76] Winstanley, *The Law of Freedom*, p. 17.

[77] Crucial in this regard was Winstanley's remarkable identification of God with 'reason', so that moderation becomes the principal work of God in the world: see Gerrard Winstanley, *Truth Lifting Up Its Head above Scandals* (London, 1649), esp. 'To the gentle reader' and pp. 1–13.

that the Norman Conquest deprived the common people of their lands and hence their liberty from domination. In the dedication, for instance, he thanked Cromwell for helping the people to 'recover our land and liberties again, by your victories, out of the Norman hand' and asked that 'free possession of the land and liberties be put into the hands of the oppressed commoners of England'.[78] He argued that the laws of England were the laws of the conquerors, except for a few 'good lines of freedom' that had been 'inserted into their laws' by those who dared to fight the crown.[79] But he also asked, in rather more explicit fashion than most Levellers dared, 'By what power do these [lords of manors] maintain their title over us? Formerly they held title from the king, as he was the Conqueror's successor, but have not the commoners cast out the king, and broke the band of that conquest? Therefore in equity they are free from the slavery of that lordly power.'[80] As he put it shortly thereafter, 'If the lords of manors and our task-masters hold title to the earth over us from the old kingly power, behold that power is beaten and cast out.'[81] Winstanley thus argued for a radical discontinuity in the landholding regime of England, just as the republicans argued for a radical discontinuity in its constitution; all previous titles to property were voided by the overthrow of the tyrannical power that had given them force.

The question, then, was if the previous landholding regime was nullified, what should replace it? This is where Winstanley offered his broadest vision: he chose not to argue for the redistribution of land, but rather that the whole principle of 'buying and selling' was itself tyrannical. This argument began from the premise that when rulers 'call the earth theirs and not ours . . . we lose our freedom'.[82] The reason was more than the conventional one that a person could not be independent without land; it was rather that, even with land, people could not be independent so long as something they needed lay on someone else's land rather than theirs. There was simply not enough land in the world for every person to be genuinely independent, in the sense of having access to all their needs without relying upon the goodwill of others. Thus domination was built into the whole system of monetary exchange. Winstanley wrote that 'true freedom lies where a man receives his nourishment and preservation, and that is in the use of the earth'. Mankind is literally made from the fruits of the earth and 'he cannot live without them; for take away the free use of these, and the body languishes, the spirit is brought into bondage'. Any

---

[78] Winstanley, *The Law of Freedom*, p. 3.     [79] *Ibid.*, p. 77.

[80] Winstanley, *The Law of Freedom*, p. 7. See also *More Light Shining in Buckinghamshire* (London, 1649), pp. 4, 13–14; *Light Shining in Buckinghamshire* (London, 1648[?]), pp. 2–5.

[81] Winstanley, *The Law of Freedom*, p. 8.     [82] *Ibid.*, p. 9.

system that requires payment for the fruits of the earth is thus unfree, because it tends towards external control over life itself, the most fundamental sort of property: 'A man had better to have had no body, than to have no food for it; therefore this restraining of the earth from brethren by brethren is oppression and bondage; but the free enjoyment thereof is true freedom.'[83]

We see here a system in which any restraint upon the enjoyment of necessary commodities – even the sort of restraint based upon so-called 'free' exchange – is *unfree* because of the uneven power relations inherent in all such transactions. The very *necessity* of food and shelter for human beings means that selling such things cannot lack coercion and thus produces a condition of dependency or unfreedom. Moreover, by this logic the accumulation of riches is the worst form of tyranny, since it is necessarily achieved at the price of other men's freedom:

All rich men live at ease, feeding and clothing themselves by the labours of other men, not by their own; which is their shame, and not their nobility. For it is a more blessed thing to give than to receive. But rich men receive all they have from the labourer's hand, and what they give, they give away other men's labours, not their own. Therefore they are not righteous actors in the earth.[84]

This explains Winstanley's understanding of tyranny. To perceive his understanding of anarchy, we must look to Winstanley's positive system, his 'platform' for commonwealth government.[85] In essence, his system was remarkably simple, if far from complete or satisfying: there would be storehouses of commodities into which everyone would place the fruits of their labour, and out of which everyone would take what they needed. Property would continue to exist, but only in the limited sense that families genuinely owned houses and furnishings, and once someone removed a commodity from the storehouses it could not be taken from them without their consent. Government would also continue to exist, elected by the people, and it was structured to ensure that everyone worked for the common good rather than leeching off the productivity of others. In this system, Winstanley realised, anarchy or licentiousness was an enormous problem because the temptation to equate economic liberty with laxity or libertinism was so strong. Thus Winstanley argued for a surprisingly dense matrix of laws in his commonwealth. He wrote that 'there must be suitable laws for every occasion, and almost for every action that men do,

[83] *Ibid.*, pp. 17–18.    [84] *Ibid.*, p. 12.
[85] In *The Law of Freedom*, Winstanley denied that it was necessary to expropriate lands in order to implement his platform, since common lands and waste lands were sufficient for the present. *Light Shining in Buckinghamshire*, p. 9, however, called for 'putting down' the nobility and gentry as a means towards 'restitution of our rights again'.

for one law cannot serve in all seasons, but every season and every action have their own particular laws attending thereupon for the preservation of right order'.[86] This, then, was no 'free' regime in the libertarian sense. As Colin Davis has noted, 'perhaps the crucial aspect of Winstanley's definition of freedom is its restrictiveness'.[87]

Winstanley especially believed that it was necessary to have laws 'to limit men's manners, because of transgressions one against another'. He thus created new civil officers with names like 'peace-makers', 'overseers' and 'task-masters' charged with the maintenance of order in the localities. These officers would be elected annually by the people under a universal male franchise, and to ensure that officers remained servants of the people rather than their lords, they were to receive no compensation for their offices.[88] This was, in other words, very much a republican vision – adapted as much from the puritan separatist tradition as from the Italian humanist one – accepting that freedom must be restrained, but arguing that a rotating bench of magistrates chosen by the people was the best way to prevent that restraint from becoming tyrannical.[89]

The most important limitation on freedom in this system was that people would be forced to work, and indeed would be forced into partic-ular sorts of employment, subjugating the individual will to the common good. Magistrates called 'overseers', for instance, would be chosen for each town and trade to 'go from house to house to view the works of the people of every house belonging to his trade and circuit, and to give directions as he sees cause, and see that no youth be trained up in idleness'.[90] Those who refused to work would 'lose their freedom' for a period of time, and the role of the 'Task-master' was to 'take those into his oversight as are sentenced by the judge to lose their freedom, and to appoint them their work and to see they do it'. Those who continued to refuse to work might be whipped or starved by the Task-master.[91] Per-haps most remarkably, in Winstanley's commonwealth there would be a standing army, intended not only to protect against invaders but to 'beat down the turbulency of any foolish spirit that shall arise to break our common peace'.[92] This was a system of external moderation, in other words, in which freedom from domination was guaranteed but freedom

---

[86] Winstanley, *The Law of Freedom*, p. 25.

[87] J. C. Davis, *Utopia and the Ideal Society: A Study of English Utopian Writing 1516–1700* (Cambridge, 1981), p. 192.

[88] Winstanley, *The Law of Freedom*, p. 35–6.

[89] On the connection between Winstanley and republicanism, see Nigel Smith, 'Gerrard Winstanley and the Literature of Revolution', *Prose Studies* 22, no. 2 (August 1999), pp. 46–60, esp. p. 55.

[90] Winstanley, *The Law of Freedom*, p. 43.    [91] *Ibid.*, pp. 47–8.

[92] *Ibid.*, pp. 64 and 55.

to act according to one's will was not; the common good, rather than the individual, was paramount.

The benefits of this system, according to Winstanley, went well beyond freedom in the political sense; they extended to the liberation of citizens' social and ethical lives, creating a godly commonwealth. So, for instance, Winstanley wrote that in a world without buying and selling, there would be no dowries in marriage, hence 'every man and woman shall have the free liberty to marry whom they love'.[93] There would be peace within families, because primogeniture had made elder brothers landlords and younger brothers servants, but true commonwealth government 'makes both elder and younger brother free men in the earth'.[94] At his most expansive, Winstanley argued that outward liberty would unlock the secret, inward liberty of human beings: 'The inward bondages of the mind, as covetousness, pride, hypocrisy, envy, sorrow, fears, desperation and madness, are all occasioned by the outward bondage that one sort of people lay upon another.'[95]

### Harrington's *Oceana*

In 1656, another writer suggested that the definition of a free commonwealth was a state where 'the whole people be landlords, or hold the lands so divided among them that no one man, or number of men, within the compass of the few or aristocracy overbalance them'. Later in his tract, the same writer argued that the commonwealth should be founded upon 'an equal agrarian; and if the earth be given unto the sons of men, this balance is the balance of justice . . . Equality, which is the necessary dissolution of monarchy, is the generation, the very life and soul of a commonwealth'. This radical plea for economic freedom was not the work of a Leveller or a Digger, however. It was rather James Harrington's 1656 epitome of neo-Roman thought, *The Commonwealth of Oceana*, described by Quentin Skinner as 'arguably the most original and influential of all the English treatises on free states'.[96] Of course, the connection between Harrington and the so-called 'radicals' has been noticed before; as Christopher Hill wrote, 'The agrarian law was to be made famous by James Harrington's advocacy of it in *Oceana* . . . but Harrington was only summing up a tradition.'[97] But this connection remains

---

[93] *Ibid.*, p. 88.  [94] *Ibid.*, pp. 17 and 27–9.  [95] *Ibid.*, p. 18.

[96] James Harrington, *The Commonwealth of Oceana and a System of Politics*, ed. J. G. A. Pocock (Cambridge, 1992), pp. 12 and 220; Skinner, *Liberty before Liberalism*, p. 15.

[97] Hill, *The World Turned Upside Down*, p. 115. John Lilburne and other Levellers likewise predated Harrington in calling for an agrarian law: see Glover, 'The Putney Debates', pp. 47 and 55, and Scott, *Commonwealth Principles*, ch. 1. Eric Nelson explores debates

a puzzle, especially considering Harrington's broad rejection of the sort of popular politics envisioned by Levellers and Diggers.

Describing how and why Harrington sometimes sounds like a radical and at other times sounds like a conservative is thus the goal of the remainder of this chapter. I want to suggest that the neo-Roman theory of moderate liberty advocated by Marchamont Nedham, Eutactus Philodemius and their ilk fundamentally failed to answer the challenge of the Levellers and the Diggers: why some English people should be free in a neo-Roman free state and others should not. This was the problem Harrington set himself to solving, and he did so, brilliantly but with profoundly disturbing implications, by borrowing freely from his polemical opponents to redefine the middle way between anarchy and tyranny and the ways that government moderated liberty. In essence, Harrington coopted the whole premise of the radicals that any structural limitation on voting rights or economic independence was a species of domination; in other words, he accepted a radical view of tyranny. His crucial manoeuvre, however, was to marry this position with a view of anarchy that was borrowed from conservatives, especially constitutional royalists, and was far more repressive than anything his erstwhile republican colleagues had imagined.[98] This squaring of the circle, this marriage of a radical view of tyranny with a reactionary view of anarchy, was Harrington's unique articulation of the rule of moderation, and it was what allowed him to appear so broadminded to later reformers in England and America while utterly denouncing populism.

The first thing to note about Harrington's view of the relationship between liberty and tyranny is that it foregrounds the significance of economic tyranny. This is something none of Harrington's republican compatriots had seriously considered, and it puts Harrington's work in an altogether different category.[99] Of course, all discussions of liberty had some economic component, but in previous republican models

---

over the agrarian law, but he has little interest in Harrington's relationship to the radical tradition: Eric Nelson, *The Greek Tradition in Republican Thought* (Cambridge, 2004), ch. 3.

[98] On this issue, it is relevant that Harrington became a close friend of Charles I in the months before the regicide: see Blair Worden, 'James Harrington and "The Commonwealth of Oceana", 1656', in David Wootton (ed.), *Republicanism, Liberty, and Commercial Society, 1649–1776* (Stanford, 1994). p. 83. See also Scott, *Commonwealth Principles*, p. 143 for a cogent discussion of Harrington combining opposed positions. Arihiro Fukuda has also perceptively argued that the novelty of Harrington's position was to merge ideas of absolute sovereignty with principles of mixed government: Fukuda, *Sovereignty and the Sword*.

[99] Here I disagree with Jonathan Scott, who has seen a 'commitment to greater economic equality and social justice' as a hallmark of all republican writing: 'What Were Commonwealth Principles?', p. 602 and *passim*.

tyranny was seen as *producing* poverty by robbing citizens of their property or undermining trade; never had it been claimed that economic dependence was *ipso facto* a sign of tyranny, nor that poverty was itself slavery, nor that riches were tyrannical.[100] In fact, as we have already seen, Marchamont Nedham explicitly denounced as mere anarchy the Roman 'agrarian laws . . . whereby it was made criminal for any man to grow richer than ordinary'.[101] Nedham had certainly worried about men becoming too rich, but this was because they might become *affectatio regni* and try to claim the throne; in the same breath that he condemned excessive riches, he stressed that the danger was not riches *per se* but that politicians might become 'too powerful and popular'.[102] Harrington, by contrast, was to make economic dependence and the evils of riches the centrepiece of his vision of tyranny, and his antidote was the very agrarian law that Nedham despised.

In recounting the history of medieval England, for instance, Harrington described how the commons assembled at Westminster were no more than the 'mere name' of a parliament, because the land of the kingdom was divided among nobles and the Church; knights were vassals and thus lacked independence, so nothing they did in parliament was genuinely free. By this logic, too, Magna Carta provided no liberty for the English people but was a mere 'wrestling match' between king and nobles, because the people were in a state of dependence upon the nobility in whose tenure they held their lands. It was only with the dissolution of the monasteries in the reign of the Tudors that power 'came to fall into the hands of the people' because they 'did in effect amortise a great part of the lands unto the possession of the yeomanry, or middle people, who, not living in a servile or indigent fashion, were much unlinked from dependence upon their lords'.[103] This was theoretically equivalent to the Levellers' attacks on 'base tenures' as incompatible with freedom.

We can see this concern with economic dependence equally clearly in the very first of the thirty fundamental laws by which Harrington hoped to govern the Commonwealth of Oceana. This law divided the people into 'freemen or citizens' on the one hand and 'servants' on the other, with 'servants' defined as those who, however temporarily, could not 'live of

---

[100] As is often the case, John Milton may be a partial exception, but his critiques of 'excessive wealth and luxury' were relatively clichéd attacks on the nobility rather than arguments against capitalist accumulation: see Pincus, 'Neither Machiavellian Moment nor Possessive Individualism', p. 726.

[101] Nedham, *The Case of the Common-Wealth of England Stated*, pp. 78–86.

[102] *Mercurius Politicus* 101 (13 May 1652), p. 1587.

[103] Harrington, *Oceana*, pp. 52–55. Harrington sounds particularly like a Leveller when suggesting that 'the aristocracy is ravenous, and not the people': p. 180.

themselves'. According to Harrington, this fundamental division needed no explanation, because servitude is 'inconsistent with freedom or participation of government in a commonwealth'.[104] Here economic independence is a *sine qua non* of political participation, and those who answered to masters were *ipso facto* unfree. However, according to Harrington those unfree people might *become* free by achieving economic independence, which they could do not only by owning land but by earning wages; land ownership was desirable for free people, but it was not a precondition of freedom. Instead, Harrington argued (against both the communists and those who saw land as the only marker of independence) that it would *diminish* liberty if the land were divided equally among all the people, because 'he that hath a cow upon the commons and earns his shilling by the day at his labour, hath twice as much already as this would come unto for his share, because if the land were thus divided, there would be nobody to set him on work'. These industrious wage-earners, in their 'innumerable trades', might not only vote but 'become also purchasers of greater estates', thus guaranteeing their future independence.[105]

The most important element of Harrington's conception of economic tyranny was that excessive riches – that is, too much land and wealth in too few hands – was antithetical to the freedom of the commonwealth. Harrington instead wanted a nation of the middle sort: 'There is a mean in things: as exorbitant riches overthrow the balance of a commonwealth, so extreme poverty cannot hold it nor is by any means to be trusted with it.'[106] Moreover, Harrington did not merely praise those of moderate wealth but actually constructed a scheme to redistribute wealth and make as many men 'moderate' as possible. At the heart of this scheme was the limitation of inheritance. No child was allowed to inherit lands worth more than £2,000 *per annum*, nor could daughters be given dowries in excess of £1,500 for fear that they would inordinately enrich their husbands. On top of these limitations, no man would be allowed to purchase lands amounting to more than a total estate of £2,000 *per annum*. The goal was that, over subsequent generations, the great estates of the realm would be broken into (at most) £2,000 lots, so that the number of landed men in the country would expand exponentially.[107]

---

[104] *Ibid.*, p. 75.

[105] *Ibid.*, pp. 181–2. This suggests that Steve Pincus was not altogether correct when he argued that Harrington had a zero-sum, anti-commercial view of political economy. Harrington did indeed place more trust in the virtue of landed men and did not trust 'mechanics' to hold office, but this hardly means that he did not see their value: 'The revenue of industry in a nation, at the least in this, is three- or four-fold greater than that of mere rent . . . If the people then obstruct industry, they obstruct their own livelihood' (p. 182). See Pincus, 'Neither Machiavellian Moment nor Possessive Individualism'.

[106] Harrington, *Oceana*, p. 77. See Chapter 6 above.    [107] *Ibid.*, pp. 1–14.

Of course, Harrington did not go so far as to suggest with Winstanley that ownership of land was itself tyrannical. But interestingly, they had many theoretical elements in common. For one thing, Harrington, like Winstanley before him, explicitly denounced primogeniture as tyranny, unsuitable to a commonwealth: 'I marvel how much it comes to pass that we should use our children as we do our puppies: take one, lay it on the lap, feed it with every good bit, and drown five.'[108] Another similarity was Harrington's claim that the agrarian laws promoted love. Harrington condemned the 'wretched custom of marrying for money', and he argued that limiting wealth would eliminate the need for such mercenary considerations: 'There is in this agrarian an homage unto pure and spotless love.' In fact, in arguing that only after a redistribution of wealth would the 'marriage bed . . . be truly legitimate, and the race of the commonwealth not spurious', Harrington came close to saying not only that financially arranged marriages were tyrannical, but that the fruits of such marriages were illegitimate.[109]

So, to summarise, here we have a system where economic dependence constituted unfreedom. Harrington's goal was thus to increase the number of free people in England by giving many more people their own land, or by giving them freer access to the fruits of that land through employment. He did not favour giving *every* person their own land, since this would stifle industry and merely make every person equally impoverished. Rather, he wanted a large, *moderately* wealthy landed class who could then pay unlanded people for their industry. Even servants could theoretically work their way out of servitude, and they were instantly enfranchised when they did so. Tyranny, then, lay in the propagation of an economic system that restricted freedom. Being a landlord did not make someone a tyrant, *if* his tenants might through their industry become independent and hence enfranchise themselves. However, a landlord *was* a tyrant if his greed and acquisitiveness prevented his tenants from becoming free, and the constitution of the kingdom must therefore prohibit this.

So this is how Harrington drew the line between tyranny and liberty, an interpretation that took seriously, if not always adopting, the criticisms by Levellers and Diggers that republicanism defined freedom correctly but then simply left the mass of Englishmen unfree. So how did Harrington get away with this radicalism and become the most important author in the English republican tradition? The answer lies on the other side of liberty's middle way: Harrington's interpretation of anarchy. In essence, because Harrington's interpretation of tyranny was so economic

---

[108] *Ibid.*, pp. 108–9.     [109] *Ibid.*, pp. 111–12.

in orientation, it left him free to offer a reading of anarchy in the political sphere that was far more authoritarian than anything his republican
colleagues had proposed, suggesting that civil liberty required a particularly vigorous bridling of the people. As we have seen, other republicans
like Eutactus Philodemius and Marchamont Nedham defined anarchy or
licentiousness as 'underived' popular power that was not properly chan-
nelled through elected representatives, or (more philosophically) as the
action of unbridled individual desire over the common good. Harrington,
however, argued that the common people always put their own interests
over the common good, hence their politics was by definition immoderate; there should ideally be no popular politics of any sort, for as he put
it in a later defence of *Oceana*, 'debate in the people makes anarchy'.[110]
He thus argued that even a properly elected representative assembly was
a form of anarchy if the representatives in that assembly were allowed
to debate, propose legislation, or even speak. Indeed, Harrington wrote
that if 'any person or persons shall go about to introduce debate into any
popular assembly', they should be put to death immediately and 'without
appeal'.[111]

How was this possible? At its heart was Harrington's famous principle
that in any situation where two people are asked to share power – like two
girls sharing a cake, in Harrington's analogy – one must divide, and the
other must choose. From this commonsensical approach to consensus-
building, Harrington deduced the need for a bi-cameral legislature in
which one chamber must propose legislation and the other must confirm
or deny it. But by this logic, he argued, the second or lower chamber must
not propose its own legislation, nor must it debate; it has the right only
to vote yes or no. Harrington thus argued that the upper house should
be the senate, selected from an aristocracy of merit who were educated
and reasonable enough to propose laws for the common good; the role
of the lower house or representative of the people, by contrast, was to
vote on this legislation to ensure that the senate did not pass any laws
infringing the people's liberties. 'That which is proposed by the authority
of the senate, and confirmed by the command of the people, is the law
of Oceana.'[112]

There is obviously a large gap from the premise that 'one divides, the
other chooses' to the conclusion that the elected representatives of the

---

[110] Quoted in Rahe, *Against Throne and Altar*, p. 332.     [111] Harrington, *Oceana*, p. 126.
[112] *Ibid.*, p. 167. This is very different from the system proposed by Marchamont Nedham,
who put the ability of the people's representatives to propose legislation at the centre of
his programme: 'The people, who are most sensible of their own burdens, being once
put into a capacity and freedom of acting, are the most likely to provide remedies for
their own relief': *Mercurius Politicus* 81 (25 December 1652), p. 1287.

people must keep silent and merely give consent. To leap this divide, Harrington adopted the anti-populist vitriol of the constitutional royalists and the belief, outlined most influentially in *His Majesties Answer to the XIX Propositions* and latterly by Thomas Hobbes, that anarchy developed whenever the people's representatives intruded upon the *arcana imperii*. According to Cicero, Harrington wrote, 'the commonwealths of Greece were all shaken or ruined by the intemperance of their *comitia*, or assemblies of the people'; the only exception was Lacedaemon, where 'the people... had no power at all of debate'. Harrington continued, 'Nor shall any commonwealth where the people in their political capacity is talkative ever see half the days of one of these [where they keep silent], but being carried away by vainglorious men (that, as Overbury says, piss more than they drink) swim down the sink.'[113]

Behind this vitriol lay the premise that the common people were naturally submissive and had no desire to debate when they were genuinely free. Generally speaking, Harrington argued, 'where there is liquorishness in a popular assembly to debate, it proceedeth not from the constitution of the people, but of the commonwealth'; in Oceana, where the people had their veto power and thus could not be oppressed by the senate, there was no such 'intemperance'.[114] The common people, unless wronged by their superiors, demonstrate 'bashfulness in the presence of the better sort or wiser men'.[115] In the Roman republic, for example, only after the patricians and nobility began 'injuring the people beyond all moderation' did the people first begin to debate – a version of the derivation of anarchy not unlike John Lilburne's, but with anarchy now understood in terms almost wholly antithetical to Lilburne's as any popular voice in government.[116]

The moral of this story was that peace was only possible when the people were given the most limited sort of freedom possible: enough to prevent their own enslavement, but not enough to provoke disorder by raising or debating their own concerns. By contrast, 'a people, when they are reduced unto misery and despair, become their own politicians, as

---

[113] Harrington, *Oceana*, p. 149. On Harrington's very unMachiavellian fear of tumults, see Worden, 'James Harrington and "The Commonwealth of Oceana"', pp. 92–3. One possible source here is Livy: 'Indeed, that is the nature of crowds: the mob is either a humble slave or a cruel master. As for the middle way of liberty, the mob can neither take it nor keep it with any respect for moderation or law': Livy, *The War with Hannibal: Books XXI–XXX of the History of Rome from Its Foundation*, trans. Aubrey de Sélincourt (London, 1972), p. 262.

[114] Harrington, *Oceana*, p. 163.

[115] *Ibid.*, pp. 149–50. Paul Rahe sees this view of the populace as quintessentially Machiavellian: see Rahe, *Against Throne and Altar*, pp. 50–2.

[116] *Ibid.*, p. 150.

certain beasts when they are sick become their own physicians'. This excessive freedom was dangerous precisely because of its immoderation: 'If you do not take the due dose of your medicines . . . it may chance to be poison; there being a like taste of the politics that inclines to confusion.'[117] As Vickie Sullivan has noted, 'moderation in this case is clearly imposed from without'.[118]

This system, as Harrington designed it, is really quite extraordinary in its attempt to square the circle between ideas at opposite ends of the contemporary political spectrum. On the one hand, it accepts the tyranny inherent in gross economic inequality and admits a great deal of property redistribution towards the goal of levelling the economic playing field. It also allows a future in which the vast majority might acquire the economic independence necessary to become enfranchised citizens of the commonwealth. All of this is beyond the pale of what Cromwell or Ireton were willing to allow at Putney, or what Nedham and Philodemius were willing to allow in their republican writings. But on the other hand, because enfranchisement and citizenship are so radically attenuated in Harrington's scheme, the dangers of anarchy envisioned by Cromwell, Ireton, Nedham and Philodemius melt away. The majority cannot legislate an end to private property, as Ireton and Cromwell feared, because they cannot propose legislation. They cannot put their private interests over the common good, as Nedham feared, because they have no forum to express those interests. Indeed, in Harrington's scheme it would not even matter if the popular will remained 'underived' and expressed through plebiscite rather than through an elected assembly, as Philodemius feared, because the people would still only have the power to vote up or down on the legislation offered by their wise and educated superiors.

Freedom, in this system, was the very quintessence of republican non-domination: the people had the ability to veto any aspect of the government, hence nothing could be done against their will. Indeed, Harrington gave the people the very 'negative voice' that earlier republicans and Levellers had seen as the epitome of political power.[119] But at the same time, the people were given no self-determination through their own

---

[117] *Ibid.*, p. 161.
[118] Sullivan, *Machiavelli, Hobbes and the Formation of a Liberal Republicanism*, p. 150. Sullivan also notes that Harrington's 'purpose, as he states it, is to offer a perfect government, and his definition of perfection relates not to the release of personal virtue through civic participation but rather to the manner in which its citizens are constrained, and hence, its perpetuity secured . . . Harrington presents Oceana as a model that aims at this mechanical perfection by so constricting the actions of its citizens. Release of any sort could be dangerous.'
[119] I owe this observation to Kinch Hoekstra.

will and ingenuity, no autonomy, no voice in the commonwealth.[120] All agency in this system came from the social elites, the Senate, a body 'elected' only from amongst the population qualified by their 'education and their leisure for the public, furnished by their ease and competent riches'.[121] All in all, it was a frighteningly prophetic vision of modern, moderate liberty.

### Conclusion

This chapter has argued that seventeenth-century English political writers understood proper liberty to be a middle way between extremes. I have suggested that the republicanism that emerged in the English Revolution, when understood in these terms, seems less like a discussion of how to *engender* liberty, and more like part of a debate over how best to *moderate* liberty. In particular, I have suggested that James Harrington's *The Commonwealth of Oceana*, the greatest monument of republican thought in the English Revolution, was particularly successful in limiting liberty in palatable ways because Harrington admitted some of the most expansive and radical interpretations of tyranny, even while offering an equally expansive and in many ways royalist interpretation of anarchy. Many of the authors discussed in this chapter expanded the category of tyranny, and many others expanded the category of anarchy, but Harrington's capacity to do both shrank the category of liberty almost to the limits of human observation.

I want to end, then, with two conclusions that are implied by my discussion here but transcend the particulars of the argument. One of these conclusions is specific to the debate in the English Revolution over 'where true freedom lies', as Winstanley put it, and the role of moderation in shaping that debate; the other is more general and concerns the role of moderation in shaping a distinctively English modernity.

My specific conclusion is that the structure of moderation rendered the theoretical debate over liberty in revolutionary England intensely incongruous with the actual experience of freedom in the turbulent decades of the mid seventeenth century. A vast number of English people learned in these years to imagine themselves as free, individual, rights-bearing citizens. They learned to petition the government for control of their labour, to choose their own churches, to rally outside the halls of power for the right to vote and to deploy the contents of the weekly press to debate

---

[120] This has been brilliantly described in Jonathan Scott, 'The Rapture of Motion', pp. 150–4.

[121] Harrington, *Oceana*, p. 141.

public policy. This was freedom in the English Revolution, unbowed no matter how hard successive regimes tried to stifle it.[122] Little of this, however, could be expressed in an analytical discourse of liberty that was steeped in the classicising, orderly, almost geometrical idiom of the middle way. The need to moderate freedom – to make it accountable and precise rather than overflowing and unruly – alienated it from human experience, in the writings of Diggers and Levellers barely less than in the writings of royalists and republicans. To be blunt, liberty is an intrinsically effusive and untidy process no matter how rigidly it is defined analytically; to force it onto a spectrum between tyranny and anarchy, to make it moderate, is to make it, in some meaningful sense, no longer liberty at all.

My more general conclusion is that the rule of moderation outlined here contributed to the evolution of liberty as a false universal in English modernity. The idea of 'false universals' has been developed by feminist scholars, in the English context especially Hilda Smith, as a way of analysing the exclusionary work of inclusive ideas.[123] Categories like 'man' and 'human rights' presume masculine experiences even as they subsume the feminine; their claim to universality is normative and thus delegitimises or renders invisible what they exclude. As feminist scholars have demonstrated, the concept of liberty acted in just such a way in the seventeenth century: the unfreedom of women was not addressed within the category of liberty by virtually any seventeenth-century writer, and the alleged universality of the category thus helped to render women invisible or subhuman.[124] I would argue that the rule of moderation was precisely what authorised this exclusion in its local English setting and gave it a power in English history that transcended gender. As we have seen, liberty contained an apparent contradiction – it was both limited and complete, both an opening of possibilities a circumscription of where

---

[122] For the idea of reading and writing about politics as constitutive of liberty, see Sharon Achinstein, *Milton and the Revolutionary Reader* (Princeton, 1994).

[123] Hilda Smith, *All Men and Both Sexes: Gender, Politics, and the False Universal in England 1640–1832* (University Park, Penn., 2002); Joan Scott, *Only Paradoxes to Offer: French Feminists and the Rights of Man* (Cambridge, Mass., 1996). For theoretical argument from political scientists, see Carole Pateman, *The Sexual Contract* (Stanford, 1988); Wendy Brown, *Manhood and Politics: A Feminist Reading of Political Theory* (Totowa, N.J., 1988).

[124] See Patricia Crawford, '"The Poorest She": Women and Citizenship in Early Modern England', in Michael Mendle (ed.), *The Putney Debates of 1647: The Army, the Levellers and the English State* (Cambridge, 2001); Elaine Hobby, 'Winstanley, Women and the Family', *Prose Studies* 22, no. 2 (August 1999), pp. 61–72. Both of these articles suggest, in different ways, that the arguments of the Levellers and Diggers were logically extendable to women, and were 'haunted' by that possibility, even if they never developed the case for women's liberty.

they might lead – neatly encapsulated in the early modern rule of moderation. Citizens required bounds in order to be free, while conversely the limitation of state power authorised the expansion of its power as a free state. Hence, when writers defined a state free from tyranny, they rendered its bridling of citizens a form of moderation rather than repression. I would argue therefore that the rule of moderation was crucial to the precocious development of the modern state in an English setting where more bluntly authoritarian forms of power were increasingly out of bounds.[125]

As we consider the historical evolution of the concept of liberty, then, moderation may help us to understand why, throughout the Anglo-American tradition, liberty has been such a paradoxical ideal, constructed upon the frustrated ambitions of society's most vulnerable members. Rather than celebrating our intellectual forerunners, as most historians of liberty tend to do, we might instead question whether our own claims to live in a free society still depend upon their categories. When we invoke liberty, what sort of power is authorised, and who ceases to be counted?

[125] See Michael Mendle, 'Parliamentary Sovereignty: A Very English Absolutism', in Nicholas Phillipson and Quentin Skinner (eds.), *Political Discourse in Early Modern Britain* (Cambridge, 1993).

# 8 How toleration became moderate in seventeenth-century England

## Introduction

Before the 1640s, the state's prerogative to punish religious deviance was almost unanimously praised as moderate, while broad claims for religious toleration were almost unanimously condemned as extremist. It was unimpeachable orthodoxy, backed by centuries of both Catholic and Protestant practice, that Christian princes should wield the sword of correction on behalf of the Church. In England, a self-consciously judicious and temperate defence of religious unity – prosecuting heresy and enforcing obligatory participation in the Established Church, but not 'making windows into men's souls' – had been the avowed policy of the government since Queen Elizabeth's reign, defining a middle way between the murderous Inquisition of the Catholics and the libertine permissiveness of the Anabaptists.[1] Even puritans and Catholics who dissented from this version of moderation – positing toleration for ceremonial nonconformity, or separation from the Church of England, as alternative forms of moderation – with rare exceptions would have agreed with the puritan Thomas Cartwright's demand that teachers of heresy be put to death: 'If this be bloody and extreme, I am content to be so counted with the Holy Ghost.'[2]

By 1689, however, and the passage of the law misleadingly known as the 'Toleration Act', this consensus had collapsed.[3] Many people throughout the Restoration Era continued to defend moderate religious coercion; in 1675, for instance, the Lord Keeper called the Test Act 'a moderate

---

[1] See Ethan Shagan, 'The English Inquisition: Constitutional Conflict and Ecclesiastical Law in the 1590s', *HJ* 47, no. 3 (September 2004), pp. 541–65. For examples, see Burton, *The Anatomy of Melancholy*, sig. BBB5v; Hall, *Christian Moderation*, part II *passim*.

[2] Cartwright, *The Second Replie of Thomas Cartwright*, pp. 112–15, quote on p. 115. The exception that proves the rule is *Arguments for Toleration Published for the Satisfaction of All Moderate Men* (London, 1647), an anti-toleration pamphlet that proposed a series of wholly sarcastic arguments linking moderation to toleration.

[3] Technically the 'Act for exempting their majesties' Protestant subjects, dissenting from the Church of England, from the penalties of certain laws'.

security to the Church and crown'.[4] But now competing visions of moderation suggested that *any* legal compulsion in matters of conscience constituted an excessive use of magisterial power. Thus, whereas in the 1640s defences of religious coercion routinely contained title phrases like 'Moderation Justified' and the 'Advantages of Moderation', by 1686 William Penn could write *A Perswasive to Moderation* defending religious toleration;[5] by 1687 a Yorkshire Justice of the Peace, when asked if he could live 'friendly with those of all persuasions', replied that he could do so 'in as much as I have always loved moderation'[6]; and by 1714 an embattled defender of the old orthodoxy could lament that toleration was now widely accepted by 'fashionable moderate men'.[7]

This chapter thus seeks to understand how toleration became moderate; or, more precisely, it seeks to understand the arguments by which proponents of toleration successfully claimed the mantle of moderation. These arguments were crucial to the growth and success of liberty of conscience, and they take us quickly into the dark underbelly of toleration, for if toleration was to be a middle way – between, in the most generic terms, intolerance of the tolerable and tolerance of the intolerable – then it had to foreground its restraint of intolerable excesses. Arguments for toleration as moderation thus distanced themselves from mere permissiveness or anarchy by emphasising *active* moderation, attacking genuinely intolerable beliefs and practices – often conveniently relocated outside the sphere of 'religion' or 'conscience' in order to render 'liberty of conscience' universal – and demanding their restraint as an essential element of a virtuous society. Of course, no toleration can ever be absolute; as Michael Walzer puts it, 'To argue that different groups and/or individuals should be allowed to coexist in peace is not to argue that every actual or imaginable difference should be tolerated.'[8] But because seventeenth-century toleration was imbricated with the ideal of moderation in ways that have never before been seriously considered, the content of that toleration was structured by and predicated upon restraint in significant and unexpected ways.

Analysing how toleration became moderate, instead of tracing the growth of toleration, can thus rescue us from a great deal of teleology,

---

[4] Quoted in Anthony Ashley Cooper, *A Letter from a Person of Quality to His Friend in the Country* (London, 1675), p. 9.
[5] Printed in William Penn, *The Political Writings of William Penn*, ed. Andrew Murphy (Indianapolis, 2002), pp. 289–329.
[6] Bodleian Library, MS Rawlinson A.139A, fo. 77v. For another example of similar wording, also from the North Riding of Yorkshire, see fos. 75v–76r.
[7] Thomas Brett, *True Moderation: A Sermon on Phil. IV. 5.* (London, 1714), p. 6.
[8] Michael Walzer, *On Toleration* (New Haven, 1997), p. 6.

anachronism and liberal self-aggrandisement. The traditional approach
to the history of religious toleration was to admit that virtually all arguments for toleration in the seventeenth century 'fell short' of modern
beliefs, but to suggest that thinkers like William Walwyn, William Penn
and John Locke came as close as they could within the limits of their
society. In other words, historians argued (and some continue to argue)
that modern liberalism was the natural endpoint of seventeenth-century
tolerationist thought, even if seventeenth-century thinkers did not themselves reach that *telos*. The exceptions and provisos early modern thinkers
placed upon toleration were thus seen as in some sense extrinsic to tolerationist thought rather than ingredients of it; they were foreign con-
taminants, gradually shed as toleration achieved its pristine form.[9] Some
recent historians have worked hard to correct this teleology. Alexandra
Walsham has argued that there was no progression from persecution to
toleration but rather 'tolerance and intolerance interacted with and fed
off each other in a recurrent and unending cycle'.[10] John Marshall and
Gordon Schochet have put salutary emphasis on the many limitations
of seventeenth-century toleration.[11] Andrew Murphy has seen toleration emerging from and remaining imbedded in the decidedly illiberal
theologies of radical sectarianism.[12] But even these scholars still imagine toleration as constituted despite, rather than through, its exceptions;
condemnations of Catholicism, atheism, drunkenness or sodomy are still
imagined as failures of an ideal toleration not yet achieved in the seventeenth century.

[9] See most recently John Coffey, *Persecution and Toleration in Protestant England, 1558–
1689* (New York, 2000), pp. 56–8 and *passim*; Perez Zagorin, *How the Idea of Religious
Toleration Came to the West* (Princeton, 2003). John Rawls wrote of the intolerance shown
by John Locke and his successors to Catholics and atheists: 'Presumably a greater
historical experience and a knowledge of the wider possibilities of political life would
have convinced them they were mistaken': John Rawls, *A Theory of Justice* (Cambridge,
Mass., 1971), pp. 215–16. This view is endorsed in the political science literature in
Alex Tuckness, 'Rethinking the Intolerant Locke', *American Journal of Political Science*
46, no. 2 (April 2002), pp. 288–98. There is also a political science literature arguing
that Locke was fundamentally illiberal in his toleration, exemplified by John Dunn, *The
Political Thought of John Locke* (Cambridge, 1969); Jeremy Waldron, 'Locke, Toleration,
and the Rationality of Persecution', in his *Liberal Rights: Collected Papers 1981–1991*
(Cambridge, 1993).

[10] Alexandra Walsham, *Charitable Hatred: Tolerance and Intolerance in England, 1500–1700*
(Manchester, 2006), p. 287.

[11] John Marshall, *John Locke, Toleration and Early Enlightenment Culture: Religious Intolerance and Arguments for Religious Toleration in Early Modern and Early Enlightenment
Europe* (Cambridge, 2006), ch. 22 and *passim*; Gordon Schochet, 'From Persecution
to "Toleration"', in J. R. Jones (ed.), *Liberty Secured? Britain Before and After 1688*
(Stanford, 1992).

[12] Andrew Murphy, *Conscience and Community: Revisiting Toleration and Religious Dissent in
Early Modern England and America* (University Park, Penn., 2001).

Yet within the rule of moderation, toleration was constituted precisely by normalising and naturalising its limitations: the coercive restraint of excess was not the opposite of moderation but fundamental to its operation. Realising that toleration had to become moderate before it could become virtuous forces us to put the exceptions and provisos of seventeenth-century toleration back into the content of toleration instead of imagining them as somehow external to it. Exceptions were the building blocks out of which toleration was constructed, moderating an otherwise extreme position and constructing it as a middle way. Seventeenth-century writers thus never imagined a toleration that was not always already a concomitant restraint; their intellectual projects justified the state's toleration of certain dubious beliefs and practices by arguing that such toleration more firmly established the state's capacity to restrain other dubious beliefs and practices. Hence modern historical definitions of toleration – like 'the concession of liberty to those who dissent in religion' in Henry Kamen's influential formulation[13] – obfuscate one half of the tolerationist project in favour of the half that fits with modern preconceptions. Moderate toleration was a technique of government, not the withdrawal or absence of government.

This chapter will thus argue that the ideological drive for religious toleration was built upon, rather than merely condoning, a concomitant drive to suppress such intolerable excesses as adultery, blasphemy, drunkenness, atheism, Arianism, Socinianism and of course Catholicism. By defining the restraint of these offences as not merely consistent with universal religious toleration but constitutive of it, proponents of toleration found new ways to assail their enemies within the rule of moderation.

### The moderate case for religious persecution

The default position of virtually all English subjects in the century between Reformation and Revolution was to accept at least some religious coercion, when used judiciously and without malice, as a form of virtuous moderation. The conformist firebrand Gabriel Powel summarised this opinion in a 1605 diatribe against puritans who dared to demand of the government 'a more moderate course of proceeding in matters of religion': he exclaimed 'As if the proceedings against Papists hitherto were immoderate!' and he offered 'such reasons as (in my simple opinion) may move any reasonable, moderate and sober man, fearing God,

[13] Henry Kamen, *The Rise of Toleration* (London, 1967), p. 7.

to detest factious toleration'.[14] As Powel's ironic reference to tolerance of Catholicism suggests, while his puritan opponents believed that toleration of their own nonconformity was moderate, they emphatically did not endorse broad religious toleration; that would have been excessive by definition, failing to provide necessary protections for legitimate religion and bridles on heresy and superstition. As such, virtually all puritans, like virtually all conformists, demanded state supervision of religion, as had virtually all Christians for more than a millennium. Before we can understand the arguments by which a minority tried to make toleration moderate in the seventeenth century, then, we need first to understand the moderate case for religious persecution.[15]

The idea that the civil state should wield its sword on behalf of the Church was a direct result of the conversion of the Roman Empire to Christianity by the Emperor Constantine, and early modern Christians remembered this moment as a crossroads in Christian history. Previously, the primitive Church of the apostles had been a voluntary society of men and women called by the Holy Spirit; it had needed no physical force to make new converts, and indeed God had decreed that the Church should be powerless and persecuted precisely to emphasise the miracle of its growth and success. In the fourth century, however, this primitive age of the Church came to an end when God decreed that Christians would cease to be persecuted and instead would wield civil power themselves. This break from the New Testament model of pacific Christianity was most influentially theorised by St Augustine, whose tireless work defending doctrinal orthodoxy and attacking schism led him to endorse religious coercion. In Augustine, especially his writings against the Donatists, temperate and measured persecution was a superior alternative to either toleration of heresy, which perpetuated sin, or the uncharitable destruction of heretics, which left them no opportunity to rejoin the Church. The use of religious coercion was thus virtuously moderate precisely when it developed out of care for the sinner: 'There is a righteous persecution, which the Church of Christ inflicts upon the impious . . . She persecutes in the spirit of love.'[16] Heretics and

---

[14] Gabriel Powel, *A Refutation of an Epistle Apologeticall Written by a Puritan-Papist* (London, 1605), pp. 46–7.

[15] See Mark Goldie, 'The Theory of Religious Intolerance in Restoration England', in Ole Peter Grell, Jonathan Israel and Nicholas Tyacke (eds.), *From Persecution to Toleration: The Glorious Revolution and Religion in England* (Oxford, 1991); Walsham, *Charitable Hatred*; Marshall, *John Locke, Toleration and Early Enlightenment Culture*. For the sixteenth century and the broader European tradition, see Brad Gregory, *Salvation at Stake: Christian Martyrdom in Early Modern Europe* (Cambridge, Mass., 1999).

[16] From St Augustine of Hippo, *A Treatise Concerning the Correction of the Donatists*, in Philip Schaff (ed.), *A Select Library of the Nicene and Post-Nicene Fathers of the Christian Church* (New York, 4 vols., 1886–90), IV, p. 637.

schismatics could not be persecuted without due bounds; authorities should use limited coercive measures which fit the offence and produced the desired result. Only utterly obstinate heretics might be killed; all others should receive penalties to compel them back into the Church, because their mere presence would contribute to their salvation.[17] These Augustinian arguments for moderate coercion provided a model for early modern Protestants, who habitually portrayed their coercion as moderate because they enforced conformity but did not practise Catholic-style Inquisitions and *autos-de-fé*. This claim was still vibrant in the 1680s, when William Saywell, master of Jesus College, Cambridge, argued for 'moderate discipline, to make them hear and consider', and when John Locke's great sparring partner Jonas Proast argued that 'moderate penalties may do good service toward the procuring of conviction and change of men's minds'.[18]

Augustine, of course, knew, because his opponents reminded him, that Christ and the Apostles had never used coercion to save souls, so he had to invent a series of theological rationales for persecution. The Old Testament provided numerous examples of civil power used to compel religion, but these texts were slippery theological ground: they could all too easily be glossed as carnal figures of a New Testament Church which was merely spiritual and hence used persuasion rather than force. So, while Augustine used Old Testament precedents when they were convenient, he chose to concentrate on two post-Incarnation arguments. First, he argued for the historical transformation of the Church, with the conversion of Constantine, into a religion aligned with civil power. Second, he relied upon Christ's parable of the feast, where a lord tells his servants to invite guests to a great supper, and when those guests fail to come he tells his servants, 'Go out into the highways and hedges, and compel them to come in.' Augustine specifically glossed 'highways and hedges' as 'heretics and schisms'.[19] In his letter to Donatus, Augustine wove these two arguments into a single thread:

Just notice the phrase used of those who came first: 'bring them in', not the phrase 'compel them to come in'. That symbolised the incipient stage of the Church, still developing to the point where it would have the strength to compel men to it. Accordingly, since it was right that when it had grown stronger in power and extent, men should actually be compelled to the feast of everlasting salvation, the

---

[17] When the threat of punishment brought Donatists into the Church, for instance, 'those who feigned conformity, becoming by degrees accustomed to our communion, and hearing the preaching of the truth . . . were to a great extent brought to a right belief': Augustine, *A Treatise Concerning the Correction of the Donatists*, p. 644.

[18] Goldie, 'The Theory of Religious Intolerance', p. 349; Jonas Proast, *The Argument of the Letter Concerning Toleration Briefly Consider'd and Answer'd* (Oxford, 1690), p. 24.

[19] Augustine, *A Treatise Concerning the Correction of the Donatists*, p. 642.

words were afterwards added: 'It is done as thou hast commanded, and still there is room. And the lord said, "Go out into the highways and hedges and compel them to come in."' . . . He who is compelled is forced to go where he had no wish to go, but when he has come in, he partakes of the feast right willingly.[20]

These Augustinian arguments, with the arguments of other post-Nicene Church Fathers like St Jerome, delineated moderate religious persecution for all subsequent Christians. But early modern English writers, raised in a uniquely Erastian Church-state with the monarch as its Supreme Head, developed these arguments in two different directions, which we might (with some simplification) call conformist and puritan. To begin with the conformist position, as we saw in Chapter 3 much of the rhetoric of the Church of England's purported *via media* was predicated upon the ideal of moderate religious coercion. The crucial framework of conformist moderation was obedience: subjects remained part of the *via media* while they obeyed laws governing religious conformity, and magistrates supported that *via media* when they enforced those laws. When John Aylmer became Bishop of London, for instance, he was given explicit instructions to enforce a middle way: 'to cut off (even as her majesty termed it) and to correct offenders on both sides which swerve from the right path of obedience'.[21] Later, Richard Bancroft was promoted to the same office in part because, 'though he hath been careful and zealous to suppress some sort of sectaries, yet hath he therein showed no tyrannous disposition, but with mildness and kind dealing, when it was expedient, hath reclaimed diverse'.[22]

In the Restoration Era, conformist arguments for coercion as moderation found newly elaborate expression, undoubtedly because what was once obvious was now contested. Perhaps the most explicit discussion of the issue was *Samaritanism*, written in 1664 against 'papists and puritans now plotting and pleading for toleration', by Richard Perrinchief, a High Anglican doctor of divinity who was already famous as a biographer of Charles I and one of the editors of the royal martyr's collected works. One whole chapter was devoted to 'removing vulgar mistakes' concerning 'extremes and moderation' – suggesting that the ancient affinity between coercion and moderation was under strain. Perrinchief complained bitterly that according to vulgar opinion 'moderation is the same in effect with . . . cutting or chopping a thing in the middle, and dividing the live child into two equal parts between the unjust pretender and the true mother'. The rabble think that persecution is excessive just because it is

---

[20] Ep. CLXXIII, in *St. Augustine: Select Letters*, ed. J. H. Baxter (London, 1930), pp. 301–3.
[21] Collinson, *The Elizabethan Puritan Movement*, pp. 201–5.
[22] CUL MS Mm.I.47, pp. 333–5.

so far removed from their own licentious desires, 'not considering that it is in the power of any man to declare or denominate a thing extreme by his own act of departing from it, as easily as it is in his power by turning himself about to cause a thing to stand to the left or right hand'. Perrinchief argued, on the contrary, that England cannot 'come to a mediocrity' through toleration because it would 'quickly dispatch and destroy all virtue, all religion and all justice'. Rather than moderation lying at the arithmetic mean of all available positions, true moderation is chosen 'rather because of some special virtue proper to it'.[23]

In context, Perrinchief was arguing primarily against Presbyterian demands to be included in a comprehensive national Church, a position far less unthinkable than universal toleration. Nonetheless, he was furious at the Presbyterian John Corbet for arguing in *The Interest of England* (1660) that the 'prelatists' [i.e. Anglicans] ought to 'descend to the Presbyterians in the proposed middle way' of mutual accommodation. Perrinchief responded, 'According to what rule does it appear, which is here weakly and childishly taken for granted, that the prelatists (as this Jack Straw miscalls those of the Church of England) are so high? Let it be showed what is the mean they have so far exceeded.' It was absurd pretence for the Presbyterians to make 'their discipline the mean', whereas in fact 'we, being the only legal, visible Church of this nation . . . have a right to judge them and rather condemn them of the extreme on the contrary side'.[24] In this argument, because legal conformity was the basis for order, the idea that enforcement of that conformity constituted moderation was nearly a tautology.

The middle way represented by the Church of England, however, did not merely persecute nonconformists willy-nilly. Perrinchief sounded almost like a tolerationist when he argued, 'It is worse than barbarous to attach or oppress any people merely upon account of their religion . . . There is no need for force or injury, for as much as religion cannot be compelled.' He argued against capital punishment for heretics, following St Augustine, who 'proceeds in a milder, and middle way, that is, neither to tolerate the heresy nor condemn the heretic to death, because that were to cut off all possibility of repentance and reconciliation'. Yet the moderate use of coercion by the state in matters of religion was nonetheless absolutely necessary, both in order to preserve order and decency in the Church, and because virtually all religious heterodoxy contained the seeds of civil sedition, as the Revolution had proved.[25] Perrinchief

[23] Richard Perrinchief, *Samaritanism: or, a Treatise of Comprehending, Compounding and Tolerating Several Religions in One Church* (London, 1664?), pp. 8–13.
[24] *Ibid.*, pp. 19–20.    [25] *Ibid.*, pp. 24, 38–9.

argued that what his opponents called Christian Liberty – 'that every man should do as he pleases in things so indifferent' – would 'inevitably produce differences, and differences in such inconsiderable matters will infallibly produce animosities and divisions in greater matters, and there terminate in the overthrow of all discipline or government'.[26] Hence to maintain order in the Church through coercion was not to persecute people merely for their religion but to forestall the inevitable effects of their religion, as every government must if it is to survive. This was the essence of the conformist vision of coercion as moderation, the position which after 1660 we may call 'Anglican': conformity must be enforced with the sword, because even toleration limited to *adiaphora* tended ultimately to anarchy.

Quite distinct from this Anglican position, there was another argument for coercion as moderation – a quintessentially puritan argument which after 1644 became the default position of the Presbyterians – defining so-called 'Christian liberty' as the moderate middle way between toleration and persecution. In this framework, nonconformity in indifferent ceremonies could be tolerated – indeed freedom of conscience in things indifferent was guaranteed by St Paul in scripture – but heresy and schism (however broadly or narrowly defined) could not. As one author put it, 'Much of the mistake that hath been about a Toleration hath come to pass by not duly considering this golden mean of liberty only in unnecessary things in religion, between the two extremes of unnecessary impositions, and an unlimited toleration. But as the former is bad, being against Christian liberty and charity, yet the latter is much worse, because it tends to subvert the Christian faith and to overthrow all government in the matters of religion.'[27] This explains why puritans have so often been wrongly accused of hypocrisy for demanding liberty of conscience for themselves while simultaneously persecuting those who disagreed with them; in fact the idea of 'Christian liberty' never admitted universal toleration but rather sanctioned a version of moderation entirely within the Augustinian consensus.

We can see this argument entering the mid century toleration debates in George Gillespie's *Wholsome Severity Reconciled with Christian Liberty* (1645), which sought a 'middle way betwixt popish tyranny and schismatising liberty' in response to the newly articulated tolerationist positions of Roger Williams and William Walwyn.[28] Gillespie argued that if the

---

[26] *Ibid.*, p. 11.
[27] *Four Grand Questions Proposed and Briefly Answered* (London, 1689), p. 23.
[28] George Gillespie, *Wholsome Severity Reconciled with Christian Liberty* (London, 1645). The quote about the middle way is in the extended title.

Christian magistrate remained 'keeper' of the second table of the Ten Commandments, responsible for public order, he had to be keeper of the first table as well, with responsibility for the soul as well as the body.[29] The new dispensation of Christ did not excuse the magistrate from punishing sins, including sins against God through false religion. What Christ did, however, was provide 'Christian liberty': the right of every Christian to decide in his or her conscience whether to perform actions neither required nor forbidden by scripture. These indifferent matters included ceremonies, clothing and other outward forms over which the Jewish law had claimed dominion, and which Catholics and conformists had tried to enforce. 'If the thing be indifferent', Gillespie wrote, 'I confess no man is to be compelled to it against his conscience, for this hath been the tyranny of papists and prelates'. However, in matters not indifferent people should yield to immutable divine law: 'Liberty of heresy and schism is no part of the liberty of conscience which Christ hath purchased to us at so dear a rate.'[30] This was the basis for Gillespie's middle way between tyrannical persecution and sinful toleration: 'Concerning this question there are three opinions: two extremes and one in the middle.' The first extreme belonged to the papists, 'who hold it to be not only no sin but good service to God to extirpate by fire and sword all that are adversaries'. The second extreme, which 'doth fall short as far as the former doth exceed', is that 'the magistrate ought not to inflict any punishment, nor put forth any coercive power, upon heretics or sectaries, but on the contrary grant them liberty and toleration'. The middle way, however, was for the magistrate to tolerate nonconformity in outward ceremonial matters, and to 'exercise his coercive power in suppressing heretics and sectaries, less or more, according as the nature and degree of the error, schism, obstinacy and danger of seducing others doth require'.[31]

To summarise, then, to most seventeenth-century English Protestants religious coercion was necessary precisely because it was a virtuous middle way between licentious tolerance of sin and cruel intolerance of human imperfection. None of these authors suggested that people could or should be 'forced to believe'. They all understood that law could not penetrate the conscience, that God had endowed different people with different levels of understanding, and that significant variation in belief and worship was tolerable in some circumstances. Yet these authors nonetheless argued that to allow heresy to flourish could no more be

---

[29] *Ibid.*, pp. 6–7, and see also p. 12 and sig. A3r.    [30] *Ibid.*, pp. 24–5.
[31] *Ibid.*, sig. A2r–p. 3. For more examples in the Presbyterian tradition, see Josiah Hunter, *Loves Companion, or a Short Treatise of the Nature, Necessity, and Advantages of Moderation* (London, 1656); Thorowgood, *Moderation Iustified*.

'moderate' than to allow murder or rape to flourish, because moderation was governance rather than its absence; religious moderation was the reasonable restraint of error.

### Moderate toleration and vice

The principal arguments made by tolerationists in later Stuart England have been described by historians so often that they need only be summarised here.[32] There was a theological argument that the New Testament allowed only spiritual rather than physical force, abrogating Old Testament examples of religious violence. There was a separation of powers argument that the conscience belongs only to God and is thus outside the magistrate's jurisdiction. There was an argument that violating one's own conscience is a greater sin than sincerely erroneous belief, so forcing consciences actually condemns people to hell. There was an argument from the Golden Rule: if people expected their own beliefs to be tolerated by other regimes, they had to be tolerant themselves. There were more prudential arguments: that toleration promoted civil peace and trade; that since Englishmen could never agree in all their beliefs they should fall back upon a baseline religion which all could accept for the sake of order; that in a free market of ideas the Truth would naturally prevail; that persecution was counterproductive and made martyrs rather than extirpating error. There were also more liberal arguments: that civil rights should not depend upon beliefs but only upon citizenship, or that religious persecution threatened rights of property, or even that individual personhood depended upon freedom from prior restraint. None of these arguments in the seventeenth century ever demanded as broad a toleration as the later liberal tradition would presume. But it is not my purpose to measure early modern theorists against modern, liberal expectations – so many points awarded for tolerating atheism, so many points deducted for banning the mass – or to challenge the genuineness of their toleration. Rather, it is crucial for us to recognise that these theories really were different from nearly all earlier demands for liberty of conscience precisely insofar as they spoke in abstract, permanent and universalising terms.

The unprecedented breadth and theoretical totality of these claims, however, marked them as dangerously excessive, hence none of these arguments could develop unless they repositioned such open-ended toleration as moderate. That is, toleration paradoxically had to bind, restrain

---

[32] See most recently Walsham, *Charitable Hatred*; Marshall, *John Locke, Toleration and Early Enlightenment Culture*; Coffey, *Persecution and Toleration in Protestant England*; and Murphy, *Conscience and Community*.

or bridle society's passions and excesses. Within the framework of the *via media*, then, moderate toleration required not only the construction of an extreme, persecuting 'right' but also the construction of an extreme, permissive 'left' in need of moderation, in order to redefine even the most abstract and universal religious toleration as an instrument of restraint. This process developed in earnest not with the initial flowering of revolutionary tolerationist thought in 1644–6 but with subsequent writers who worked to make their ideas palatable to the mainstream of the Church of England.

The first element of this framework that I want to explore is the tolerationist assault on immorality. It has long been recognised that there was a connection between arguments for the toleration of religion and arguments for the prosecution of vice. It can hardly be a coincidence that the great statutory campaign known as the Reformation of Manners was closely associated with the success of the Revolution of 1688–9 and the passage of the so-called 'Toleration Act'.[33] More broadly, Blair Worden has argued that post-Restoration England experienced a 'shift of emphasis from faith to conduct', a 'retreat of theology, and the concomitant shift of Protestantism from a religion of faith towards a religion of works'.[34] Mark Knights has stressed that the growth of toleration in the 1680s helped spur the Reformation of Manners by removing morality from the sphere of 'religion' and hence making it ripe for state intervention.[35] Most recently, Alexandra Walsham has argued that 'toleration stimulated revived efforts to promote personal godliness not least because conservatives feared that it had "let loose the reins" to "licentious practices"', while John Marshall has noted that 1689 fulfilled two parallel desires to 'see "libertinism" and "debauchery" punished and orthodox nonconformist religious worship tolerated'.[36] What has not been fully appreciated even in these excellent studies, however, is that the assault on immorality was neither a byproduct of tolerationist thought nor a response to

---

[33] See Dudley Bahlman, *The Moral Revolution of 1688* (New Haven, 1957); Tony Claydon, *William III and the Godly Revolution* (Cambridge, 1996), pp. 110–21; Shelley Burtt, *Virtue Transformed: Political Argument in England 1688–1740* (Cambridge, 1992); Isabel Rivers, *Reason, Grace, and Sentiment: A Study of the Language of Religion and Ethics in England, 1660–1780* (Cambridge, 2 vols., 1991–2000), I.

[34] Blair Worden, 'The Question of Secularisation', in Alan Houston and Steve Pincus (eds.), *A Nation Transformed: England after the Restoration* (Cambridge, 2001), pp. 38–40.

[35] Mark Knights, '"Meer Religion" and the "Church-State" of Restoration England: the Impact and Ideology of James II's Declarations of Indulgence', in Alan Houston and Steve Pincus (eds.), *A Nation Transformed: England after the Restoration* (Cambridge, 2001).

[36] Walsham, *Charitable Hatred*, p. 321; Marshall, *John Locke, Toleration and Early Enlightenment Culture*, p. 132.

conservative criticism, but was embedded in a new vision of moderate toleration. Universalising arguments for religious toleration became moderate and hence virtuous precisely because they bridled sin.

Connections were drawn between the Restoration government's intolerance of conscience and their notorious tolerance of vice as early as the 1660s, as Tim Harris has shown.[37] By the time of the political crises of the 1680s many texts can be found linking the two. To take an example from cheap print, in 1682 *A Word of Advice to the Two New Sherriffs of London* argued poetically:

> Meetings have been disturbed too oft by those
> That to a bawdy house were never foes:
> Thus preaching seems a crime, and whoring none.[38]

Higher up the social ladder, in 1687 a defender of James II's indulgence argued: 'Never was any prince's court freer from debauchery and more orderly in the disposal of all officers ... The diligent, virtuous, sober, ingenuous and loyal are received without censure of their religion; the slothful, turbulent, factious, debauched and irreligious are as much discouraged, as is most manifest by his severe charges against swearing and drunkenness.'[39] In the same year, the incomparable Gilbert Burnet suggested strong parallels between modern persecutors and their ancient Roman predecessors who had 'delivered themselves up to all the brutalities of sensual pleasure'.[40]

Such claims were commonplace in Restoration politics, but the simplicity of these anecdotes fails to capture the theoretical sophistication that often underlay them. Tolerationism attacked not merely government persecution but government permissiveness, both of which resulted from the same misunderstanding of civil power; proper understanding of the just limits of government would create a middle way that moderated both errors. One of the foundational texts in this line of reasoning was the massively influential *Theologia Eklektike: A Discourse of the Liberty of Prophesying*, written in 1647 by Charles I's chaplain, Jeremy Taylor. Taylor's approach to moderate religious toleration was to delineate a least common denominator Christianity in which moral rectitude, rather than doctrinal orthodoxy, was the litmus test of inclusion. He constructed his

---

[37] Tim Harris, 'The Bawdy House Riots of 1688', *HJ* 29, no. 3 (1986), pp. 537–56; Tim Harris, *London Crowds in the Reign of Charles II: Propaganda and Politics from the Restoration until the Exclusion Crisis* (Cambridge, 1987), ch. 4.

[38] *A Word of Advice to the Two New Sherriffs of London* (London, 1682).

[39] Cited in Knights, '"Meer Religion"', pp. 64–5.

[40] Gilbert Burnet, *A Relation of the Death of the Primitive Persecutors* (Amsterdam, 1687), pp. 8, 19, 44.

treatise around the distinction between necessary and unnecessary religion, suggesting that virtually all questions of theology were indifferent, to be believed or not believed according to the conscience of the individual (a position theoretically distinct from puritan arguments because it accepted not merely ceremonies but beliefs, and even positive laws of scripture, as indifferent). Only the Apostles' Creed was necessary to salvation, and all other beliefs consistent with it should thus be tolerated as mere 'superstructures'.[41] But there was a second, coequal side to Taylor's 'common principles of Christianity': toleration was to be extended to those 'believing the creed, and living good lives'.[42] Christianity was, in its pure state, 'a simple profession of the articles of belief, and a hearty prosecution of the rules of good life'.[43] Hence 'because faith is not only a precept of doctrines but of manners and holy life', any position which 'teaches an ill life, that's heresy'.[44] Given this second, practical side to simple Christianity, Taylor asked, 'Why is not any vicious habit as bad or worse than a false opinion? Why are we so zealous against those we call heretics, and yet great friends with drunkards, and fornicators, and swearers, and intemperate and idle persons?'[45] He continued, 'If we consider that drunkenness is certainly a damnable sin, and that there are more drunkards than heretics, and that drunkenness is parent of a thousand vices, it may be better said of this vice than of most of those opinions which we call heresies, it is infectious and dangerous, and the principle of much evil, and therefore as fit an object for a pious zeal to contest against, as is any of those opinions which trouble men's ease or reputation.'[46]

For Taylor, there was a close relationship between heresy – that is, true heresy, which was intolerable, rather than mere difference of opinion – and immoral living. Violations of the Apostles' Creed were to be accounted 'criminal' not only because they called 'God's veracity into question' but because they caused 'a destruction also of good life'.[47] On the opposite side, moral vices were the wellspring of doctrinal error, and true heresies 'sprang from the too nice distinguishing the faith from the piety and good life of a Christian; they are both but one duty. However they may be distinguished if we speak like philosophers, they cannot be distinguished when we speak like Christians.'[48] Generally speaking, in

---

[41] Jeremy Taylor, *Theologia Eklektike: A Discourse of the Liberty of Prophesying* (London, 1647), pp. 44–7. For 'superstructures' see epistle, p. 14. Taylor attacked even so orthodox a repository of doctrine as the Nicene Creed for taking the beautiful simplicity of the Apostles' Creed and making it 'more curious and articulate', leading to confusion and schism.

[42] Taylor, *A Discourse of the Liberty of Prophesying*, epistle p. 29.    [43] *Ibid.*, p. 191.

[44] *Ibid.*, p. 58.    [45] *Ibid.*, epistle pp. 37–8.    [46] *Ibid.*, epistle pp. 41–2.

[47] *Ibid.*, epistle p. 40.    [48] *Ibid.*, p. 24.

scripture 'faith and good life are made one duty, and vice is called opposite to faith, and heresy opposed to holiness'.[49] This led Taylor to the
remarkable conclusion that it was the morals of believers, rather than the
content of their beliefs, that distinguished true Christians from heretics:
'In the condemnation of heretics, the personal iniquity is more considerable than the obliquity of the doctrine . . . It is not the opinion, but the
impiety that condemns and makes the heretic.'[50]

The result was that Taylor reframed the legitimate scope of religious
coercion around what he termed 'practical impiety' rather than doctrinal
error: 'I deny not but certain and known idolatry or any other sort of
practical impiety with its principiant doctrine may be punished corpo-
rally, because it is no other but matter of fact; but no matter of mere
opinion, no errors that of themselves are not sins are to be persecuted
or punished.'[51] Doctrinal errors *in themselves* were not punishable, but
'if ever error be procured by a vice it hath no excuse but becomes such
a crime, of so much malignity, as to have influence upon the effect and
consequent, and by communication makes it become criminal'.[52] Even
though beliefs were outside the jurisdiction of magistrates, nonetheless
'it concerns the duty of a prince because it concerns the honour of God,
that all vices and every part of ill life be discountenanced and restrained.
And therefore in relation to that, opinions are to be dealt with. For the
understanding being to direct the will, and opinions to guide our practices, they are considerable only as they teach impiety and vice.'[53] This
led Taylor to a vicious diatribe against Roman Catholicism, since 'many
of their doctrines do accidentally teach or lead to ill life'. Because this
tendency was 'accidental' rather than direct, Catholicism was not always
intolerable, but the ease with which the Catholic economy of salvation
forgave sin meant that 'the fear of hell is quite removed' and there was
nothing in Catholic doctrine to 'impede and slacken their proclivity to
sin', hence, 'if men would consider things upon their true grounds, the
Church of Rome should be more reproved upon doctrines that infer ill
life than upon such as are contrariant to faith'.[54]

Taylor's arguments for toleration were cited incessantly by Restoration authors who argued that a permissive and libertine left and an
intolerant and tyrannical right were two sides of the same coin: persecution of conscience produced a culture of immorality that needed
restraint. A forceful statement of the moral rather than strictly doctrinal
basis for unity was Samuel Bolde's *A Plea for Moderation Towards Dissenters* (1682), which combined puritan-style arguments for ceremonial

---

[49] *Ibid.*, p. 23.    [50] *Ibid.*, p. 42.    [51] *Ibid.*, p. 191.
[52] *Ibid.*, p. 184.    [53] *Ibid.*, p. 216.    [54] *Ibid.*, pp. 251–2.

nonconformity with the so-called 'latitudinarian' arguments of Jeremy Taylor, John Wilkins and Edward Stillingfleet.[55] Bolde was a conforming minister in the Church of England who had become infamous among Anglicans for his *Sermon Against Persecution* (1682), and the *Plea* was very much an attempt to reclaim the mantle of moderation after the alleged excesses of that earlier text. It thus began with a furious assault on persecutors for undermining the morality of the nation: 'It is undeniably evident that the primitive strict discipline of the Church with relation to manners did decay answerably to the proportion of warmth and zeal men were allowed to lay out about little differences.' Persecutors attacked godly men for their differences in religious practices, while neglecting moral actions, 'those things in which religion doth indeed consist', as if attention to morality were but 'preciseness'. He utterly rejected the conformist position, which he caricatured as arguing that 'men might be as vicious as they pleased, swear and be drunk and commit all manner of lewdness, and yet be admirable zealous Christians, because they were for the Church'.[56] Later, he told a (surely apocryphal) story of an overzealous churchwarden who wanted to persecute everyone in his parish who refused to receive the sacrament, but who later agreed to let off those who 'will swear and be drunk' because they did not 'scruple to receive the sacrament on their knees'.[57] More significantly, Bolde (like Taylor) managed to translate his 'plea for moderation' into a vicious assault on Catholicism, since 'the very fundamentals of Christianity are now assaulted by the papists'.[58] Bolde described papists as perennial drunkards and immoral louts, but he also painted them as the masterminds of a sophisticated plot to undermine morality in England by convincing Anglicans to persecute nonconformists.[59]

Outside the Church of England, other theorists also argued that governors who misunderstood their powers not only wrongly persecuted conscientious subjects but also inevitably tolerated vice. Again, this was not a coincidental connection but resulted firstly from the fact that persecution pushed people to ignore their own consciences, and secondly from the fact that persecution was itself a sin which, in Gilbert Burnet's words, 'does extremely vitiate the morals of the party that manages it'.[60] As early

[55] I use the word 'latitudinarian' with inverted commas to refer to a set of related seventeenth-century arguments about the legitimate latitude of beliefs within the English Church, but without meaning to imply either that there was a coherent 'latitudinarian' party or that 'latitudinarians' were particularly broadminded. See John Spurr, '"Latitudinarianism" and the Restoration Church', *HJ* 31, no.1 (March 1988), pp. 61–82; Ashcraft, 'Latitudinarianism and Toleration'.

[56] Samuel Bolde, *A Plea for Moderation Towards Dissenters* (London, 1682), pp. 1–2.

[57] *Ibid.*, p. 41.     [58] *Ibid.*, p. 8.     [59] *Ibid.*, pp. 6–8, 32, 36.

[60] Burnet, *A Relation of the Death of the Primitive Persecutors*, p. 44.

as 1647 these sorts of arguments can be found in *A Still Soft Voice From the Scriptures* by the Leveller William Walwyn, who stressed that 'it is a hard thing unto men, bred so vainly as most men are, to keep the golden mean in natural or moral reformations'. For Walwyn, this meant that men who avoided the first extreme of 'worldly politicians' usually fell into the opposite extreme of haughty rejection of the world. The solution to both extremes was a middle way defined by an activist morality, labouring 'to reclaim those many thousands of miserable people that are drenched all their life long in gross ignorance and notorious, loathsome wickedness'.[61] Among the earliest Restoration texts to develop these arguments was *The Case of Free Liberty of Conscience in the Exercise of Faith and Religion* (1661) by the Quaker firebrand Edward Burroughs. This text repeatedly invoked a sphere of conscience over which the magistrate had no authority: 'Lordship in and over conscience, and the exercise thereof in all matters of faith, worship and duty to God-wards, is God's alone ... and he hath reserved this power and authority in himself and not committed the lordship over conscience, nor the exercise thereof in the cases of faith and worship, to any upon earth.'[62] In making this argument, however, Burroughs contrasted the unjust persecution of 'just and upright men', who might conscientiously err in matters of belief, with the equally unjust toleration of 'drunkards and profane persons ... in their stage-playing and gaming and the like'.[63] Indeed, the two were intimately connected, because forcing men to conform to the Church of England and deny their own professed principles naturally made them false-hearted hypocrites, encouraging them afterwards to all manner of vice.[64] Toleration became moderate because it limited one sphere of activity even as it liberated another.

A far more elaborate version of this sort of argument for moderate toleration came from John Locke, who argued in his first *Letter Concerning Toleration* that the state can ban practices for civil reasons but has no competence in religion; a banned practice must be banned for everyone

---

[61] William Walwyn, *A Still and Soft Voice from the Scriptures* (London, 1647), pp. 4, 10, and *passim*. In Walwyn's case, the argument that conscience is involuntary and hence cannot be punished (developed in his *The Compassionate Samaritane* (London, 1644), p. 7, among other places) carried the clear corollary that 'punishment is the recompense of voluntary actions', so voluntary actions could be punished regardless of their content. Hence Walwyn, who unlike most tolerationists even wanted to tolerate blasphemy, sought the active suppression of those whose 'uncontrolled liberty has generally been taken publicly to reproach and make odious' himself and his Leveller allies: William Walwyn, *Gold Tried in the Fire*, reproduced in Sharp (ed.), *The English Levellers*, p. 89.

[62] Edward Burroughs, *The Case of Free Liberty of Conscience in the Exercise of Faith and Religion, Presented unto the King and Both Houses of Parliament* (London, 1661), p. 5.

[63] *Ibid.*, p. 13.    [64] *Ibid.*, p. 10.

regardless of beliefs, while conversely a licit practice must be licit for everyone regardless of beliefs.[65] This argument, while ostensibly devoted to the liberation of religion from the shackles of civil coercion, in fact spent much of its energy displacing coercion from doctrine to morality.[66] For instance, Locke based his arguments for the hypocrisy of persecutors on the fact that, while they pretended to be concerned for people's souls, they tolerated immorality. He wrote that he would not believe that persecutors had the people's interests truly at heart until he saw 'those fiery zealots correcting in the same manner their friends and familiar acquaintances for the manifest sins they commit against the precepts of the gospel; when I shall see them prosecute with fire and sword the members of their own communion that are tainted with enormous vices'. If the government imprisoned and tormented men to make them Christians and procure their salvation, 'why then do they suffer whoredom, fraud, malice and such like enormities', why do they 'pass by those moral vices and wickednesses without any chastisement'? In general, 'uncleanness', 'lasciviousness' and other moral failings were the real threats to men's salvation, and Locke attacked anyone who persecuted nonconformity but was 'indulgent to such iniquities and immoralities as are unbecoming the name of a Christian'.[67] The 'business of true religion' is not dominion or compulsion but rather 'the regulating of men's lives according to the rules of virtue and piety'.[68]

Of course, in these passages Locke was exposing the excessive permissiveness of his opponents rather than making substantive policy suggestions for the restraint of vice, but elsewhere he did more or less precisely that. The stated reason why he sought to 'distinguish exactly the business of civil government from that of religion, and to settle the just bounds that lie between the one and the other' was to ensure that men 'under pretense of religion, may not seek impunity for their libertinism and licentiousness'.[69] Unlike many tolerationist writers, Locke denied that the government had any obligation to punish sin *per se*; he made the test of proper magisterial involvement whether that sin was 'prejudicial to other men's rights' or 'break[s] the public peace of societies'.[70] But on the other hand, Locke also argued that 'a good life, in which consists not the

---

[65] John Locke, *A Letter Concerning Toleration, Licensed, Octob. 3. 1689. The Second Edition Corrected* (London, 1690), pp. 45–6. The famous example here is that the state can ban human sacrifice because murder is everywhere forbidden, but if a Church wishes to sacrifice a calf, that cannot be banned unless for some reason (e.g. a shortage of calves) all calf killing is forbidden.

[66] Here I depart substantially from the argument in Marshall, *John Locke, Toleration and Early Enlightenment Culture*, pp. 540–1 and ch. 17 *passim*.

[67] *Ibid.*, pp. 2–5.    [68] *Ibid.*, p. 2.    [69] *Ibid.*, pp. 7–8.    [70] *Ibid.*, p. 50.

least part of religion and true piety, concerns also the civil government, and in it lies the safety both of men's souls and of the commonwealth'. Thus, unlike religious actions which belong solely to the spiritual sphere, 'moral actions belong therefore to the jurisdiction both of the outward and inward court . . . I mean both the magistrate and conscience'.[71] If we move to the *Second Letter Concerning Toleration* (1690), Locke was somewhat more explicit that proper religious toleration was predicated upon intolerance of debauchery: 'I will boldly say that if the magistrates will severely and impartially set themselves against vice in whomsoever it is found, and leave men to their own consciences in their articles of faith and ways of worship, true religion will be spread wider and be more fruitful in the lives of its professors than ever hitherto it has been by the imposition of creeds and ceremonies.' Men should always seek to live morally, hence magistrates 'should, by their laws and penalties, force them to a good life'.[72]

The supreme example of a moral crusade through the rhetoric of toleration can be found in the writings of the Quaker leader and prophet of pacifism William Penn. Throughout his career, Penn was explicitly concerned to redefine toleration as moderate. As early as a 1671 draft of a petition to parliament that Penn wrote from prison, the theme of toleration as moderation appeared, but it is indicative of how unfamiliar that argument at first seemed that he wrote, and then crossed out, the claim that if the government ended its persecution 'such moderation will be well pleasing both to God and good men'.[73] By 1675, it had already become much easier to argue that toleration was 'a medium, something that may compass the happy end of good correspondence and tranquility'.[74] As such, Penn was always deeply concerned about what could *not* be tolerated by moderate men. It would not do, he wrote in 1681, for 'all the world's libertines to plead the light within for their excesses'.[75] In his 1686 *A Perswasive to Moderation* he wrote that 'conscience . . . [must] keep within the bounds of morality, and . . . be neither frantic nor mischievous, but a good subject, a good child, a good servant'.[76]

Penn's most extensive argument tying religious toleration to intolerance of vice was his *An Address to Protestants upon the Present Conjuncture* (1679). This was an overtly heterodox tract that asserted the possibility for human perfection and denied the basic Protestant ideals of imputed

[71] *Ibid.*, p. 57.
[72] John Locke, *A Second Letter Concerning Toleration. Licensed, June 24. 1690* (London, 1690), p. 5.
[73] *The Papers of William Penn*, ed. Mary Dunn and Richard Dunn (Philadelphia, 5 vols., 1981–87), I, p. 207.
[74] Penn, *Political Writings*, p. 66.    [75] *Ibid.*, p. 284.    [76] *Ibid.*, p. 292.

righteousness and salvation by faith alone.[77] No wonder, then, that Penn incessantly referred to himself throughout the tract as 'a Protestant' and repeatedly claimed the mantle of moderation. Even when he made the radical argument that 'freedom from actual sinning . . . was the great reason of Christ's coming', Penn presented this as a middle way between the standard Protestant argument that only the guilt of sin was removed by Christ rather than sin itself, and the argument that Christ gives 'liberty to do that now, which ought not to have been done before (as the Ranters interpret it)'.[78] On the subject of toleration, which was the principal focus of *An Address to Protestants*, Penn repeatedly equated toleration and moderation. He referred to the pagan philosopher Themistius as more Christian than the Christians for having 'commended and advised the emperor Jovianus to exercise moderation and to give that liberty of conscience which professed Christians refused to do to each other'.[79] In describing the Synod of Dort, he wrote that whenever any Calvinists 'appeared moderate in their behaviour, gentle in their words and for accommodation in some particulars with the Remonstrants or Freewillers', their intolerant coreligionists 'reproached their tenderness and began to fix treachery upon their sober endeavors of accommodation'.[80]

So what made toleration moderate in Penn's argument? At heart, he argued that moderation required a proper understanding that human sins are 'of two great sorts, the one relating more particularly to the State, and the other to the Church'.[81] Part Two of *An Address to Protestants* was a discussion of the second sort, the sins of the Church, 'those capital sins and errors that relate to the ecclesiastical state'.[82] Here Penn argued, citing Jeremy Taylor among others, that outward morality rather than doctrinal belief was the true test of intolerability. He argued that anything more than the plain sense of scripture is unnecessary for salvation, that the plain sense 'can with ease be discerned by every honest and conscientious person', and that more complex theology can never be compulsory for Christians.[83] As such, anyone who accepts salvation through Christ should be tolerated within the Christian communion, and the test for such acceptance is moral living rather than doctrine:

---

[77] William Penn, *An Address to Protestants upon the Present Conjuncture* (London, 1679), esp. pp. 109–33. For this tract, I cite the original rather than Andrew Murphy's edition in *Political Writings*, since Murphy omitted the entire first half of the tract, creating the impression of a far more liberal William Penn than the one who actually wrote in 1679.

[78] Penn, *An Address to Protestants*, pp. 126–9.    [79] *Ibid.*, p. 66.

[80] *Ibid.*, pp. 64–5.    [81] *Ibid.*, p. 7.    [82] *Ibid.*, p. 61.

[83] *Ibid.*, pp. 76–9. Penn's heterodox belief in perfectionism and freedom from sin gave these arguments about morality a somewhat different meaning than similar arguments coming from more orthodox Church of England writers.

'So shall men know them that sincerely believe and confess Christ, by their sanctified manners and blameless conversation.'[84]

On the other side, however, Part One was concerned with civil sins, 'those impieties that relate more to the state to correct'.[85] This amounted to a frontal assault upon the culture of permissiveness and libertinism created by Charles II and his court, the 'degeneracy of the age we are fallen into', in which all manner of vice was tolerated and even promoted while 'sober' Christians were persecuted for their beliefs.[86] Indeed, Penn drew explicit connections between persecution and the promotion of vice, arguing that there is 'not so ready a way to atheism as this extinguishing the sense of conscience for worldly ends . . . This sacred tie of conscience thus broken, say farewell to all heavenly obligation in the soul'.[87] Hence toleration was posited against libertines as well as persecutors, moderating the excessive liberties of the debauched court.

When we look more deeply at Penn's discussion of state sins, moreover, we see how thoroughly his vision of toleration was dependent upon a co-equal prosecution of vice. Penn first defined state sins as follows: 'Those impieties that relate more particularly to the state to correct are drunkenness, whoredoms and fornications; excess in apparel and furniture and living; profuse gaming; and finally oaths, profaneness and blasphemy.'[88] Let us consider these sins in some detail. To begin with 'drunkenness, or excess in drinking', Penn regarded this sin as subject to state jurisdiction because it robs us of our reason, leading us to commit all manner of murders and robberies in 'drunken fits', as well as leaving us 'unfit for trust or business'.[89] Second, there is 'whoredom and fornication', which Penn regarded as a new sin in England imported, naturally enough, from France. Here the culture of libertinism was particularly to blame, a culture where 'lust [is] called love, and wantonness good humour. To introduce which, nothing hath been so pernicious as the use of plays and romances amongst us.' This was a particularly civil constellation of sins because 'it pollutes houses, and makes the issue of the nation spurious'. Significantly, Penn attacked the 'ungodly latitude' that had led to the growth of such sexual sins in England, and he called on the government to institute civil penalties: 'Let then both cities, courts, households and streets be swept of such iniquity; let the law have its course, let not God be provoked to destroy us.' The reference to 'courts' here was clearly a condemnation of the court of Charles II and its epic unwillingness to enforce laws regulating sexual practice.[90]

---

[84] *Ibid.*, p. 99.     [85] *Ibid.*, p. 7.     [86] *Ibid.*, p. 30.
[87] *Ibid.*, p. 201.     [88] *Ibid.*, p. 7.     [89] *Ibid.*, pp. 7–9.     [90] *Ibid.*, pp. 9–13.

Penn's third sin under state jurisdiction was 'great excess . . . in apparel, in furniture, [and] in feasting', and he defined excess as 'the misusing of any thing, by not observing its moderation'; even something which was 'lawful in itself' might be 'abused in the use of it'. Among his particular complaints were the use of clothing for ornament, pride and lust rather than mere necessity; the 'inexcusable superfluity' of rich china, costly pictures and painted windows; the 'immoderate eating and drinking, with that strain of mirth and jollity, that is the mode and practice of the times'; the new culture of epicurean cooking by which 'the book of cookery is grown as big as the Bible'; and the generally excessive sin of gambling. These sins of excess were to be punished by the state. On the issue of excessive apparel, for which there were already statutes on the books, Penn called for laws to be 'refreshed and enforced' and demanded 'just severity' for violators. For gambling, he argued that it 'deserves to be suppressed' and he called for new laws to 'prevent that extravagancy in the future'. On food, Penn begged 'the supreme authority of this land to put a speedy check to these exorbitances, to discountenance these excesses by the revival of those old laws, and in making of such new ones, as may be convenient to prevent such pride and prodigality'. He argued that 'the very preventing of that excess which is amongst us will be pleasing to almighty God, and one way or other beneficial to the government'.[91]

As for Penn's attack on oaths, profaneness and blasphemy, here he offered no systematic explanation of what made these state sins rather than Church sins, except the general argument that blasphemy had extended even to 'men of quality' by whose example the whole realm would be corrupted. But regardless of their dubious status under the magistrate's jurisdiction, on these sins Penn was most insistent in calling for magistrates to 'be a terror to evil-doers' as the Bible commanded. Blasphemy had become so rampant in England that Penn felt 'obliged in conscience' to complain to those who 'have power in their hands to punish and suppress them'. In the 'degeneracy' of the current age 'profaneness does not only go unpunished, but boldly lays claim to wit'.[92]

In general, then, Penn argued that on moral issues the magistrate was required to declare standards of conduct, erect laws and punish violators, and no one so punished could count themselves persecuted. Indeed, his whole argument for toleration as genuine moderation was predicated on the idea that toleration would restrain the current government's permissive libertinism. He thus reprimanded the government of Charles II:

---

[91] *Ibid.*, pp. 13–23.    [92] *Ibid.*, pp. 25–32.

Be pleased to consider your commission and examine the extent of your authority. Ye will find that God and the government hath empowered you to punish these impieties, and it is so far from being a crime, that it is your duty. This is not troubling men for faith, nor perplexing people for tenderness of conscience; for there can be no pretence of conscience to be drunk, to whore, to be voluptuous, to game, to swear, curse, blaspheme and profane. No such matter; these are sins against nature and against government, as well as against the written laws of God. They lay the ax to the root of humane society and are the common enemies of mankind. 'Twas to prevent these enormities that government was instituted, and shall government indulge that which it is instituted to destroy? This were to render magistracy useless, and the bearing of the sword in vain. There would be then no such thing in government as a terror to evil-doers, *but everyone would do that which he thought right in his own eyes. God almighty defend us from this anarchy!*[93]

Such were the words of seventeenth-century England's greatest defender of liberty of conscience. This was not hypocrisy or incoherence, but rather a coherent statement of a distinctively early modern vision: moderate toleration.

## Moderate toleration and natural religion

As this last quotation hints with its mention of 'sins against nature', another functionally overlapping but formally distinct constellation of arguments for moderate toleration involved maintaining the boundaries of so-called 'natural religion'. That is, many Restoration intellectuals, working in the 'latitudinarian' tradition of William Chillingworth and Jeremy Taylor, developed categories of 'natural religion' that were independent of revealed religion and were supposedly imprinted upon the consciences of all human beings. Some of these arguments, developed by Deists like John Toland and (maybe) John Locke, overlapped significantly with so-called 'reasonable religion' and were intended to challenge the monopoly of orthodox Trinitarianism. But others, like the arguments of John Wilkins and Henry More, were intended to reduce Christianity to principles of 'moral certainty' that could form the basis of a broad Christian peace.[94] For these authors and many less famous ones, beliefs and practices which violated natural religion – often identified with atheism, blasphemy and idolatry – were external to religious toleration because they were by definition non-religious. These authors thus redefined

---

[93] *Ibid.*, p. 33. My emphasis.
[94] See discussion in Worden, 'The Question of Secularisation'; Rivers, *Reason, Grace, and Sentiment*; Gordon Cragg, *From Puritanism to the Age of Reason* (Cambridge, 1966). For some of the formal, philosophical aspects of this tradition, see John Wilkins, *Of the Principles and Duties of Natural Religion* (London, 1675); Ralph Cudworth, *The True Intellectual System of the Universe* (London, 1678).

toleration as moderate in the sense that it restrained subjects within the bounds of nature. Indeed, John Wilkins's vision of natural religion – 'I call that natural religion, which men might know and should be obliged unto by the mere principles of reason, improved by consideration and experience, without the help of revelation' – had coercion built into its definition.[95] It does not take much imagination to see how, through broad application of the idea of unnaturalness, 'latitudinarian' demands for toleration could become, in Richard Ashcraft's words, 'the acceptable face of the persecution of religious dissent'.[96]

One of the major statements of this position in the early 1680s was the anonymous *Liberty of Conscience in Its Order to Universal Peace* (1681), a long treatise describing the 'rock of certainty' of natural religion upon which 'universal' religious peace could be built. Playing with themes not only from Taylor and Wilkins but also from Aquinas's *Summa Contra Gentiles*, the author made a fundamental distinction between natural religion and revealed religion; the latter was not less true than the former, but because humans were fallible and their judgements varied, revealed religion could not be the basis of human peace. Instead, differences in revealed religion should be tolerated so long as they were consistent with natural religion. When we begin to examine the fundamental principles of natural religion, however, we see how the author redefined 'universal' religious peace. First, rather conventionally, he concluded that belief in God, and belief in a single God, were fundamental to natural religion; hence anyone who disbelieved in God 'may without any brand of cruelty be dealt with as a traitor to the universe', and belief in more than one God is 'justly to be punished by the judge, being the first and prime idolatry'.[97] Next, somewhat more contentiously, 'worship and service' of God, publicly and by communities rather than merely by individuals, was constitutive of natural religion, and hence the requirement of public, communal worship was also 'most deservedly under the public eye of authority'.[98] Next, and rather remarkably, natural religion required that public worship contain only the simplest ceremonies, for too much ceremony inevitably tends to idolatry; moreover, there should be a learned ministry in natural religion rather than uneducated preachers, and in natural religion preaching always takes precedence over prayer, while prayer takes precedence over ceremony.[99] The tract specifically referred to this version of natural religion as a virtuous 'middle place' in which God has

---

[95] Quoted in Rivers, *Reason, Grace, and Sentiment*, I, p. 66.
[96] Ashcraft, 'Latitudinarianism and Toleration', p. 155.
[97] *Liberty of Conscience in Its Order to Universal Peace* (London, 1681), pp. 12–13.
[98] *Ibid.*, pp. 13–14.      [99] *Ibid.*, pp. 15–25.

set mankind between superstition and irreligion.[100] This begins to look like a rather traditional framework with its exclusions dressed up in fancy new garb.

At the heart of this attack on unnecessary ceremonies was traditional anti-popery: 'Romish religion not only is not, but cannot be true'; it is a 'synagogue of Satan . . . the very spirit of Antichrist'.[101] Natural religion fits perfectly with Christianity insofar as Christianity is 'not ceremonial', for 'the darker any religion is, the more are the ceremonies like the shadows of the evening stretched out'. The great example of this unnatural corruption of Christianity was that 'the Lord's Supper was at length corrupted into the idolatrous mass'. The author thus attacked the 'empty formalist' who adorns religion and the 'vulgar, unlearned, irrational minds who must be catched with shows and pompous appearances'. However, on the other side, this author's *via media* also attacked radical anti-formalism. While the author detested *empty* ceremonies, or ceremonies for their own sake, he admitted that 'substantial' elements of natural religion did indeed require some ceremonies, easy and intelligible, symbols of God's grace and presence. More remarkably, he also admitted that natural religion could tolerate some ceremonies 'as the results of human prudence or national decency', leaving the door open for magisterial authority in *adiaphora*.[102]

The author also made explicit which brands of 'opinions' were intolerable because they were unnatural. These included Socinianism and Arianism; 'image worship', prayers to saints and 'adoration of the bread in the sacrament'; and most broadly 'all fanatic principles turning religion into Ranterism'. These various transgressions were 'excluded and shut out of that universal peace and quietness' that the author proposed: 'So far as natural religion extends, so far the magistrate's power extends. Here he is the minister of God and bears not the sword in vain . . . These are the ancient landmarks that ought not to be removed.'[103] The author also excluded women preachers and other forms of disorder as incompatible with natural religion, hence effectively excluding Quakers from his 'universal peace'.[104] Here, again, toleration becomes moderate explicitly because of what it refuses to tolerate; the author called for 'severe natural religion, enforced and strictly pursued'.[105]

Natural religion also had nasty surprises awaiting non-Christians. The author asserted that natural religion resided in the hearts of all human beings, whether Christian or not, hence non-Christian (monotheistic)

---

[100] *Ibid.*, p. 143.     [101] *Ibid.*, pp. 80, 108–9.
[102] *Ibid.*, pp. 30–1. On ceremonies for the sake of order and decency, see also p. 99.
[103] *Ibid.*, pp. 42–3, and 48.     [104] *Ibid.*, pp. 119–20.     [105] *Ibid.*, p. 76.

religions could in some circumstances be tolerated. However, the author also asserted that anyone who truly lived by natural religion would inevitably convert to Christianity when it was offered to them, allowing an easy syllogism to prove that all those who refused the gift of Christianity were not really tolerable after all. As such, ex-Christians or outward Christians who apostatised from Christianity should be brutally punished by the magistrate.[106]

Lastly, despite his many claims about the moral equivalency of all opinions within the bounds of natural religion, the author supported the maintenance of an Established Church of England. He argued that:

> When sovereigns and nations have considered the wisdom, rationality and heavenliness of proposals in religion, and settled upon what they find of the highest character as the religion of their nation by law to be established, to which they allow the encouragement of their public honours and maintenance, and taken care for the propagation of it by instructions, arguments, reasons and good examples, they have done all that God expects from them to do, and so have delivered their own souls.[107]

Magistrates may not forbid beliefs that are consistent with natural religion, but it was entirely natural and within 'the right of national powers to dispose of their own according to their own reason and judgment'.[108] Moreover, even dissenters who fulfilled their duties to natural religion in separate congregations were, by the requirements of order and peace, 'still bound to promote and encourage national religion, so far as it extends, to avoid as much as possible all divisions and professed separation from it, by putting the fairest construction and the kindest hopes upon those things that seem doubtful, and as little infringing upon the authority of laws as may be consistent with sentiments of conscience'.[109] In sum, then, *Liberty of Conscience in Its Order to Universal Peace* turned natural religion into an argument for active rather than passive moderation.

Other authors who ostensibly favoured liberty of conscience based upon natural religion nonetheless found this vision too permissive. The author of *Liberty of Conscience Explicated and Vindicated, and the Just Limits Betwixt It and Authority, Sacred and Civil, Cleared* (1689) began by suggesting that in the recent 'sharp contests between authority sacred and civil, and liberty of conscience in matter of religion', the 'sober and moderate have been pleased with neither extreme, yet few of them have used half so much diligence to point out the right path as these in either extreme have used to stray from it'.[110] The author particularly objected to those who 'make the rule and measure of civil authority to be only the

---

[106] *Ibid.*, pp. 53–9.  [107] *Ibid.*, p. 73.  [108] *Ibid.*, p. 116.  [109] *Ibid.*, p. 137.
[110] *Liberty of Conscience Explicated and Vindicated* (London, 1689), p. 1.

law of nature, but not to extend to instituted and revealed religion'. The problem with this argument was that natural religion was the command of God imprinted upon men's hearts, and part of that command was that 'wherever the command of God doth appear, his vicegerents are obliged no less to promote it than the light of nature, in so far as they and their subjects acknowledged divine principles known by revelation'. In other words, part of natural religion was to enforce the revealed law of God when it manifestly appeared, so in Christian commonwealths the revealed law of God essentially attained the status of natural religion. The author thus argued that, while non-Christians should enjoy liberty of conscience for all things consonant with the law of nature, for Christians there should be liberty of conscience only for those who followed the fundamental 'principles of Christianity'.[111]

In practice, the implications of this argument were little different than the implications of *Liberty of Conscience in Its Order to Universal Peace*. It accepted the usefulness of an Established Church but allowed Christians to meet freely in separate congregations, shrinking the bounds of legitimate separatism only slightly: they not only had to accept natural religion but also those things which are necessary to salvation according to Christian scripture. In other words, only essential points of doctrine were to be compelled – although the author gave a hint of how far this doctrine could be pushed by listing not only Trinitarianism but 'the free election of the father' (i.e. a Calvinist stance on predestination) as necessary doctrine.[112] More remarkably, the author explained that the least common denominator of Christianity, the version that most perfectly captured natural religion and combined it with revelation, was none other than 'the Reformed Churches . . . for there is no doctrine they hold concerning faith and holiness which is not held by all national Christian Churches, with whom they differ only in refusing to believe the peculiar doctrines which any of them do profess'.[113] By this feat of logic, then, an argument for universal liberty of conscience became an argument for the broad communion of Reformed Churches; reading between the lines, we can see a bitter argument against the new Arminianism of the Restoration Church.

Besides eliding the distinction between natural religion and Reformed Christianity, the author also used the idea of natural religion to explain which ideas and practices could not be tolerated. Once again, idolatry and

---

[111] *Ibid.*, pp. 8–11.
[112] *Ibid.*, p. 2. For anti-Trinitarianism, see p. 16. Lutheran-style belief in the Real Presence, however, was listed as inessential and hence tolerable, as long as it was not accompanied by outward idolatry: pp. 4–5.
[113] *Ibid.*, p. 5.

polytheism were banned because worshippers of 'heathen gods ... could no more plead liberty of conscience than murderers, robbers, adulterers or sodomites'.[114] Likewise, magistrates should compel 'all their subjects to perform public worship to God' because the need for such worship was part of natural religion, regardless of the sort of worship performed. Most interestingly, this author also demanded a series of remarkable restrictions on Roman Catholics. The author suggested that 'if civil authority should establish a Protestant Church, they ought not to compel papists to conform thereto'. However, because natural religion had to be enforced:

They ought to compel them to perform a public worship of God, forbearing these things that are against the light of nature, as the worshipping of anything which is not God, with religious worship directly or indirectly, and particularly the invocation of angels, or the souls of men, of the Host at the elevation thereof in the time of consecration, or in processions (without inquiring on what account they kneel at receiving) and forbearing the worshipping of images, crosses, relics, without regard to their coined distinction ... And therefore they ought not to hinder priests to perform their worship in the way it is allowed, yet they ought to exclude Jesuits and such firebrands as trafficking seminary priests from coming into the country, but only such parochial priests as shall be found sober and willing to abstain from the forenamed idolatrous practices. They may be also compelled to forbear any doctrine or practice against the light of nature, as equivocation, mental reservation, not observing of engagements with these they call heretics, or subjecting the sovereign civil powers to the pope or Church of Rome.[115]

Besides these minor exceptions, Catholicism could be tolerated in England.

Another argument in the 'natural religion' tradition was *Liberty of Conscience Asserted and Vindicated* (1689), written by the 'learned country gentleman' and erstwhile defender of James II's indulgence for Catholics, George Care. This tract cited such luminaries of Protestant ecumenism as Jeremy Taylor, Henry More and the newly installed Bishop of Salisbury Gilbert Burnet, adopting their arguments that much of scripture was too opaque to be used as a judge of controversies and that only fundamentals of Christianity were legitimate grounds for exclusion. It also made some rather more daring statements about ecclesiastical property, calling for disestablishment and for the temporal goods of the Church to be redistributed.[116] More importantly for our purposes, it explicitly presented itself as moderate on several counts, both in its proposed treatment of Catholics and in its middle way between over-scrupulousness and idolatry.[117] It is all the more interesting, then, how vigorously Care

[114] *Ibid.*, pp. 8–11.   [115] *Ibid.*, p. 15.   [116] *Ibid.*, pp. 19, 13–14.   [117] *Ibid.*, pp. 22–4.

denounced excessive tolerance of *unnaturalness*. The very first words of the preface advised the courteous reader,

My purpose in the following treatise is not to satisfy all the questions which may be put, as, what if anyone should preach in the pulpit (*in terminis*) that Jesus is not the Christ, or against the resurrection of the dead, or any other article of our faith which all who call themselves Christians do acknowledge, or affront the minister at the communion, and pull the cloth and utensils off the table. Such things by the place and manner of doing them may be reduced to moral impiety, and punished as crimes against natural light.[118]

This notion that crimes against natural light were intolerable was extended not only to the examples mentioned here – which were obvious jabs at Quakers and Socinians – but also to moral offences, on the grounds that no one's conscience could violate the laws of nature. These alleged moral offences aligned very closely with those commonplace offences of popular culture, formerly coded spiritual, that had so goaded puritans. So, he continued,

I think there are in our Church others who deserve toleration less than any dissenters whom I know, as notorious profaners of the Lord's day, haunters of alehouses at unseasonable times of the night or when according to their consciences they should be at Church; and other debauched persons whom we hear daily in the streets cursing and swearing, bidding God to damn themselves and others. Now that they are grossly mistaken, who tolerate such persons as these that offend against their own consciences and yet fiercely punish dissenters in matters of mere religion, will be sufficiently proved in the following discourse.[119]

In such conditions, not only would God punish the sinner but so should the king, and 'the greater the error is as to the clearness of the light against which it is committed, or as to the mischief and malignity of it, the more punishable it is; for else we should introduce a liberty for professed atheism, blasphemy, murder, adultery, theft, etc'. Of particular interest here is the inclusion of 'adultery' as a crime against natural religion, which according to the author was punishable by death. As the author summarised his position, the magistrate may not punish mere doctrinal heresies, but he must punish 'moral errors and impieties by due coercion' – and he must even punish heresies when those heresies do not occur alone but contain a 'mixture of moral impiety, proved by sufficient witnesses' – precisely because 'if the conscience be erroneous by any great fault against the common light of nature, we cannot assert any freedom to it'.[120]

---

[118] *Ibid.*, first page of preface (unpaginated).
[119] *Ibid.*, second page of preface (unpaginated).    [120] *Ibid.*, pp. 1–3.

These and other visions of natural religion thus managed to combine pleas for toleration with rigorous new arguments for external restraint. Generally speaking, historical analyses of 'latitudinarianism' have stressed its emphasis on epistemological limitation: because human beings can know so little with moral certainty, we must agree to disagree on all but the most fundamental issues. Hence proponents of 'natural religion' might adopt either broad tolerationist positions or, as Richard Ashcraft and Richard Kroll have noted, an almost Hobbesian abandonment of individual conscience in favour of the commands of civil authority.[121] Here, however, by looking at the categories deemed unnatural and hence external to religious toleration, we can see the obverse of epistemological limitation: on those issues on which human beings *can* be certain, no latitude can be accepted. Within this framework, then, some beliefs and practices previously persecuted might now be (at least theoretically) tolerated, but others were pronounced 'unnatural' and hence subject to the strictest restraint. As such, these 'unnatural' beliefs and practices could not be prudentially tolerated when circumstances demanded it; they could not be liberally tolerated when they supported civil government or trade; they could not be conscientiously tolerated as sincere but wrong. With moderation newly framed around naturalness, those who fell on the wrong side of this moving line found themselves outside the mercy of God or man.

### Moderate toleration and the state

A third, overlapping but distinct argument for toleration as moderation was one which restrained or excluded ideas and activities that tended to undermine the state, positioning toleration as moderate because it provided a bulwark for civil authority. If there was a distinct sphere of religion outside the jurisdiction of the magistrate, as so many tolerationists argued, then obviously that sphere ended wherever activities inside spilled over into the sphere defined by civil authority. So, most bluntly, while tolerationists wanted to legalise independent religious conventicles, none would have suggested that it was legal to denounce the king at those conventicles. This principle was so obvious that some Quakers used it to claim that conventicles were *already* legal in the 1660s: the Conventicle Act explicitly stated that conventicles were banned because they were

---

[121] Richard Kroll, 'Introduction', in Richard Kroll, Richard Ashcraft and Perez Zagorin (eds.), *Philosophy, Science and Religion in England 1640–1700* (Cambridge, 1992); Ashcraft, 'Latitudinarianism and Toleration'. See also Murphy, *Conscience and Community*, pp. 106–10.

surreptitiously used to plot sedition, but Quakers did not plot sedition at their meetings, *ergo* their meetings were not banned by the Conventicle Act, QED.[122] But more broadly, tolerationists argued that they were moderate because it was they, and not their opponents, who could bridle the factious civil strife that had ravaged the English state for much of the seventeenth century.

In practice, of course, determining exactly what sorts of beliefs and practices tended to the dissolution of the state was not so simple, and depending upon how broadly one interpreted this category it could expand almost indefinitely, to the point that arguments against toleration sometimes looked little different from arguments for toleration. We have already seen, for instance, Richard Perrinchief's *anti-toleration* argument that 'it is worse than barbarous to attach or oppress any people merely upon account of their religion'; he argued instead that nonconformists should be punished not for their religion but because nonconformity would 'inevitably . . . terminate in the overthrow of all discipline or government'.[123] Roger L'Estrange concurred: 'The State that allows the people a freedom to choose their religion is reasonably to expect that they will take a freedom likewise to choose their government.'[124] Joseph Glanville argued that 'liberty of conscience must be given', but he meant merely pure and internal conscience rather than its practical application, because 'to strive for toleration is to contend against all government'.[125] There was, in other words little *theoretical* difference between these anti-toleration theorists and their opponents on this issue, merely a *practical* difference on what constituted danger to the State.

Among those who considered themselves proponents of liberty of conscience, however, the most common categories of intolerable dangers to the civil state were the same old bogeymen we have already seen: atheism, blasphemy, idolatry and of course Catholicism. Edward Whitaker's 1681 *Argument for Toleration and Indulgence*, for instance, made it plain that 'I never did intend that atheists, blasphemers of the true God, and enemies to natural religion (without which no government or commonwealth can stand) should be exempted from punishment; for not to punish these is to be false and treacherous to government itself.' Atheists and blasphemers should be 'punished capitally as enemies to all government', and

---

[122] See, e.g., R. F., *Christian Toleration* (1664), pp. 1–2, 9.
[123] Perrinchief, *Samaritanism*, p. 11.    [124] Cited in Knights, 'Meer Religion', p. 47.
[125] Cited in Scott Mandelbrote, 'Religious Beliefs and the Politics of Toleration in the Late Seventeenth Century', *Nederlands Archief voor Kerkgeschiedenis* 81, no. 2 (2001), pp. 93–114, at p. 105.

popery was likewise 'a malignant influence upon the state' which deserved punishment.[126]

An early and interesting version of these arguments can be found in *A Discourse Concerning Liberty of Conscience* (1661) by Peter Pett, a lawyer and original fellow of the Royal Society. This was a Machiavellian treatise suggesting that broad religious toleration was beneficial not because it was ethically necessary – the author claimed no interest in writing about 'moral things' – but because it tended to 'the people's good' and served the 'political interest'. As such, Pett made support of the civil state the prime condition for liberty of conscience, and he defended his arguments as a middle way by condemning 'querulous persons' who reject restraint of religion but do not say 'how far they would have it removed'.[127] Pett's version of what exactly made certain religious beliefs and practices dangerous to the state was informative. Anabaptists he was willing to tolerate, on the grounds that their past disruptions to civil order had been contingent on their circumstances rather than intrinsic to their beliefs: 'For though those of that persuasion were in Germany as so many fire-ships among the states of the Empire, it doth not follow that others here must necessarily prove incendiaries in the same manner.' Quakers were a more liminal case, and since Pett was uncertain what the civil consequences of their beliefs might be, 'the Quakers may for a while be tolerated, 'til we have seen what effects their light within them will produce' – although he did believe that because Quakers were so often 'idle, and go from town to town, neglecting their callings' the state should compel them to work. Fifth Monarchists were even more suspicious: while it was true that some in the early Church had held similar beliefs without sedition, and hence their opinions alone should not be prosecuted, in practice modern Fifth Monarchists 'disturb civil societies', threaten property rights, and want to erect a theocracy in violation of lawful civil authority, and hence they have little if any claim to toleration.[128] Finally, Catholics had virtually no claim to toleration at all: the papacy was 'a commonwealth of increase by arms' that would continuously threaten invasion if its followers were tolerated in England.[129] Catholics did not have to do anything to be intolerable in this model. Rome was a foreign enemy of the English state and loyalty to both was simply impossible.

The most famous exponent of the argument that political sedition and other forms of civil illegality invalidated toleration was, of course,

---

[126] Edward Whitaker, *An Argument for Toleration and Indulgence* (London, 1681), pp. 9 and 12.

[127] Pett, *A Discourse Concerning Liberty of Conscience*, pp. 1–4.     [128] *Ibid.* pp. 8–12.

[129] *Ibid.*, pp. 23–4. See also pp. 115–17, possibly not written by Pett.

John Locke. For Locke, unlike many theorists of toleration, churches were voluntary societies wholly distinct from civil society, hence they were welcome to create any doctrinal tests for membership they pleased and exclude whomever they wanted, so long as exclusion carried no penalties to 'body or estate'.[130] The state, however, had no authority to ban opinions, with one huge category of exceptions: 'No opinions contrary to human society, or to those moral rules which are necessary to the preservation of civil society, are to be tolerated by the magistrate.' For example, the state could not tolerate any religion which held that 'men are not obliged to keep their promise; that princes may be dethroned by those that differ from them in religion; or that dominion in all things belongs only to themselves'. These were clear seventeenth-century Protestant stereotypes of Catholicism. Likewise, since for Locke toleration was the basis of civil peace, the state cannot tolerate 'those that will not own and teach the duty of tolerating all men in matters of mere religion' – an intolerance of intolerance that was common in tolerationist arguments. And lastly, the state cannot tolerate atheists who 'deny the being of a God', since 'promises, covenants and oaths, which are the bonds of human society, can have no hold upon an atheist'.[131]

In Locke's tracts, the anti-Catholicism of these arguments is perhaps secondary, although historians continue to debate their significance.[132] But if we want to see anti-popery take centre stage we need only turn to Locke's occasional ally William Penn. There was no more slippery proponent of religious toleration than Penn, who was notoriously willing to adapt all manner of competing and sometimes contradictory arguments in hopes of securing liberty of conscience for his beloved Quakers. During the reign of James II he supported the Declaration of Indulgence for Catholics as well as Protestants.[133] Earlier in his career, however, he had

---

[130] Locke, *A Letter Concerning Toleration*, p. 18.     [131] *Ibid.*, pp. 64–7.

[132] Marshall, *John Locke, Toleration and Early Enlightenment Culture*, esp. pp. 686–94, denies the intrinsic anti-Catholicism of Locke's arguments and suggests that they need to be seen as far more nuanced and changing over time; Mark Goldie, 'John Locke's Circle and James II', *HJ* 55, no. 3 (1992), pp. 557–86, argues that Locke's principal allies were willing to compromise on toleration for Catholics. For anti-Catholicism as central to Locke's theories, see Richard Ashcraft, 'Religion and Lockean Natural Rights', in Irene Bloom, J. Paul Martin and Wayne Proudfoot (eds.), *Religious Diversity and Human Rights* (New York, 1996).

[133] Historians have now stressed that before the birth of a Stuart heir in 1688 many nonconformists were willing to compromise on this issue: Gary De Krey, 'Reformation and Arbitrary Government: London Dissenters and James II's Polity of Toleration, 1687–88', in James McElligott (ed.), *Fear, Exclusion and Revolution: Roger Morrice and Britain in the 1680s* (Aldershot, 2006); Mark Goldie, 'John Locke's Circle and James II'.

furiously opposed Catholic toleration when it was politically expedient to do so. One tract in particular, *One Project for the Good of England* (1679) – opportunistically dedicated to the first Exclusion parliament in the midst of the anti-Catholic furor surrounding the Popish Plot – was perhaps the clearest statement ever written that toleration in England should not merely exclude Catholics but actually depended upon the state's power to restrain them.[134]

*One Project* was based upon the premise that religion was theoretically the 'best bond of human society' but that in practice, religion in England was so divisive and misunderstood that it was 'yet too early in the day to fix such a religion upon which mankind will readily agree as a common basis for civil society'. Thus, if religious unity could not bind human beings together peacefully for the common good, instead 'we must recur to some lower but true principle for the present'. This 'lower but true principle' was 'civil interest', the common understanding of all Englishmen that they 'owe allegiance and subjection unto the civil government of England'. Anything that contributed to this unanimous principle should be tolerated, and Penn stressed that, while dissenters and Anglicans disagreed about religion, all Protestants shared a common civil interest and worked together for the common good: 'Let us go together as far as our way lies, and preserve our unity in those principles, which maintain our civil society. This is our common and our just interest, all Protestant dissenters agree in this, and it is both wise and righteous to admit no fraction upon this pact, no violence upon this concord.'[135] Here, then, common political allegiance was not merely incidental to toleration but its foundation.

This opened the door for some extraordinary anti-Catholic polemic, because for Penn the proof that all Protestants participated in a common 'civil interest' was precisely that they all opposed popery.

First, all English Protestants, whether conformists or nonconformists, agree in this, that they only owe allegiance and subjection unto the civil government of England, and offer any security in their power to give of their truth in this matter. And in the next place, they do not only consequently disclaim the pope's supremacy and all adhesion to foreign authority under any pretence, but therewith deny and oppose the Romish Religion, as it stands degenerated from scripture and the first and purest ages of the Church, which makes up a great Negative Union.

---

[134] William Penn, *One Project for the Good of England* (London, 1679), reprinted in Penn, *Political Writings*, pp. 120–36. Here I disagree with Murphy, *Conscience and Community*, ch. 5.

[135] Penn, *Political Writings*, pp. 120–7.

It was in the interest of both Anglicans and dissenters that the pope should have no power in England because papists would suppress them all, and this shared interest was the basis of civil peace.[136] A bit later, Penn came close to saying outright that the 'lower but true principle' that bound English people together in harmony was anti-popery, and hence if dissent had been tolerated over the previous eighteen years then the Popish Plot could never have happened:

Now because the civil interest of this nation is the preservation of the free and legal government of it from all subjection to foreign claim, and that the several sorts of Protestants are united, as in the common Protestancy, that is, a general renunciation of Rome, so in the maintenance of this civil government as a common security (for it strikes at both their rights, civil and sacred, their conscience, religion and law, to admit any foreign jurisdiction here) it must follow, that had these several as well English as Protestant parties been timely encouraged to the united civil interest, they had secured the government from this danger by rendering it too formidable for the attempt.[137]

Moreover, Catholics who themselves called for liberty of conscience were liars and hypocrites, because, while the differences among Protestants were 'purely religious' and hence irrelevant to their common civil interest, the main difference between Protestant and Catholics was 'merely civil, and should never be otherwise admitted or understood'. To be sure, there was also 'vast contrariety of doctrine and worship', but this was irrelevant compared to 'that fundamental inconsistency they carry with them to the security of the English government and constitution'.[138] As such, Penn proposed at the end of the tract a new and much harsher Test Act to root out English Catholics. The new Test required subjects to 'acknowledge and declare' that 'the Roman Catholic Church is both superstitious and idolatrous', to denounce transubstantiation and to deny that 'there is a purgatory after death, or that saints should be prayed to, or images in any sense be worshipped'.[139] These doctrinal elements could be included, even though Penn claimed that the Test was purely about preserving the 'civil interest', because, as he put it elsewhere in the tract, for Catholics 'religion . . . is nothing else but a softer word for civil empire'.[140] This Test was not merely to be administered to candidates for office but to the entire population once a year, and punishment for violation 'can scarcely be too severe'.[141] In the context of England's greatest paroxysm of anti-Popish paranoia, this was brilliant propaganda to establish

---

[136] *Ibid.*, pp. 122–3.    [137] *Ibid.*, p. 128.    [138] *Ibid.*, pp. 128–9.
[139] *Ibid.*, pp. 133–4. This was phrased as a 'declaration' because Quakers opposed obligatory oaths.
[140] *Ibid.*, p. 125.    [141] *Ibid.*, pp. 134–5.

Quakers and other dissenters as allies of Anglicans and the Stuart monarchy against a shadowy terrorist menace. As such, we need not presume that Penn actually believed his own words (although there is likewise no reason to presume that he believed his later arguments for toleration of Catholics in James II's reign). What we can say, however, is that in *One Project for the Good of England* dissenters were to be tolerated precisely because they refused to tolerate Catholics, and the shared boundaries that Anglicans and Dissenters placed upon the 'intolerable' was what allowed Penn to claim the mantle of moderation for his programme.

### Conclusion

Liberty of conscience was an aggressive language of boundary formation in seventeenth-century England. When John Locke and other writers claimed that 'absolute liberty' was their goal – and then defined absolute liberty as a moderate middle way between persecution of conscience on the one hand and toleration of vice, blasphemy, atheism or Catholicism on the other hand – they performed a crucial task of ideological violence firmly rooted in the rule of moderation. This chapter has suggested that this manoeuvre was not peripheral to the project of religious toleration; rather, exclusions rendered toleration moderate, forming a sort of negative space – 'a great Negative Union' in William Penn's ominous words – that gave toleration its shape.

Historians of toleration, even those most sensitive to the dangers of anachronism and teleology, have not much analysed this crucial constitutive process because they have themselves written within an ideology of moderation shaped by the winners of this story and indebted to their interpretive categories. Virtually no modern scholar can write about toleration debates in early modern England without describing toleration as moderate. So, for instance, Alexandra Walsham has written that 'notwithstanding their reputation for moderation' the Latitudinarians were unwilling to relax laws restraining dissent.[142] John Marshall has written that the 'Latitudinarian stress on the need for civility, persuasion and compromise . . . flowed directly into the moderate strands of early European Enlightenment thought.'[143] Mark Greengrass has argued, in reference to the execution of Mary Stuart by the Elizabethan regime, that 'the voice of the Old Testament was heard all too often in the sixteenth

---

[142] Walsham, *Charitable Hatred*, p. 236. For another example, see p. 148.
[143] John Marshall, 'Some Intellectual Consequences of the English Revolution', *The European Legacy* 5, no. 4 (2000), pp. 515–30, at p. 520. For other examples see p. 519.

century alongside the voice of moderation'.[144] John Coffey has written that, 'although most Christian humanists did not break with the Augustinian assumption that religious coercion was legitimate . . . Erasmus provided the inspiration for both Catholic and Protestant moderates'.[145] Mark Knights argued that 'the call for moderation had been drowned out by the din of persecution in the early 1680s, but by 1687 the prevailing rhetoric was tolerationist'.[146] The examples are nearly endless.

The result is that, even though scholars have learned to be far more careful than they once were in describing seventeenth century toleration – it can no longer be unproblematically grafted onto modern liberalism or described as intrinsically 'secularising' – the great intellectual transformation which undoubtedly occurred in this period nonetheless retains its patina of equanimity and reasonableness. To give just one example from perhaps the most astute scholar of the period: Blair Worden has described the process by which Anglicans and dissenters chose to tolerate theological difference, and turn instead to the enforcement of morals, as a retreat to an 'innocuous middle way'.[147] But in what sense is redefining the Other as offensive to civil society, morality or natural law, rather than offensive to revealed religion, so 'innocuous' or moderate? Only in the sense that modern historians inevitably adopt categories of analysis from our subjects, in this case men like Gilbert Burnet and John Locke who sought to consolidate their Revolution by redefining a legal reformation of manners and a permanent exclusion of Catholics from government as virtuously moderate rather than extreme.

As long as we continue to accept these categories in our historiography, and to accept religious toleration as a purely irenic project without acknowledging its obverse, it is virtually impossible to see in this subject anything other than the origins of the Enlightenment. The delineation of a bounded category of religion was absolutely essential to the intellectual inheritance of the eighteenth century. If religion were everywhere and imbued everything, as it was so often portrayed in the writings of England's long Reformation, then toleration of its free expression could never be moderate. If, on the other hand, religion were bounded and limited, confined to safe spaces and unable to compromise public order, then toleration of its free expression could be virtuously moderate. This manoeuvre is so fundamental to modern, Western thought that we rarely stop to notice that its categories are not natural categories of

[144] Mark Greengrass, 'Moderate Voices, Mixed Messages', in Luc Racaut and Alec Ryrie (eds.), *Moderate Voices in the European Reformation* (Aldershot, 2005), p. 203.
[145] Coffey, *Persecution and Toleration in Protestant England*, p. 210.
[146] Knights, 'Meer Religion', p. 57.
[147] Worden, 'The Question of Secularisation', p. 38.

transhistorical human experience. As such, not only do we follow the
thinkers of the early Enlightenment in re-describing all who came before
them as immoderate because they opposed religious toleration, we are
also categorically bound to accept the moderation of those who supported religious toleration no matter how violently their moderation was
pursued. If we wish to transcend the aggressive moderation of our subjects, then, we need to change the terms of our analysis and much more
energetically reject the values of moderation encoded in our historical
language.

# Conclusion

This book has argued that a cluster of ancient ethical ideals organised around 'moderation' and the 'middle way' acquired new meaning and singular importance in English public life between Henry VIII's break with Rome and the Glorious Revolution. Yet unexpectedly, these ubiquitous moral principles often functioned as aggressive polemical weapons and tools of social, religious and political power. Understanding how and why has taken us back and forth across two centuries, through topics ranging from Reformation theology to imperial expansion to political theory, and deep into the ideological heart of early modern England.

We began with the observation that moderation meant government, with no firm boundary between the ethical governance of the passions and the political governance of subjects. Claims for moderation thus routinely combined notions of interior virtue and exterior restraint in ways that would make little sense today. A moderate person – or, by extension, a moderate Church, state or society – was one in equipoise, neither excessive nor deficient, but that equipoise might result from external government as well as self-control. Conversely, moderation was the active process of restraint that resulted in a virtuous middle way, and that process might entail an array of external pressures ranging from polite admonition to public execution. The early modern concept of moderation, in other words, combined and subsumed the conditions of peace, equanimity and reasonableness with the coercion, exclusion or violence that produced them.

This framework was by no means unique to England – it was an inheritance of the European Renaissance developed from a variety of classical and Christian sources – but beginning in the second quarter of the sixteenth century the unique institutional and intellectual contexts of the English Reformation combined to give it special potency. The crucial institutional context was the assumption of the royal supremacy over the Church by Henry VIII and the subduction of religious authority in England under the jurisdiction of the state. The concept of moderation provided a powerful language with which to authorise this

326

Reformation-from-above, not only because the Church of England was usefully described as a *via media* between Rome and radicalism (as were so many other churches in Reformation Europe), but because moderation perfectly captured the Tudor regime's claim that amplified royal government guaranteed religious peace. Moderation, in the official mind of the English Reformation, was simultaneously the coercive enforcement of obedience by the Church-state and the peaceful and unified middle way that ideally resulted from such governance.

However, when this Erastian framework of moderation was grafted onto an ostensibly Protestant Church after 1559, it ignited more than a century of furious debate over the appropriate limits of such moderation and the conditions under which the external moderation of Christian subjects devolved into tyranny; in a Protestant Church built upon ideals of Christian liberty, moderation necessarily included the restraint of government itself. Thus, to an extent rivalled nowhere else in Europe, religious conflict in England broke along issues of Church government: the English Reformation was the ecclesiological Reformation. And since moderation meant government, moderation became the essential language through which English Reformation debates were fought, a language which made no distinction between the middle ways reformers sought and the repression and exclusion through which they hoped to achieve them.

The concurrent intellectual context was the rapid growth of Protestantism amongst England's socio-political elite beginning in the middle of the sixteenth century. The development of a Protestant culture meant that internal or ethical moderation was increasingly taken to be extremely difficult to achieve, beyond the native capacity of most if not all subjects, thus legitimating the growth of external moderation and the intervention of ministers and magistrates in public life. Given the depths of human depravity, in most circumstances ethical moderation was simply unequal to the task of producing a virtuous society, so public government became necessary. This Protestant framework, it should be noted, resonated with the new, civic humanist stress on the necessity of virtue for the regeneration of public life, emphasising the role of law and public policy in restraining the excesses of the commonwealth. The result was that increasingly robust assertions of authority were justified as instances of moderation, necessary restraints upon the rebellious impulses and appetites of the fallen world. In this model, the middle way became in essence a path of regulation to keep unruly subjects in line.

The result was the development of what I have called the 'rule of moderation'. Assertions of authority, whether in the public life of the kingdom or in the quotidian lives of its people, were justified as examples of moderation insofar as they bridled the excesses to which human beings were inevitably prone. But at the same time, those assertions of authority themselves had to be moderate and restrained rather than excessive in order to be legitimate, not only producing but also proceeding from restraint and regulation. The consequence was that government in England – not only official government but a wide variety of less formal claims to power – came to be authorised by its limitation, resulting in an apparent paradox: the exponential growth of moderate government. Claims to moderation came to dominate English public life, producing a 'politics of restraint' through which power was contested. In this context, moderation could become exceedingly violent as conflicting visions of the middle way clashed and excesses were forcibly restrained. But this is not to deny that moderation was *also* at heart a language of peace, equanimity and reason. I have been careful not to accuse my sources of subterfuge when they used moderation for aggressive purposes; the point is not that they disguised coercion within the language of moderation, but rather that the language of moderation wore its coercion openly alongside peace and equanimity in ways that did not become unsustainable until later generations differentiated them. The project of analysing the rule of moderation, then, is not about accusing early modern subjects of hypocrisy or exposing their inconsistencies, but rather about re-illuminating a coherent and powerful early modern system of thought whose existence has been obscured by the huge shadow of the Enlightenment.

Having mapped the contours of this system and described its development in the ecclesiological controversies of the English Reformation, this book then analysed the rule of moderation in a series of discrete case studies chosen because of both their centrality to seventeenth-century English history and their importance to the long-term development of English modernity. Seen though a reconstructed early modern lens in which ethical moderation was inseparable from external authority and in which government was authorised by its limitation, some of the most important events and ideas in early modern English history look very different. For instance, the emergence of the English empire in the New World, insofar as it was identified as fundamentally moderate, can be seen as an amplification of restraint, justifying limitless expansion on the grounds of its moderation. Likewise, the new social category of the middle sort, insofar as it was identified with a moderate middle way between riches and poverty, can be seen as a new and controversial argument about political participation and the governance of the commonwealth. The assertion of political liberty in the English Revolution, insofar as it was identified as a middle way between tyranny and anarchy, can be seen as part of an argument about how best to restrain subjects from their own dangerous excesses. And the rise of religious toleration, insofar as it was identified as a middle way between persecution and permissiveness, can be seen as a new technique of government rather than the withdrawal of government, an attempt to restrain the moral and political excesses that the rampant persecution of religious minorities had ignored or encouraged.

This book thus offers two core conclusions. First, the omnipresent invocations of moderation in early modern England were never the simple claims for reason, equanimity and consensus that they sometimes appear to modern eyes. Rather, they embodied to some degree or another – and I am happy to admit a wide range of possibilities here – an understanding of moderation in which the microcosm of self-restraint through reason was fully articulated with the macrocosm of external restraint through government. As such, the middle way was not only a valuable and contested piece of ideological real estate; it was also by its very nature a claim for authority. Second, we historians (and I certainly count myself here) who have used moderation as an analytical category in our discussions of early modern England, and who have all too often taken at face value claims to moderation by our subjects, need to rethink both the location and the magnitude of conflict in the period. If moderation was a claim for power, then the very place where we have assumed early modern violence to end is where our search for that violence must instead begin.

None of this is to suggest that the rule of moderation described in this book survived in anything like its Tudor-Stuart form into the eighteenth century or beyond. This book has described a particular historical configuration, not a snapshot of a timeless structural framework, and early modern associations of moderation with governance rapidly passed into oblivion in the eighteenth century as the ancient link between the microcosm of human beings and the macrocosm of their environment was severed.[1] Moderation and the middle way remained central to English public life, but their meanings and uses changed in the eighteenth century, befitting the new milieu of commercial society and the Enlightenment. Thus, while a serious treatment of eighteenth-century developments is beyond the scope of this book, it is important at least to glance forward to see how the years around 1700 were a significant

---

[1] Here I am indebted to Debora Shuger's analysis of the characteristic permeability of intellectual boundaries in the Renaissance and the fact that 'the movement from premodern to modern thought describes a thickening of boundaries': Debora Shuger, *Habits of Thought in the English Renaissance: Religion, Politics, and the Dominant Culture* (Berkeley, 1990), p. 11.

boundary (and hence the *terminus ad quem* of this book) but also a porous one through which a great deal of cultural and intellectual material passed.

The major transition from the seventeenth to eighteenth centuries was a shift from *equating* inward and outward moderation – a framework dependent upon Renaissance ideas of correspondence between microcosm and macrocosm – to a more limited sense that inward moderation *authorised* public action.[2] Writers of the seventeenth century had routinely and instinctively fused ethics and politics, so that moderation might equally result from the restraint of reason or the restraint of the magistrate, while an act of moderation was both a product and an agent of restraint. Writers of the eighteenth century, by contrast, privileged inward self-restraint. At a vernacular or cultural level this was essentially the transition from 'moderation' to 'politeness' as the core value of public discourse, the overwhelming emphasis on self-control, manners and affect that historians of the eighteenth century have seen as developing from the commercialisation of society. Of course, politeness was often still coercive, but it was coercive in substantially different ways. While, as Lawrence Klein has shown, politeness was 'aligned' with moderation insofar as it privileged restrained sociability over enthusiasm, few writers in the eighteenth century would have argued that it was polite to restrain *other* people's enthusiasms the way seventeenth-century writers routinely claimed that it was moderate to restrain other people's excesses.[3] This transition did not diminish either the magnitude or the ferocity of public restraint – state violence at the local, national and imperial levels was central to the emergence of 'political stability', as Edward Thompson and his many successors have shown – but that violence was gradually separated from ethics. While coercion had been understood as an outcome or even a facet of moderation, it was an exception to politeness.

Within this general transition from moderation to politeness, we can trace changes in a variety of different public domains. In the religious sphere, in the century after the Toleration Act the idea of moderation and the middle way increasingly focused on the dangers of 'enthusiasm' and the improper leakage of religious expression into civil life, a meaning

---

[2] I do not wish to suggest that this process was too abrupt; new paradigms were slowly taking hold in Restoration society, while older models still held currency in the eighteenth century. See Pincus, *1688: The First Modern Revolution*; Alan Houston and Steve Pincus (eds.), *A Nation Transformed: England after the Restoration* (Cambridge, 2001); Shapin, *A Social History of Truth*; Markku Peltonen, *The Duel in Early Modern England: Civility, Politeness and Honour* (Cambridge, 2003); Cowan, *The Social Life of Coffee*; Rivers, *Reason, Grace and Sentiment*.

[3] Lawrence Klein, 'Politeness and the Interpretation of the British Eighteenth Century', *HJ* 45, no. 4 (December 2002), pp. 869–98.

it had only slowly developed in the seventeenth century.[4] As the Church of England settled into a life of comfortable partnership with the rural squirearchy, enjoying wealth and privilege but no longer monopoly or unimpeachable necessity to the survival of the state, the clergy helped to enforce morality and order in the countryside but cared much less for issues of theology or ecclesiology. Quakers, for instance, became paragons of moderation, regardless of their heterodoxies, because of their reputation for orderliness and sobriety. The great new emphasis on moderation in the early nineteenth century, then, culminating in John Henry Newman's *The Via Media of the Anglican Church* (1836), was ironically a response to liberalisation and secularisation more than an attack on radical religion.

The most important legacy of the early modern religious *via media* for the eighteenth century, then, lay not in the Church at all but in political thought. The trajectory of religious conformity from Henry VIII's reign to the early seventeenth century generated a vision of civil authority in which law was the essence of moderation. In Richard Hooker's vision in particular, government was legitimate precisely insofar as it was limited by law, so that law itself rendered moderate what might otherwise be excessive, potentially legitimating an almost infinite expansion of legally constituted power for the state to discipline its subjects. Likewise, the trajectory of puritanism generated a vision of self-government in which the people were given increasingly robust authority over their religious lives, but the obverse of this democratisation of authority was its dependence upon the restraint or exclusion of those deemed unfit to exercise it. It should be no surprise, then, that the development of political liberalism in the eighteenth century found ample use for frameworks of moderation that showed how individual liberty could be reconciled with exclusivity and restraint, and that explained how to reconcile liberal anxiety about government with admiration for what gradually became the most powerful state the world had ever seen.

In the sphere of government, then, it is possible to draw significant lines of influence between Tudor-Stuart ideals of moderation and their eighteenth-century successors, especially as parliamentary government confronted first the radicalism of the French Revolution and then the demotic energies of the nineteenth-century Reform Movement. So, for instance, an April 1793 print entitled *Britannia between Scylla & Charybdis* depicted William Pitt the Younger steering the allegorical figure of Britannia in a vessel called 'The Constitution' between the 'Rock of

[4] J. G. A Pocock, 'Enthusiasm: The Antiself of the Enlightenment', *Huntington Library Quarterly* 60, nos. 1 and 2 (1998), pp. 7–28.

Figure 9. *Britannia between Scylla & Charybdis*. Broadside dated 8 April 1793, published in London by H. Humphrey.

Democracy' (topped by a distinctively French *chapeau*) and the 'Whirlpool of Arbitrary Power'. Pursued by sharks that looked suspiciously like the Whig icons Richard Sheridan, Charles James Fox and Joseph Priestley, they sailed towards a castle with a flag inscribed 'Haven of Public Happiness'.

This print seems as if, *mutatis mutandis*, it might have emerged from the seventeenth century. Yet some scholars of eighteenth-century political philosophy would stress that here, too, politeness at least partially trumped moderation with the advent of a new political philosophy of 'manners', befitting a government increasingly organised around 'commerce and the arts'.[5] Edmund Burke, for instance, wrote, 'Men are qualified for civil liberty in exact proportion to their disposition to put chains upon their own appetites', a sentiment in some ways compatible with earlier ideas but conspicuously absent the concept that the role of government is to chain the appetites of the people to reduce them to moderate subjects.[6] We might at least speculate, then, that the similarities between this eighteenth-century print and its Renaissance predecessors

---

[5] J. G. A. Pocock, 'Virtues, Rights, and Manners: A Model for Historians of Political Thought', *Political Theory* 9, no. 3 (August 1981), pp. 353–68.

[6] Quoted in Jenny Davidson, *Hypocrisy and the Politics of Politeness: Manners and Morals from Locke to Austen* (Cambridge, 2004), p. 8.

were not as profound as they seem. It is notable, for instance, that Pitt's physical comportment plays an inordinate role in the print; he guides 'The Constitution' to its destination with his firm countenance as much as the ship's rudder. It is also notable that, while he is sailing a middle course, he is not actively restraining anybody; he does not, for instance, attempt to bridle Charles James Fox.

If we turn to the imperial sphere, here, too, other issues and agendas quickly displaced the particulars of early modern moderation explored in this book, but nonetheless the moderation of the newly 'British' Empire continued to be a major theme. Most importantly, moderation increasingly referred to the commercial nature of imperialism. As the British Empire became dependent upon slave labour, for instance, moderation was invoked on both sides of the slavery issue. In a 1792 debate in the House of Commons over abolition, to take one example, Henry Dundas and Henry Addington repeatedly called for 'moderation' in the slave trade and asked for some 'middle measure' short of abolition that protected property rights and trade, while Charles James Fox responded that a moderate slave trade was no more possible than moderate murder.[7] For a different sort of example, Philip Stern has stressed that, beginning late in the seventeenth century, the East India Company combined elements of a polity and elements of a business in a new sort of middle way that may have a lot to tell us about the role of commerce in redefining eighteenth-century government. Likewise, Robert Travers has shown that British political thought in eighteenth-century Bengal found in the supposed Mughal 'ancient constitution' precedents for the fiscal 'moderation' of the colonial state, the 'moderate' collection of rents and taxes rather than oriental despotism.[8] This enormous new emphasis on commerce and the moderation of political economy was both continuity and change, developing one strand of Tudor-Stuart ideas while diminishing many others.

The most seemingly profound continuities appear in the sphere of social moderation and the growth of the middle sort of people. Throughout the first half of the eighteenth century, influential publications like *The Tatler* and *The Spectator* defined British society around the new public voice of the middle sort. And if English society in the eighteenth century

---

[7] W. O. Blake (ed.), *The History of Slavery and the Slave Trade* (Columbus, Ohio, 1861), pp. 230–1.
[8] Armitage, *The Ideological Origins of the British Empire*, pp. 144, 194–5 and ch. 6 *passim*; Philip Stern, '"A Politie of Civill & Military Power": Political Thought and the Late Seventeenth-Century Foundations of the East India Company-State', *JBS* 47, no. 2 (April 2008), pp. 253–83; Robert Travers, *Ideology and Empire in Eighteenth-Century Bengal* (Cambridge, 2007), pp. 54, 175, 240–2.

was normatively associated with its 'polite and commercial' classes, as Paul Langford has written, those classes were themselves normatively associated with moderation. At the start of Daniel Defoe's *Robinson Crusoe* (1719), for instance, the eponymous hero's father tells him what turns out to be one of the morals of the story:

> He told me it was men of desperate fortunes on one hand, or of aspiring, superior fortunes on the other, who went abroad upon adventures, to rise by enterprise, and make themselves famous in undertakings of a nature out of the common road; that these things were all either too far above me or too far below me; that mine was the middle state, or what might be called the upper station of low life, which he had found, by long experience, was the best state in the world, the most suited to human happiness, not exposed to the miseries and hardships, the labour and sufferings of the mechanic part of mankind, and not embarrassed with the pride, luxury, ambition and envy of the upper part of mankind.[9]

Such sentiments were commonplace, and, as Dror Wahrman has shown, in the crisis of the French Revolution they took on a far more politicised tone in which alternative claims to middling identity involved real contests for power.[10]

Yet new developments in eighteenth-century economic thought also gave these claims significantly new meanings, especially the idea, associated with Bernard Mandeville, that 'middling' identity did not require the restraint of avarice and ambition but rather a certain form of their expression. As Albert Hirschman has shown, this expression was itself re-imagined as a form of moderation, a rational calculation of interest rather than a release of passions, and as such it was compatible with politeness, the new watchword of the age.[11] But it was also largely incompatible with earlier views of moderation in which the governance of the self was microcosmically linked to the governance of the commonwealth. Now, increasingly, the summation of private vices was imagined to engender public benefits.[12]

This is, of course, no more than a very brief and partial survey, and historians of the eighteenth century will undoubtedly find much to criticise in it. My goal is not to be definitive or profound but to make a rather simple point about continuity and change. In all of these different spheres, the rule of moderation was displaced and refracted as commerce and politeness, rather than godliness and obedience, became the new

---

[9] Daniel Defoe, *The Life and Strange Surprising Adventures of Robinson Crusoe* (London, 1719), pp. 2–3. I owe this reference to Tom Laqueur.

[10] Wahrman, *Imagining the Middle Class.*

[11] Albert Hirschman, *The Passions and the Interests: Political Arguments for Capitalism before Its Triumph* (Princeton, 1977).

[12] Bernard Mandeville, *The Fable of the Bees*, ed. Phillip Harth (Harmondsworth, 1970).

cornerstones of public life, and moderation itself thus lost many of its early modern connotations. There was still a politics of restraint, but now it was largely a politics of self-restraint that was much less firmly tied to the restraint of others. Yet nonetheless, in every sphere where moderation mattered in eighteenth-century British life, even if that moderation now meant self-control rather than public control, early modern developments had left their mark in an important sense. The seventeenth century bequeathed to its successors a politics of restraint in which public action, and indeed government itself, was authorised by its limitation; even if that limitation was now encoded in the new language of politeness, the rule of moderation was inscribed in modern English society.

And this brings us, finally, to the last and largest claim that I want to make in this book. That is, I want to suggest that the early modern rule of moderation potentially offers a new genealogy for some of the core contradictions of English modernity.

The concept of 'modernity' is slippery and contested. While the modernisation theory of the 1960s described England's progress since the seventeenth century as a universal template for development, a series of revisionist movements successfully argued that this historical paradigm was itself part of the universalising, Enlightenment project of rationalising modernity it ostensibly described. Thus, since the 1970s scholars have largely replaced the process of 'modernisation' with the condition of 'modernity'. In so doing, they have retained little agreement about what exactly modernity entails, where and when it might be found, or whether it is singular or multiple in form.[13] With regard to England or Britain in particular, some see the beginnings of modernity in the late seventeenth century while others do not see it until the twentieth.[14] Some

[13] See Frederick Cooper, *Colonialism in Question: Theory, Knowledge, History* (Berkeley, 2005), ch. 5; Alan O'Shea, 'English Subjects of Modernity', in Mica Nava and Alan O'Shea (eds.), *Modern Times: Reflections on a Century of English Modernity* (London, 1996). Simon Gunn and James Vernon, 'Introduction: What Was Liberal Modernity and Why Was It Peculiar in Imperial Britain?' in Simon Gunn and James Vernon (eds.), *The Peculiarities of Liberal Modernity in Imperial Britain* (Berkeley, 2011). I am indebted to James Vernon for sharing this introduction with me prior to publication, and to both James Vernon and Steve Pincus for valuable discussions of English/British modernity.

[14] For the seventeenth century, see Houston and Pincus (eds.), *A Nation Transformed*; Pincus, *1688: The First Modern Revolution*. For the eighteenth century, see John Brewer, *The Sinews of Power: War, Money, and the English State, 1688–1783* (Cambridge, Mass., 1990); Roy Porter, *The Creation of the Modern World: The Untold Story of the British Enlightenment* (New York, 2000); A. L. Beier, David Cannadine and James Rosenheim (eds.), *The First Modern Society: Essays in English History in Honour of Lawrence Stone* (Cambridge, 1989). For nineteenth century, see J. C. D. Clark, *English Society, 1688–1832: Ideology, Social Structure and Political Practice during the Ancien Regime* (Cambridge, 1985);

see British modernity as a totalising condition while others argue for a series of disconnected micro-modernities.[15] Some see British modernity as internally generated and exceptional – that is to say, insular – while others place it within larger European and global patterns.[16]

It is not my intention to intervene explicitly in these debates, but rather to use them as a point of departure. For despite these differences, there is now a broad consensus that the difficulty of defining or precisely locating modernity results from the fact that modernity is itself identified by its agonisms and contradictions.[17] That is, the speed and instability of modernity, and the existential dilemma of predicating a stable society upon constant change, means that the modern condition is always self-negating. Modernity is rationalised order combined with rage against that order; it is neither the bourgeois restraint of Dr Jekyll nor the atavistic violence of Mr Hyde but the yoking together of the two.[18]

In Britain in particular, the contradictions of modernity have revolved around a series of interrelated projects tied to liberalism in the broadest

---

Harold Perkin, *The Origins of Modern English Society* (London, 1969); Richard Price, *British Society, 1680–1880: Dynamism, Containment and Change* (Cambridge, 1999). For the twentieth century, see Arno Mayer, *The Persistence of the Old Regime: Europe to the Great War* (New York, 1981); Martin Daunton and Bernhard Rieger (eds.), *Meanings of Modernity: Britain from the Late-Victorian Era to World War II* (Oxford, 2001); Becky Conekin, Frank Mort and Chris Waters (eds.), *Moments of Modernity: Reconstructing Britain, 1945–1964* (London, 1998); Callum Brown, *The Death of Christian Britain: Understanding Secularisation, 1800–2000* (London, 2001). Bruno Latour, *We Have Never Been Modern*, trans. Catherine Porter (Cambridge, Mass., 1993) powerfully argues that modernity was a fantasy of the Enlightenment, a desire to separate man from nature that paradoxically produced the very hybridities it was designed to overcome, hence any claim for the origins of modernity is also a fantasy.

[15] See Antoinette Burton (ed.), *Gender, Sexuality and Colonial Modernities* (London, 1999); Laura Doan and Jane Garrity (eds.), *Sapphic Modernities: Sexuality, Women and National Culture* (New York, 2006); David Gilbert, David Matless and Brian Short (eds.), *Geographies of British Modernity* (Oxford, 2003).

[16] See Dipesh Chakrabarty, *Provincializing Europe: Postcolonial Thought and Historical Difference* (Princeton, 2000); Dipesh Chakrabarty, *Habitations of Modernity* (Chicago, 2002); Nasser Hussein, *The Jurisprudence of Emergency: Colonialism and the Rule of Law* (Ann Arbor, 2003).

[17] For the dynamics of this consensus, see Mary Poovey, *Making a Social Body: British Cultural Formation, 1830–1864* (Chicago, 1995), and its critique in Ian Burney, 'Bone in the Craw of Modernity', *Journal of Victorian Culture* 4, no. 1 (Spring 1999), pp. 104–16.

[18] See Jürgen Habermas, 'Modernity: An Incomplete Project', trans. Nicholas Walker, in Seyla Benhabib and Maurizio D'Entreves (eds.), *Habermas and the Unfinished Project of Modernity: Critical Essays on the Philosophical Discourse of Modernity* (Cambridge, Mass., 1997); Jürgen Habermas, *The Philosophical Discourse of Modernity: Twelve Lectures*, trans. Frederick Lawrence (Cambridge, Mass., 1987), esp. lectures I and XII; Marshall Berman, *All That Is Solid Melts into Air: The Experience of Modernity* (New York, 1982). On the particularly English context, see Alison Light, *Forever England: Femininity, Literature and Conservatism between the Wars* (London, 1991); O'Shea, 'English Subjects of Modernity'.

sense of the term. Within the political sphere, for instance, English modernity has been identified with parliamentary government, the rule of law, individual liberty and the peaceful transition to participatory democracy. Yet at the same time, political modernity domesticated popular politics, displacing the turbulent crowd onto the circumscribed ballot box; freedom was always predicated upon restraint. Within the economic sphere, English modernity has been defined by industriousness, improvement, the free market and the rational reorganisation of labour and capital. Yet at the same time, economic modernity naturalised the political triumph of the middle class and produced new forms of dependency. In the imperial sphere, English modernity was associated with an empire that was Protestant, commercial, maritime and free. Yet at the same time, imperial modernity naturalised racial hierarchy and was predicated upon forms of coerced labour that belied metropolitan claims to liberty and industriousness. All of these projects shared a liberal suspicion of government, but they also paradoxically authorised the exponential growth of the very government they sought to limit. From a variety of perspectives, then, scholars have realised that the elemental agonism of British modernity was the discord between liberty and authority, what Patrick Joyce has called 'the central contradiction of ruling through freedom'.[19]

Scholars disagree significantly about the sources of these contradictions: some focus on their development on the imperial periphery, others focus on their gendered qualities, others see them as expressions of new forms of knowledge and expertise. But in general, the Tudor-Stuart era is implicated in these discussions only in refracted and limited ways. When the category 'early modern' was developed in the 1960s, historians presumed a teleology in which the novelties of the period – notably proto-industrialisation, the scientific revolution and the rationalisation of the state – were steps towards modernisation. Likewise, Renaissance claims for the 'dignity of man' were seen as the intellectual foundation of modernisation, while the Reformation was credited with the secularisation of society and the birth of the modern individual. But since the 1970s, to the extent that the 'process of modernisation' has yielded to the 'condition of modernity', the Tudor-Stuart period has largely dropped out of the picture and even the epithet 'early modern' has begun to feel old-fashioned and teleological. Certainly from the 1660s onwards English people talked a great deal about the rapid pace of change they experienced, hence Steve Pincus and Alan Houston have made valiant

---

[19] Patrick Joyce, *The Rule of Freedom: Liberalism and the Modern City* (London, 2003), p. 102. For a very different view of this problem, see Peter Mandler (ed.), *Liberty and Authority in Victorian Britain* (Oxford, 2006).

claims for the 'modernity' of Restoration England, but even in their work the 'early modern' field is divided into 'early' and 'modern' halves with a sharp break in the mid seventeenth century.[20] For most other scholars concerned with 'modernity', Tudor-Stuart England has become more or less irrelevant to the real story: the totalising project of the Enlightenment, 'the hubris of those who would remake the world by the dictates of their own notions of rationality'.[21] Hence the whole view of modernity in which it is defined by its contradictions and ambivalences presumes that they emerged in the eighteenth century as part of a secularising, rationalising project.

This consensus has developed in part because two of the most influential late twentieth-century critics of liberal modernity – Michel Foucault and Pierre Bourdieu – predicated their theoretical models upon the Enlightenment. Foucault's analysis of the 'microphysics of power' stressed that the advent of modern state power depended upon the invention of 'a regime of its exercise within the social body, rather than from above it'.[22] Individuals and institutions notionally separate from the state became implicated in the propagation of 'governmentality', a term Foucault coined to describe new technologies of knowledge, expertise and administration that rendered populations governable. Foucault explicitly argued that governmentality was an outcome of the eighteenth century and that what came before was mere prolegomena. Early modern developments like the 'art of government' and 'reason of state' remained obstacles rather than pathways to modernity because they focused attention on sovereignty and the artificial role of the ruler rather than the abstract exercise of power within society. The great leap forward, then, only occurred when the invention of 'political economy' allowed sovereignty to yield to techniques and practices that transcended the state. It was only in the Enlightenment that societies learned to create orderly subjects not through violent repression but through the normalisation of observation and control in everyday life.

---

[20] Houston and Pincus (eds.), *A Nation Transformed*.

[21] Cooper, *Colonialism in Question*, p. 115.

[22] Michel Foucault, *Power/Knowledge: Selected Interviews and Other Writngs 1972–1977*, ed. Colin Gordon, trans. Colin Gordon, Leo Marshall, John Mepham and Kate Soper (New York, 1980), p. 39. See also Michel Foucault, *Security, Territory, Population: Lectures at the Collège de France 1977–1978*, ed. Michel Senellart, trans. Graham Burchell (New York, 2007), *passim* but especially ch. 4; Michel Foucault, *Discipline and Punish: The Birth of the Prison*, trans. Alan Sheridan (New York, 1979); Michel Foucault, *The Birth of the Clinic: An Archaeology of Medical Perception*, trans. A. M. Sheridan Smith (New York, 1994); Graham Burchell, Colin Gordon and Peter Miller (eds.), *The Foucault Effect: Studies in Governmentality with Two Lectures and an Interview with Michel Foucault* (Chicago, 1991).

Developing from but also critiquing Foucault, Bourdieu's 'theory of practice' stressed from a social-scientific perspective how modern virtues like 'civility' were the inculcated habits of the ruling elite, so that the production of moral systems assigning value to those virtues served as unconscious and disguised pillars of the existing hierarchy.[23] Bourdieu described the routine socialisation of authority in the modern world through the concept of 'symbolic power', the mode of power which, rather than telling a person what he must do, instead tells a person what he is, and through the cultural and political capital of the teller is able to make that nomination real. Symbolic power is 'the imposition of political systems of classification beneath the legitimate appearance of philosophical, religious, legal (etc.) taxonomies', the ability to prescribe while appearing to describe.[24] Bourdieu thus defined symbolic *violence* as the force exercised through symbolic power, a force altogether more potent because it is misrecognised as merely descriptive. If political violence is domination, symbolic violence is the production of orthodoxy, belying the distinction between freedom and constraint because its victims are habituated to accepting it as natural by the same social conditions that create such violence in the first place.[25] But again, Bourdieu's framework was predicated upon post-Enlightenment institutions, like political parties or public school systems, through which habits are inculcated and symbolic power is won; in earlier eras individuals pursued strategies aimed directly at the domination of others.[26] Moreover, Bourdieu's theories presumed the existence of semi-autonomous 'fields' with their own rules and structures – economic, political, educational, religious and so forth – which were only differentiated in the Enlightenment.

Now, some of the claims advanced in the current book clearly resemble arguments by Foucault and Bourdieu. I have claimed, for instance, that the early modern English ideology of moderation, with its parallel levels of policing by moralists, ministers and magistrates, embedded strategies of rule within a normative language of peace and reason. I have likewise claimed that the moral system linking moderation to authority was not intentionally repressive, and indeed was committed to peace and equanimity, yet nonetheless the deployment of such a system as orthodoxy, and the bitter debates over who possessed its virtues, enacted real violence. Readers would not be wrong to detect in these claims

---

[23] Pierre Bourdieu, *Outline of a Theory of Practice*, trans. Richard Nice (Cambridge, 1977).

[24] Pierre Bourdieu, *Language and Symbolic Power*, ed. John Thompson, trans. Gino Raymond and Matthew Adamson (Cambridge, Mass., 1991), pp. 52, 170, 236–7.

[25] Bourdieu, *Language and Symbolic Power*, pp. 165, 51; Pierre Bourdieu, *The State Nobility: Elite Schools in the Field of Power*, trans. Loretta Clough (Stanford, 1996), pp. 386–7.

[26] Bourdieu, *Language and Symbolic Power*, editor's introduction, p. 24.

the subtle scent of French social theory. Yet it is crucial to understand that neither Foucault nor Bourdieu, with their eyes stubbornly focused on post-Enlightenment rationality, would allow for the argument presented here: that a specifically English version of what Foucault called 'government of one's self and others' emerged in the sixteenth century, establishing restraint as the basis of authority, paradoxically authorising the asymptotic growth of moderate government. Perhaps because of their perspective from France, where early modern government can so easily be caricatured as synonymous with emergent absolutism, neither Foucault nor Bourdieu could have imagined an early modern rule of moderation that was always in some sense internal to the body politic rather than above it, constituted immanently through a reciprocal process of restraining and restraint. We might call this, *pace* Norbert Elias, the moderating process.

The present book, then, offers an alternative genealogy for some of the core contradictions of (specifically English) modernity in which Reformation rather than Enlightenment was the organising principle, the Church was the primary (although far from the only) institution whose structures were in dispute, and moderation was the matrix that reconciled political authority and ethical authorisation. In this model, English adaptations of governance – political liberty, a religious *via media*, the middle sort, the empire – emerged from debates over, and as versions of, the rule of moderation: how power is authorised by its limitation. These adaptations were all fully established before the consolidation of state power and its alliances with liberal capitalism in the eighteenth century, and in fact it could not have been otherwise, for it was these adaptations that underwrote later expansions as properly moderate rather than excessive.

This book thus suggests that while the *conditions* of English modernity may have been a product of the Enlightenment and Industrialisation, the *contradictions* of English modernity emerged from the early modern rule of moderation. Most importantly, the central agonism of English modernity, the contradiction between liberty and authority, developed in its uniquely English form around the ideal of moderation, a concept that in the sixteenth and seventeenth centuries *simultaneously represented both sides* of this dialectic and mediated between them in complex and powerful ways. Even though the dilemma of reconciling government and freedom is an ancient one, then, and even though other liberal regimes in the modern world produced their own solutions, the English iteration developed out of a very peculiar context: a Reformation process that made possible the birth of the modern state as an engine of moderation. This context may explain something of England's tortured and existential relationship to the dilemma of liberty over the last 400 years.

Virtually all theorists who have studied the paradoxes and contradictions of English modernity – ruling through freedom, exclusive universalism, creative destruction – have told an essentially secular story, and they have traced the genealogy of these paradoxes to the Enlightenment project of rationality. This book, by contrast, has suggested that those paradoxes and contradictions emerged from the English Reformation's peculiar project of moderation. The result of this analysis is not a new understanding of English modernity but perhaps a new way of thinking about why that version of modernity was at the same time so precocious and so ambivalent. As such, it offers a new, if necessarily incomplete, window into the subtle violence of English history.

# Bibliography

## PRIMARY SOURCES

### MANUSCRIPTS

LPL MS 3497, fos. 121–35: Matthew Hale's unfinished manuscript treatise 'Of Moderation'.

PRO SP 12: State Papers Domestic, Elizabeth I.

BL Harleian MS 2127, fo. 15r–v: anonymous royalist poem of the Civil War.

PRO SP 1: State Papers Domestic, Henry VIII.

PRO SP 6: Theological Tracts, Henry VIII.

BL Lansdowne MS 45, fo. 125v: Andrew Perne to Lord Burghley, 1 September 1585.

BL Lansdowne MS 36, no. 65, fo.164r: 'a copy of certain texts of scripture painted near the royal arms in a church at Bury', 1582.

CUL MS Mm.I.47, pp. 333–5: 'reasons alleged by the Archbishop of Canterbury, for Dr. Bancroft's being promoted to the bishopric of London'.

Bodleian Library, MS Rawlinson A.139A: documents related to James II's 'three questions', 1687–88.

## PRINTED BOOKS

Abel, Thomas, *Inuicta Veritas* (Antwerp, 1532).

Aesop, *The Fables of Esope in Englishe* (London, 1570).
　*Here Begynneth the Book of the Subtyl Historyes and Fables of Esope*, trans. William Caxton (Westminster, 1484).

Ainsworth, Henry, *An Animadversion to Mr Richard Clyftons Advertisement* (Amsterdam, 1613).
　*A Defence of the Holy Scriptures* (Amsterdam, 1609).

Andrewes, Lancelot, *XCVI Sermons* (London, 1629).

Aquinas, St Thomas, *Summa Theologica*, translated by the Fathers of the English Dominican Province (New York, 5 vols., 2007).

Aquinas, St Thomas and Peter of Auvergne, *Sententia Libri Politicorum*, available at www.corpusthomisticum.org/iopera.html.

Arboreus, Joannes, *Commentarii Ioannis Arborei Laudunensis, Doctoris Theologi, in Proverbia Salomonis* (Paris, 1549).

*Arguments for Toleration Published for the Satisfaction of All Moderate Men* (London, 1647).

Aristotle, *Aristotles Politiques*, trans. I. D. (London, 1598).

The *Ethiques of Aristotle, That Is to Saye, Preceptes of Good Behauoute [sic] and Perfighte Honestie, Now Newly Tra[n]slated into English*, trans. John Wilkinson (London, 1547).

*Nicomachean Ethics*, trans. Martin Ostwald (New York, 1962).

*The Politics and the Constitution of Athens*, trans. Stephen Everson (Cambridge, 1996).

Arnway, John, *The Tablet or Moderation of Charles the First Martyr* (The Hague, 1649).

Augustine, St, *The City of God against the Pagans*, trans. R. W. Dyson (Cambridge, 1998).

*St. Augustine: Select Letters*, trans. J. H. Baxter (London, 1930).

Ash, John, *The New and Complete Dictionary of the English Language* (London, 1775).

Atkins, William, *A Discourse Shewing the Nature of the Gout* (London, 1694).

Atkyns, Robert, *The Power, Jurisdiction and Priviledge of Parliament* (London, 1689).

*A Treatise of the True and Ancient Jurisdiction of the House of Peers* (London, 1699).

Aylett, Robert, *Ioseph, or, Pharoah's Fauorite* (London, 1623).

*Thrifts Equipage viz. Fiue Diuine and Morall Meditations* (London, 1622).

B., J. [John Bullokar], *An English Expositor* (London, 1616).

Bacon, Francis, *The Essayes or Counsels* (London, 1625).

*The Historie of the Reigne of King Henry the Seuenth* (London, 1629).

*The Letters and the Life of France Bacon*, ed. James Spedding (London, 7 vols., 1861–74).

Bacon, Nicholas, *The Recreations of His Age* (Oxford, 1919).

Baldwin, William, *A Treatise of Morall Phylosophie* (London, 1547).

Bancroft, Richard, *Dangerous Positions and Proceedings* (London, 1593).

Barckley, Richard, *A Discourse of the Felicitie of Man* (London, 1598).

Barnes, Barnabe, *Foure Bookes of Offices* (London, 1606).

Barnes, Robert, *A Supplication Made by Robert Barnes* (Antwerp, 1531).

Barnfield, Richard, *The Encomion of Lady Pecunia: or the Praise of Money* (London, 1598).

Barret, Robert, *The Theorike and Practike of Moderne Warres Discoursed in Dialogue Wise* (London, 1598).

Barrow, Henry, *The Writings of Henry Barrow 1587–1590*, ed. Leland Carson (London, 1962).

Barrow, Henry and John Greenwood, *A Plaine Refutation of M. G. Giffardes Reprochful Booke* (Dordrecht?, 1591).

Baxter, Richard, *The Practical Works of the Rev. Richard Baxter*, ed. William Orme (London, 23 vols., 1830).

*Reliquiae Baxterianae* (London, 1696).

Baylor, Michael (ed.), *The Radical Reformation* (Cambridge, 1991).

Bede, The Venerable, *In Proverbia Solomonis*, in *Corpus Christianorum*, Series Latina (177 + vols, Turnholti, 1953–), CXIX B.

Bell, Thomas, *The Regiment of the Church as It Is Agreeable with Scriptures* (London, 1606).

Bernard of Clairvaux, St, *Sermo VI in Quadragesima. De Oratione Dominica*, available at http://pld.chadwyck.com.

Bilson, Thomas, *The Perpetual Gouernement of Christes Church* (London, 1593).

Black, Joseph (ed.), *The Martin Marprelate Tracts: A Modernized and Annotated Edition* (Cambridge, 2008).

Blackstone, William, *Commentaries on the Laws of England* (Oxford, 4 vols., 1765–9).

Blake, W. O. (ed.), *The History of Slavery and the Slave Trade* (Columbus, Ohio, 1861).

Blandie, William, *The Castle, or Picture of Pollicy Shewing Forth Most Liuely, the Face, Body and Partes of a Commonwealth* (London, 1581).

Blount, Thomas, *Glossographia: or, a dictionary* (London, 1656).

*Nomo-Lexikon, a Law-Dictionary* (London, 1670).

Bodin, Jean, *The Six Bookes of a Common-Weale*, trans. Richard Knolles (London, 1606).

Bolde, Samuel, *A Plea for Moderation Towards Dissenters* (London, 1682).

Botero, Giovanni, *A Treatise, Concerning the Causes of the Magnificencie and Greatnes of Cities*, trans. Robert Peterson (London, 1606).

Boyle, Robert, *The Early Essays and Ethics of Robert Boyle*, ed. John Harwood (Carbondale, Ill., 1991).

Bradshaw, William, *A Treatise of the Nature and Use of Things Indifferent* (London?, 1605).

*The Unreasonablenesse of the Separation* (Dort?, 1614).

Brathwaite, Richard, *The English Gentleman* (London, 1630).

Bredwell, Stephen, *The Rasing of the Foundations of Brownisme* (London, 1588).

Brett, Thomas, *True Moderation: A Sermon on Phil. IV. 5.* (London, 1714).

Brewer, J. S. *et al.* (eds.), *Letters and Papers, Foreign and Domestic, of the Reign of Henry VIII* (London, 21 vols. in 33, 1862–1932).

Bridges, John, *A Defence of the Gouernment Established in the Church of Englande* (London, 1587).

*A Briefe and Plaine Declaration* (London, 1584).

Brinkelow, Henry, *The Complaint of Roderyck Mors* (Strasbourg, 1542).

*Brittania between Scylla & Charybdis* (1793).

Brunel, Antoine de, *A Journey into Spain* (London, 1670).

Buckeridge, John, *A Sermon Preached at Hampton Court before the Kings Maiestie* (London, 1606).

Bullein, William, *A New Booke Entituled the Government of Healthe* (London, 1558).

Burnet, Gilbert, *A History of the Reformation of the Church of England*, new edition (Oxford, 3 vols., 1816).

Burnet, Gilbert, *The Ill Effects of Animosities among Protestants in England* (London, 1688).

*A Relation of the Death of the Primitive Persecutors* (Amsterdam, 1687).

Burroughs, Edward, *The Case of Free Liberty of Conscience in the Exercise of Faith and Religion, Presented unto the King and Both Houses of Parliament* (London, 1661).

Burton, Robert, *The Anatomy of Melancholy* (Oxford, 1621).

Butler, Samuel, *The Second Volume of the Posthumous Works of Mr. Samuel Butler* (London, 1715).

*Calendar of State Papers Relating to English Affairs in the Archives of Venice* (London, 38 vols., 1864–1947).

*Camp-Bell: or, the Ironmongers Faire Field* (London, 1609).

Care, Henry, *An Answer to a Paper* (London, 1688).

Cartwright, Thomas (1535–1603), *Commentarii Succincti & Dilucidi in Proverbia Salomonis* (Leiden, 1617).

*The Rest of the Second Replie* (Basel, 1577).

*The Second Replie of Thomas Cartwright* (Heidelberg, 1575).

Cartwright, Thomas (1634–89), *The Danger of Riches, Discovered in a Sermon* (London, 1662).

Case, John, *Sphaera Civitatis* (Oxford, 1588).

Cawdrey, Robert, *A Table Alphabetical* (London, 1604).

Chaderton, Laurence, *A Fruitfull Sermon, vpon the 3.4.5.6.7.&8. Verses of the 12. Chapiter of the Epistle of S. Paule to the Romanes* (London, 1584).

Chamberlayne, Edward, *Angliae Notitia: Or, the Present State of England* (London, 1669).

Charles I?, King of England, *Eikon Basilike: The Porvtraictvre of his Sacred Maiestie in His Solitudes and Svfferings* (London, 1649).

*His Majesties Answer to the XIX Propositions of Both Houses of Parliament* (Oxford, 1642).

Charleton, Walter, *Natural History of the Passions* (London, 1673).

Cicero, *De Officiis*, available at www.thelatinlibrary.com/cicero/off.shtml, accessed 27 September 2010.

*The Five Days Debate at Cicero's House in Tusculum*, trans. Christopher Wase (London, 1683).

*Marcus Tullius Ciceroes Thre Bokes of Duties*, trans. Nicholas Grimald (London, 1556).

Clapham, Henoch, *A Chronological Discourse* (London, 1609).

Clark, Andrew (ed.), *'Brief Lives', Chiefly of Contemporaries, Set Down by John Aubrey, between the Years 1669 & 1696* (Oxford, 2 vols., 1898).

Cocker, Edward, *Cocker's English Dictionary* (London, 1704).

Cockeram, Henry, *The English Dictionarie: or, an Interpreter of Hard English Words* (London, 1623).

*The English Dictionary: or, an Expositor of Hard English Words* (London, 1670).

Colby, Thomas (ed.), *Ordnance Survey of the County of Londonderry* (Dublin, 1837).

Coles, Elisha, *An English Dictionary* (London, 1684).

Cooper, Anthony Ashley, *A Letter from a Person of Quality to His Friend in the Country* (London, 1675).

Cooper, Thomas, *The Mysterie of the Holy Government of Our Affections* (London, 1620).

Cope, Michael, *Godly and Learned Expositions upon the Proverbs of Solomon* (London, 1580).

Copland, Patrick, *Virginia's God Be Thanked* (London, 1622).

*Corpus Reformatorum* (Leipzig, 101 + vols., 1834–).

Cosin, Richard, *Conspiracie, for Pretended Reformation* (London, 1592).

Cotton, John, *God's Promise to His Plantation* (London, 1630).

Crashaw, William, *A Sermon Preached in London before the Right Honourable the Lord Lawarre, Lord Governour and Captaine Generall of Virginea* (London, 1610).

Cudworth, Ralph, *The True Intellectual System of the Universe* (London, 1678).

Cuff, Henry, *The Differences of the Ages of Mans Life* (London, 1607).

Dallison, Charles, *The Royalist's Defence* (London, 1648).

Davenant, William, *Gondibert an Heroick Poem* (London, 1651).

*A Declaration of the Wel-Affected in the Country of Buckinghamshire* (London, 1649).

*A Declaration or Representation of the Actions, Intentions and Resolutions of Divers of the Inhabitants of the County of Hartford* (London, 1649?).

Dee, John, *John Dee: The Limits of the British Empire*, ed. Ken MacMillan with Jennifer Abeles (Westport, Conn., 2004).

Defoe, Benjamin, *A Compleat English Dictionary* (Westminster, 1735).

Defoe, Daniel, *The Life and Strange Surprising Adventures of Robinson Crusoe* (London, 1719).

Descartes, René, *The Passions of the Soule* (London, 1650).

*A Dialogue Between Riches, Poverty, Godliness, Gravity, Labour and Content* (London, 1659).

Dod, John, *Foure Godlie and Fruitful Sermons* (London, 1611).

Donne, John, *A Sermon of Commemoration of the Lady Danvers, Late Wife of Sir John Danvers* (London, 1627).

  *A Sermon upon the Eighth Verse of the First Chapter of the Acts of the Apostles* (London, 1624).

Drayton, Michael, *Poly-Olbion* (London, 1612).

Dryden, John, *Absalom and Achitophel* (London, 1681).

Dyche, Thomas, *A New General English Dictionary* (London, 1740).

Eburne, Richard, *A Plaine Path-Way to Plantations* (London, 1624).

Elizabeth I, Queen of England, *Elizabeth I: Collected Works*, ed. Leah Marcus, Janel Mueller and Mary Beth Rose (Chicago, 2000).

Elyot, Thomas, *Bibliotheca Eliotae* (London, 1542).

  *The Boke Named the Gouernour* (London, 1531).

  *The Castel of Health* (London, 1539).

*The English Reports* (Edinburgh, 176 vols., 1900–30).

Erasmus, Desiderius, *Apophthegmes that Is to Saie, Prompte, Quicke, Wittie and Sentencious Saiynges* (London, 1542).

  *Collected Works of Erasmus: Adages II.i.1 to II.vi.100*, trans. R. A. B. Mynors (Toronto, 1991).

  *Familiarum Colloquiorum Opus* (London, 1571).

Estienne, Robert, *Dictionariolum Puerorum, Tribus Linguis Latina, Anglica & Gallica Conscriptum* (London, 1552).

F., R., *Christian Toleration* (1664).

Farindon, Anthony, *Fifty Sermons Preached at the Parish-Church of St. Mary Magdalene Milk-Street, London, and Elsewhere* (London, 1674).

Ferrarius, Johannes, *A Woorke of Ioannes Ferrarius Montanus, Touchynge the Good Orderynge of a Common Weale*, trans. William Bavand (London, 1559).

Filmer, Robert, *The Anarchy of a Limited or Mixed Monarchy* (London, 1648).

*Patriarcha and Other Writings*, ed. Johann Sommerville (Cambridge, 1991).

Flavell, John, *Husbandry Spiritualized. or, the Heavenly Use of Earthly Things* (London, 1669).

Forset, Edward, *A Comparatiue Discourse of the Bodies Natural and Politique* (London, 1606).

Foster, George, *The Sounding of the Last Trumpet* (London, 1650).

*Four Grand Questions Proposed and Briefly Answered* (London, 1689).

Foxe, John, *Acts and Monuments* (London, 1563), available at www.hrionline. shef.ac.uk/foxe/, accessed 1 October 2010.

*Acts and Monuments* (London, 1583).

*The Acts and Monuments of John Foxe*, ed. G. Townshend and S. R. Cattley (London, 8 vols., 1837–41).

Fulbecke, William, *A Booke of Christian Ethicks* (London, 1587).

Fuller, Thomas, *The Holy State* (Cambridge, 1642).

*Jacobs Vow: A Sermon Preached before His Majesty* (London, 1644).

Gainsford, Thomas, *The Glory of England, or, a True Description of Many Excellent Prerogatives and Remarkeable Blessings* (London, 1618).

Galfridus, Anglicus, *Ortus Vocabularum Alphabetico* (London, 1509).

Gardiner, Ralph, *England's Grievance Discovered, in Relation to the Coal-Trade* (London, 1655).

Gardiner, Stephen, *De Vera Obedientia* (1553).

*The Letters of Stephen Gardiner*, ed. J. A. Muller (Cambridge, 1933).

Gifford, George, *A Short Treatise against the Donatists of England, whome We Call Brownists* (London, 1590).

Gillespie, George, *Wholsome Severity Reconciled with Christian Liberty* (London, 1645).

Gray, Robert, *A Good Speed to Virginia* (London, 1609).

Greenham, Richard, *The Workes of the Reverend and Faithfull Servant of Iesus Christ M. Richard Greenham* (London, 1601).

Greville, Fulke, *The Remains of Sir Fulk Grevill Lord Brooke Being Poems of Monarchy and Religion* (London, 1670).

Grotius[?], Hugo, *Politick Maxims and Observations* (London, 1654).

Guild, William, *A Yong Mans Inquisition, or Triall* (London, 1608).

H., I., Gentleman, *A Strange Wonder or a Wonder in a Woman* (London, 1642).

Hakluyt, Richard, *A Discourse Concerning Western Planting*, ed. Charles Deane (Cambridge, Mass., 1877).

Hall, David (ed.), *The Antinomian Controversy, 1636–1638: A Documentary History*, 2nd edn (Durham, N.C., 1990).

Hall, Edward, *The Vnion of the Two Noble and Illustre Famelies of Lancastre [and] Yorke* (London, 1548).

Hall, Joseph, *Cases of Conscience Practically Resolved* (London, 1654).

*Christian Moderation in Two Books* (London, 1640).

*Meditations and Vowes, Divine and Morall* (London, 1605).

*Quo Vadis? A Iust Censure of Travell as It Is Commonly Vndertaken by the Gentlemen of Our Nation* (London, 1617).

Hardy, Nathaniel, *The Arraignment of Licentious Liberty and Oppressing Tyranny* (London, 1647).

Harrington, James, *The Commonwealth of Oceana and a System of Politics*, ed. J. G. A. Pocock (Cambridge, 1992).

Harrison, Edward, *Plain Dealing: or, the Countreymans Doleful Complaint and Faithful Watchword, to the Statesmen of the Times* (London, 1649).

Hawke, Michael, *The Right of Dominion, and Property of Liberty* (London, 1656).

Helwys, Thomas, *An Advertisement or Admonition unto the Congregations* (Amsterdam?, 1611).

Heylyn, Peter, *Lord Have Mercie Upon Us* (Oxford, 1643).

*An Historicall Discoverie and Relation of the English Plantations in New England* (London, 1627).

Hobbes, Thomas, *Behemoth: Or, the Long Parliament*, ed. Ferdinand Tönnies (Chicago, 1990).

*Leviathan*, revised student edn, ed. Richard Tuck (Cambridge, 1996).

Holinshed, Raphael, *The First and Second Volumes of Chronicles* (London, 1587).

*The Firste Volume of the Chronicles* (London, 1577).

Hooker, Richard, *The Folger Library Edition of the Works of Richard Hooker*, ed. W. Speed Hill (Cambridge, Mass., 7 vols. in 8, 1977–1998).

*Of the Lawes of Ecclesiastical Politie* (London, 1611).

Horace, *Certain Selected Odes of Horace, Englished*, trans. John Ashmore (London, 1621).

*Horace His Arte of Poetrie, Pistles and Satyrs Englished*, trans. Thomas Durant (London, 1567).

*House of Lords, Journal of*, available at www.british-history.ac.uk/catalogue.aspx?gid=44, accessed 24 August 2010.

Howard, Henry, *Songes and Sonettes, Written by the Right Honourable Lorde Henry Haward Late Earle of Surrey, and Other* (London, 1557).

Hudson, William and John Cottingham Tingley (eds.), *The Records of the City of Norwich* (Norwich, 2 vols., 1906–10).

Hughes, Paul and James Larkin (eds.), *Tudor Royal Proclamations* (New Haven, 3 vols., 1964–9).

Hugo de Sancto Charo, *Opera Omnia in Universum Vetus & Novum Testamentum* (Coloniae Agrippinae, 8 vols., 1621).

Hunter, Josiah, *Loves Companion, or a Short Treatise of the Nature, Necessity, and Advantages of Moderation* (London, 1656).

Hyde, Edward, *The History of the Rebellion and Civil Wars in England* (Oxford, 3 vols., 1707).

Jacob, Henry, *The Divine Beginning and Institution of Christs True Visible or Ministeriall Church* (Leiden, 1610).

*Reasons Taken out of Gods Word and the Best Humane Testimonies Proving a Necessitie of Reforming our Churches in England* (Middelburg, 1604).

Jansen, Cornelius, *Paraphrasis in Psalmos Omnes Dauidicos . . . Eiusdem in Prouerbia Salomonis & Ecclesiasticum Accuratissima Commentaria* (Lugduni, 1592).

Jerome, St, *S. Eusebii Hieronymi Stridonensis Presbyteri Commentariorum in Isaiam Prophetam Libri Duodeviginti*, available at http://pld.chadwyck.com, accessed 24 August 2010.

Johnson, Edward, *Wonder-Working Providence of Sion's Saviour*, ed. William Frederick Poole (Andover, Mass., 1867).

Johnson, Francis, *A Short Treatise Concerning the Exposition of Those Words of Christ, Tell the Church, &c. Mat. 18.17* (Amsterdam?, 1611).

Johnson, Robert, *Nova Britannia: Offering Most Excellent Fruites by Planting in Virginia* (London, 1609).

Johnson, Samuel, *A Dictionary of the English Language*, 2nd edn (London, 1755–6).

Kaulek, Jean (ed.), *Correspondance Politique de MM. de Castillon et de Marillac, Ambassadeurs de France en Angleterre (1537–1542)* (Paris, 1885).

Kersey, John, *Dictionarium Anglo-Britannicum: or, a General English Dictionary* (London, 1708).

*The Lambs Defence against Lyes* (London, 1656).

Latimer, Hugh, *Certayn Godly Sermons* (London, 1562).

*A Most Faithfull Sermon Preached before the Kinges Most Excellente Maiestye* (London, 1550).

Lawne, Christopher, John Fowler, Clement Sanders and Robert Bulward, *The Prophane Schisme of the Brownists or Separatists* (London, 1612).

Lawrence, John, *Politica Decorum Commentationes* (London, 1590).

Lemnius, Levinus, *The Touchstone of Complexions*, trans. Thomas Newton (London, 1576).

L'Estrange, Roger, *The State and Interest of the Nation* (London, 1680).

*Liberty of Conscience Explicated and Vindicated* (London, 1689).

*Liberty of Conscience in Its Order to Universal Peace* (London, 1681).

Lilburne, John, *The Legall Fundamentall Liberties of the People of England Revived, Asserted and Vindicated* (London, 1649).

*Light Shining in Buckinghamshire* (London, 1648?).

Lipsius, Justus, *Six Bookes of Politickes or Ciuil Doctrine*, trans. William Jones (London, 1594).

Livy, *The Romane Historie Written by T. Livius of Padua*, trans. Philemon Holland (London, 1600).

*The War with Hannibal: Books XXI–XXX of the History of Rome from Its Foundation*, trans. Aubrey de Sélincourt (London, 1972).

Lloyd, David, *Memoires of the Lives, Actions, Sufferings & Deaths . . . for the Protestant Religion and the Great Principle Thereof, Allegiance to Their Soveraigne, in Our Late Intestine Wars* (London, 1668).

Locke, John, *An Essay Concerning Human Understanding* (Amherst, New York, 1995).

*A Letter Concerning Toleration, Licensed, Octob. 3. 1689. The Second Edition Corrected* (London, 1690).

*A Second Letter Concerning Toleration. Licensed, June 24. 1690* (London, 1690).

Loe, William, *The Incomparable Jewell Shewed in a Sermon* (London, 1632).

Lyly, John, *Midas* (London, 1592).

Mandeville, Bernard, *The Fable of the Bees*, ed. Phillip Harth (Harmondsworth, 1970).

Marsilius of Padua, *The Defence of Peace* (London, 1535).

Mason, Francis, *The Authoritie of the Church in Making Canons and Constitutions Concerning Things Indifferent* (London, 1607).

Mason, John, *A Briefe Discourse of the New-Found-Land* (London, 1620).

Mediolano, Johannes de, *Regimen Sanitatis Salerni*, trans. Thomas Paynell (London, 1528).

Melanchthon, Philip, *The Loci Communes of Philip Melanchthon*, trans. Charles Leander Hill (Boston, 1944).

*Mercurius Politicus* (London, published 514 weekly issues, June 1650–April 1660).

Meres, Francis, *Wits Common Wealth the Second Part* (London, 1634).

Milton, John, *A Defence of the People of England* (Amsterdam?, 1692).

　*Ioannis Miltoni Angli Pro Populo Anglicano Defensio* (London, 1650).

　*A Soveraigne Salve to Cure the Blind* (London, 1643).

*The Moderate* (London, published in 63 weekly issues, June 1648–September 1649).

*More Light Shining in Buckinghamshire* (London, 1649).

More, Henry, *An Account of Virtue: or, Dr. Henry More's Abridgment of Morals, Put into English* (London, 1690).

More, St Thomas, *A Fruteful, and Pleasaunt Worke of the Beste State of a Publyque Weale, and of the Newe Yle called Vtopia*, trans. Ralph Robinson (London, 1551).

Morley, George, *The Bishop of Winchester's Vindication* (London, 1683).

Morton, Thomas, *New English Canaan* (London, 1632).

*A Most Grave, and Modest Confutation of the Errors of the Sect, Commonly Called Brownists, or: Separatists* (London, 1644).

Mulcaster, Richard, *Positions Wherin Those Primitiue Circumstances Be Examined, which Are Necessarie for the Training Vp of Children* (London, 1581).

Munda, Constantia, *The Worming of a Mad Dogge: Or, a Soppe for Cerberus the Iaylor of Hell No Confutation but a Sharpe Redargution of the Bayter of Women* (London, 1617).

Mure, Eleanor, *The Story of the Three Bears* (Toronto, 1967).

Nash, Thomas, *An Almond for a Parrat, or Cutbert Curry-Knaues Almes Fit for the Knaue Martin* (London, 1589).

Nedham, Marchamont, *The Case of the Common-Wealth of England Stated* (London, 1650).

　*The Excellencie of a Free-State* (London, 1656).

Neville, Henry, *Plato Redivivus* (London, 1681).

Nichols, J. G. (ed.), *Narratives of the Days of the Reformation*, Camden Society, old series 77 (Westminster, 1859).

Ormerod, Oliver, *The Picture of a Puritane* (London, 1605).

Osborne, Francis, *A Perswasive to a Mutuall Compliance under the Present Government* (Oxford, 1652).

Owen, David, *Herod and Pilate Reconciled: Or, the Concord of Papist and Puritan* (Cambridge, 1610).

Parker, Henry, *Observations upon Some of His Majesties Late Answers and Expresses* (London, 1642).

Parker, Matthew, *A Briefe Examination* (London, 1566).

Parker, Samuel, *A Discourse of Ecclesiastical Politie* (London, 1671).

Patrizi, Francesco, *A Moral Methode of Ciuile Policie*, trans. Richard Robinson (London, 1576).

Peacham, Henry, *Minerva Britanna or a Garden of Heroical Deuises* (London, 1612).

Pearson, John, *Critici Sacri* (London, 1660).

Penn, William, *An Address to Protestants upon the Present Conjuncture* (London, 1679).

*The Papers of William Penn*, ed. Mary Dunn and Richard Dunn (Philadelphia, 5 vols., 1981–7).

*The Political Writings of William Penn*, ed. Andrew Murphy (Indianapolis, 2002).

Perkins, William, *Christian Oeconomie: or, a Short Survey of the Right Manner of Erecting and Ordering a Familie* (London, 1609).

*A Commentarie or Exposition, Vpon the Fiue First Chapters of the Epistle to the Galatians* (Cambridge, 1604).

*Epieikeia: or, a Treatise of Christian Equitie and Moderation* (Cambridge, 1604).

*A Godlie and Learned Exposition upon the Whole Epistle of Iude* (London, 1606).

*The Whole Treatise of the Cases of Conscience* (Cambridge, 1608).

*The Workes of that Famous and Worthy Minister of Christ in the Vniversitie of Cambridge, Mr. William Perkins* (Cambridge, 2 vols., 1612–13).

Perrinchief, Richard, *Samaritanism: or, a Treatise of Comprehending, Compounding, and Tolerating Several Religions in One Church* (London, 1664?).

Pett, Peter, *A Discourse Concerning Liberty of Conscience* (London, 1661).

Phillips, Edward, *The New World of English Words* (London, 1658).

Philodemius, Eutactus, *The Original & End of Civil Power* (London, 1649).

Plato, *Republic*, trans. G. M. A. Grube and C. D. C. Reeve (Indianapolis, 1992).

Playfere, Thomas, *The Pathway to Perfection* (London, 1596).

Plot, Robert, *The Natural History of Stafford-Shire* (Oxford, 1686).

Powel, Gabriel, *De Adiaphoris: Theological and Scholastical Positions, Concerning the Nature and Use of Things Indifferent* (London, 1607).

*A Refutation of an Epistle Apologeticall Written by a Puritan-Papist* (London, 1605).

Price, Richard, *Sauls Prohibition Staide* (London, 1609).

Primaudaye, Pierre de la, *The French Academie wherein is Discoursed the Institution of Manners*, trans. Thomas Bowes (London, 1586).

Proast, Jonas, *The Argument of the Letter Concerning Toleration Briefly Consider'd and Answer'd* (Oxford, 1690).

Prynne, William, *A New Discovery of Free-State Tyranny* (London, 1655).

Purchas, Samuel, *Purchas His Pilgrimage. Or Relations of the World and the Religions Observed in All Ages* (London, 1613).

Quinn, David (ed.), *New American World: a Documentary History of North America to 1612* (New York, 5 vols., 1979).

R., E., *Two Fruitfull Exercises* (London, 1588).

R., M., *The Mothers Counsell or, Live Within Compasse. Being the Last Will and Testament to Her Dearest Daughter* (London, 1630).

Raleigh, Walter, *The Discouerie of the Large, Rich, and Bevvtiful Empire of Guiana* (London, 1596).

Raleigh[?], Walter, *The Prince, or Maxims of State* (London, 1642).

Reyner, Edward, *Precepts for Christian Practice, or, the Rule of the New Creature New Model'd* (London, 1655).

Reynolds, Edward, *A Treatise of the Passions and Faculties of the Soul* (London, 1640).

Rider, John, *Riders Dictionary Corrected and Augmented* (London, 1606).

*Salus Populi Solus Rex. The Peoples Safety Is the Sole Sovereignty, or the Royalist Out-Reasoned* (London, 1648).

Sanderson, William, *A Compleat History of the Life and Raigne of King Charles from His Cradle to His Grave* (London, 1658).

Sandys, Edwin, *A Relation of the State of Religion* (London, 1605).

Schaff, Philip (ed.), *A Select Library of the Nicene and Post-Nicene Fathers of the Christian Church* (New York, 4 vols., 1886–90).

Scott, Thomas, *Vox Populi, or Newes from Spayne* (London, 1620).

*Vox Regis* (Utrecht, 1624).

Secker, William, *A Wedding-Ring Fit for the Finger* (London, 1664).

Senault, Jean-François, *The Use of the Passions*, trans. Henry, Earl of Monmouth (London, 1649).

Seneca, *The Eyght Tragedie of Seneca. Entituled Agamemnon*, trans. John Studley (London, 1566).

*The Lamentable Tragedie of Oedipus*, trans. Alexander Neville (London, 1563).

*Moral and Political Essays*, ed. John Cooper and J. F. Procopé (Cambridge, 1995).

Sharp, Andrew (ed.), *The English Levellers* (Cambridge, 1998).

Sibbes, Richard, *The Spirituall-Mans Aime* (London, 1637).

Smith, John, *The Generall Historie of Virginia, New-England, and the Summer Isles* (London, 1624).

Smith, Thomas, *De Republica Anglorum* (London, 1583).

Smyth, John, *The Character of the Beast, or the False Constitution of the Church* (Middelburg, 1609).

*The Differences of the Churches of the Separation* (Middelburg, 1608).

Some, Robert, *A Godly Treatise, Wherein Are Examined and Confuted Many Execrable Fancies* (London, 1589).

Southey, Robert, *The Doctor, &c.* (London, 7 vols., 1834–47).

Spenser, Edmund, *A View of the State of Ireland*, ed. Andrew Hadfield and Willy Maley (Oxford, 1997).

*A Spirit Moving in the Women-Preachers* (London, 1646).

Standish, John, *A Lytle Treatyse Composed by John Standysshe* (London, 1540).

Starkey, Thomas, *A Dialogue between Pole and Lupset*, ed. Thomas Mayer (London, 1989).

*An Exhortation to the People, Instructynge Theym to Vnitie and Obedience* (London, 1536).

*State Papers Published under the Authority of Her Majesty's Commission, King Henry VIII* (London, 11 vols., 1830–52).

*The Statutes of the Realm (1225–1713) Printed by Command of His Majesty George the Third* (London, 12 vols., 1810–28).

Stoughton, William, *An Assertion for True and Christian Church-Policie* (Middelburg, 1604).

Stow, John, *A Survay of London* (London, 1598).

Strype, John, *Ecclesiastical Memorials, Relating Chiefly to Religion* (Oxford, 3 vols., 1822).

Swetnam, Joseph, *The Araignment of Lewde, Idle, Froward, and Unconstant Women* (London, 1615).

Swinnock, George, *The Works of George Swinnock* (London, 1665).

Taylor, Jeremy, *Theologia Eklektike: A Discourse of the Liberty of Prophesying* (London, 1647).

Taylor, Thomas, *A Commentarie vpon the Epistle of S. Paul Written to Titus* (Cambridge, 1612).

Thomas, A. H. (ed.), *Calendar of Plea and Memoranda Rolls Preserved among the Archives of the Corporation of the City of London at the Guild-Hall* (Cambridge, 6 vols., 1926–61).

Thorowgood, Thomas, *Moderation Iustified, and the Lords Being at Hand Emproved* (London, 1644).

Tichborne, John, *A Triple Antidote, against Certain Very Common Scandals of this Time* (London, 1609).

*To His Excellency Thomas Lord Fairfax . . . The Humble Representation of the Desires of the Officers and Souldiers in the Regiment of Horse, for the County of Northumberland* (London, 1648).

*A True Declaration of the Estate of the Colonie in Virginia* (London, 1610).

Trundle, John, *Keepe within Compasse* (London, 1619).

Tutchin, John, *A New Martyrology* (London, 1693).

*A Two-Fold Treatise* (Oxford, 1612).

Tyndale, William, *The Obedience of a Christian Man*, ed. David Daniell (London, 2000).

Tyrrell, James, *Bibliotheca Politica: or an Enquiry into the Ancient Constitution of the English Government* (London, 1694).

Udall, John, *A Demonstration of the Trueth of that Discipline* (1588).

Venner, Tobias, *A Briefe and Accurate Treatise, Concerning, the Taking of the Fume of Tobacco* (London, 1621).

Victor, Veritie, *A Plea for Moderation in the Transactions of the Army* (London, 1648).

Vincent, Philip, *A True Relation of the Late Battell Fought in New England* (London, 1637).

Walwyn, William, *The Compassionate Samaritane* (London, 1644).

*A Still and Soft Voice from the Scriptures* (London, 1647).

Ward, Samuel, *A Coal from the Altar* (London, 1615).

Warmington, E. H. (ed.), *Greek Geography* (London, 1934).

Warner, William, *Albions England a Continued Historie of the Same Kingdome* (London, 1597).

Warr, John, *The Priviledges of the People* (London, 1649).

Waterhouse, Edward, *A Declaration of the State of the Colony and Affaires in Virginia* (London, 1622).

Webbe, George, *Agurs Prayer: Or, the Christians Choyce* (London, 1621).

Wharton, Henry, *Anglia Sacra* (London, 1691).

Whitaker, Edward, *An Argument for Toleration and Indulgence* (London, 1681).

Whitaker, Tobias, *The Tree of Humane Life* (London, 1638).

Whitbourne, Richard, *A Discourse and Discovery of New-Found-Land* (London, 1620).

White, John, *The Planters Plea* (London, 1630).

Whitgift, John, *The Works of John Whitgift*, ed. John Ayre (Cambridge, 3 vols., 1851–3).

Whitney, Geffrey, *A Choice of Emblemes, and Other Devises* (Leiden, 1586).

Wilkins, John, *Of the Principles and Duties of Natural Religion* (London, 1675).

Winstanley, Gerrard, *The Law of Freedom in a Platform* (London, 1652).

  *Truth Lifting Up Its Head above Scandals* (London, 1649).

Wither, George, *A Collection of Emblemes, Ancient and Moderne* (London, 1635).

Wood, William, *New Englands Prospect* (London, 1634).

*A Word of Advice to the Two New Sherriffs of London* (London, 1682).

Wright, Thomas, *The Passions of the Minde* (London, 1601).

## SECONDARY SOURCES

Achilleos, Stella, 'The *Anacreontea* and a Tradition of Refined Male Sociability', in Adam Smyth (ed.), *A Pleasing Sinne: Drink and Conviviality in 17th-Century England* (Cambridge, 2004).

Achinstein, Sharon, *Milton and the Revolutionary Reader* (Princeton, 1994).

Almasy, Rudolph, 'Language and Exclusion in the First Book of Hooker's *Politie*', in W. J. Torrance Kirby (ed.), *Richard Hooker and the English Reformation* (Dordrecht, 2003).

Amussen, Susan, 'Being Stirred to Much Unquietness: Violence and Domestic Violence in Early Modern England', *Journal of Women's History* 6, no. 2 (Summer 1994), pp. 70–89.

  *An Ordered Society: Gender and Class in Early Modern England* (Oxford, 1988).

Armitage, David, *The Ideological Origins of the British Empire* (Cambridge, 2000).

  'The New World and British Historical Thought', in Karen Kupperman (ed.), *America in European Consciousness 1493–1750* (Chapel Hill, 1995).

Armstrong, Catherine, *Writing North America in the Seventeenth Century: English Representations in Print and Manuscript* (Aldershot, 2007).

Artese, Charlotte, 'King Arthur in America: Making Space in History for *The Faerie Queene* and John Dee's *Brytanici Imperii Limites*', *Journal of Medieval and Early Modern Studies* 33, no. 1 (Winter 2003), pp. 125–41.

Ashcraft, Richard, 'Latitudinarianism and Toleration: Historical Myth Versus Political History', in Richard Kroll, Richard Ashcraft and Perez Zagroin (eds.), *Philosophy, Science and Religion in England 1640–1700* (Cambridge, 1992).

  'Religion and Lockean Natural Rights', in Irene Bloom, J. Paul Martin and Wayne Proudfoot (eds.), *Religious Diversity and Human Rights* (New York, 1996).

Atkinson, Nigel, *Richard Hooker and the Authority of Scripture, Tradition and Reason* (Carlisle, 1997).

Axtell, James, *Native and Newcomers: The Cultural Origins of North America* (Oxford, 2001).

Aylmer, G. E., 'Presidential Address: Collective Mentalities in Mid Seventeenth-Century England: IV. Cross Currents: Neutrals, Trimmers, and Others', *TRHS* fifth series 39 (1989), pp. 1–22.

Bahlman, Dudley, *The Moral Revolution of 1688* (New Haven, 1957).

Balis, Arnout (ed.), *The Ceiling Decoration of the Banqueting House*, part XV of the *Corpus Rubenianum* (London, 2 vols., 2005).

Barbour, Reid, *English Epicures and Stoics: Ancient Legacies in Early Stuart Culture* (Amherst, 1998).

Barry, Jonathan, 'Civility and Civic Culture in Early Modern England: The Meanings of Urban Freedom', in Peter Burke, Brian Harrison and Paul Slack (eds.), *Civil Histories: Essays Presented to Sir Keith Thomas* (Oxford, 2000).

Barry, Jonathan and Christopher Brooks (eds.), *The Middling Sort of People: Culture, Society and Politics in England, 1550–1800* (New York, 1994).

Beier, A. L., David Cannadine and James Rosenheim (eds.), *The First Modern Society: Essays in English History in Honour of Lawrence Stone* (Cambridge, 1989).

Bennett, Martyn, 'Between Scylla and Charybdis: The Creation of Rival Administrations at the Beginning of the English Civil War', reprinted in Peter Gaunt (ed.), *The English Civil War* (Oxford, 2000).

Berman, Marshall, *All That Is Solid Melts into Air: The Experience of Modernity* (New York, 1982).

Bernard, George, *The King's Reformation: Henry VIII and the Remaking of the English Church* (New Haven, 2005).

Bloomfield, Edward, *The Opposition to the English Separatists, 1570–1625* (Washington, D.C., 1981).

Boose, Lynda, 'Scolding Brides and Bridling Scolds: Taming the Woman's Unruly Member', *Shakespeare Quarterly* 42, no. 2 (Summer 1991), pp. 179–213.

Bourdieu, Pierre, *Language and Symbolic Power*, ed. John Thompson, trans. Gino Raymond and Matthew Adamson (Cambridge, Mass., 1991).

*Outline of a Theory of Practice*, trans. Richard Nice (Cambridge, 1977).

*The State Nobility: Elite Schools in the Field of Power*, trans. Loretta Clough (Stanford, 1996).

Bouwsma, William, 'The Two Faces of Humanism', in his *A Usable Past: Essays in European Cultural History* (Berkeley, 1990).

Brachlow, Stephen, *The Communion of Saints: Radical Puritan and Separatist Ecclesiology, 1570–1625* (Oxford, 1988).

Breen, T. H., *The Character of the Good Ruler: A Study of Puritan Political Ideas in New England, 1630–1730* (New Haven, 1970).

Brewer, John, *The Sinews of Power: War, Money, and the English State, 1688–1783* (Cambridge, Mass., 1990).

Brigden, Susan, *London and the Reformation* (Oxford, 1989).

Brown, Callum, *The Death of Christian Britain: Understanding Secularisation, 1800–2000* (London, 2001).

Brown, Wendy, *Manhood and Politics: A Feminist Reading of Political Theory* (Totowa, N.J., 1988).

*Regulating Aversion: Tolerance in the Age of Identity and Empire* (Princeton, 2006).

Bunbury, E. H., *A History of Ancient Geography*, 2nd edn (New York, 2 vols., 1959).

Burchell, Graham, Colin Gordon and Peter Miller (eds.), *The Foucault Effect: Studies in Governmentality with Two Lectures and an Interview with Michel Foucault* (Chicago, 1991).

Burgess, Glenn, *Absolute Monarchy and the Stuart Constitution* (New Haven, 1996).

Burgess, Glenn, and Matthew Festenstein (eds.), *English Radicalism, 1550–1850* (Cambridge, 2007).

Burney, Ian, 'Bone in the Craw of Modernity', *Journal of Victorian Culture* 4, no. 1 (Spring 1999), pp. 104–16.

Burton, Antoinette (ed.), *Gender, Sexuality and Colonial Modernities* (London, 1999).

Burtt, Shelley, *Virtue Transformed: Political Argument in England 1688–1740* (Cambridge, 1992).

Bushnell, Rebecca, *A Culture of Teaching: Early Modern Humanism in Theory and Practice* (Ithaca, 1996).

Canny, Nicholas, 'The Origins of Empire: An Introduction', in Nicholas Canny (ed.), *The Origins of Empire* (Oxford, 1998).

'The Permissive Frontier: The Problem of Social Control in English Settlements in Ireland and Virginia 1550–1650', in K. R. Andrews, N. P. Canny and P. E. H. Hair (eds.), *The Westward Enterprise: English Activities in Ireland, the Atlantic, and America 1480–1650* (Liverpool, 1978).

Carlin, Norah, 'The Levellers and the Conquest of Ireland in 1649', *HJ* 30, no. 2 (1987), pp. 269–88.

Cave, Alfred, 'Canaanites in a Promised Land: The American Indians and the Providential Theory of Empire', *American Indian Quarterly* 12, no. 4 (Fall 1988), pp. 277–97.

Chakrabarty, Dipesh, *Habitations of Modernity* (Chicago, 2002).

*Provincializing Europe: Postcolonial Thought and Historical Difference* (Princeton, 2000).

Chaplin, Joyce, *Subject Matter: Technology, the Body, and Science on the Anglo-American Frontier, 1500–1676* (Cambridge, Mass., 2001).

Clark, J. C. D., *English Society, 1688–1832: Ideology, Social Structure and Political Practice during the Ancien Regime* (Cambridge, 1985).

Clark, Stuart, *Thinking with Demons: The Idea of Witchcraft in Early Modern Europe* (Oxford, 1997).

Claydon, Tony, *William III and the Godly Revolution* (Cambridge, 1996).

Coffey, John, *Persecution and Toleration in Protestant England, 1558–1689* (New York, 2000).

Cohn, Samuel, *The Black Death Transformed* (London, 2003).

Collinson, Patrick, *The Elizabethan Puritan Movement* (Oxford, 1989; first published 1967).

'Hooker and the Elizabethan Establishment', in Arthur McGrade (ed.), *Richard Hooker and the Construction of Christian Community* (Tempe, Ariz., 1997).

'"A Magazine of Religion Patterns"; An Erasmian Topic Transposed In English Protestantism', in Derek Baker (ed.), *Studies in Church History* 14 (Oxford, 1977), pp. 223–49.

'The Monarchical Republic of Queen Elizabeth I', in his *Elizabethan Essays* (London, 1994).

'Sir Nicholas Bacon and the Elizabethan *Via Media*', in his *Godly People: Essays on English Protestantism and Puritanism* (London, 1983).

Como, David, *Blown by the Spirit: Puritanism and the Emergence of an Antinomian Underground in Pre-Civil-War England* (Stanford, 2004).

Condren, Conal, *The Language of Politics in Seventeenth-Century England* (Basingstoke, 1994).

Conekin, Becky, Frank Mort and Chris Waters (eds.), *Moments of Modernity: Reconstructing Britain, 1945–1964* (London, 1998).

Coolidge, John, *The Pauline Renaissance in England* (Oxford, 1970).

Cooper, Frederick, *Colonialism in Question: Theory, Knowledge, History* (Berkeley, 2005).

Cooper, James, *Tenacious of Their Liberties: The Congregationalists in Colonial Massachusetts* (Oxford, 1999).

Corfield, Penelope, 'Class by Name and Number in Eighteenth-Century England', *History* 72, no. 234 (February 1987), pp. 38–61.

Corfield, Penelope (ed.), *Language, History and Class* (Oxford, 1991).

Corns, Thomas, 'Milton and the Characteristics of a Free Commonwealth', in David Armitage, Armand Himy and Quentin Skinner (eds.), *Milton and Republicanism* (Cambridge, 1995).

Cowan, Brian, *The Social Life of Coffee: The Emergence of the British Coffeehouse* (New Haven, 2005).

Cragg, Gordon, *From Puritanism to the Age of Reason* (Cambridge, 1966).

Craig, John, *Reformation, Politics and Polemics: The Growth of Protestantism in East Anglian Market Towns, 1500–1610* (Aldershot, 2001).

Crane, Mary, *Framing Authority: Sayings, Self, and Society in Sixteenth-Century England* (Princeton, 1993).

Crawford, Patricia, '"The Poorest She": Women and Citizenship in Early Modern England', in Michael Mendle (ed.), *The Putney Debates of 1647: The Army, the Levellers and the English State* (Cambridge, 2001).

Daly, James, *Cosmic Harmony and Political Thinking in Early Stuart England*, printed in *Transactions of the American Philosophical Society* 69 (Philadelphia, 1979).

Daunton, Martin and Bernhard Rieger (eds.), *Meanings of Modernity: Britain from the Late-Victorian Era to World War II* (Oxford, 2001).

David, Zdenek, *Finding the Middle Way: The Utraquists' Liberal Challenge to Rome and Luther* (Washington, D.C., 2003).

Davidson, Jenny, *Hypocrisy and the Politics of Politeness: Manners and Morals from Locke to Austen* (Cambridge, 2004).

Davies, Catherine, *A Religion of the Word: The Defence of the Reformation in the Reign of Edward VI* (Manchester, 2002).

Davis, Charles, '"For Conformities Sake": How Richard Hooker Used Fuzzy Logic and Legal Rhetoric against Political Extremes', in Arthur McGrade (ed.), *Richard Hooker and the Construction of Christian Community* (Tempe, Ariz., 1997).

Davis, J. C., 'Gerard Winstanley and the Restoration of True Magistracy', *PP* 70 (1976), pp. 76–93.

'Levellers and Democracy', *PP* 40 (1968), pp. 174–80.

*Utopia and the Ideal Society: A Study of English Utopian Writing 1516–1700* (Cambridge, 1981).

Davis, Stevie, *Unbridled Spirits: Women of the English Revolution: 1640–1660* (London, 1998).

Dean, David, *Law-Making and Society in Late Elizabethan England: The Parliament of England, 1584–1601* (Cambridge, 1996).

Dickens, A. G., *The English Reformation* (New York, 1964).

Diethe, Jürgen, 'The Moderate: Politics and Allegiances of a Revolutionary Newspaper', *History of Political Thought* 4, no. 2 (Summer 1983), pp. 247–79.

Doan, Laura and Jane Garrity (eds.), *Sapphic Modernities: Sexuality, Women and National Culture* (New York, 2006).

Dodds, Gregory, *Exploiting Erasmus: The Erasmian Legacy and Religious Change in Early Modern England* (Toronto, 2009).

Dunn, John, *The Political Thought of John Locke* (Cambridge, 1969).

Dzelzainis, Martin, 'History and Ideology: Milton, the Levellers, and the Council of State in 1649', *Huntington Library Quarterly* 68, no. 1 (2005), pp. 269–87.

Earle, Peter, *The Making of the English Middle Class: Business, Society, and Family Life in London, 1660–1730* (Berkeley, 1989).

Elias, Norbert, *The Civilizing Process: Sociogenetic and Psychogenetic Investigations*, revised edn, trans. Edmund Jephcott (Maldon, Mass., 1994).

Elliott, J. H., Empires of the Atlantic World: Britain and Spain in America, 1492–1830 (New Haven, 2006).

Elms, Alan, '"The Three Bears": Four Interpretations', *The Journal of American Folklore* 90, no. 357 (July–September 1977), pp. 257–73.

Elton, G. R., 'Thomas Cromwell's Decline and Fall', *Cambridge Historical Journal* 10, no. 2 (1951), pp. 150–85.

Eppley, Daniel, *Defending Royal Supremacy and Discerning God's Will in Tudor England* (Aldershot, 2007).

Ferguson, Arthur, *The Articulate Citizen and the English Renaissance* (Durham, N.C., 1965).

Ferrell, Lori Anne, *Government by Polemic: James I, the King's Preachers, and the Rhetorics of Conformity, 1603–1625* (Stanford, 1998).

Finkelstein, Andrea, *Harmony and the Balance: An Intellectual History of Seventeenth-Century English Economic Thought* (Ann Arbor, 2000).

Fitzmaurice, Andrew, *Humanism and America* (Cambridge, 2003).

Foster, Stephen, *The Long Argument: English Puritanism and the Shaping of New England Culture, 1570–1700* (Chapel Hill, N.C., 1991).

*Their Solitary Way: The Puritan Social Ethic in the First Century of Settlement in New England* (New Haven, 1971).

Foucault, Michel, *The Birth of the Clinic: An Archaeology of Medical Perception*, trans. A. M. Sheridan Smith (New York, 1994).

*Discipline and Punish: The Birth of the Prison*, trans. Alan Sheridan (New York, 1979).

*Power/Knowledge: Selected Interviews and Other Writings 1972–1977*, ed. Colin Gordon, trans. Colin Gordon, Leo Marshall, John Mepham and Kate Soper (New York, 1980).

*Security, Territory, Population: Lectures at the Collège de France 1977–1978*, ed. Michel Senellart, trans. Graham Burchell (New York, 2007).

*The Use of Pleasure: Volume 2 of the History of Sexualtiy*, trans. Robert Hurley (New York, 1990).

Foxley, Rachel, 'John Lilburne and the Citizenship of "Free-Born Englishmen"', *HJ* 47, no. 4 (2004), pp. 849–74.

Foyster, Elizabeth, 'Male Honour, Social Control and Wife Beating in Late Stuart England', *TRHS* sixth series, 6 (1996), pp. 215–24.

*Marital Violence: An English Family History, 1660–1875* (Cambridge, 2005).

French, H. R., *The Middle Sort of People in Provincial England 1600–1750* (Oxford, 2007).

'Social Status, Localism and the "Middle Sort of People" in England 1620–1750', *P&P* 166, no. 1 (2000), pp. 66–99.

Fukuda, Arihiro, *Sovereignty and the Sword: Harrington, Hobbes and Mixed Government in the English Civil Wars* (Oxford, 1997).

Gal, Stéphane, 'Malaise et Utopie Parlementaires au Temps de la Ligue: Les "Moyenneurs" du Parlement de Dauphiné', *Revue Historique* 303 (2001), pp. 403–31.

George, Charles and Katherine George, *The Protestant Mind of the English Reformation 1570–1640* (Princeton, 1961).

Gibbs, Lee, 'Richard Hooker: Prophet of Anglicanism or English Magisterial Reformer?' *Anglican Theological Review* 84, no. 4 (Fall 2002), pp. 952–4.

Gilbert, David, David Matless and Brian Short (eds.), *Geographies of British Modernity* (Oxford, 2003).

Gillies, John, 'Shakespeare's Virginian Masque', *English Literary History* 53, no. 4 (Winter, 1986), pp. 673–707.

Glover, Samuel, 'The Putney Debates: Popular versus Elitist Republicanism', *P&P* 164 (1999), pp. 47–80.

Goldie, Mark, 'John Locke's Circle and James II', *HJ* 55, no. 3 (1992), pp. 557–86.

'The Theory of Religious Intolerance in Restoration England', in Ole Peter Grell, Jonathan Israel and Nicholas Tyacke (eds.), *From Persecution to Toleration: The Glorious Revolution and Religion in England* (Oxford, 1991).

'The Unacknowledged Republic: Officeholding in Early Modern England', in Tim Harris (ed.), *The Politics of the Excluded, c.1500–1850* (New York, 2001).

Gordon, Colin, 'Governmental Rationality: An Introduction', in Graham Burchell, Colin Gordon and Peter Miller (eds.), *The Foucault Effect: Studies in Governmentality with Two Lectures and an Interview with Michel Foucault* (Chicago, 1991).

Gowing, Laura, *Domestic Dangers: Women, Words, and Sex in Early Modern London* (Oxford, 1996).

Greenblatt, Stephen, *Renaissance Self-Fashioning: From More to Shakespeare* (Chicago, 1980).

Greene, David, 'The Identity of the Emblematic Nemesis', *Studies in the Renaissance* 10 (1963), pp. 25–43.

Greengrass, Mark, *Governing Passions: Peace and Reform in the French Kingdom, 1576–1585* (Oxford, 2007).

'Mixed Messages', in Luc Racaut and Alec Ryrie (eds.), *Moderate Voices in the European Reformation* (Aldershot, 2005).

Gregory, Brad, *Salvation at Stake: Christian Martyrdom in Early Modern Europe* (Cambridge, Mass., 1999).

Gilbert, David, David Matless and Brian Short (eds.), *Geographies of British Modernity* (Oxford, 2003).

Gunn, Simon and James Vernon, 'Introduction: What Was Liberal Modernity and Why Was It Peculiar in Imperial Britain?' in Simon Gunn and James Vernon (eds.), *The Peculiarities of Liberal Modernity in Imperial Britain* (Berkeley, 2011).

Habermas, Jürgen, 'Modernity: An Incomplete Project', trans. Nicholas Walker, in Seyla Benhabib and Maurizio D'Entreves (eds.), *Habermas and the Unfinished Project of Modernity: Critical Essays on the Philosophical Discourse of Modernity* (Cambridge, Mass., 1997).

*The Philosophical Discourse of Modernity: Twelve Lectures*, trans. Frederick Lawrence (Cambridge, Mass., 1987).

Harris, Tim, 'The Bawdy House Riots of 1688', *HJ* 29, no. 3 (1986), pp. 537–56.

*London Crowds in the Reign of Charles II: Propaganda and Politics from the Restoration until the Exclusion Crisis* (Cambridge, 1987).

Harrison, William, 'The Church', in Torrance Kirby (ed.), *A Companion to Richard Hooker* (Leiden, 2008).

Hart, Vaughan and Richard Tucker, 'Imaginacy Set Free: Aristotelian Ethics and Inigo Jones's Banqueting House at Whitehall', *RES: Anthropology and Aesthetics* 39 (Spring 2001), pp. 151–67.

Hartwig, Joan, 'Horses and Women in *The Taming of the Shrew*', *Huntington Library Quarterly* 45, no. 4 (Autumn 1982), pp. 285–94.

Hill, Christopher, *Puritanism and Revolution: Studies in Interpretation of the English Revolution of the Seventeenth Century* (London, 1958).

*The Religion of Gerard Winstanley* (Oxford, 1978).

*The World Turned Upside Down: Radical Ideas in the English Revolution* (London, 1975).

Hill, W. Speed, 'Works and Editions II', in Torrance Kirby (ed.), *A Companion to Richard Hooker* (Leiden, 2008).

Hindle, Steve, *On the Parish? The Micro-Politics of Poor Relief in Rural England c.1550–1750* (Oxford, 2004).

*The State and Social Change in Early Modern England, c.1550–1640* (New York, 2000).

Hirschman, Albert, *The Passions and the Interests: Political Arguments for Capitalism before Its Triumph* (Princeton, 1977).

Hobby, Elaine, 'Winstanley, Women and the Family', *Prose Studies* 22, no. 2 (August 1999), pp. 61–72.

Holstun, James, *Ehud's Dagger: Class Struggle in the English Revolution* (London, 2000).

Houlbrooke, Ralph, 'Civility and Civil Observances in the Early Modern English Funeral', in Peter Burke, Brian Harrison and Paul Slack (eds.), *Civil Histories: Essays Presented to Sir Keith Thomas* (Oxford, 2000).

House, Seymour Baker, 'An Unknown Tudor Propaganda Poem c.1540', *Notes and Queries*, new series 39, no. 3 (September 1992), pp. 282–5.

Houston, Alan, '"A Way of Settlement": The Levellers, Monopolies, and the Public Interest', *History of Political Thought* 14, no. 3 (Autumn 1993), pp. 381–420.

Houston, Alan and Steve Pincus (eds.), A *Nation Transformed: England after the Restoration* (Cambridge, 2001).

Howell, Roger, 'The Structure of Urban Politics in the English Civil War', *Albion* 11, no. 2 (Summer 1979), pp. 111–27.

Howell, Roger and David Brewster, 'Reconsidering the Levellers: The Evidence of the Moderate', *P&P* 46 (February 1970), pp. 68–86.

Hunt, Margaret, *The Middling Sort: Commerce, Gender, and the Family in England 1680–1780* (Berkeley, 1996).

Hussein, Nasser, *The Jurisprudence of Emergency: Colonialism and the Rule of Law* (Ann Arbor, 2003).

Ingalls, Ranall, 'Sin and Grace', in Torrance Kirby (ed.), *A Companion to Richard Hooker* (Leiden, 2008).

James, Susan, *Passion and Action: The Emotions in Seventeenth-Century Philosophy* (Oxford, 1997).

   'Reason, the Passions and the Good Life', in Daniel Garber and Michael Ayers (eds.), *The Cambridge History of Seventeenth-Century Philosophy* (Cambridge, 2 vols., 2003).

Jennings, Francis, *The Invasion of America: Indians, Colonialism, and the Cant of Conquest* (Chapel Hill, 1975).

Jones, Norman, *God and the Moneylenders: Usury and the Law in Early Modern England* (Oxford, 1989).

Jordan, W. K., *The Development of Religious Toleration in England* (Cambridge, Mass., 4 vols., 1932–40).

Joyce, Patrick, *The Rule of Freedom: Liberalism and the Modern City* (London, 2003).

Kahn, Victoria, 'The Passions and the Interests in Early Modern Europe: The Case of Guarini's *Il Pastor fido*', in Gail Paster, Katherine Rowe and Mary Floyd-Wilson (eds.), *Reading the Early Modern Passions: Essays in the Cultural History of Emotion* (Philadelphia, 2004).

Kamen, Henry, *The Rise of Toleration* (London, 1967).

Kaye, Joel, *Economy and Nature in the Fourteenth Century: Money, Market Exchange, and the Emergence of Scientific Thought* (Cambridge, 1998).

   'The (Re)Balance of Nature, c.1250–1350', in Barbara Hanawalt and Lisa Kiser (eds.), *Engaging with Nature: Essays on the Natural World in Medieval and Early Modern Europe* (Notre Dame, 2008).

Kenyon, Timothy, *Utopian Communism and Political Thought in Early Modern England* (London, 1989).

Kirby, W. J. Torrance, 'Reason and Law', in W. J. Torrance Kirby (ed.), *A Companion to Richard Hooker* (Leiden, 2008).

*Richard Hooker's Doctrine of the Royal Supremacy* (Leiden, 1990).

Kishlansky, Mark, *Parliamentary Selection: Social and Political Choice in Early Modern England* (Cambridge, 1986).

*The Rise of the New Model Army* (Cambridge, 1979).

Klein, Lawrence, 'Politeness and the Interpretation of the British Eighteenth Century', *HJ* 45, no. 4 (December 2002), pp. 869–98.

Knapp, Jeffrey, *An Empire Nowhere: England, America, and Literature from Utopia to The Tempest* (Berkeley, 1992).

*Shakespeare's Tribe: Church, Nation, and Theater in Renaissance England* (Chicago, 2002).

Knights, Mark, '"Meer Religion" and the "Church-State" of Restoration England: the Impact and Ideology of James II's Declarations of Indulgence', in Alan Houston and Steve Pincus (eds.), *A Nation Transformed: England after the Restoration* (Cambridge, 2001).

'Occasional Conformity and the Representation of Dissent: Hypocrisy, Sincerity, Moderation and Zeal', *Parliamentary History* 24, no. 1 (2005), pp. 41–57.

Knockles, Peter, *The Oxford Movement in Context: Anglican High Churchmanship, 1760–1857* (Cambridge, 1994).

Krey, Gary De, 'Reformation and Arbitrary Government: London Dissenters and James II's Polity of Toleration, 1687–88', in James McElligott (ed.), *Fear, Exclusion and Revolution: Roger Morrice and Britain in the 1680s* (Aldershot, 2006).

Kroll, Richard, 'Introduction', in Richard Kroll, Richard Ashcraft and Perez Zagorin (eds.), *Philosophy, Science and Religion in England 1640–1700* (Cambridge, 1992).

Kupperman, Karen, 'The Beehive as a Model for Colonial Design', in Karen Kupperman (ed.), *America in European Consciousness 1493–1750* (Chapel Hill, 1995).

'Climate and Mastery of the Wilderness in Seventeenth-Century New England', in David Hall and David Allen (eds.), *Seventeenth-Century New England: A Conference* (Boston, 1984).

'Errand to the Indies: Puritan Colonization from Providence Island through the Western Design', *WMQ* 45, no. 1 (January 1988), pp. 70–99.

'Fear of Hot Climates in the Anglo-American Colonial Experience', *WMQ* 41, no. 2 (April 1984), pp. 213–40.

*The Jamestown Project* (Cambridge, Mass., 2007).

'The Puzzle of the American Climate in the Early Colonial Period', *AHR* 87, no. 5 (December 1982), pp. 1262–89.

*Settling with the Indians: The Meeting of English and Indian Cultures in America, 1580–1640* (Totowa, N.J., 1980).

Lake, Peter, *Anglicans and Puritans? Presbyterianism and English Conformist Thought from Whitgift to Hooker* (London, 1988).

'Joseph Hall, Robert Skinner and the Rhetoric of Moderation at the Early Stuart Court', in Lori Anne Ferrell and Peter McCullough (eds.), *The English Sermon Revised: Religion, Literature and History 1600–1750* (Manchester, 2001)

'The Moderate and Irenic Case for Religious War: Joseph Hall's *Via Media* in Context', in Susan Amussen and Mark Kishlansky (eds.), *Political Cultures and Cultural Politics in Early Modern England: Essays Presented to David Underdown* (Manchester, 1995).

*Moderate Puritans and the Elizabethan Church* (Cambridge, 1982).

'Order, Orthodoxy and Resistance: The Ambiguous Legacy of English Puritanism or Just How Moderate Was Stephen Denison?' in Michael Braddick and John Walter (eds.), *Negotiating Power in Early Modern Society: Order, Hierarchy and Subordination in Britain and Ireland* (Cambridge, 2001).

Langford, Paul, *Public Life and the Propertied Englishman, 1689–1798* (Oxford, 1991).

Latour, Bruno, *We Have Never Been Modern*, trans. Catherine Porter (Cambridge, Mass., 1993).

Lehmberg, Stanford, *The Later Parliaments of Henry VIII, 1536–1547* (Cambridge, 1977).

Levine, Joseph, 'Latitudinarians, Neoplatonists and Ancient Wisdom', in Richard Kroll, Richard Ashcraft, and Perez Zagorin (eds.), *Philosophy, Science, and Religion in England 1640–1700* (Cambridge, 1992).

Lewis, J. E., *The Trial of Mary Queen of Scots: A Brief History with Documents* (Boston, 1999).

Light, Alison, *Forever England: Femininity, Literature and Conservatism between the Wars* (London, 1991).

Louthan, Howard and Randall Zachman (eds.), *Conciliation and Confession: The Struggle for Unity in the Age of Reform* (Notre Dame, 2004).

Lovejoy, Arthur, *The Great Chain of Being: A Study of the History of an Idea* (Cambridge, Mass., 1936).

McClendon, Muriel, *The Quiet Reformation: Magistrates and the Emergence of Protestantism in Tudor Norwich* (Stanford, 1999).

McCrea, Andrea, *Constant Minds: Political Virtue and the Lipsian Paradigm in England 1584–1650* (Toronto, 1997).

MacCulloch, Diarmaid, 'Richard Hooker's Reputation', *EHR* 117, no. 473 (2002), pp. 773–812.

*Suffolk and the Tudors: Politics and Religion in an English County* (Oxford, 1986).

McDiarmid, John (ed.), *The Monarchical Republic of Early Modern England: Essays in Response to Patrick Collinson* (Aldershot, 2007).

McGinnis, Timothy, *George Gifford and the Reformation of the Common Sort* (Kirksville, Miss., 2004).

McGrade, A. S., 'Episcopacy', in W. J. Torrance Kirby (ed.), *A Companion to Richard Hooker* (Leiden, 2008).

McLaren, Anne, *Political Culture in the Reign of Elizabeth I: Queen and Commonwealth, 1558–1585* (Cambridge, 1999).

MacMillan, Ken, *Sovereignty and Possession in the English New World: The Legal Foundations of Empire, 1576–1640* (Cambridge, 2006).

Macpherson, C. B., *The Political Theory of Possessive Individualism* (Oxford, 1962).

McRae, Andrew, *God Speed the Plough: The Representation of Agrarian England, 1500–1660* (Cambridge, 1996).

Maddox, Graham, 'The Limits of Neo-Roman Liberty', *History of Political Thought* 23, no. 3 (Autumn 2002), pp. 418–31.

Maltby, Judith, *Prayer Book and People in Elizabethan and Early Stuart England* (Cambridge, 1998).

Maltby, William, *The Black Legend in England: The Development of Anti-Spanish Sentiment, 1558–1660* (Durham, N.C., 1971).

Mandelbrote, Scott, 'Religious Beliefs and the Politics of Toleration in the Late Seventeenth Century', *Nederlands Archief voor Kerkgeschiedenis* 81, no. 2 (2001), pp. 93–114.

Mandler, Peter (ed.), *Liberty and Authority in Victorian Britain* (Oxford, 2006).

Manning, Brian, *The English People and the English Revolution, 1640–1649* (London, 1976).

Marshall, John, *John Locke: Resistance, Religion and Responsibility* (Cambridge, 1994).

*John Locke, Toleration and Early Enlightenment Culture: Religious Intolerance and Arguments for Religious Toleration in Early Modern and Early Enlightenment Europe* (Cambridge, 2006).

'Some Intellectual Consequences of the English Revolution', *The European Legacy* 5, no. 4 (2000), pp. 515–30.

Mayer, Arno, *The Persistence of the Old Regime: Europe to the Great War* (New York, 1981).

Maza, Sarah, *The Myth of the French Bourgeoisie: An Essay on the Social Imaginary, 1750–1850* (Cambridge, Mass., 2003).

Mendle, Michael, *Dangerous Positions: Mixed Government, the Estates of the Realm, and the Making of the Answer to the xix Propositions* (University, Ala., 1985).

'Parliamentary Sovereignty: A Very English Absolutism', in Nicholas Phillipson and Quentin Skinner (eds.), *Political Discourse in Early Modern Britain* (Cambridge, 1993).

Merchant, Carolyn, *The Death of Nature: Women, Ecology, and the Scientific Revolution* (San Francisco, 1980).

Miller, John, 'Containing Division in Restoration Norwich', *EHR* 121, no. 493 (September 2006), pp. 1019–47.

'A Moderate in the First Age of Party: The Dilemmas of Sir John Holland, 1675–85', *EHR* 114, no. 458 (September 1999), pp. 844–74.

Milton, Anthony, *Catholic and Reformed: The Roman and Protestant Churches in English Protestant Thought, 1600–1640* (Cambridge, 1995).

Morrill, John, 'Provincial Squires and "Middling Sorts" in the Great Rebellion', *HJ* 20, no. 1 (March 1977), pp. 229–36.

'The Religious Context of the English Civil War', *TRHS* fifth series 34 (1984), pp. 155–78.

*Revolt in the Provinces: The People of England and the Tragedies of War, 1634–48* (London, 1999).

Muldrew, Craig, *The Economy of Obligation: The Culture of Credit and Social Relations in Early Modern England* (New York, 1998).

Murphy, Andrew, *Conscience and Community: Revisiting Toleration and Religious Dissent in Early Modern England and America* (University Park, Penn., 2001).

Neale, John, 'The Via Media in Politics: A Historical Parallel', in his *Essays in Elizabethan History* (London, 1958).

Nelson, Eric, *The Greek Tradition in Republican Thought* (Cambridge, 2004).

North, Helen, *Sophrosyne: Self-Knowledge and Self-Restraint in Greek Literature* (Ithaca, 1966).

Nugent, Donald, *Ecumenism in the Age of Reformation: The Colloquy of Poissy* (Cambridge, Mass., 1974).

Nussbaum, Martha, *The Therapy of Desire: Theory and Practice in Hellenistic Ethics* (Princeton, 1994).

Opie, Iona and Peter Opie, *The Classic Fairy Tales* (Oxford, 1974).

O'Shea, Alan, 'English Subjects of Modernity', in Mica Nava and Alan O'Shea (eds.), *Modern Times: Reflections on a Century of English Modernity* (London, 1996).

Pagden, Anthony, *Lords of All the World: Ideologies of Empire in Spain, Britain and France c.1500–c.1800* (New Haven, 1995).

Paster, Gail, Katherine Rowe and Mary Floyd-Wilson (eds.), *Reading the Early Modern Passions: Essays in the Cultural History of Emotion* (Philadelphia, 2004).

Pateman, Carole, *The Sexual Contract* (Stanford, 1988).

Patterson, W. B., *King James VI and I and the Reunion of Christendom* (Cambridge, 1997).

Pears, David, 'Courage as a Mean', in Amélie Rorty (ed.), *Essays of Aristotle's Ethics* (Berkeley, 1980).

Peltonen, Markku, *The Duel in Early Modern England: Civility, Politeness and Honour* (Cambridge, 2003).

Perkin, Harold, *The Origins of Modern English Society* (London, 1969).

Peterson, Mark, *The Price of Redemption: The Spiritual Economy of Puritan New England* (Stanford, 1997).

Pincus, Steve, *1688: The First Modern Revolution* (New Haven, 2009).

'Neither Machiavellian Moment nor Possessive Individualism: Commercial Society and the Defenders of the English Commonwealth', *AHR* 103, no. 3 (June 1998), pp. 705–36.

Pocock, J. G. A., *The Ancient Constitution and the Feudal Law: A Study of English Historical Thought in the Seventeenth Century* (Cambridge, 1957).

'Enthusiasm: The Antiself of the Enlightenment', *Huntington Library Quarterly* 60, nos.1 and 2 (1998), pp. 7–28.

*The Machiavellian Moment: Florentine Political Thought and the Atlantic Republican Tradition* (Princeton, 1975).

'Virtues, Rights, and Manners: A Model for Historians of Political Thought', *Political Theory* 9, no. 3 (August 1981), pp. 353–68.

Pollock, Linda, 'Honor, Gender, and Reconciliation in Elite Culture, 1570–1700', *JBS* 46 (January 2007), pp. 3–29.

Poovey, Mary, *Making a Social Body: British Cultural Formation, 1830–1864* (Chicago, 1995).

Porter, H. C., 'Hooker, the Tudor Constitution, and the *Via Media*', in W. Speed Hill (ed.), *Studies in Richard Hooker: Essays Preliminary to an Edition of His Works* (Cleveland, 1972).

Porter, Roy, *The Creation of the Modern World: The Untold Story of the British Enlightenment* (New York, 2000).

Price, Richard, *British Society, 1680–1880: Dynamism, Containment and Change* (Cambridge, 1999).

Prior, Charles, *Defining the Jacobean Church: The Politics of Religious Controversy, 1603–1625* (Cambridge, 2005).

Racault, Luc and Alec Ryrie (eds.), *Moderate Voices in the European Reformation* (Aldershot, 2005).

Rahe, Paul, *Against Throne and Altar: Machiavelli and Political Theory under the English Republic* (Cambridge, 2008).

'The Classical Republicanism of John Milton', *History of Political Thought* 25, no. 2 (Summer 2004), pp. 243–75.

*Republics Ancient and Modern: Classical Republicanism and the American Revolution* (Chapel Hill, 1992).

Rasmussen, Barry, 'The Priority of God's Gracious Action in Richard Hooker's Hermeneutic', in W. J. Torrance Kirby (ed.), *Richard Hooker and the English Reformation* (Dordrecht, 2003).

Rawls, John, *A Theory of Justice* (Cambridge, Mass., 1971).

Read, David, 'Colonialism and Coherence: The Case of Captain John Smith's General Historie of Virginia', *Modern Philology* 91, no. 4 (May 1994), pp. 428–48.

Redemaker, Adriaan, *Sophrosyne and the Rhetoric of Self-Restraint: Polysemy and Persuasive Use of an Ancient Greek Value Term* (Leiden, 2005).

Remer, Gary, 'James Harrington's New Deliberative Rhetoric: Reflection of an Anticlassical Republicanism', *History of Political Thought* 16, no. 4 (Winter 1995), pp. 532–57.

Rex, Richard, 'The Crisis of Obedience: God's Word and Henry's Reformation', *HJ* 39, no. 4 (1996), pp. 863–94.

Rivers, Isabel, *Reason, Grace, and Sentiment: A Study of the Language of Religion and Ethics in England, 1660–1780* (Cambridge, 2 vols., 1991–2000).

Roberts, Penny, 'The Languages of Peace during the French Religious Wars', *Cultural and Social History* 4, no. 3 (September 2007), pp. 297–315.

Rogers, Michael, 'Gerard Winstanley on Crime and Punishment', *SCJ* 27, no. 3 (1996), pp. 735–47.

Rust, Martha, 'The ABC of Aristotle', in Daniel Kline (ed.), *Medieval Literature for Children* (New York, 2003).

Schmitt, Charles, *John Case and Aristotelianism in Renaissance England* (Kingston, 1983).

Schochet, Gordon, 'From Persecution to 'Toleration'', in J. R. Jones (ed.), *Liberty Secured? Britain Before and After 1688* (Stanford, 1992).

Scodel, Joshua, *Excess and the Mean in Early Modern English Literature* (Princeton, 2002).

Scott, Joan, *Only Paradoxes to Offer: French Feminists and the Rights of Man* (Cambridge, Mass., 1996).

Scott, Jonathan, *Commonwealth Principles: Republican Writings of the English Revolution* (Cambridge, 2004).

'"The Rapture of Motion": James Harrington's Republicanism', in Nicholas Phillipson and Quentin Skinner (eds.), *Political Discourse in Early Modern Europe* (Cambridge, 1993).

'What Were Commonwealth Principles?' *HJ* 47, no. 3 (2004), pp. 591–613.

Seaberg, R. B., 'The Norman Conquest and the Common Law: The Levellers and the Argument from Continuity', *HJ* 24, no. 4 (1981), pp. 791–806.

Secor, Philip, *Richard Hooker and the Via Media* (Bloomington, Ind., 2006).

Selement, George, 'The Covenant Theology of English Separatism and the Separation of Church and State', *Journal of the American Academy of Religion* 41, no. 1 (March 1973), pp. 66–74.

Shagan, Ethan, 'The Battle for Indifference in Elizabethan England', in Luc Racault and Alec Ryrie (eds.), *Moderate Voices in the European Reformation* (Aldershot, 2005).

'Beyond Good and Evil: Thinking with Moderates in Early Modern England', *JBS* 49, no. 3 (July 2010), pp. 488–513.

'The English Inquisition: Constitutional Conflict and Ecclesiastical Law in the 1590s', *HJ* 47, no. 3 (September 2004), pp. 541–65.

*Popular Politics and the English Reformation* (Cambridge, 2003).

Shapin, Steven, *A Social History of Truth: Civility and Science in Seventeenth-Century England* (Chicago, 1994).

Shepard, Alexandra, *Meanings of Manhood in Early Modern England* (Oxford, 2003).

Shuger, Debora, *Habits of Thought in the English Renaissance: Religion, Politics, and the Dominant Culture* (Berkeley, 1990).

'"Societie Supernaturall": The Imagined Community of Hooker's *Lawes*', in Arthur McGrade (ed.), *Richard Hooker and the Construction of Christian Community* (Tempe, Ariz., 1997).

Shulman, George, *Radicalism and Reverence: The Political Thought of Gerard Winstanley* (Berkeley, 1989).

Skinner, Quentin, *Hobbes and Republican Liberty* (Cambridge, 2008).

'John Milton and the Politics of Slavery', *Prose Studies* 23, no. 1 (April 2000), pp. 1–22.

*Liberty Before Liberalism* (Cambridge, 1998).

'Rethinking Political Liberty', *History Workshop Journal* 61 (Spring 2006), 156–70.

Smail, John, *The Origins of Middle-Class Culture: Halifax, Yorkshire, 1660–1780* (Ithaca, 1994).

Smith, David, *Constitutional Royalism and the Search for Settlement, c.1640–1649* (Cambridge, 1994).

Smith, Hilda, *All Men and Both Sexes: Gender, Politics, and the False Universal in England 1640–1832* (University Park, Penn., 2002).

Smith, Nigel, 'Gerrard Winstanley and the Literature of Revolution', *Prose Studies* 22, no. 2 (August 1999), pp. 46–60.

'Popular Republicanism in the 1650s: John Streater's "Heroick Mechanicks"', in David Armitage, Armand Himy and Quentin Skinner (eds.), *Milton and Republicanism* (Cambridge, 1995).

Smuts, Malcolm, 'Force, Love and Authority in Caroline Political Culture', in Ian Atherton and Julie Sanders (eds.), *The 1630s: Interdisciplinary Essays on Culture and Politics in the Caroline Era* (Manchester, 2006).

Sommerville, Johann, 'English and Roman Liberty in the Monarchical Republic of Early Stuart England', in John McDiarmid (ed.), *The Monarchical Republic of Early Modern England: Essays in Response to Patrick Collinson* (Aldershot, 2007).

Spurr, John, '"Latitudinarianism" and the Restoration Church', *HJ* 31, no. 1 (March 1988), pp. 61–82.

*The Restoration Church of England, 1646–1689* (New Haven, 1991).

Stanwood, P. G., 'Works and Editions I', in Torrance Kirby (ed.), *A Companion to Richard Hooker* (Leiden, 2008).

Stern, Philip, '"A Politie of Civill & Military Power": Political Thought and the Late Seventeenth-Century Foundations of the East India Company-State', *JBS* 47, no. 2 (April 2008), pp. 253–83.

Stevens, Paul, '"Leviticus Thinking" and the Rhetoric of Early Modern Colonialism', *Criticism* 35, no. 3 (Summer 1993), pp. 441–61.

Stevenson, Laura, *Praise and Paradox: Merchants and Craftsmen in Elizabethan Popular Literature* (Cambridge, 1984).

Strier, Richard, 'Donne and the Politics of Devotion', in Donna Hamilton and Richard Strier (eds.), *Religion, Literature and Politics in Post-Reformation England 1540–1688* (Cambridge, 1996).

Stuurman, Siep, 'The Canon and the History of Political Thought: Its Critique and a Proposed Alternative', *History and Theory* 39, no. 2 (May 2000), pp. 147–66.

Sullivan, Vickie, *Machiavelli, Hobbes and the Formation of a Liberal Republicanism in England* (Cambridge, 2004).

Tadmor, Naomi, *The Social Universe of the English Bible: Scripture, Society and Culture in Early Modern England* (Cambridge, 2010).

Tawney, R. H., *Religion and the Rise of Capitalism: a Historical Study* (London, 1926).

Thomas, Keith, 'The Levellers and the Franchise', in Gerald Aylmer (ed.), *The Interregnum: The Quest for Settlement 1646–1660* (London, 1972).

Thompson, W. D. J. Cargill, 'The Philosopher of the "Politic Society": Richard Hooker as a Political Thinker', in W. Speed Hill (ed.), *Studies in Richard Hooker: Essays Preliminary to an Edition of His Works* (Cleveland, 1972).

Thrupp, Sylvia, *The Merchant Class of Medieval London* (Ann Arbor, 1962).

Tillyard, E. M. W., *The Elizabethan World Picture* (London, 1958).

Todd, Margo, *Christian Humanism and the Puritan Social Order* (Cambridge, 1987).

'Seneca and the Protestant Mind: The Influence of Stoicism on Puritan Ethics', *Archiv für Reformationgeschichte* 74 (1983), pp. 182–99.

Travers, Robert, *Ideology and Empire in Eighteenth-Century Bengal* (Cambridge, 2007).

Tuck, Richard, *Philosophy and Government, 1572–1651* (Cambridge, 1993).

Tuckness, Alex, 'Rethinking the Intolerant Locke', *American Journal of Political Science* 46, no. 2 (April 2002), pp. 288–98.

Tully, James, *An Approach to Political Philosophy: Locke in Contexts* (Cambridge, 1993).

Turner, James, *Libertines and Radicals in Early Modern London: Sexuality, Politics, and Literary Culture, 1630–1685* (Cambridge, 2002).

Tyacke, Nicholas, *Anti-Calvinists: The Rise of English Arminianism c.1590–1640* (Oxford, 1987).

Urmson, J. O., 'Aristotle's Doctrine of the Mean', in Amélie Rorty (ed.), *Essays of Aristotle's Ethics* (Berkeley, 1980).

Vaughan, Alden, 'From White Man to Red Skin: Changing Anglo-American Perceptions of the American Indian', *AHR* 87 (1982), pp. 917–53.

Verkamp, Bernard, *The Indifferent Mean: Adiaphorism in the English Reformation to 1554* (Athens, Ohio, 1977).

Vickers, Brian, 'Authority and Coercion in Elizabethan Thought', *Queen's Quarterly* 87, no. 1 (Spring 1980), 114–23.

Vickers, Daniel, 'Competency and Competition: Economic Culture in Early America', *WMQ* 3rd series, 47, no. 1 (January 1990), pp. 3–29.

Voak, Nigel, *Richard Hooker and Reformed Theology: A Study of Reason, Will, and Grace* (Oxford, 2003).

Wahrman, Dror, *Imagining the Middle Class: The Political Representation of Class in Britain, c.1780–1840* (Cambridge, 1995).

Waldron, Jeremy, 'Locke, Toleration and the Rationality of Persecution', in his *Liberal Rights: Collected Papers 1981–1991* (Cambridge, 1993).

Walsham, Alexandra, *Charitable Hatred: Tolerance and Intolerance in England, 1500–1700* (Manchester, 2006).

Walzer, Michael, *On Toleration* (New Haven, 1997).

Warnicke, Retha, *The Marrying of Anne of Cleves* (Cambridge, 2000).

Webb, Darren, 'The Bitter Product of Defeat? Reflections on Winstanley's Law of Freedom', *Political Studies* 52 (2004), pp. 199–215.

Webster, Tom, *Godly Clergy in Early Stuart England: The Caroline Puritan Movement, c.1620–1643* (Cambridge, 1997).

White, Peter, *Predestination, Policy, and Polemic: Conflict and Consensus in the English Church from the Reformation to the Civil War* (Cambridge, 1992).

Winship, Michael, 'Freeborn (Puritan) Englishmen and Slavish Subjection: Popish Tyranny and Puritan Congregationalism, c.1570–1606', *EHR* 124, no. 510 (October 2009), pp. 1050–74.

'Godly Republicanism and the Origins of the Massachusetts Polity', *WMQ* 63, no. 3 (July 2006), pp. 427–62.

*Making Heretics: Militant Protestantism and Free Grace in Massachusetts, 1636–1641* (Princeton, 2002).

Withington, Phil, *The Politics of Commonwealth: Citizens and Freemen in Early Modern England* (Cambridge, 2005).

'Public Discourse, Corporate Citizenship, and State Formation in Early Modern England', *AHR* 112, no. 4 (October 2007), pp. 1016–38.

Wood, Andy, *The 1549 Rebellions and the Making of Early Modern England* (Cambridge, 2007).

Wood, Diana, *Medieval Economic Thought* (Cambridge, 2002).

Wooding, Lucy, *Rethinking Catholicism in Reformation England* (Oxford, 2000).

Wootton, David (ed.), *Republicanism, Liberty, and Commercial Society, 1649–1776* (Stanford, 1994).

Worden, Blair, 'James Harrington and "The Commonwealth of Oceana", 1656', in David Wootton (ed.), *Republicanism, Liberty, and Commercial Society, 1649–1776* (Stanford, 1994).

'Marchamont Nedham and the Beginnings of English Republicanism', in David Wootton (ed.), *Republicanism, Liberty, and Commercial Society, 1649–1776* (Stanford, 1994).

'The Question of Secularisation', in Alan Houston and Steve Pincus (eds.), *A Nation Transformed: England after the Restoration* (Cambridge, 2001).

'Wit in a Roundhead: The Dilemma of Marchamont Nedham', in Susan Amussen and Mark Kishlansky (eds.), *Political Culture and Cultural Politics in Early Modern Europe: Essays Presented to David Underdown* (Manchester, 1995).

Wright, Jonathan, 'Marian Exiles and the Legitimacy of Flight from Persecution', *Journal of Ecclesiastical History* 52, no. 2 (April 2001), pp. 220–43.

Wrightson, Keith 'Estates, Degrees and Sorts: Changing Perceptions of Society in Tudor and Stuart England', in Penelope Corfield (ed.), *Language, History and Class* (Oxford, 1991).

'The Social Order in Early Modern England: Three Approaches', in Lloyd Bonfield, Richard Smith and Keith Wrightson (eds.), *The World We Have Gained: Histories of Population and Social Structure* (New York, 1986).

'"Sorts of People" in Tudor and Stuart England', in Jonathan Barry and Christopher Brooks (eds.), *The Middling Sort of People: Culture, Society and Politics in England, 1550–1800* (New York, 1994).

Zagorin, Perez, *How the Idea of Religious Toleration Came to the West* (Princeton, 2003).

# Index